ι

SPOILED
ROTTEN

SPOILED ROTTEN

HOW THE POLITICS OF PATRONAGE

CORRUPTED THE ONCE NOBLE

DEMOCRATIC PARTY

AND NOW THREATENS

THE AMERICAN REPUBLIC

JAY COST

BROADSIDE BOOKS
An Imprint of HarperCollins*Publishers*
www.broadsidebooks.net

HarperCollins books may be purchased for educational, business, or sales promotional use. For information, please write: Special Markets Department, HarperCollins Publishers, 10 East 53rd Street, New York, NY 10022.

Broadside Books™ and the Broadside logo are trademarks of HarperCollins Publishers.

FIRST EDITION

Designed by Joy O'Meara

Library of Congress Cataloging-in-Publication Data
Cost, Jay.
Spoiled rotten : how the politics of patronage corrupted the once noble Democratic party and now threatens the American republic / Jay Cost.—1st ed.
p. cm.
Includes bibliographical references and index.
ISBN: 978-0-06-204115-9   *48 71 8638*   */12*
1. Democratic Party (U.S.)—History. I. Title.
JK2316.C67   2012
324.2736—dc23   2011041796

12 13 14 15 16   OV/RRD   10 9 8 7 6 5 4 3 2 1

For Lindsay

The great desideratum in Government is such a modification of the Sovereignty as will render it sufficiently neutral between the different interests and factions, to controul one part of the Society from invading the rights of another, and at the same time sufficiently controuled itself, from setting up an interest adverse to that of the whole Society.

—JAMES MADISON, *"Vices of the Political System of the United States"*

There are no necessary evils in government. Its evils exist only in its abuses. If it would confine itself to equal protection, and, as Heaven does its rains, shower its favors alike on the high and the low, the rich and the poor, it would be an unqualified blessing.

—ANDREW JACKSON, *Veto Message, July 10, 1832*

[Speaker of the House Nancy Pelosi] tracked down Rep. Jim Cooper (D-Tenn.) in a Tennessee airport, returning to Washington for the final week. . . . "The store is open," Cooper recalled Pelosi telling him. "We're crafting the manager's amendment. Now is the time to get your provisions."

—CECI CONNOLLY, *Landmark: The Inside Story of America's New Health-Care Law and What It Means for Us All*

Contents

SPOILED
ROTTEN

Introduction

It wasn't supposed to be like this.

Barack Obama entered the White House in January 2009 with all signs pointing toward major liberal policy reforms. He had campaigned unabashedly as a reformer, promising "change we can believe in," and won the largest popular-vote majority of any Democrat in more than forty years. He had an outsize congressional majority in both chambers, dominated by the kinds of northern Democrats who had long been the prime movers of liberal reform. The Republican opposition was seemingly discredited, taking the blame for a terrible economy as well as a congressional faction of so-called conservatives who had spent money like drunken sailors during their years in the majority. To top it all off, his job approval upon entering office was nearly 70 percent, higher than that of any incoming president in decades.

Within twenty months it was all over. In November 2010 the country elected more Republicans to the House of Representatives than in any election since the 1940s. President Obama's job approval had fallen below 50 percent, and his rating among the all-important group of independent voters who swing elections had dropped into the danger zone of the low forties. The new Republican majority in the House promised a return to the party's role as a responsible steward of the economy and the federal budget, and the reform era of the Obama administration was well and truly finished.

How could this have happened? Sure, some of it can be chalked up to the midterm blues—the sitting party of the president almost always loses seats in off-year elections. Some of it can be chalked up to the weak economy—twenty months into his administration, President Obama had to share at least some of the blame with George W. Bush. Yet the breadth and depth of Democratic losses in November 2010—

with a net of sixty-two House seats flipping from blue to red, most of which came in the Midwest and the South—suggested that something more was at play.

That something was symbolized by the Patient Protection and Affordable Care Act (PPACA), which represented for liberal Democrats the culmination of nearly a century of struggle. Harry Truman included universal health care reform in his Fair Deal package in the 1940s. Before that, Teddy Roosevelt's Progressive party, dominated by future New Dealers like Harold Ickes, called for a national health service in 1912. No wonder Obama and the Democratic leadership in Congress wanted to use their outsize majority to remake the nation's health care system.

But health care reform turned out to be the Democratic party's undoing. Almost as soon as the legislative process began, moderate Democrats from the South and Midwest started bolting, finally forcing a showdown between "Blue Dogs" and liberal chairman Henry Waxman in the House Energy and Commerce Committee in the summer of 2009. Meanwhile, Obama's job approval plummeted nearly 20 points in just seven months, and by August it stood at an anemic 50 percent in the Gallup poll. By that point, poll after poll found a plurality, if not an outright majority, of Americans disapproving of the Democratic health care plan. Of course, the Democrats did not stop there. Despite mounting public pressure, evidenced by a Republican victory in the battle to fill the seat left behind by the late Ted Kennedy, Democrats pushed forward with the bill, finally passing it in the spring of 2010 via an unprecedented legislative sleight of hand. Public opinion by that point had completely soured and was never to sweeten again on "Obamacare."

Democrats blamed the collapse of the public's support for reform on Republican smear tactics, while Republicans blamed it on Americans' distaste for big government. Neither answer makes much sense. By the middle of 2009, "Republican" had become the political equivalent of a four-letter word—hardly anybody trusted the Republican party enough to believe its claims about the health care bill. What's more, Obama occupied the bully pulpit, the most effective tool for communicating to the mass public, while the Republicans struggled to get any media attention for their message. As for the mass public's supposed dislike of big government, how does one account for the enduring popularity of Medicare, which is "socialized medicine" if anything is? Furthermore, Americans overwhelmingly approved of many specific items within the legislation, in particular tougher regulations on the insurance companies, which are not held in high esteem.

The real problem with the health reform efforts was the controversial manner by which it was passed. Rather than propose a bill to Congress, President Obama allowed the legislature to draft health care reform basically from scratch, and the result was a political disaster. Dozens upon dozens of "stakeholders" (the buzzword the Obama administration used for special-interest groups aligned with the Democratic party) emerged out of nowhere to demand this exceptional consideration or that particular carve-out. The line of groups demanding to wet their beaks seemed endless: big businesses, labor unions, liberal activist groups, medical groups representing doctors, nurses, drug companies, and so on. And of course, wavering legislators were able to extract significant concessions, the most infamous of which was Nebraska senator Ben Nelson's "Cornhusker Kickback" that exempted only Nebraska from having to pay additional costs for the expanded Medicaid rolls. The only ones who did not get a seat at the table were the American people, the supposed beneficiaries of the reform effort.

Despite the severe losses the party suffered in 2010 and the seemingly irreparable damage done to President Obama's approval rating, many liberals still do not fully appreciate the significance of this political debacle—in particular, how it challenges the very notion of what the Democratic party is *supposed* to be. The Democratic party, since its founding nearly two hundred years ago, has aspired to be a reform party for and of the people. Now here it is pushing for reforms that the people don't want and that cater to the very kinds of special interests Democrats have opposed for generations.

What would Andrew Jackson think of all this? Old Hickory founded the Democratic party in the 1820s in response to the rampant corruption that had overwhelmed the federal government, culminating in the "Corrupt Bargain" of 1824, wherein Henry Clay and John

Quincy Adams supposedly conspired to deprive Jackson of the presidency, despite his having won a clear popular-vote victory that year. In response, Jackson formed the new Democratic party out of his loyal base in the West as well as the "radical" Jeffersonians who had long opposed leaders like Clay and Adams. The party promised to stand up for the little guy against the enroachments of the well-to-do—pledging to cut the size of government down to its constitutional limits and institute "rotation in office" to remove the new aristocracy from positions of power. In 1832, Jackson vetoed a bill to recharter the Second Bank of the United States, and his veto message remains a kind of mission statement for the Democratic party even to this day:

> It is to be regretted that the rich and powerful too often bend the acts of government to their selfish purposes. Distinctions in society will always exist under every just government. Equality of talents, of education, or of wealth can not be produced by human institutions. In the full enjoyment of the gifts of Heaven and the fruits of superior industry, economy, and virtue, every man is equally entitled to protection by law; but when the laws undertake to add to these natural and just advantages artificial distinctions, to grant titles, gratuities, and exclusive privileges, to make the rich richer and the potent more powerful, the humble members of society—the farmers, mechanics, and laborers—who have neither the time nor the means of securing like favors to themselves, have a right to complain of the injustice of their Government.[1]

This is the kind of rhetoric that Americans have heard from the Democratic party ever since—the people versus the powerful, with the Democrats standing up for the "humble members of society" and the Republicans (and before them the Whigs) doing the bidding of the "rich . . . and the potent."

Yet during the health care debate, many Americans felt that the roles had been reversed. Obamacare did not "shower its favors alike on the high and the low," but instead picked winners and losers based largely on which groups had the right political connections. During the first half of Obama's tenure, the Democrats seemed to be not the

Jacksonian party of the people but rather the party of the very kinds of special interests Old Hickory had railed against.

Why has this happened? Why has the Democratic party gone from being the people's party of reform to the party of special interest carve-outs? This is the question we will answer in the pages that follow. Over the next twelve chapters, we shall tell the story of the Democratic party from the end of the Civil War to the present day, tracking the tragic decline of a once noble political coalition that is now no longer capable of living up to its lofty Jacksonian ideals.

As we shall see, the critical piece of the puzzle is *clientelism*—transforming factions of voters into loyal members of a party's coalition by offering them special privileges. The Democrats have been very good at this over the years—too good, in fact—and the result has been a kind of subtraction by addition. The more client groups the party has brought on board, the more it is obliged to tend to their needs, and the less able it is to govern for the people as a whole.

Clientelism is as old as government itself, and it has been an endemic feature of the American experiment in self-rule. James Madison—the father of the Constitution—believed clientelism to be a core defect of the original state governments. Politicians on the state level would regularly "join in a perfidious sacrifice" of the public good to appeal to *factions,* which Madison defined as groups of citizens "united and actuated by some common impulse of passion, or of interest, adverse to the rights of other citizens, or to the permanent and aggregate interests of the community." Politicians, desperate for reelection and lusting after ever more power, were happy to turn factions into clients—to make them dependent upon the government to take care of their needs. And if the public good was sacrificed, so what? As Madison astutely noted, concern for the interests of the people as a whole was rarely, if ever, the paramount motivation for politicians.

To "break and control the violence of faction," as Madison put it in "Federalist" Number 10, the framers of the Constitution carefully designed a government that combined many aspects—a large geographical reach, a federal system, a bicameral legislature, a series of checks and balances between the branches, and finally a Bill of Rights—to prevent narrow-interest groups from railroading the rest of the country. The hope was that these constitutional features would serve as circuit breakers, preventing the government from exercising its expansive powers except when a broad majority of the country approved of the action. The American system was to be one where factions were tamped down and government clientelism would not exist.

But what Madison and his cohorts failed to anticipate was the rise of political parties—an ironic oversight, because the framers were also the originators of the American party system. If our constitutional system disperses political power to prevent factionalism and clientelism, the party system concentrates it to help the government actually function. The political parties are essentially extragovernmental conspiracies of political actors who coordinate their actions to win control of, then manage, the government. So, for instance, the Constitution separates the Congress from the presidency, but the party system links the fate of the president and his partisans in Congress, giving them all an incentive to work together. Because the parties are meant to overcome the limitations inherent in the constitutional system, they have been a breeding ground for the kind of clientelism that Madison feared. Factions might not be able to take control of the government directly, but if they can dominate a party, and that party takes control of the government, factions can indeed control things indirectly.

We have seen parties undermined by this kind of factionalism time and again. For instance, the old Jeffersonian Republican party that had dominated politics since 1798 had all but eliminated its Federalist opposition by the end of the War of 1812. In time, it fell prey to rampant corruption as government officials seemed more interested in catering to the special interests than the public interest. The low point, at least according to Jackson, came when the House of Representatives defied the will of the people and made John Quincy Adams president in 1825.

What's more, the Jacksonians came to perpetrate the very clientelism they had pledged to root out. Old Hickory had initiated "rotation in office" as a way to drive out the established interests from the bureaucracy and hand power over to the people. In time, however, this seemingly democratic practice devolved into the "spoils system," wherein government officials would hand out extensive patronage—in the form of jobs, contracts, licenses, and so on—to their supporters. The spoils system became the centerpiece of the urban machines of the late nineteenth century, most of which were run by Irish Democrats. That the Jacksonians failed to reform and democratize the government is an enduring testament to the tenacity of clientelism: so long as politicians are looking to be reelected, there is always a chance that it will rear its ugly head.

Eventually, the modern Democratic party would also fall prey to clientelism.

As the nineteenth century gave way to the twentieth, the Jacksonian spirit of fighting for the "humble members of society" was revived within the Democratic party; however, rather than push for a small government, as Jackson preferred, the modern party would be a progressive one, promising active intervention in the private economy to make sure the downtrodden are treated fairly. This turn to progressivism would only enhance the prospects of clientelism. After all, clients depend on governmental largesse—so the bigger the government, the greater the possible payoffs. And during the tenure of Franklin Roosevelt, the Democratic party would begin using big government not only to solve public problems but also to cultivate clientelistic relationships with scores of factions within society.

For the next forty years, we'd see a similar modus operandi in Democratic leadership. While he was battling the Depression, Franklin Roosevelt added organized labor as a party client, transformed the big-city machines, and secured the privileged position of the segregationist South in the party. Harry Truman's Fair Deal sought to level the playing field for all citizens but also give party supporters a little extra for their votes in 1948. John F. Kennedy inspired the country to go to the moon while also aiding the cause of labor by recognizing government unions. Lyndon Johnson's Great Society sought to finish the Rooseveltian project of national reform, but it sowed the seeds for new clients in African Americans, environmentalists, feminists, and other groups from the "New Politics" left.

Practiced on a modest scale, clientelism may be noxious, but it is to be expected, and is not really harmful to our republican system of government. It's silly to expect a political party not to offer its own side some of the spoils of political victory, even if the public treasury pays out those private benefits. So long as party leaders are able to tend to those clients without forsaking the national interest, the final result may be occasionally unseemly, but it does not endanger the republican character of our government. The real problem with clientelism is when it overwhelms a party, when a party is no longer capable of governing for the public good because the demands of the clients have grown too onerous.

Through the presidency of Lyndon Johnson, Democratic leaders were more or less able to manage the party's client groups while simultaneously pursuing the national interest, at least as they saw it. Sure, there were exceptions, like Harry Truman vetoing the Taft-Hartley Act in 1947 to keep organized labor on board with his reelection bid, despite the widespread unrest that had prompted Congress to enact it (not to mention Truman's promise to reform labor relations). But by and large Democratic presidents could keep the balancing act going, tending to clients and the mass public at the same time. At the end of the 1960s, however, a series of new groups entered the Democratic coalition, each with its own unique set of demands and its own ways of making sure that the party paid attention to them. With these new groups added to the old clients, the whole apparatus began to collapse under its own weight. All of a sudden, there seemed to be no way for party leaders to keep every client group happy and also tend to the public good. It was like a juggler who'd added one too many balls to the routine, only to see them all come crashing down.

For the Democrats, this has meant an effective end to its role as a populist reform party. Party leaders since the 1970s have been faced with a stark choice: govern for the public interest or govern for the party's client groups; it now appears impossible to do both at the same time. The three Democratic leaders since the 1960s—Jimmy Carter, Bill Clinton, and now Barack Obama—have each tried different approaches to squaring this circle, but none has found a way to do it. The result is a political coalition that cannot be trusted with full power of the government: at best, it will produce no valuable policy during its tenure in charge of government; at worst, it will actually legislate against the public interest, as it has done during the Obama tenure.

• • •

The title of this book is a reference to the old "spoils system" of the nineteenth century, and as we shall see, the metaphor is an apt one. During the "Gilded Age," the forty years or so following the Civil War, the practice of rotation in office, once intended as a leveling force in American politics under Jackson, devolved into a corrupt patronage regime that enabled the politically privileged to keep their special place in society. In time, the perfidy of the spoils system threatened the republican character of the government itself, as the two parties forsook the public good to divide up the spoils of office.

There are two parallels between the politics of the Gilded Age and today's Democratic party that are worth keeping in mind as we move through our investigation. First, many of the political leaders of the nineteenth century were honorable people by the standards of their day, and many of them hold up even by contemporary standards. Similarly, today's Democratic party is full of good guys and bad guys in equal proportions to today's Republican party, or any large group of people. This means that our story will not be a pitched battle between the forces of good and evil.

Second, the honor of the political class does not matter if the institutions in which it operates are dysfunctional. That is why upright men were nevertheless forgettable presidents during the Gilded Age. For instance, few presidents were as upstanding in their public life as Grover Cleveland, who served in the 1880s and 1890s. Yet today he is not remembered for having enacted any lasting reforms, or for taming the wild excesses of his day. The reason is that Cleveland, like everybody else in the Gilded Age, had to operate within the dysfunctional political institutions of the time. Institutions are really just the rules—be they informal or formal—that govern behavior for sinners and saints alike. And the institutions that governed party politics in the Gilded Age, which mandated a relentless focus on patronage and a scrupulous avoidance of the most important issues, were such that honorable men could not become great presidents.

The same goes for today's Democratic party. Though it is as full of upstanding people as any other organization, that does not matter here. This is a story not about morality but about institutions, or rules. And the rules of modern clientelism have *broken* the Democratic party; regardless of the men who lead it, the party is no longer capable of governing in the spirit of republicanism that inspired the national founding. Instead, Democratic leaders, good and bad alike, must provide a never-ending stream of benefits to the party clients, at the expense of the public interest.

Put simply, clientelism has rendered the Democratic party incapable of governing a republic such as ours. The following pages will explain why.

CHAPTER ONE

All the Toiling Masses

William Jennings Bryan and the Jacksonian Revival

Ask the average American today to recall which presidents have been shot, and he will probably mention Abraham Lincoln and John F. Kennedy. If he's older than forty, he might also note the attempt on Ronald Reagan's life. The odd history buff here or there might mention William McKinley's murder in 1901, but almost nobody will talk about James A. Garfield, the twentieth president of the United States, who was shot just four months into his tenure, in July 1881.

Garfield's assassination has largely been forgotten, but if it were remembered, people today would surely be puzzled by it. After all, here was a chief executive murdered by a scorned federal office seeker. After the dirty deed was done, his assassin—Charles Guiteau—famously shouted, "I am a Stalwart!" These "Stalwarts" were not some radical faction, but rather a clique of Republicans who wanted Ulysses S. Grant to be renominated in 1880, in large part so they could collect the patronage he was bound to dole out upon returning to the White House. That makes Garfield the only president ever murdered because of the spoils system.[1]

It is indeed strange that such a narrow concept would animate the body politic, let alone induce somebody to murder over it. But the fact of the matter was that patronage was the mother's milk of politics for decades after the Civil War. Politics was not organized around the big issues of the day, or between the great ideological systems that we today call liberalism and conservatism. Of course, there had been great ideological struggles in the earlier periods of our history; Thomas Jefferson and Alexander Hamilton fought in the 1790s over the role of government in American life, as did Andrew Jackson and Henry Clay in the 1830s. However, by the middle of the 1840s, politics started to realign into a North-South divide over the issue of slavery. After the peace was signed at Appomattox in 1865, those regional divides remained mostly in place, and parties held their coalitions together in part by distributing patronage.

Guiteau was insane, of course, and Stalwarts and Half-Breeds (the rival GOP faction) alike were rightly horrified, but in historical retrospect, Garfield's death stands as a stark illustration of the moral bankruptcy of American politics after the Civil War. Indeed, as Henry Adams noted, "One might search the whole list of Congress, Judiciary, and the Executive during the twenty five years 1870–1895 and find little but damaged reputations."[2]

The Democratic party of this period was, accordingly, nothing like what it is today, or even what it had been in Old Hickory's day. The party after the Civil War was dominated by the urban political bosses of the North and the plantation gentry of the South, hardly representative of the "humble members of society" whom Jackson claimed to defend when he vetoed the Bank of the United States. Instead, what really bound the Democrats together was enmity toward of the Republicans as well as the spoils they expected to collect after electoral victory had been secured.

This sorry state of affairs finally began to change in the 1890s. The economic crisis of that decade had driven western farmers into the radical populist movement, which in turn overtook the Democratic party in 1896. A young, brash Nebraskan named William Jennings Bryan would capture the party nomination and reorient the Democrats back toward the old Jacksonian vision—a party of "all the toiling masses" that stood up to the financial magnates back East. Though Bryan's efforts to win the presidency were ultimately unsuccessful, his candidacy nevertheless marks the beginning of the modern Democratic party.

The Democratic party that emerged on the other side of the Civil War was an ideological hodgepodge of three major groups that had little in common with one another, except for a shared hatred of the Republicans. The first and most prominent group in the party was the Solid South. In the states of the former Confederacy, all the old political divisions that had enlivened the Whig-Democratic contests were put aside, at least when it came to national politics, as whites in the South flocked to the Democratic party with the common goal of keeping African Americans from the ballot box. The most aggressive opponents of black enfranchisement, and thus the vanguards of the southern wing of the party, were the conservative plantation owners from majority black counties in the Black Belt (the band of counties stretching in a southward crescent from Norfolk, Virginia, up the Mississippi River and to Memphis, Tennessee, originally named after the dark soil that was amenable to cotton farming), who had actually been in the opposing Whig party prior to the war. Now they were the defenders of party orthodoxy, and so the southern Democrats shifted noticeably to the right.[3]

Second, the Jacksonian Democrats had done well with western voters prior to the Civil War, when the frontier was mostly east of the Mississippi River, in states like Indiana and Ohio. The postwar Democratic party managed to hold many of its old Jacksonian bastions, which typically meant that plenty of electoral votes were up for grabs from this region. But the frontier had moved west of the Mississippi as states like Iowa, Kansas, Minnesota, and Nebraska came into the Union. These states were rock-ribbed Republican in the decades following the Civil War, typically giving the GOP twenty-point victory margins.

The third major faction in the Democratic coalition was the ethnic vote, especially the Irish Catholics and the German Lutherans. Immigrants had been partial to the Jeffersonian Republicans as early as 1798, when the Federalists passed the Alien Acts and the Scots-Irish Jackson also enjoyed their support. They stuck with the Democrats in the decades following the Civil War—and that was sufficient to deliver to the party several big cities, including Boston, Brooklyn, and New York.[4]

Taken together, these groups consistently put the Democrats within striking distance of electoral victory. From 1876 through 1892, the party always won at least 49.9 percent of the two-party vote for president, and in the battle for the House, it actually won a majority of the two-party vote every time.[5] Even so, both the Democrats and the Republicans lacked a coherent ideology, a belief system that tied together the party's positions on all the relevant issues. Instead the political coalitions of both parties during this period were held together primarily by old prejudices, with both sides voting based upon Civil War loyalties or age-old ethnic tensions rather than the big issues, like industrialization, urbanization, and western expansion. Another source of party unity was the patronage regime, or the practice wherein political officeholders won the right to staff the government with their supporters.

This spoils system was a vestige of the Jacksonian Democracy, but its once admirable purpose had become lost in a haze of postwar partisan turpitude.[6] Prior to Andrew Jackson's presidency, the federal bureaucracy was a "government by gentlemen," staffed largely by the landed gentry. All of the early presidents preferred to install their supporters in open posts, but they were generally content to leave the old bureaucrats in place, even if they were from the opposing party.[7] Jackson brought about a shift in attitude regarding the bureaucracy; it's not that Old Hickory diverged dramatically from his predecessors in terms of dismissals or appointments, but he elevated the spoils system to a republican virtue. Rotation in office became a way to clean out the established interests from the government and thus promote the new Democratic goal of entrusting the people with control of the government.

Jackson's use of patronage might have been cautious and judicious, but his underlings and successors were not so modest. The spoils system soon became a way to raid the federal treasury to reward party supporters for their campaign efforts. When the Whig Zachary Taylor assumed the presidency in 1849, roughly 30 percent of all federal jobs were assigned according to the demands of the patronage system,[8] and the Democrat James Buchanan went so far as to redistribute government jobs to his supporters, even though he was of the same party as his predecessor.[9] The Republican Abraham Lincoln was the undisputed champion of federal patronage, replacing nearly 90 percent of eligible offices with supporters as he struggled to hold his coalition together through the Civil War.[10]

This did not make much of an impact until the unprecedented sleaze of the Grant administration. As scandal mounted upon scandal, it became increasingly clear not only that Grant was not up to the top job but that the spoils system itself had to go. Reform-minded Republicans created the Liberal Republican party to oppose Grant in his 1872 reelection campaign, advocating tough new civil service reforms. The party vanished after Grant's decisive victory, but the reformers who had inspired it did not.[11] After all, they had the virtue of being right: whatever noble, democratic purpose the spoils system once served was now overwhelmed by rampant corruption and inefficiency. One reformer wrote that the system represented "a wide-spread evil, which defrauds the country in the collection of taxes on a scale so gigantic that the commissioners of revenue, collectors, assessors, and Treasury officers—at least those of them who are honest—bow their heads in shame and despair."[12]

Tragically, an American president would have to die for the country to find the political courage to reform the patronage system. On July 2, 1881, Charles Guiteau shot President James Garfield as he was walking through the Sixth Street Station in Washington, D.C. Garfield had won the Republican nomination in 1880 after a protracted struggle between the "Half-Breeds" and the "Stalwarts," two factions within the party that had been divided over whether Grant should be renominated. Garfield was a Half-Breed, so to balance the ticket, Stalwart Chester Arthur was nominated for the vice presidency. Guiteau's "reasoning" was that Arthur, in the role of president, would push out the Republican Half-Breeds who had denied him a federal job.[13] Garfield lingered for more than 10 weeks, then finally passed away in September, leaving Arthur as the most unqualified person ever to hold the office of president.[14] The country was rightly horrified by the depraved state of the Grand Old Party, and in the 1882 midterms the Democrats won a massive majority. The lame-duck Republican Congress recognized that it had better do something to redeem itself or else it would get walloped again in the 1884 election. So it dusted off an old proposal by Senator George H. Pendleton, a Democrat from Ohio, that would slowly eliminate federal patronage jobs and replace them with a permanent bureaucratic class.[15]

The Pendleton Civil Service Act ultimately transformed the federal bureaucracy, but it had no authority over state and local governments, where the use of patronage would grow markedly through the rest of the century, thanks to the legendary "party machines." Some machines were state-based, like those in Pennsylvania, under Matthew Quay, and New York, under Thomas Platt, both Republican.[16] But the most notorious machines were the big-city versions, and the most infamous of those was Tammany Hall, the Democratic machine that controlled New York City politics for eighty years. The "Tiger"—as Tammany was also known—took the patronage system to a whole different level from what Jackson or Lincoln had ever envisioned. Jackson had used it to promote democracy, and Lincoln to hold together his fragile coalition, but for Tammany and the rest of the postwar machines, patronage was the whole point of government. Parties competed for office not to enact some noble vision but merely to pay off the supporters who had put them there.

The big-city machines were an outgrowth of the rapid urbanization occurring in the decades before and after the war. In 1820, New York City had a population of about 125,000; thirty years later it passed 500,000, and in 1890 an astounding 1.5 million Americans called it their home.[17] This population explosion created economic, political, and social problems, and the federal welfare and regulatory state that we know today simply did not exist back then, so the machines stepped in to impose order on the urban chaos. While a handful of city machines—like Philadelphia's and Pittsburgh's—were Republican- and Yankee-run, Irish Democrats dominated most of the urban machine governments, including Albany, Brooklyn, Buffalo, Jersey City, New York City, and San Francisco.[18] The Irish Potato Famine of 1845–1852 brought waves of Irish to the shores of the United States, so that by 1870 the census counted more than 1.8 million Irish-born Americans, nearly two-thirds of whom lived in the Northeast.[19] The Sons of Hibernia created complex networks of political patrons and clients that exchanged jobs, services, licenses, and franchises for votes, all organized hierarchically from the bosses (or, in the Tammany lexicon, "sachems") at the top of the pyramid to local ward heelers at the bottom.[20]

The machine approach to politics is vastly different from what Americans know in the twenty-first century. Today we expect the two major parties to present us with a plan for how the whole country would improve under their control, and we vote for which one we think has the best vision for the nation's future. Most of us do not think about what personal benefits our vote can buy for us, but that's how politics worked in the urban machines. In fact, machine bosses thought politics as we know it today was impossible. They figured that without material inducements, people would not participate in democracy at all. When reformers began promoting civil service reform, George Washington Plunkitt—a Tammany Hall sachem—decried it in these colorful terms:

> [C]ivil service is sappin' the foundation of the whole shootin' match. Let me argue it out for you. I ain't up on sillygisms, but I can give you some arguments that nobody can answer.
>
> First this great and glorious country was built up by political parties; second, parties can't hold together if their workers don't get the offices when they win; third, if the parties go to pieces, the government they built up must go to pieces, too; fourth, then there'll be h— to pay . . .
>
> How are you goin' to keep up patriotism if this thing goes on? You can't do it. Let me tell you that patriotism has been dying out fast for the last twenty years. Before then when a party won, its workers got everything in sight. That was somethin' to make a man patriotic. Now, when a party wins and its men come forward and ask for their reward, the reply is, "Nothin' doin," unless you can answer a list of questions about Egyptian mummies and how many years it will take for a bird to wear out a mass of iron as big as the earth by steppin' on it once in a century?[21]

Plunkitt's point is overstated, but it does have some merit. Voter turnout in the election of 1880—a dull, drab affair in which there were few if any differences between the candidates on the issues—reached an impressive 81 percent.[22] Politics back then may not have been organized around big issues, but it had a broader appeal than it does today.

From a certain perspective, it's possible to appreciate the social utility of the machine system, especially when articulated by a character like Plunkitt (who was known to philosophize from his "rostrum," the bootblack stand at the New York County Courthouse). For poor Irish immigrants who were scorned by the native-born, the urban machines transformed them into citizens and offered them a path to prosperity. Under the tenure of Tammany's infamous Boss William Tweed, the electorate of New York City expanded quickly, as the machine worked hard to register new voters. During this period, Tammany also expanded the size of the city government to provide patronage to its scores of new supporters, dubbed the Shiny Hat Brigade during the Tweed reign.[23] The basic structure has some merit, at least on paper: voters supported the machines, which in turn helped them establish themselves in the United States and eventually rise to the middle class.

Practically speaking, however, it was riddled with defects. For starters, the perspective of scale is necessary: Tammany might have boasted a patronage army in the tens of thousands, but the size of the labor force in New York City was roughly one million, making it a drop in the bucket.[24] Additionally, the machine's generosity while it was pursuing a majority quickly turned into stinginess after victory was secured. Between 1880 and 1900, the golden age of the Irish machines, the per capita spending of machine-dominated governments actually declined.[25] What's more, the machines were hardly progressive advocates of social welfare or workers' rights; the patronage the machines doled out came mostly from property taxes, which meant that the machines needed to keep the business community and middle-class property owners happy.[26] The urban machines also engaged in rampant voter fraud, like stuffing ballot boxes and registering dead dogs, to a massive degree.[27] Finally and most outrageously, Tammany pols regularly turned public service into private profit. Plunkitt famously distinguished between "dishonest graft" and "honest graft"; dishonest graft included illegal activities like blackmail and the thievery that landed Boss Tweed in the Ludlow Street Jail, but honest graft was something entirely different:

> I might sum up the whole thing by sayin': "I seen my opportunities and I took 'em."
> Just let me explain by examples. My party's in power in the city, and it's goin' to undertake a lot of public improvements. Well, I'm tipped off, say, that they're going to lay out a new park at a certain place.

I see my opportunity and I take it. I go to that place and I buy up all the land in the neighborhood. Then the board of this or that makes its plan public, and there is a rush to get my land, which nobody cared particular for before.

Ain't it perfectly honest to charge a good price and make a profit on my investment and foresight? Of course, it is. Well, that's honest graft.[28]

Nowadays, this sort of behavior would land Plunkitt in the slammer, but it was par for the course in the days of urban machines. Politics was a for-profit enterprise.

If the politics of the period was small, the economic changes the country was experiencing were great. This was a time of rapid, unchecked industrialization that brought with it frequent recessions, several of which were long and deep. People were moving from the countryside into big cities, which created a host of new social problems for which the nation was unprepared. Wealth was becoming concentrated in the hands of just a few industrial and financial magnates, challenging notions of property rights first developed in a time of much greater equality of riches. Advances in technology—inventions like barbed wire and dry irrigation—enabled farmers to pour into the Great Plains, but this was a mixed blessing. Factor in cheap land, easy credit, and a quickly developing railroad system and there was a recipe for overexpansion and all its attendant problems. Yet despite the monumental changes that were reshaping American society, the two political parties contributed very little to the growth of the republic in this period, focused as they were on patronage and the conflicts of days long gone by.

Then came the election of 1896, perhaps the most consequential presidential contest between the Civil War and the Great Depression, all because of a thirty-six-year-old Nebraska Democrat by the name of William Jennings Bryan. Later known as the "Great Commoner," Bryan remains one of the more colorful figures in American history. For starters, he might be the best populist orator the country has ever seen, but there was more to Bryan than great speechifying. Although previous candidates had taken campaign swings through the country, nobody had toured as relentlessly as Bryan in 1896, and nobody had focused on the so-called swing states as Bryan did. By setting that precedent, he helped make subsequent presidential campaigns a little more democratic.[29] Above all, in an age when the two political parties were most interested in blurring differences so that they could scrape out a small victory and claim the spoils of patronage, Bryan actually stood for something greater than himself. He stood for the American farmer.

The condition of many farmers—which was never terribly strong—had declined in the decades after the Civil War. The number of southern farmers who were tenants—i.e., who farmed land that somebody else owned—was on the rise during this period, and they took the collapse in world cotton prices at the end of the century especially hard.[30] In the Midwest, rapid expansion had produced a glut of agricultural output, which drove down crop prices. Tariffs remained at the "emergency" levels set during the Civil War, which made it difficult for farmers to purchase the equipment necessary to run a farm, while railroad monopolies squeezed them for every last penny they had. The biggest threat to farmers, however, was the money supply. The Union government had printed greenbacks during the Civil War as a way to conserve the gold reserve, and the bankers who had snatched them up expected to have them redeemed in gold after the war. Rather than hike taxes, the government tightened the money supply so that the greenback's value would increase. In the short term, this might have been a politically smart move, but it spread the pain of the correction across decades as the country entered a long period of deflation. Combine that with massive population and economic growth and it meant that dollars were quite hard to come by, which put the squeeze on indebted farmers everywhere.[31]

Yet one would not recognize any of this by looking only at the two parties' quadrennial platforms, which mostly ignored the farmers. In the Jacksonian era, when the two parties refused to deal with the slavery issue, abolitionists found political expression through outside groups like the Liberty and Free Soil parties. Similarly, farmers in the late nineteenth century organized in response to the two parties' indifference, forming the National Grange of the Order of Patrons of Husbandry (or the "Grange," for short) in the 1860s to promote greater cooperation between farmers, and the more political Farmers' Alliance in the 1870s to push for higher agricultural prices.[32] In 1880, Iowa's James Weaver ran on the pro-inflation Greenback party ticket, which won more than 3 percent of the vote thanks to support from indebted farmers in the South and the Great Plains.[33] In 1892, the Populist party, an outgrowth of the Farmers' Alliance, also nominated Weaver, on a platform that called for the unlimited coinage of silver, direct election of senators, government control of the railroads, and other radical ideas (at least for the age).[34] The Populists won nearly 9 percent of the presidential vote, carrying Colorado, Idaho, Kansas, Nevada, and North Dakota.[35]

For indebted farmers, silver coinage became the hot-button issue. The United States Treasury had historically accepted it for coinage on a 16:1 basis with gold, but the Coinage Act of 1873 had demonetized silver at the behest of eastern financial interests. Large silver deposits had been discovered in the Mountain West; these were bound to push the value of silver downward and inflation upward, so debt owners in the East pressed Congress to stop coining silver and thus adopt a de facto gold standard. Farmers caught on to what became known as the "Crime of '73," and they later prevailed upon Congress to allow for modest coinage of silver, first with the Bland-Allison Act of 1878 and then with the Sherman Silver Purchase Act of 1890, yet neither was sufficient to produce the inflation farmers so desperately needed.[36] The collapse of the National Cordage Company on May 4, 1893, precipitated a series of bank failures, and the ensuing "Panic of 1893" plunged the nation into a deep recession, pushing the silver issue from the margins into the mainstream.[37] Wheat prices plummeted, and the plight of the yeomen farmer went from bad to worse. Pro-gold president Grover Cleveland, a Democrat, blamed the recession on the Sherman Silver Purchase Act, and he convinced Congress to repeal it, which contributed to a quick depletion of the gold supply as owners of silver coins hastily traded them in for gold ones.[38] With the nation's gold reserves running low, Cleveland cut a deal with a banking syndicate headed by J. P. Morgan to replenish the reserve at a tidy profit for the bankers. Farmers in the Midwest were outraged; it seemed as though the fix was in.[39]

When the Democrats assembled in Chicago for their quadrennial convention in 1896, they were in an ornery mood. President Cleveland did not attend, and that turned out to be a good thing for the portly chief executive, as he did not have to witness "Pitchfork Ben" Tillman of South Carolina giving a fiery speech denouncing him.[40] Meanwhile, Bryan knew that a majority of delegates were pro-silver but had no firm preferences for a presidential nominee, and he thought he might be able to swing the nomination his way.[41] He had secured the closing pro-silver speech in the debate over whether to add a silver plank to the party platform, and he made full use of his opportunity, giving one of the all-time great convention speeches in American history:

> *When you come before us and tell us that we shall disturb your business interests, we reply that you have disturbed our business interests by your action. We say to you that you have made too limited in its application the definition of a businessman. The man who is employed for wages is as much a businessman as his employer. . . . The farmer who goes forth in the morning and toils all day, begins in the spring and toils all summer, and by the application of brain and muscle to the natural resources of this country creates wealth, is as much a businessman as the man who goes upon the Board of Trade and bets upon the price of grain. . . .*
>
> *Having behind us the commercial interests and the laboring interests and all the toiling masses, we shall answer their demands for a gold standard by saying to them, you shall not press down upon the brow of labor this crown of thorns. You shall not crucify mankind upon a cross of gold!*[42]

Ultimately, the convention nominated Bryan on the fifth ballot and endorsed a platform that, though not as radical, was certainly reminiscent of the 1892 program offered by the Populist party, which subsequently endorsed Bryan at its convention later in the summer.[43]

It was the Bryan candidacy of 1896 that finally revived that old Jacksonian spirit, which had been idle for half a century. While the issues had changed since Jackson's day—Jackson's foe was the Bank of the United States, while Bryan's was the gold standard—both Jackson and Bryan were prepared to stake their political fortunes on the working class. What's more, they both conceived of politics as a struggle between the haves and the have-nots, with the haves controlling the levers of power to manipulate public policy toward their own ends. Like Old Hickory before him, a President Bryan would turn the tables and force the moneyed interests to respect the power of the people.

But it wasn't to be. The Republicans nominated William McKinley of Ohio, who pulled out a 52–45 victory on Election Day—practically a blowout, considering how close the presidential contests of the late nineteenth century usually were.[44] How do we account for this? How was it that Bryan, who basically reran the old Jacksonian campaign of 1832, would fail where the Old General had succeeded? Two problems stand out. First, Bryan's haves-versus-have-nots approach to politics simply did not appeal to a lot of farmers, many of whom were more secure economically than Bryan's hard-core supporters in Kansas and Nebraska, having improved their agricultural methods and diversified their crops over the years. They had a vested interest in the status quo, and the idea of a radical departure under a Bryan presidency was just not appealing to them.[45]

Second, while Bryan hoped to forge a coalition of all have-nots—laborers and farmers alike—his actual campaign strategy failed miserably. For starters, his tone was far too evangelical, which pushed Catholics to McKinley, who eschewed making divisive statements on the hot-button cultural issues of the day. Beyond Bryan's evangelical fervor, there was the fact that the Democratic platform really offered nothing for laborers or urban residents. If anything, they must have viewed Bryan as a real threat, thanks to his rhetorical excesses. For instance, this line in his "Cross of Gold" speech must have terrified city folk when they read it in the newspaper:

> *You come to us and tell us that the great cities are in favor of the gold standard; we reply that the great cities rest upon our broad and fertile prairies. Burn down your cities and leave our farms, and your cities will spring up again as if by magic. But destroy our farms and the grass will grow in the streets of every city in the country.*[46]

A Democrat might have been able to get away with such an anti-urban campaign fifty years prior, but not anymore. The country was now substantially more urban, industrial, and interconnected than in the days of Jackson. A populist pitch geared primarily to the hardscrabble farmers in the Great Plains simply was not going to work anymore.

There are two ways to take the election of 1896 for the Democrats. From the perspective of those who had to endure the defeat, it was an unmitigated disaster, and a sign of worse things to come. The Panic of 1893 would be the last severe recession until after World War I, and so McKinley's promise during the campaign that he was the "advance agent of prosperity" turned out to be more or less true. In the decade before 1896, real GDP per capita was basically flat, hovering right around $3,700 per person for the whole decade (in 2000 dollars); however, it increased by 44 percent in the decade after 1896, making for one of the most robust economic expansions in the country's history.[47] With that kind of prosperity, the Democrats had little hope of a return to form back in the East. Meanwhile, a rebound in agricultural prices meant that the farmers who'd bolted the GOP in 1896 were back in line by 1900. So all the Democrats really had left by then were Tammany Hall and a handful of other Irish machines, the Solid South, and some sparsely populated states in the Mountain West that stuck with them because coining silver would help the mining industry.[48]

Yet from today's perspective, the Bryan candidacy was an important milestone in the development of the Democratic party. In 1896, Bryan had a vision of a political coalition that would unite the farmers and laborers by advocating unabashedly for their interests over those of the wealthy. In his "Cross of Gold" speech, he said:

> *There are two ideas of government. There are those who believe that if you just legislate to make the well-to-do prosperous, that their prosperity will leak through on those below. The Democratic idea has been that if you legislate to make the masses prosperous their prosperity will find its way up and through every class that rests upon it.*[49]

This kind of rhetoric should sound familiar to modern ears, for it is basically the same point that Democrats have made in every campaign ever since. This return to a Jacksonian "people versus the powerful" theme begins with the Great Commoner, whose candidacy ends a fifty-year period in which the Democratic party was a tangle of sectional and ethnic gripes, unable to offer much of anything besides patronage. The fact that most of "the toiling masses" voted Republican that year was terrible news for Democrats of the day, but in our story it simply signals that this was the start, not the conclusion, of the party's transformation.

CHAPTER TWO

Bryanism with a Princeton Accent

Woodrow Wilson and the Founding of the Modern Democratic Party

---

At their core, the major American political parties are a lot like businesses—but instead of seeking profit, the parties seek electoral victory. To achieve this goal, they engage in all sorts of electioneering practices, nowadays running television advertisements, sponsoring phone banks, printing and distributing yard signs, holding rallies, and so on. They also promote political ideologies—governing philosophies that tie together their various positions on the issues—as a way to attract voters. A party's ideology is adopted in service of its quest for victory, not the other way around—and here it's necessary to distinguish the purists from the insiders, or the *National Review* from the Republican National Committee.[1] One is driven by the quest for the good society, the other by victory next November.

Any time a party suffers a stinging defeat, there is always some element within it that encourages reform, revision, and rethinking of the old electoral strategies. More often than not, the grand pooh-bahs of the party decide that only modest tweaks are necessary—perhaps a change in rhetoric, a candidate from a different region, or a more moderate speaking lineup at the next convention. It's rare to see a party reshape its basic political ideology for the purpose of reclaiming office, but it's rarer still that a party must endure seemingly unending defeats like those the Democrats suffered between 1894 and 1910. The Democratic party of this age eventually had to face the stark reality that superficial adjustments were not going to return it to old glories; root-and-branch change was necessary.

As we shall see in this chapter, the need for such essential restructuring triggered an epic battle in 1912 between the new progressive forces within the party and its old conservative factions. The victors would be the progressives and their chosen candidate, Woodrow Wilson of New Jersey. Entering office in 1913 with an enormous Democratic majority in Congress, Wilson would have wide latitude in charting a new course for the party of Jackson, and after some wobbling, he would eventually choose the progressive path. His term thus marks the emergence of the modern Democratic party. Previous Democratic administrations had held, as Jackson did, that big government was ultimately a danger to the interests of average folks. Under Wilson, the Democrats began to abandon this Jacksonian notion of limited government, deciding instead that a powerful, expansive government was the best friend of the common man.

Though Bryan had suffered the worst defeat of any Democrat in nearly a quarter century, the party nevertheless nominated him for president unanimously on the first ballot in 1900, in large part because there was really nobody of sufficient stature within the party to stop him.[2] With the economic crisis having dissipated by 1900, the Democrats turned their attention to the Spanish-American War; the party's platform declared that "no nation can long endure half republic and half empire, and we warn the American people that imperialism abroad will lead quickly and inevitably to despotism at home."[3] While the issues changed, the results were basically the same: McKinley trounced Bryan by six points in the general election—a small shift relative to 1896, but enough of a swing to put all of the Farm Belt states back in the Republican column. Bryan even lost his home state of Nebraska by seven thousand votes.[4]

After Bryan's back-to-back defeats, Democrats everywhere were wondering, How can we win national office again? In 1904, the party establishment looked backward to solve this riddle, searching about for an eastern, pro-business conservative in the mold of Samuel Tilden and

Grover Cleveland, the only Democrats since the Civil War to outpoll the Republicans. Of course, one of their problems was that they had no leaders of national prominence from the East, so they were forced to run one Alton B. Parker, who had won a statewide election in New York in 1897, for chief judge of the Court of Appeals.[5] No sooner had Parker won the nomination than he inflamed the populist West, which still swore fealty to Bryan. Although the pro-gold Parker had backed the Great Commoner in 1896 and 1900 (a gesture of loyalty that not all eastern Democrats, including future president Woodrow Wilson, actually offered), he nevertheless dropped a bombshell on the convention after he won the nomination, announcing that he considered the gold standard to be "irrevocably fixed."[6] The convention voted in favor of backing Parker despite his pro-gold condition, but there was substantial dissent from the South and the West.[7] The party's hope heading into the general election was that the conservative Parker would restore the party's standing in the East, but he turned out to be mere cannon fodder for Teddy Roosevelt in the general election that year, losing everywhere except the South and carrying just 38 percent of the vote nationwide. All in all, it made for the worst drubbing in the party's history to that point.

The hapless Democrats seemed to be damned if they did and damned if they didn't: when they ran a populist/anti-imperialist, they lost; when they ran a conservative, they lost by more. Worse, the thrice-in-a-row drubbings had not unified the party in a shared goal of electoral victory, but rather exacerbated the internal divisions that had developed over the previous decade. So the party was really in a double bind: not only did it have to find a way to become competitive with the dominant Republicans, but it had to figure out how to mend fences on its own side. What to do? As the early part of the twentieth century wore on, the Democrats discovered that the solution to both problems lay in embracing progressivism, a new approach to governing that would reunite the eastern with the western/southern Democrats and give them a prayer of defeating the Republicans.

Progressivism is a very difficult philosophical movement to classify, both politically and ideologically. Politically, lots of different types of people were progressive during this period in American history. When we think about progressives, we usually think of activists who pushed for social change in the big northern cities. These were mostly educated, middle-class, Protestant do-gooders whose sense of outrage had been aroused by the problems of industrialization, urbanization, and the waves of immigrants from eastern and southern Europe.[8] Their spiritual and (oftentimes) genealogical forebears were the reformist elements of the Republican party—the "Conscience Whigs" in Lincoln's coalition, the Liberal Republicans who bolted the GOP in 1872 over the cronyism of the Grant administration, and the "Mugwumps" who supported the upstanding Democrat Grover Cleveland in 1884 over the ethically suspect Republican senator James G. Blaine of Maine.[9]

Yet progressivism was not confined simply to the big cities of the East. William Borah of Idaho was a key Republican backer of the New Deal and a leading anti-imperialist voice in the Senate, while Hiram Johnson of California was an opponent of the trusts and a crusader against bossism and graft.[10] There were southern progressives like Charles McIver, who fought for women's education, and Alexander McKelway, who was a strong advocate for child labor laws.[11] Additionally, the populists from the Farm Belt often migrated into the progressive camp—as we shall see, Bryan would be the leader of this faction. With so many types of progressives out there, it should not be surprising to learn that some were Republican while others were Democrats, and that both parties still had large contingents of conservatives in their ranks, with leaders like Rhode Island machine boss Nelson Aldrich in the GOP and Tammany Hall in the Democratic party.

Ideologically speaking, progressives generally pushed for reform of the role of government in American society, and we can identify several different tracks their proposals tended to run on. First, they favored a restructuring of the electoral process, which on the federal level meant the direct election of senators, and on the state and local levels resulted in the widespread adoption of recall and referendum initiatives. They also advocated the secret ballot, as well as suffrage for women. Yet the progressive commitment to democracy was not unconditional; they abhorred the city machines, like those found in New York and Philadelphia, and they promoted city managers and unelected officials to govern city affairs. Second, progressives sponsored programs to deal with the growing problem of urban poverty, and the country's first class of social workers and sociologists can rightly be called progressive. Tracing their roots back to the thinly veiled anti-Catholic initiatives of the middle of the nineteenth century, the progressives sought to "reform" the morals of the new immigrants, and succeeded in getting many states—and finally the whole country—to ban the sale of alcohol.[12]

Third, progressives pushed for a more expansive role for the federal government to counter the runaway power of big business, an economic force that had been nonexistent when the country ratified the Constitution and its minimal scope for federal activity. In this way, the progressives introduced a new, distinct ideology into the American political world. The Democrats had long favored a small, lean government to protect the rights of average citizens, while the Whigs and later the Republicans supported a more active and dynamic state that facilitated commerce and industry. The government had implemented antitrust and interstate commerce regulations in the 1880s, but neither reform represented much of an expansion in federal regulatory authority over business. The progressives were the first significant force in the country to lobby hard for an active and vigorous federal government that defended the rights of average citizens against the ill effects of the Industrial Revolution. Most notably, this meant greater regulation of the trusts, consumer protection, and labor reforms.[13]

Teddy Roosevelt—or T.R., as he is also known—is often remembered as the political leader of the progressive movement, which is a fair characterization in many respects: after all, Roosevelt's exuberance certainly matched the spirit of the movement, and his term was filled with many substantial reforms. Still, it's important to keep in mind that Roosevelt often had to rely on the congressional Democrats, including the southerners, to get progressive reforms through Congress, as the leadership of his party was dominated by conservatives like House Speaker Joe Cannon of Illinois and Aldrich. What's more, despite T.R.'s list of accomplishments, he was still never to the left of William Jennings Bryan—no national leader in either of the two major parties ever really was during this period—and Bryan remains an unsung hero in the story of how progressivism came of age in American politics. As the decade wore on, Bryan had evolved from an agrarian populist into an uncompromising advocate of all things progressive. This was a fairly easy transition for the Great Commoner, who always had a knack for placing himself on the frontier between the mainstream and out-and-out radicalism. For instance, he returned from a world tour in 1906 to give a speech in Madison Square Garden in which he borrowed a page from the Populist platform of 1892, urging the nationalization of the rail lines.[14]

The Democratic party did not include public ownership of the railroads in its 1908 platform, but it did nominate Bryan on the first ballot.[15] The conservative forces tried desperately to find an alternative, but the problem that had plagued the party in the last two presidential cycles—the lack of a solid bench of would-be candidates—had only gotten worse by 1908.[16] Bryan remained the only figure of any prominence still around, and he won the nomination on the first ballot, with nearly 90 percent of all convention delegates in support.[17] He made sure that the party adopted a very progressive platform, laying out specific and detailed proposals to reduce tariffs, curb the trusts, regulate the railroads, reform the banking system, guarantee the right of workers to organize into labor unions, and initiate a national health bureau. T.R.'s panache aside, the 1908 Democratic platform should be remembered as the first unabashed progressive program to come from a major party.[18]

Once again, the Democrats had to graft the urban vote—which had backed conservative Democrats in the 1880s but not since—onto Bryan's agrarian base. Populism, anti-imperialism, and conservatism had failed in three straight attempts, so in 1908 the party embraced "Bryanism 3.0," the progressive version. Yet once again, its strategy failed. Bryan improved modestly on Parker's terrible showing, but he still did worse in 1908 than he had in 1896 or 1900, pulling just 43 percent of the popular vote.[19] The Republicans had happily endorsed T.R.'s handpicked successor, Secretary of War William Howard Taft, and had approved a more conservative platform than the Democrats.[20] Still, Taft had T.R.'s blessing, and that was good enough for the United States in 1908.

Bryan was genuinely surprised by the defeat, and in historical retrospect, it is indeed a bit of a puzzle. Although T.R. was an immensely popular leader—much like Andrew Jackson and Ronald Reagan, who similarly had enough national credibility to secure the election of their successors—at least after Jackson and Reagan the opposition had stanched the bleeding. Why couldn't the magnetic Bryan at least match the performance of the insipid Michael Dukakis? This becomes all the more peculiar when we factor in the Panic of 1907, the yearlong recession that followed,[21] and the fact that the Democratic platform came much closer to the progressive zeitgeist of the age than did the Republican program. These factors should have aided the Democratic cause, so how could Taft trounce Bryan by an even bigger margin than McKinley ever had?

Ultimately, Bryan's problem in 1908 was the same as it had been in 1896 and 1900: he scared the living daylights out of easterners—conservative and progressive alike. Though the two-party system was now beginning to split along ideological lines, regional prejudices were still a major factor. Eastern progressives were simply more comfortable with Taft, a moderate from Ohio, than Bryan, a populist-progressive from Nebraska. What the Democrats really needed to secure their long-sought farmer-labor alliance was a "cultivated" progressive who could put the "respectable" elements of society at ease, i.e., an easterner who could play on his home turf without losing the agrarian vote out west. That person would be not Bryan but rather Woodrow Wilson of New Jersey. As historian David Sarasohn has observed, Wilson advocated "Bryanism with a Princeton accent," which made him perfect for the Democrats.[22]

Taft was a reluctant successor to T.R., and he brought to the White House a less aggressive view of the presidency than his predecessor.[23] In consequence, he could not manage the growing rift in his party between the conservative leadership and progressive insurgents like Robert La Follette of Wisconsin and Albert Cummins of Iowa. The result was a political coalition that was beginning to crack into pieces, evidenced most notably by the debate over the Payne-Aldrich Tariff Bill. Progressives hoped it would enact a downward revision and a streamlining of rates. However, conservatives in the Senate, led by Aldrich, dominated the process, and the final result raised many tariff rates for well-connected special interests and split the Republican party sharply in two, with the bill passing just narrowly in the House despite a GOP majority of forty-seven seats.[24]

In a rebuke to the Taft administration, the public in 1910 elected a Democratic majority to the House for the first time in nearly twenty years.[25] The newly empowered progressive Democrats buzzed with activity, passing a constitutional amendment providing for the direct election of senators and approving trade reciprocity, tariff reductions, more than a dozen pro-labor measures, and stricter railroad regulations. House Democrats had to deal with President Taft and a Republican-dominated Senate, so many of these reforms were for naught. Still, they gave the party much-needed momentum heading into the 1912 presidential campaign. What's more, the Democratic surge in 1910 finally gave the party a better crop of national candidates as Democrats picked up Senate seats and governorships in big eastern states, including New Jersey and New York.[26]

Bryan promised not to be a candidate for president in 1912, but he came to the party convention in Baltimore determined that the standard-bearer would be a bona fide progressive. When the proceedings began, there were four major contenders vying for the nomination. Oscar Underwood of Alabama had the backing of the South, while Ohio governor Judson Harmon was the darling of the party's conservative wing.[27] Meanwhile, there were two seemingly progressive candidates from the North, with whom Bryan initially expressed satisfaction.[28] The first was Champ Clark, the affable Speaker of the House of Representatives, who had a solid record of accomplishment upon which to found a candidacy. The other progressive in the field was Wilson, the former president of Princeton University and now governor of New Jersey, whose political preferences had shifted along with his party's in the preceding twenty years.

Wilson had opposed Bryan in 1896, instead supporting the pro-gold National Democratic ticket,[29] and as late as 1907 he had written a letter to a former Princeton trustee lamenting, "Would that we could do something, at once dignified and effective, to knock Mr. Bryan once for all into a cocked hat!"[30] An early Wilson backer was noted conservative Colonel George Harvey, who was influential in getting the New

Jersey Democratic machinery to nominate him for governor in 1910. Yet Wilson was an ambitious and perceptive political player who sensed the changing mood within his party and the country. Upon election as governor, he had immediately defied the bosses, going so far as to persuade the legislature to deny his machine sponsor, James Smith, a seat in the United States Senate.[31] Wilson then enacted a series of progressive reforms, including workplace regulations, women and child labor laws, an act granting a public utilities commission new powers, a revision of electoral rules, school reform, and a new commission form of government for New Jersey cities.[32] He had been in office for less than a year, yet by the end of 1911 his record in this key eastern state made him a prime contender for the party's presidential nomination.

When the convention met in June 1912, Wilson had secured the support of some three hundred delegates, and Clark had more than four hundred committed to him. Yet the indomitable Bryan would once again rule the proceedings, as he had the previous four conventions. When the national committee backed Parker as the temporary convention chairman, Bryan asked Clark and Wilson for help in opposing the New York judge. This was a test to smoke out which of the two was a true progressive and which might be willing to bend to the New York delegation, Tammany Hall, and its patrons on Wall Street. As front-runners often do, Clark equivocated in his response to Bryan, offering instead to make Bryan permanent chairman.[33] Meanwhile, Wilson—who had been courting the Commoner for some time—stood firmly with him. "You are quite right," Wilson replied, "a convention of progressives . . . must, if it is not to be put in a wrong light before the country, express its convictions in its organization and its choice of the men who are to speak for it."[34]

So, early on, Clark positioned himself to the right of Bryan and Wilson, and the convention seemingly was of a similar mind, electing Parker to the chairmanship, 579 to 510. In the first round of balloting, Clark had a sizable lead over Wilson—440½ to 324, with the rest going to other candidates—and his strength grew steadily thereafter. On the tenth ballot, the New York delegation left Harmon and swung to Clark, giving him a majority of the convention delegates; however, this was not sufficient for victory because, ever since 1832, a candidate had to obtain two-thirds of the delegates to win the nomination. To prevent a stampede to Clark, who Bryan believed was in cahoots with Tammany and Wall Street, the Great Commoner informed the convention that he would not support Clark so long as he had the backing of the New York delegation.[35] This stalled the Speaker's progress, and subsequent ballots came and went with little change. When it became clear that the anti-Clark factions would not budge, the convention wound its way over to Wilson, who as an eastern progressive was an acceptable compromise for the exhausted delegates. In a testament to just how divided the Democrats were that year, it took forty-six ballots to nominate the New Jersey governor for the presidency, more than any number since the 1860 convention, when the party deadlocked without a nominee.[36]

What possessed Bryan to take such a hard stand against New York? After all, he had made peace with Tammany Hall in 1908—why was it suddenly so unworthy of a political alliance? Bryan might have wanted to swing a deadlocked convention to himself, but he might also have realized that this year the progressives did not have to compromise with the reviled Tammany forces. Victory was all but ensured, because the Republicans were hopelessly torn in two. T.R. had returned to the States after a world tour in 1909, and he found his party a shambles. At first he was charitable toward Taft, but he soon decided that his successor was too comfortable with the conservative factions in the party. He declared himself a candidate for the party's nomination and dominated the Republican primaries, hoping to force the GOP convention to recognize him as the choice of the people.[37] However, Taft's control of the national committee as well as the southern delegations—which did not represent Republican voters so much as recipients of federal patronage—meant that the result was a foregone conclusion. Ultimately, T.R. requested that his name not be placed in nomination, and before the balloting began, he all but said he planned to run as a third-party candidate.[38]

Taft was pretty much a nonentity in the general election. He gave a few speeches, then retired to the White House to await his impending electoral rebuke. So Wilson had to deal primarily with T.R., who had taken a much more progressive turn since leaving office. Roosevelt's new Progressive party—nicknamed the Bull Moose party, after a characteristic Roosevelt turn-of-phrase—promoted a robust agenda for "social and industrial justice," including a minimum wage, a six-day workweek, an eight-hour industrial workday, workers' compensation, the right of workers to organize, and the prohibition of child labor. The Progressives acknowledged the inevitability of the trusts, distinguished between good ones and bad, and promised vigorous regulation.[39] T.R. called his program the "New Nationalism," and attracted the backing of notable progressives like Herbert Croly and Walter Lippmann.[40]

There was much overlap between the Progressive and Democratic platforms, but Wilson managed to carve out several important distinctions. He campaigned—as Democrats long had—on tariff reductions, and he connected protectionism to the emergence of the trusts. He railed against the paternalism of T.R.'s program and promised a "New Freedom" instead. This was billed as a neo-Jeffersonian ideology that would return the individual to a place of preeminence, in opposition to the big government advanced by T.R. or the big business tolerated by the conservatives. In particular, Wilson denied the inescapability of what the Progressives called "the concentration of modern business," promising instead to end the trusts for good by vigorous prosecution of unfair practices, although he never really clarified what these were.[41]

With the Republican vote split, Wilson was bound for a huge victory. On Election Day, the New Jersey governor won 435 electoral votes to T.R.'s 88, leaving just eight for the luckless Taft, who never really wanted to be president in the first place.[42] The Democrats also captured more than 60 new House seats, extending their majority in the lower chamber to 291 seats.[43] Even so, the Democrats did not so much win as the Republicans lost. Though he was an eastern governor, Wilson was still hampered by the regional prejudices that were attached to his political coalition; many northerners still viewed the Democrats as an illegitimate collection of southern secessionists and Tammany hacks and saw the Republican party as the only respectable coalition, despite the presence of anti-reform reactionaries. These voters split their support between Taft and T.R., leaving Wilson with little more than the old

Bryan vote.[44] Meanwhile, the public's interest in the campaign did not nearly match the excitement that accompanied the raucous nomination conventions that had resulted in three major candidates—turnout was actually down in 1912 relative to four years prior.[45]

So Wilson would assume power under very strange circumstances. His party had just achieved one of the largest governing majorities in the history of the country, yet it clearly did not represent a majority of public opinion. The Democrats had no mandate to speak of—they were still nothing more than the relatively narrow faction that had spent the previous decade in the political wilderness. This gave Wilson a unique opportunity, as he was free to govern without worry about the minority Republicans in Congress, but it also made for a tremendous challenge: if he did not quickly and effectively consolidate his political position, surely a reunited Republican party would drive him out of power in 1916 as quickly as he had been swept in. As if all this were not enough, he was leading a political coalition still full of internal disagreements along ideological and geographical lines—for although the progressives had won a victory over the conservatives at the Baltimore convention, the latter were far from vanquished. Indeed, Tammany Hall remained the entrenched Democratic power in the Empire State, by far the largest and politically most important in the Union.

The fate of the Democratic party, in particular its budding progressive wing, would therefore depend on how well Wilson utilized the vast powers the country had handed him. Would the Republicans position themselves as the truly progressive party, thus crowding out Wilson, Bryan, and the progressive Democrats? Would the conservative forces within the Democratic party recover the power they had lost? Would the two parties simply return to their old regional divisions, leaving the progressive-conservative split a historical peculiarity? None of these questions had been resolved by the election of 1912; instead, they would all be left up to Wilson as he took office in March 1913.

Though Wilson had been elected president on a highly progressive platform and had been backed by Bryan, the party's leading progressive, the first half of his first term saw only modest achievements for the movement. This was due to reticence not so much from congressional

Democrats but rather from Wilson himself, who preferred not to have the government involve itself in "social justice" projects as actively as many progressives demanded, and who particularly balked at proposals designed to advance the interests of one particular class or group.

Even so, Wilson could boast three significant accomplishments in the Sixty-third Congress, which convened in 1913. The first was the Underwood Tariff, on which Congress began work when Wilson called it into special session in April. The new president showed himself to be the most able manager of the Democratic caucus in seventy years, and his skill and dedication paid off. The Underwood Tariff sailed through the House, but it was Wilson's careful supervision of the process that helped it pass the Senate, which had strong protectionist factions in it. Wilson also reorganized the nation's banking infrastructure under the Federal Reserve System, which utilized a mix of public and private interests to manage the currency. Third, he instituted the Federal Trade Commission (FTC), which had broad authority to regulate unfair business practices. The FTC was closer to the New Nationalism than the New Freedom, but Wilson changed course as he realized that trying to enumerate unfair business practices would produce a byzantine and draconian piece of legislation.[46]

Still, many progressives were disappointed, and they saw Wilson as being too friendly with the conservatives in both parties.[47] For instance, Wilson originally favored a more conservative reorganization of the banking system, and it was Bryan—now the secretary of state—who pushed him to the left. The final result still left many elements in the party unsatisfied.[48] He also appointed lackluster board members to the FTC, discouraging progressives who wanted a robust regulatory agency.[49] More annoying to progressives was what Wilson did not do. He generally wanted legislation that would not play favorites between groups, so he did not embrace the cause of labor, refusing to put his weight behind an effort to grant unions an antitrust exemption, despite the pledge of his party's platform to do just that; instead, labor unions secured only a few vaguely worded sentences in the Clayton Act, which expanded the government's antitrust rules.[50] Additionally, he refused to offer banking assistance—known as "rural credits"—to farmers who were concerned that the new banking system would inevitably favor the

East. He also opposed progressive measures like proposals to curb child labor.[51]

The midterm elections of 1914 indicated that the president had failed to enlarge his political coalition beyond the core vote from 1912. Instead, the Republicans captured sixty-three seats in the House as most of the Progressive vote returned to the GOP. The Republicans rebounded in the East and the Midwest, where they won scores of new seats, including ten in Ohio and eleven in New York. The only bright spot for Wilson's party came in the West, where much of the Progressive vote seemed comfortable remaining with the Democrats, who picked up House seats in Colorado, Kansas, and Washington.[52] Nevertheless, this was but a silver lining amid dark clouds. Bryan's defeat in 1896 had demonstrated quite clearly that a sweep of the West and the South would not be sufficient to carry the White House without at least a few electoral votes back East, which was quickly rejoining the Republican fold. The Democrats had long been in pursuit of a coalition of farmers and laborers, and Wilson had not yet built it. If the trend continued, he would be voted out of office in 1916.

Yet Wilson had already proved himself to be an adept political chess player—as evidenced by his thorough turnaround on William Jennings Bryan: in 1896 he voted against him, and in 1907 he lamented to a friend that the party could not get rid of him, but in 1912 he allied with him at the convention, and in 1913 he named him secretary of state. Similarly, Wilson had moved from the conservative to the progressive end of the political spectrum in relatively short order, so he was perfectly capable of making more political adjustments, and that's exactly what he did.[53] If progressives in the East didn't think he had been progressive enough, well then, Wilson would just shift further left to accommodate them.

So as the presidential campaign season approached, he flip-flopped on many key issues in an effort to hold down his rural base and expand his support among urban workers and eastern progressives. An early signal of his shift came when he nominated Louis Brandeis—a progressive hero and Wilson adviser—to the Supreme Court in January 1916. Through the remainder of the legislative session, Wilson and the Sixty-fourth Congress busily implemented one progressive reform after another: the Federal Farm Loan Act offered rural credits to farmers;

the Kern-McGillicuddy Act offered workers' compensation to federal employees; the Keating-Owen Act regulated child labor; the Adamson Act gave the labor unions a big win by establishing an eight-hour workday for railroad workers; the Warehouse Act required federal inspection and licensing of storage sites for agricultural products; and the Revenue Act redistributed the tax burden from labor to capital.[54] Preeminent Wilson historian Arthur Link has observed that "the Democratic Congressional majority had, by the fall of 1916, enacted almost every important plank in the Progressive platform of 1912."[55] Whatever differences there had been between the New Nationalism and the New Freedom were now moot.

But would this pivot work against a united GOP front? The Republicans and the Progressives met in June 1916 with the common goal of securing peace between the warring factions. While the conservatives agreed to reform the nominating process, they refused to nominate the apostate T.R., who once again was in pursuit of the White House, so former New York governor and sitting Supreme Court justice Charles Evans Hughes emerged as a compromise candidate. Nominally, the Republicans were reunited, but in reality big philosophical disagreements remained between the conservative and progressive wings of the party, leaving Hughes to bridge a very wide intraparty divide.[56] This was not an easy job, and he spent most of his time attacking Wilson's administration, in particular the Adamson Act, and offering only vague indications of what a Hughes administration would look like. His candidacy turned off the progressive elites, and many of T.R.'s high-profile backers—including Croly and Lippmann—eventually embraced Wilson, albeit with some reluctance.[57]

The Democrats, meanwhile, put aside their disagreements to rally behind the surging Wilson, whom they nominated by acclamation in St. Louis on a platform trumpeting progressivism and peace. Europe by then had become embroiled in World War I, and, as in the 1790s and 1810s, European conflict threatened the United States' commercial rights on the high seas. Wilson took a pro-British posture and pushed for military preparedness at home but nevertheless refused to commit the nation to the war effort. This stand probably helped him with swing voters, but it noticeably damaged him with two key Democratic constituencies that didn't much care for the Brits: the Irish and the Germans. Adding to

Wilson's problem with the Irish vote was his strained relationship with the urban machines, especially Tammany Hall. The Tiger had also been a thorn in the side of the incorruptible Grover Cleveland during his tenure, and though Wilson wanted to be rid of it, he was unable to defang it.[58] Ultimately, New York County gave Wilson a disappointing 52 percent of the vote as the Empire State went to Hughes.[59]

Even with weak support from the Irish and Germans, Wilson's turn to progressivism and his peace campaign helped secure reelection, albeit narrowly. He won 49.2 percent of the vote, a smaller share than any victorious incumbent except Bill Clinton; he also carried just 52 percent of the Electoral College vote, which remains the smallest share a victorious incumbent has ever won. A shift of fewer than four thousand votes in California—where Hughes famously, albeit accidentally, snubbed the state's progressive Republican governor, Hiram Johnson, during a campaign swing through the state—would have tipped the White House to the GOP.[60] Wilson even lost his home state of New Jersey by a wide margin.[61] Yet despite all this, his victory in 1916 remains a noteworthy accomplishment; it was the best popular-vote performance by a Democratic candidate since the Tilden candidacy some forty years before, and it greatly advanced the party's transformation into a progressive coalition, thus paving the way for FDR's New Deal.

Generally speaking, Wilson's voting coalition in 1916 was a hybrid of what Bryan and Cleveland had forged in the 1890s. The conservative Cleveland had won the great American cities in the Northeast and the Midwest but ran poorly in the West. The populist Bryan was the hero of the farmers in the Great Plains, but he had failed to make eastern urbanites comfortable. Wilson embraced progressivism to discover a comfortable median between these extremes, pulling in farmers and laborers alike. He generally matched Bryan in the West, and though Cleveland ran stronger in the cities, Wilson did well enough. This balanced approach can be seen most clearly in Wilson's narrow victories in Ohio, which Bryan could never carry, and Nebraska, which Cleveland lost thrice. Wilson won them both, and with them the presidency.

In his second inaugural address, President Wilson declared of his first term:

*Perhaps no equal period in our history has been so fruitful of
important reforms in our economic and industrial life or so full
of significant changes in the spirit and purpose of our political action. We have sought very thoughtfully to set our house in order,
correct the grosser errors and abuses of our industrial life, liberate
and quicken the processes of our national genius and energy, and
lift our politics to a broader view of the people's essential interests.*[62]

The vanity of this boast helps explain why Wilson has been remembered with mixed emotions by successive generations. It is very rare,
after all, to see a chief executive suggest that his tenure to date has been
perhaps the most important in history.

And still, there is something to be said for the claim. Woodrow
Wilson was the only Democrat to win reelection between Andrew
Jackson and Franklin D. Roosevelt, and his first term marks a decisive
shift in the party toward progressivism. Sure, many conservatives would
remain within the Democratic coalition, but they would never again
control the main levers of power. Bryan had reoriented the party toward
the common folk, while Wilson had shown that a progressive Democratic government could win their support.

Yet Wilson had overlooked the need to build an enduring political
coalition, as evidenced by the 1920 election. He and the progressives
loathed the patronage regimes in the big cities, especially Tammany
Hall, yet the machines understood something that they had not yet
grasped: every party experiences bad times sooner or later, so you'd
better have enough loyal voters to ride out the storm. The new progressive movement would have to learn this the hard way. Wilson had won
election in 1916 trumpeting the fact that he'd "kept us out of war," but
the country entered World War I just a few months after his second inauguration. After the war's successful conclusion, Wilson spent most of
his political capital in an effort to rally the country behind the League
of Nations. Americans, however, were in an isolationist mood, and the
Republican-led Senate defeated Wilson's treaty. This, combined with
a postwar recession and a series of anarchist terror attacks, created the
impression that the country had headed in the wrong direction, and
the Republicans won an enormous victory in the 1920 presidential elec-

tion, pledging a "return to normalcy."[63] Over the next decade, the GOP would dominate the national government, returning the Democrats to the same position they were in after the defeat of 1896.

This points to a missed opportunity during Wilson's tenure. The Republican voters who had briefly backed him in 1916 ultimately felt comfortable returning to the GOP fold at decade's end because, for all his progressive governance, he had failed to turn them into loyal Democratic clients. He never really offered them any policies that required their continued support of the party, as Tammany Hall had done by creating its "Shiny Hat Brigade" and giving Irish voters patronage jobs, or the GOP by giving its business allies generous tariff protections during the Gilded Age. In both cases, the clients knew that if they didn't back their patrons, their benefits would run dry. However, the Wilson voters of 1916 were free to wind their way back to the GOP, which they did in large numbers in 1920.

This was a mistake that FDR would not make when his turn came in 1932. He would build a Democratic party on the progressive foundations of Bryan and Wilson, designed to use the vast powers of the federal government to ensure social justice for all Americans. However, Roosevelt's party would also use those powers to build electoral levies, strong enough to endure the inevitable resurgence of Republicanism, which came roaring back in 1938. For FDR and later party leaders, that would mean the creation and maintenance of new client groups dependent upon and loyal to the Democratic party.

CHAPTER THREE

A Mediator of Interests

FDR and the Establishment of the New Deal Order

In the 1920s, the Democratic party was stuck in the same terrible spot where it had found itself in the first decade of the century, limited to the Solid South and a handful of Democratic bastions in the big cities. The Republican conservatism once expounded by William McKinley was again triumphant, and President Calvin Coolidge summed up the philosophy of the Grand Old Party with characteristic succinctness when he said, "The business of America is business." The country agreed, and delivered the GOP three straight presidential and six straight congressional victories from 1920 through 1928.

The Democrats, meanwhile, were left fighting among themselves. The alliance between the urban faction in the North and the rural factions in the South and West had always depended more on shared dislike of Republicanism than a unifying ideology, and without the leadership of the progressive Woodrow Wilson to harmonize the various interests, they fell back to counterproductive infighting. The nadir came in 1924 when the rural South and the urban North deadlocked in the national convention, squabbling over Prohibition and whether an anti–Ku Klux Klan plank should be inserted into the party platform. It took the party a record-shattering 103 ballots to settle on a nominee, John Davis of West Virginia, who went on to win just 29 percent of the vote in November.[1] Four years later, the urban North managed to nominate its preferred candidate, New York governor Al Smith, a Catholic who favored the repeal of Prohibition. The South responded in

November by doing something that for eighty years had been unthinkable: it supported a Republican. Herbert Hoover won Florida, North Carolina, Tennessee, Texas, and Virginia, and took 47 percent of the southern vote as a whole.[2]

Then the Great Depression hit and everything changed.

The longer the Depression lasted, the further the Republicans were bound to fall. After all, they had to take full political responsibility for the economic collapse, as the Democrats had had no share of governmental power since Wilson left in 1921. By the 1932 election, the economy had been in steep decline for more than three years, and GDP was more than 25 percent off its 1929 peak.[3] The Democrats were destined to win by a huge margin; it was simply a matter of whom they chose to lead them.

Their choice was without doubt the best progressive they had for the job, Governor Franklin Delano Roosevelt of New York. In historical retrospect, it is hard not to admire him, even if one disagrees deeply with his policies or doubts their effectiveness. His extraordinary efforts to bring about victory in World War II were enough to earn him acclaim as America's greatest president since Lincoln. But FDR did much more than that. He brought a warmth and friendliness to the office that contrasted markedly with his glum and defensive predecessor, and his unflinching, unapologetic confidence in American greatness lifted the country's spirits during the Depression.[4] He fundamentally changed the role of the federal government in managing national affairs, which in time even the Republican party would accept. He developed new ways to communicate with the American people, thus bringing president and public closer to one another. And he totally redesigned the Democratic party.

It is this last point that will concern us in this chapter. William Jennings Bryan and Woodrow Wilson had infused the Democratic party with the progressive belief that an active federal government should do what it can for Jackson's "humble members of society." FDR shared this view, and he unleashed the power of Washington in ways never before seen, largely for the sake of saving America from the Great Depression. But he did one better than Bryan or Wilson: he also used the newly expanded powers of the federal government to help bring about a permanent, progressive Democratic majority. The New Deal thus pursued nation building *and* party building simultaneously.

Party building under the New Deal meant the use of the federal government to manage and grow the party's clientele, and FDR was strategic and crafty in his approach. For the sake of expediency, he was careful to kowtow to southern agricultural interests during his first term, even if that meant giving the southern gentry federal largesse that it did not deserve. When it came to the urban machines in the North, Roosevelt either protected or destroyed them, depending upon how they aided his reelection prospects. Yet the real political revolution came with how FDR handled the American working class. With the National Labor Relations Act (NLRA) of 1935, Roosevelt greatly expanded the size of the American labor union movement and brought organized labor into the Democratic party as a powerful new client.

Little did FDR realize that, far from resulting in a permanent progressive majority, the addition of organized labor would force a decades-long stalemate within the Democratic party. On issues like unionization, wages, working conditions, and taxation, the interests of organized labor were often diametrically opposed to the interests of southern Democrats. FDR tried to break this deadlock by purging southern conservatives from the party in 1938, but to no avail. The conservatives held the line in Dixie, and the result was an intraparty schism based upon enduring regional and economic differences. Ironically, it would be the minority Republican party that would swing the balance of power one way or the other for the next sixty years.

In his 1933 inaugural address, President Roosevelt emphasized the pressing problems of unemployment, collapse of farm income, lack of regulation in the banking industry, and the need to stabilize the currency.[5] During his famed First Hundred Days, Roosevelt built a broad coalition of Republicans and Democrats, conservatives and liberals, and business leaders, workers, and farmers to tackle these problems.[6]

The lawmaking began shortly after his inauguration. FDR called Congress into special session and prevailed upon it to pass the Emergency Banking Act, designed to stabilize the financial system and calm the rising panic. Also during FDR's first month, Congress passed the

Economy Act, which cut spending by trimming veterans' benefits and government salaries, and the Reforestation Relief Act, which established the Civilian Conservation Corps, putting young men from the cities to work in the country. In mid-May, Congress passed the consequential Agricultural Adjustment Act (AAA), which, according to Arthur Schlesinger, was the first major New Deal proposal in a series meant to "reorganize one after another the basic aspects of American economic life."[7] It restricted agricultural output to stabilize farm prices, in hopes that increased buying power for farmers would help restore the broader economy.[8] In a compromise with western, Bryanesque Democrats like Senator Burton Wheeler of Montana, FDR agreed to an amendment to the AAA that gave the president discretion to take the country off the gold standard. Just like that, one of the most contentious issues of the past fifty years was settled with little fanfare.

The flurry of legislative activity continued through the spring of 1933. Congress passed the Federal Emergency Relief Act, which provided grants to states to relieve rising poverty; the Farm Credit Act, which lifted the burden of taxes and mortgage payments that was crushing the family farm; the Federal Securities Act, which gave the Federal Trade Commission authority to supervise issues of new securities and mandate that relevant information be released about new stocks, and made company directors responsible for misrepresentation; the Home Owners' Loan Act, which enabled mortgagors to turn in defaulted loans for guaranteed government bonds; the Glass-Steagall Banking Act of 1933, which reformed the Federal Reserve and separated investment banking from commercial banking; and the Tennessee Valley Authority (TVA) Act, which authorized the creation of the TVA, whose purpose was to build dams and power plants in the Tennessee Valley and produce electricity and fertilizer.

On the final day of the Hundred Days, Congress passed the National Industrial Recovery Act (NIRA), which would become one of the most controversial laws of the Roosevelt administration. New Dealers believed that trade associations could give responsible businessmen the opportunity to engage in industry-wide planning, thus stabilizing the economy. However, such coordination ran afoul of the Sherman Antitrust Act, so the NIRA instituted a grand bargain: trade associations

that worked with the government to create socially responsible production codes would receive exemptions from the antitrust rules. The
NIRA created the National Recovery Administration (NRA) to negotiate the codes with industry, and also instituted new federal licensing
provisions to give the act regulatory muscle. Importantly, the NIRA included Section 7(a), which guaranteed the right of collective bargaining
for labor, the establishment of maximum hours, and minimum wages.
While the public was highly supportive of the NRA at the start, it was
soon apparent that the law was not working as planned. Cognizant that
the conservatives on the Supreme Court might very well strike it down,
NRA officials never used the coercive powers in the bill to force industries to come on board with regulatory codes. They instead tried moral
suasion, but many industries were hesitant to join up, and many others
failed to follow through on their production agreements.

Together, the AAA, the TVA, and the NIRA embodied a vision
of a broad coalition of multiple interests designed to respond to the
national economic emergency. Historian William Leuchtenburg sum-
marizes this "First New Deal" thus: "Its distinguishing characteristic
was the attempt to redress the imbalances of the old order by creating
a new equilibrium in which a variety of groups and classes would
be represented. The New Dealers sought to effect a truce similar to
that of wartime, when class and sectional animosities abated and the
claims of partisan or private economic interest were sacrificed to the
demands of national unity." Leuchtenburg sees the First New Deal as
managing a "parallelogram of pressures," with Roosevelt acting as the
"mediator of interests."[9]

Yet as the economy came back from the brink in 1933 and 1934, the
sense of emergency faded and business grew restless under increased
governmental oversight. Also growing restless were conservative
Democrats like Virginia senator Carter Glass, whose early opposition
to the New Deal foreshadowed the North–South congressional rift
that would emerge by 1938.[10] Meanwhile, northern conservatives—
including former Democratic National Committee chair John Jakob
Raskob and former presidential nominees John Davis and Al Smith—
backed the American Liberty League to oppose the New Deal.[11] FDR
also increasingly faced pressure on his left—from Louisiana senator

Huey Long and his Share Our Wealth movement; Father Charles Edward Coughlin, host of a popular radio show; and Francis Townsend, who advocated a generous old-age pension insurance program.[12]

Regardless of the growing pressure from his left and right, FDR retained the trust of the American people. With the economy stabilized by the 1934 midterms, Roosevelt and the Democrats could take credit, and despite the seemingly ironclad rule that the sitting president's party loses seats in midterm elections, the party expanded its majorities to 320 seats in the House and 69 in the Senate.[13] Still, New Dealers opened the 1935 legislative session with feelings of unease, as the impetus for reform seemed to be petering out: the NIRA had, by that point, generally been deemed a failure and was soon to be struck down by the Supreme Court;[14] the AAA had not reformed the southern agricultural system, as many liberals had hoped; and the TVA had not followed through on the grand designs of regional planning.

The Court ruling against the NIRA seemed to give FDR the jolt he needed. In what has since become known as the "Second New Deal," Roosevelt quickly reinvigorated the reform drive and pushed through a series of decidedly progressive laws: the National Labor Relations Act, sponsored by Robert F. Wagner of New York, replaced Section 7(a) of the NIRA and gave the government power to protect the rights of workers; the Social Security Act offered unemployment and old-age pension insurance for most Americans; the Banking Act of 1935 further regulated the financial industry; the Public Utility Holding Company Act strictly regulated utility companies; and the Wealth Tax Act imposed higher taxes on the rich.

Combined, these policies signified that FDR no longer was interested in a coalition of all interests, but rather focused more on the "people versus the powerful" approach that had characterized Democratic politics since the election of 1896.[15] Accordingly, he further alienated business interests, provoked greater opposition from conservative Democrats in Congress, and gave the GOP a false sense of hope heading into the 1936 presidential campaign.[16] Republicans felt confident that the party's conservative base in the Northeast was ready to return to the fold, and what they needed was a presidential nominee who could bring back the western, progressive wing of the GOP,[17] so the party nominated Kansas governor Alf Landon, a former Bull Mooser and the only Republican governor who'd won reelection in 1934.[18]

However, Republican hopes of a rebound were brutally dashed on Election Day as FDR carried 61 percent of the vote and won every state except Maine and Vermont,[19] while Democrats increased their majorities in Congress to 334 House seats and 76 Senate seats.[20] It seemed as though the Republican party was doomed to go the way of the Federalists, the Whigs, and the dodo.

Of course, that never happened, thanks in no small part to FDR's missteps in his second term. Three significant blunders stand out. His first mistake was an ill-conceived attempt to reform the Supreme Court. Frustrated by the conservative court's consistent tendency to strike down New Deal legislation, Roosevelt proposed the Judicial Procedures Reform Bill of 1937, which would have given the president authority to nominate new justices for every one over the age of 70½, up to a maximum of six. This was quickly seen as a blatant attempt to force ideological change on a recalcitrant judicial branch, and the public and conservative congressional Democrats reacted negatively.[21] In response, FDR tried unsuccessfully to purge anti–New Deal Democrats from Congress; this second mistake further hurt his credibility, widened the rift between northern and southern Democrats, and emboldened Republicans in advance of the 1938 midterms. Finally, FDR had promised in the 1932 campaign to cut spending, and he resolved to keep the promise in his second term, ordering a drawdown of federal expenditures.[22] That, combined with the new taxes enacted by the Seventy-fifth Congress, pushed the economy into recession in the spring of 1937. The country responded angrily in the 1938 midterms, electing eighty-two new Republicans to the House.[23] While they were still far short of a majority, Republicans would from this point forward align with southern conservative Democrats to block further New Deal initiatives.

The reform phase of the New Deal lasted just six years, from Roosevelt's election to the 1938 midterms, yet within this short span of time, FDR fundamentally altered the American political system. The New Deal dramatically expanded the role the federal government would play in the management of the economy, a precedent that both Democrats and Republicans would accept. Not only would the government have a greater hand in the regulation of business, but thanks to FDR it would guarantee the rights of labor and provide welfare to the unemployed, indigent, and elderly. The first six years of FDR's presidency are some of the most consequential of the twentieth century in terms of domestic policy, and the New Deal continues to affect politics to this very day.

That the New Deal simultaneously engaged in national policy making and Democratic party building, few can doubt. There's nothing peculiar about this; every American president since John Adams has been concerned with maintaining and strengthening his electoral coalition, and in the party system of the United States, that means the president must forge a broad alliance that stretches from the White House down to the county commissioner. FDR had an overwhelmingly large congressional majority and an expansive vision of the role that the federal government should play in American society, which meant that not only did he have the motive; he also had the opportunity to build the Democratic party. Indeed, scholarly study after scholarly study has shown that per capita spending under the New Deal did not depend solely on issues of welfare but on issues of politics as well: FDR and his Democratic allies in Congress distributed federal tax dollars strategically to hold their coalition together for the 1936 presidential election.[24]

But there is more to the story than this. The New Deal represented the single biggest change in the size and scope of the federal government in all of American history, which gave FDR unprecedented power not just to strengthen the Democratic coalition but to reshape it in ways that went beyond the congressional pork barrel. This chapter will recount three major party-building activities: the appeasement of the Solid South, the creation of organized labor as a party client, and the transformation of the urban machines, the last of which is our next focus. FDR used the power of the New Deal as well as his unprecedented popularity to alter fundamentally the character of urban politics, and he approached this task with a simple goal: to maximize his chances of reelection. Thus, in some cities he strengthened the existing power structure; in others he destroyed it.[25]

The most famous Democratic victim of the New Deal was none other than the Tiger itself, Tammany Hall. As a reform politician from

New York, FDR had tussled with Tammany Hall before, famously opposing its selection for the United States Senate while he was a state legislator in Albany.[26] Reform-minded Democrats since Samuel Tilden had been opposed to Tammany in one form or another, but the Tiger was always too strong to defang. Presidents Cleveland and Wilson ultimately had no choice but to make peace, and so also did FDR, at least at first. In the 1932 Democratic nomination battle, Tammany and several other urban delegations backed Smith over FDR; Roosevelt had to win the nomination based upon strong support from the South and West.[27] After the convention, FDR sent his top political fixer, James Farley, to broker a truce with the sachems that ruled New York City.[28]

As discussed in Chapter 1, political machines treat politics like a business, and business was booming for the Tiger throughout the 1920s. Strict immigration laws, designed to keep the urban machines from registering second-wave immigrants as Democrats, were actually beneficial to the Tammany operation. It had already put together a minimal winning voting coalition based largely on the Irish vote; if Italians, Jews, and Poles were brought into the electorate, Tammany would have to find more resources to pay off the new voters. So the organization did little to naturalize and register the eastern and southern European immigrants who had been arriving since the 1890s, instead lavishing even more benefits on its loyal Irish voters. The booming economy of the 1920s meant there were more resources to dispense, and the rise of the early suburbs gave the Yankee middle class a place to resettle, which in turn freed Tammany to increase taxes. All told, in the 1920s the machine thrived even as the national Democratic party suffered.

Yet by the time Tammany made its move against FDR at the 1932 convention, the machine was breaking down. Tammany's longtime leader Charles Francis Murphy had died in 1924, leaving behind a power vacuum that would never fully be filled. After the Crash of 1929, the Depression vastly diminished the city's tax base and increased demand for machine services, like poor relief. What's more, the candidacy of the Catholic Al Smith brought scores of second-wave immigrants into the political process, and the Tiger had no easy way to buy their support.[29]

In 1933, the mayoral campaign of liberal Republican Fiorello La Guardia—the "Little Flower," as he was known—was the stiffest challenge that Tammany had ever faced, as he tried to combine urban progressives and the second-wave immigrants that Tammany had long ignored into a patchwork coalition big enough to defeat the Irish machine. FDR, riding high by this point in the First New Deal, played it coy in New York City and ultimately brought about big changes.

La Guardia was ideologically much closer to FDR than any Tammany pol, but the president could not come out and back a Republican, even a nominal one such as La Guardia. So the president prevailed upon Bronx boss Ed Flynn to sponsor a third-party challenge from Joseph McKee—yet FDR never explicitly threw his support, or the New Deal patronage machinery, behind the third-party challenger. Historians have since judged that Roosevelt's scheme all along was to split the Democratic vote between McKee and incumbent mayor John P. O'Brien and thus to install the progressive La Guardia as mayor of the Big Apple. That's exactly what happened; La Guardia won just 40 percent of the vote that year, but it was enough to carry the day against a split in the Democratic ranks.[30]

FDR's quiet support of La Guardia did not stop on Election Day 1933; instead, he gave La Guardia unprecedented access to the patronage boon that the New Deal relief and works agencies offered. New York State was controlled by Democrats when La Guardia came to power, and if FDR let the state party leaders handle the New Deal patronage, they would have used it to strangle the La Guardia insurgency in its infancy. So FDR established two administrators for the Empire State—one for New York City and one for the rest of the state. In 1937, FDR took a hands-off approach to the mayoral campaign, refusing to endorse or disavow the Democratic candidate, and in 1941 the president praised La Guardia for having "given to the City the most honest and, I believe, the most efficient municipal government of any within my recollection."

FDR could have saved the Tammany machine. The logic of partisan loyalty might have predicted that he would: he was a Democrat, and it was a Democratic operation that badly needed help. By providing it with support in 1933, then patronage thereafter, he could have propped it back up and maybe even bought its loyalty. Yet FDR recognized that, in the long run, the Democratic party would be better without it. Tammany Hall had been an embarrassment for reformist Democrats since the 1870s, and in the 1932 nomination battle it had lined up against FDR. That made it a threat not only to President Roosevelt but to the long-term progressive coalition FDR hoped to build among reformist Democrats, independents, and progressive Republicans. He saw an opportunity to finally put the Tiger down, and he took the kill shot. Apart from a brief resurgence in the 1950s under the leadership of Carmine DeSapio, Tammany would never again influence New York politics.[31]

FDR also used the powers of New Deal patronage to topple another infamous machine, the William Vare operation in Philadelphia. The City of Brotherly Love had long been a Republican town, with a machine that drew support and sustenance from the statewide Republican operation. Pennsylvania's loyalty to the Grand Old Party seemed nearly absolute;[32] since 1860, the Democrats had never once carried Pennsylvania's electoral votes, not even in 1912, when the GOP vote was split, or 1932, when the Keystone State voted to reelect Hoover.[33] Republicans regularly dominated the U.S. House and Senate delegations, and in Harrisburg, the GOP was so strong that as late as 1930 the Democrats held just four of fifty seats in the state senate.[34] The Philadelphia machine had thrived for seventy years as a satellite of the state machine, and the GOP organization in the city was so powerful that it actually had paid off its Democratic opponents. The leader of this "kept minority" in the early 1930s, Democrat John O'Donnell, really had no other choice but to align with the GOP; given the Republicans' total control of the city and the state, they were the only source of the patronage needed to keep the Democratic operation functioning.[35]

But as with so much else in American life, the New Deal changed everything in Philadelphia politics. FDR and his political advisers certainly were aware it had been the only major American city to vote for Hoover. This situation needed to change, and the White House played a key role in booting O'Donnell from the city Democratic leadership. When the Democrats captured the governorship in 1934, the Philadelphia Democratic organization suddenly had access to a new revenue stream in the form of federal patronage, which was carefully applied not only to swing weak Republicans to the Democratic party but also to activate the still largely inactive Italian American vote, especially in South Philly.[36] This, combined with the personal appeal of the president, the popularity of the New Deal, and the political activism of local unions, finally ended the Republican stranglehold over city politics.[37] Though the GOP would retain dominance over local politics for some time longer, FDR had secured his political position by the middle of the decade. Every House district in the city went Democratic in 1936, and FDR improved from 43 percent of the vote in 1932 to 60 percent in 1936.[38]

Generally speaking, FDR's approach to urban politics was not principled so much as it was pragmatic. Whenever he thought that attacking an entrenched machine would help him secure the city's votes in the next presidential election, he attacked the machine—hence the assault on the New York and Philadelphia operations. Yet when a machine had solid control over a city or an alliance with friendly statewide Democratic leaders, FDR gave the existing operation access to New Deal patronage. This happened, for instance, in Chicago, Albany, and Jersey City.[39] In Pittsburgh, FDR was a key player not only in the destruction of the old Republican machine but in the creation of a new Democratic machine, run by David L. Lawrence.[40]

Even so, the Depression and the New Deal marked the beginning of the end of the urban political machines. The decline of the machines was not as cut-and-dried as it was portrayed to be in *The Last Hurrah,* the popular John Ford movie starring Spencer Tracy. Machine politicians like Lawrence of Pittsburgh and Richard J. Daley of Chicago would continue to thrive for decades. Regardless, the New Deal was a significant factor in undermining the power of the urban machines, because it transferred many social welfare functions from the machines to the federal government. It also gave new life to the labor union movement, which would come to dominate city payrolls and thus reduce the patronage that machine leaders could dispense.[41] The postwar economic boom would turn out to be another factor in the demise of the urban machines; the prosperity of the 1950s and '60s gave millions of middle-class urban denizens the mobility to move the machine's tax base into the suburbs, while a third wave of newcomers, mostly African

Americans and Hispanics, came into the cities and further strained machine resources.[42]

By the 1980s, machine leaders had been forced into tight alignments with big businesses in regional development projects. The "machine" of son Richard M. Daley in Chicago in the 2000s was quite different from the one run by his father up through the 1970s; the younger Daley survived not only by deploying patronage to tens of thousands of loyal voters but by attracting businesses and private sector jobs to the Windy City. The age of towering urban machines, capable of winning elections with a loyal patronage army, is simply no more.

The relationship between the South and the Democratic party has its origins in the politics of the post–Civil War era. African Americans, grateful to Abraham Lincoln and the Grand Old Party, were bound to vote Republican if brought into the electorate;[43] this incipient Republicanism prompted the Radical Republicans to impose congressional Reconstruction in the 1860s, and it later induced President Benjamin Harrison and the "Billion Dollar Congress" of 1889–90 to push the so-called Force Bill, intended to promote fair and open elections in the South.[44] In response, the white South struck an implicit bargain with the Democratic party: the region would support northern Democrats (the only ones electable on a national level) in exchange for protection from Republican incursions into the southern way of life. This made Dixie the original client of the Democratic party, as its union with Democratic ethnics in the big northern cities was due not to a shared vision of the good society but rather to its need for blunting the advances of the GOP.

Essential to the southern modus vivendi was, of course, the racial caste system that had developed in the wake of the Civil War, one in which blacks occupied grossly inferior economic, social, and political positions than whites. Yet the South's alienation from the rest of the country—and thus the basis of the region's relationship with the Democratic party—was not reducible only to opposition to civil rights; the South would also demand from the Democratic party protection against efforts to regulate any aspects of Dixie's economy or society, which had fallen far behind the North in virtually every metric of well-being.

The reasons for southern obstinacy are many and varied, but ultimately they all get back to "King Cotton." Cotton prices boomed after the war, and cash-strapped southern farmers ceased to grow a diverse array of crops as they switched mostly, if not entirely, to cotton. This left the southern economy far too dependent upon the ebbs and flows of the world cotton market, and when cotton prices later fell, small landowners were forced into a vicious circle of indebtedness that very often led to tenancy. During the depression of the 1890s, tenancy rates increased by about 25 percent in the South as small farmers of both races were forced from property ownership into tenancy. Blacks were much more likely than whites to be sharecroppers, but by 1920 just 60 percent of white farmers owned their land.

Dependence on cotton also stalled the development of the southern industrial economy, leaving workers economically and socially impoverished relative to their northern counterparts. Though southern industry grew at a respectable rate in the latter half of the nineteenth century, it remained limited primarily to the extraction and refinement of the region's natural resources—mostly timber and textile production that added little value to nature's bounty. Again, cotton was to blame. Low-wage cotton jobs, combined with a glut of unskilled workers thanks to high southern fertility rates, pegged industrial wages in the South far below those in the North, as industrialists had no reason to pay laborers much more than what they could make in the cotton fields. These low wages created disincentives for southern industrialists to develop more advanced industry or the modern workforce required for it, as they feared that more skilled or better-educated workers would migrate northward to higher-wage jobs.

All in all, the postwar South was like a separate country. It was not simply impoverished relative to the North; it was also cut off from the rapid and transformative growth the North enjoyed in the postwar decades. Cotton had once helped enrich the South, but now it was the main factor in the region's impoverishment, promoting tenancy, low wages, and a perpetual economic and social backwardness. Today, the South is a great American success story, but in the eighty years between the Civil War and World War II, it was, to borrow a phrase from sociologist Gunnar Myrdal, an American dilemma.

Closed off from the rest of the country, the South languished while the North prospered.

Most southerners—black and white—were losers in this arrangement, and they were kept in their positions by a southern ruling class that systematically excluded them from participating in government. After the Civil War, Democratic elites used fraud, repression, and race-baiting to push African Americans out of the political process and consolidate their power, so that after the withdrawal of federal soldiers from the region, the South was solidly Democratic, apart from a few Republican pockets in the Appalachian Mountains. Still, African Americans had not been shut out of the process entirely; Benjamin Harrison managed to get 37 percent of the southern presidential vote in 1888, thanks in part to the black vote, and as late as 1894 South Carolina sent to Congress an African American Republican.[45] The informal practices of limiting black involvement in the political process were not legally formalized into Jim Crow laws until the end of the century, with the new restrictions adopted in response to the Force Bill and the populist insurgency, both of which threatened the southern aristocracy. Because of the Fifteenth Amendment, which protected the right to vote from being abridged on the basis of race, restrictions like literacy tests and poll taxes had to be technically color-blind, and this meant that poor whites were pushed out as well (though to a much lesser degree). Regionwide, the result of this mass disenfranchisement was startling: in the 1894 midterms, at the high tide of populism, some 47 percent of all eligible adults in the old Confederacy voted; thirty years later, in 1924, turnout was just 18 percent.[46]

The narrowing of the electorate tilted southern governments toward the prosperous classes—the landowners, industrialists, doctors, lawyers, and county store merchants. They installed in Congress a clique of southern congressmen happy to use the federal government to regulate northern business and push for lower tariff rates but staunchly opposed to alterations in the southern economic, social, and political systems. They usually amounted to twenty-two senators and a little over a hundred House members, and regularly controlled crucial leadership positions within Congress. So there was little that any progressive Democrat—even one as cunning as FDR—could do about this. To be sure, Roosevelt was a reformer who had firsthand knowledge of the backwardness of the American South, having recuperated from polio in Warm Springs, Georgia. As president, he hoped to rehabilitate the South, but he was also an astute political player who usually had a good sense of what was possible, and alterations of the southern system were simply not possible, at least not during his first term. Thus, illiberal southern carve-outs, especially for agricultural interests, were common throughout the early New Deal.[47]

The AAA is a prominent example of this tendency. Not only did the program fail to reform the southern agricultural system, it actually reinforced the status of the wealthier landowners. Initially, the AAA cut checks directly to southern landowners and left it to them to distribute the money to their tenants. Later this practice was reformed, but even so, the whole system incentivized landowners to reduce the number of tenants so as to pocket as much of the governmental largesse as possible. Between 1935 and 1940, the number of southern tenants declined by nearly 25 percent, with African Americans overrepresented among the dislocated. What's more, the payments from the AAA gave landowners the cash needed to begin the overdue process of mechanization. Over the long term, this helped modernize the southern farm economy, but it also served to put the already vulnerable lower classes of farmers in an even more precarious state, as fewer farmworkers were needed. African Americans were disproportionately harmed because, according to Myrdal, "to operate an expensive machine is to have a position of responsibility, which, even in the rural South, must draw 'white man's pay.' "[48] Meanwhile, New Deal programs to relocate and resettle displaced farmers—like the Resettlement Administration and the Farm Security Administration—were underfunded and ineffective, thanks in no small part to protests from southern Democrats in Congress. When liberals in the Department of Agriculture, including Alger Hiss, tried to push the federal government to reform the southern system, they were sacked.[49]

The Social Security Act was also drafted with sensitivity to the interests of elite southern landowners, who had developed a system of what economists Lee Alston and Joseph Ferrie have termed "southern paternalism." Cash-poor farmers often remunerated their tenants with non-cash services like housing, gardens, schools, churches, and forms of old-age insurance; they also provided protection to their black workers against a racist justice system (which, of course, they had played an integral role in creating). Alston and Ferrie argue, "The result was a system of thorough paternalism in which planters looked after most aspects of their workers' lives, and workers responded by offering their loyalty to their patron."[50] The federal provision of old-age or unemployment assistance to tenants would undermine this paternalistic relationship, making workers (in the view of the planters) more independent and less reliable. And so southern Democrats in Congress successfully fought to exempt farmworkers from the benefits of Social Security.

Of course, there is no more infamous example of the New Deal bending to the illiberal will of southern Democrats than the issue of lynching. This atrocious practice had become more frequent by 1933, and the next year Senators Wagner and Edward P. Costigan, a Democrat from Colorado, proposed an antilynching bill that southern Democrats promptly filibustered. The duo tried again in 1935, and when southern Democrats again filibustered, FDR refused to intervene, explaining to the NAACP's Walter White:

> *I did not choose the tools with which I must work. But I've got to get legislation passed by Congress to save America. The southerners by reason of the seniority rule in Congress are chairmen or occupy strategic places on most of the Senate and House committees. If I come out for the antilynching bill now, they will block every bill I ask Congress to pass to keep America from collapsing. I just can't take that risk.*[51]

This is the essence of political clientelism—a special carve-out to a well-placed interest group solely for the sake of expediency.

Over the next fifty years, the old southern economic and political systems would largely be dismantled, though not in the ways intended by the New Dealers. Roosevelt the progressive set out to reform the American way of life, but because Roosevelt the politician needed the votes of southern Democrats, he allowed the southern system to remain intact. On item after item, southerners were given illiberal carve-outs, not because they deserved them but because they occupied prominent positions in the party structure. And so, as FDR reformed the rest of the country, he was bound by political reality to leave the South largely as it was.

Labor as an organized interest had been around since the colonial era, when groups of workers banded together for coordinated agitation.[52] In the early days of the republic, local workingmen's parties formed to oppose mechanization and the declining value of high-skilled workers in big cities like New York and Philadelphia, and they often allied with the Jacksonian Democrats.[53] The impetus to organize accelerated with the Industrial Revolution, when the nature of work changed dramatically. Employees had to deal with faceless mega-corporations, which made it more difficult for them to bargain as individuals. Additionally, the fixed costs of industrial machinery induced corporations to push workers harder and harder—with longer hours, overnight shifts, the employment of child labor, and so on—to get the most out of their equipment.[54] In response, Terence Powderly formed the Knights of Labor, the first national union, in 1869, and by the middle of the 1880s it would peak at a membership of three-quarters of a million workers. The Knights of Labor was a reformist organization whose mission was "to secure to the toilers a proper share of the wealth they create." It promoted an alliance of all workers, skilled and unskilled, male and female, black and white, all bound together for the purpose of fundamentally altering the factory system.[55]

In the 1870s and '80s, the growth of organized labor led to strikes, many of which were violent, and the courts regularly responded by issuing severe injunctions to break up the work stoppages. Judges had an evolving view of why labor agitation was illegal—viewing it first as a criminal conspiracy, then as a violation of property rights, and after the passage of the Sherman Act as a trust in restraint of commerce. Their verdicts often carried harsh penalties for striking workers; for example, in its 1908 ruling on the Danbury Hatters strike, the Supreme Court held that the stoppage was illegal under the Sherman Act, awarding the company treble damages assessed on individual workers.[56] When the Wilsonian progressives passed the Clayton Antitrust Act of 1914, which ostensibly gave unions antitrust exemptions, the court agreed that workers could organize in theory but strictly limited sympathy strikes, secondary boycotts, and other activities unions had promoted to advance their agendas. Worse, violations of the court's rules continued to result in treble damages.[57]

The economic collapse at the end of the nineteenth century, combined with high-profile and often violent labor protests—notably the Haymarket riot, the Pullman Strike, and the Homestead steel strike—gave worker organizations a bad name and contributed to the collapse of the Knights of Labor, although the organization did not plan for any violence.[58] By the middle of the 1890s, the group was effectively no more. In its place arose the American Federation of Labor (AFL), founded in 1886 by Samuel Gompers, a Jewish cigar maker who had emigrated from England. He had a philosophy of organized labor that was markedly different from the one espoused by the Knights of Labor; whereas the Knights of Labor was interested in social reform, promoted a broad coalition of all workers, and emphasized change through political action, the AFL was most concerned about increasing wages and improving working conditions, emphasized the organization of skilled workers in the trades, and cultivated political neutrality. While it backed Bryan in 1908, the AFL was not in the pocket of either party; Gompers evaluated individual candidates on their merits and did not swear fealty to the Democrats or the Republicans. In 1896, he remarked, "The industrial field is littered with more corpses of organizations destroyed by the damning influences of partisan politics than from all other causes combined," and throughout his nearly forty years in charge of the AFL, he stuck to this view.[59]

Unionization accelerated rapidly during World War I as business, government, and labor hammered out industrial production codes in a coordinated war effort. The number of workers in unions exceeded five million by the end of Wilson's tenure, with most of the growth coming in war industries.[60] Yet the 1920s saw a significant decline in union rates for several reasons. The same industries that tolerated labor during the war stopped once the Treaty of Versailles had been signed, and the Wilson administration abided this retrenchment. Conservative Republicans dominated the political field in the 1920s and were generally unwilling to facilitate the growth of organized labor. Meanwhile, businesses worked hard to push back on unionization, adopting contrivances like company unions, yellow-dog contracts, and blacklists. By the time Hoover was sworn in, union workers numbered fewer than 3.5 million nationwide.[61]

Even the Great Depression, the election of Franklin Roosevelt, and the Democratic dominance of Congress did not deliver labor much of anything substantive at first. While the First New Deal articulated fairly clear and coherent policies toward agriculture, banking, and poverty relief, its labor policy was a muddle. Included in the ill-conceived NIRA was the famous Section 7(a); modeled on World War I's War Labor Board, of which FDR was a member, this provision was supposed to protect the rights of workers to organize by limiting the union-busting practices of big business. Yet Section 7(a) was poorly written, and businesses soon discovered that they could circumvent the spirit of the law by promoting company unions. What's more, the NRA lacked strong enforcement mechanisms for the government, and federal administrators were hesitant to use the ones it gave them for fear of rebuke from the Supreme Court.[62]

Unsurprisingly, the efforts of labor to organize under the NIRA were generally unsuccessful, despite victories in a handful of locales like Minneapolis, San Francisco, and Toledo. The result in many cities was disruptive strikes and occasional violence as workers and businesses clashed, prompting FDR to create the National Labor Board (NLB) to handle disputes and thus give meaning to Section 7(a). Composed of a mix of union and business leaders, with pro-union New York senator Robert Wagner as chairman, the NLB determined that shop elections would be the solution to the labor problem: workers could decide for themselves whether to unionize, and the verdict of a majority of workers would be binding on all. The problem was that the NLB also lacked enforcement mechanisms to ensure compliance, and as the sense of economic crisis passed, businesses began to defy the rulings of the board. Wagner, a German immigrant who had settled in New York City, grew frustrated; he was, in the words of Arthur Schlesinger, "almost alone among liberal Democrats in placing a high value on trade unions."[63] He realized that the NLB did not have the muscle to force businesses to acknowledge unions, and he set about writing a bill that would put the power of the federal government fully on the side of organized labor.[64]

The result was the National Labor Relations Act (NLRA), also known as the Wagner Act. The NLRA created the National Labor Relations Board, which would monitor labor elections for unions and ensure that businesses did not use unfair practices, now defined more broadly than ever before. Not only were businesses prohibited from firing workers who tried to organize unions; they were also not allowed to promote company unions. Initially, FDR refused to back Wagner, but after the Supreme Court struck down the NIRA as unconstitutional, the president embraced the NLRA, and it passed the Senate 63–12 and carried in the House on a voice vote.[65] In historical retrospect, this is amazing. As discussed below, the NLRA would help fundamentally realign the American party system and would reshape the political debate in the United States for the next seventy-plus years. For it to have passed so overwhelmingly is extraordinary. Just as when FDR took the nation off the gold standard, the New Deal had brought about yet another fundamental change in economics and politics that nobody seemed to appreciate fully at the time.

Except labor, that is. Industrial labor leaders like John L. Lewis of the United Mine Workers and Sidney Hillman of the Amalgamated Clothing Workers of America quickly recognized the possibilities inherent in the NLRA. Labor had been in a decades-long decline, and with little fanfare the federal government had suddenly given it the tools it needed to reinvigorate itself. Lewis, Hillman, and others started pushing for an aggressive plan to unionize workers by industry, but the old guard in the AFL resisted this innovation. The AFL had long been the domain of skilled craftsmen, and leaders like William Green, who replaced Gompers as president in 1924, had mixed feelings about organizing unskilled, ethnic workers; also, the AFL bosses strongly believed that, insofar as such workers did organize, it should be done by craft (e.g., the International Brotherhood of Boilermakers) and not by industry (e.g., the United Steelworkers). The conflict between these factions came to a head at the AFL annual meeting in Atlantic City in 1935, during which Lewis and William "Big Bill" Hutcheson of the United Brotherhood of Carpenters and Joiners of America literally came to blows, a symbol of the growing divisions within labor ranks.[66]

The leaders of ten unions formed a separate group within the AFL, the Committee for Industrial Organization, to focus on unionizing industrial workers. The next year, however, the AFL expelled the splinter faction, and the latter rechristened itself the Congress of Industrial Organizations (CIO), with Lewis as its president.[67] Over the next several years, the CIO pushed hard for new union workers, and it differed from the AFL in several important ways: the CIO organized workers by industries, rather than trades within those industries; whereas the AFL had long been a fairly conservative organization (Hutcheson, for instance, backed Republicans throughout his entire career), the CIO was much more progressive, viewing itself not just as an advocate for its workers but also as an agent of social change; the CIO was much more willing than the AFL to pursue aggressive union tactics like sit-down strikes; and the CIO did not discriminate against workers nearly to the same extent as the AFL did—by and large, blacks and whites were both welcome in the CIO.

It scored some amazing gains in 1936 and 1937. The first big breakthrough came in Flint, Michigan, where a CIO-sponsored sit-down strike—one that FDR and Michigan governor Frank Murphy refused to disavow—forced GM to recognize the United Auto Workers, led by the charismatic Walter Reuther, in early 1937. This sent shock waves through the industrial world, and a few months later the gigantic U.S. Steel Corporation recognized the Steel Workers Organizing Committee (SWOC) without a fight. All told, in 1937 there were nearly five thousand recorded strikes nationwide, involving 1.9 million American workers; about 60 percent of these strikes involved the right to unionize. By comparison, 1932 had seen about eight hundred strikes involving 325,000 workers; less than 25 percent of these involved the right to unionize.[68]

One region to defy the trend, however, was the South, for many reasons. Perhaps the most significant was a broad alliance of southern elites who wanted to attract new business to Dixie and thus opposed unionization. As was the case with everything else in the South during this period, race was also an important factor; Communist-backed groups had tried to organize black sharecroppers in Alabama earlier in the decade, and the Communist factions within the CIO handed south-

ern officials a perfect rhetorical club with which to beat back the forces
of unionization. Geography was also an issue: it was harder to organize
workers in the rural South than in densely packed urban areas like
New York and Philadelphia.[69]

Thus, the revolution in working relations was largely a northern
phenomenon. Even so, the growth in the number of unionized workers
was stunning. The Bureau of Labor Statistics estimates that in 1933, 2.9
million workers were part of a labor union—just 11 percent of the nonagricultural workforce. By 1940, prior to the outbreak of hostilities in
World War II, that number had increased to 8.9 million, or 27 percent
of non-farmworkers. The CIO could claim 3.6 million members that
year, so its growth had vastly outstripped that of the nineteenth-century
Knights of Labor; by the time of FDR's death in 1945, the CIO had basically reached parity with the AFL.[70]

Such a dramatic change in the economic foundations of the country
was bound to have a major impact on the political process as well. The
Republican party had long argued that the interests of workers and
businesses were inseparable, and that what was good for one was good
for the other. For thirty-five years between the Panic of 1893 and the
Great Depression, the public basically agreed, and the Republicans won
sweeping national victories. However, the NLRA embodied a markedly different view: the belief that the workingman's long-term interests
were not identical to those of capital owners, that he should organize
with fellow workers to protect those interests, and that the federal government was duty-bound to facilitate this organization. In so doing, it
gravely damaged the Republican coalition as millions of newly unionized industrial workers began to see the unions and Democrats—rather
than businesses and Republicans—as the protectors of their interests.
Not only did old working-class Republicans abandon the party, but Italians, Poles, Jews, and other immigrants who had come to the United
States in the past fifty years entered the electorate as Democrats. These
ethnic voters typically worked industrial jobs in the big northern cities,
and with Roosevelt promoting unionization, his Democratic party was
the obvious choice for them.

The big change came in 1936, the first election after the NLRA
became law, when Landon suffered the biggest blowout in GOP his-

tory, thanks to the great American cities. FDR increased his number of voters between 1932 and 1936 by roughly five million nationwide, and 40 percent of his gains came from just ten cities: Buffalo, Chicago, Cleveland, Detroit, Los Angeles, Milwaukee, New York, Philadelphia, Pittsburgh, and San Francisco. In many other cities—Baltimore, Boston, Cincinnati, Denver, Hartford, Kansas City, Memphis, Oakland, Portland, and Seattle—the president added tens of thousands of new voters to his coalition.[71] What makes this haul all the more amazing is that, apart from Philadelphia, FDR had defeated Hoover by wide margins in these cities four years prior.

Labor's political mobilization played an integral role in FDR's landmark victory that year. Lewis argued that "it is the duty of labor to support Roosevelt 100 percent,"[72] and the CIO established Labor's Non-Partisan League to raise funds for FDR's reelection and conduct an extensive nationwide get-out-the-vote drive for FDR and pro-labor politicians, most of whom were Democrats.[73] Philadelphia in particular saw a tremendous amount of political agitation by the Democrats and labor. Union leaders worked with the WPA-funded Workers' Education Project in Philadelphia to bring workers into the political process, and the Amalgamated Clothing Workers of America—one of the more politically active unions in the country—sponsored a massive voter registration drive, campaign rallies, and even poll watching to maximize the Democratic vote, especially in south Philadelphia, which had long been a Republican bastion but had a large number of garment workers. The coordinated WPA, labor, and Democratic effort paid off: in 1936, Philadelphia voted for a Democratic president for the first time since 1856.[74]

CIO campaign efforts were not limited to the big cities; Lewis and the United Mine Workers (UMW) also helped drive up the Democratic vote in mining counties nationwide. For instance, FDR did poorly in 1932 in the coal country of southern West Virginia, but four years later he dominated the region. McDowell County is the most extraordinary example: in 1932, Roosevelt won just 43 percent of the vote, but in 1936 he carried 72 percent and an additional 13,000 votes (out of just 35,000 cast).[75] Similarly, the anthracite counties of northeastern Pennsylvania, as well as the bituminous counties in southwestern Pennsylvania, came out more heavily for FDR in 1936, as did the mining towns in the Mountain West, like Butte, Montana, and Coeur d'Alene, Idaho. These gains clearly demonstrate the efforts of the UMW and the CIO.[76]

Labor's politicization in 1936 marked quite a change in its long-standing approach to politics. Why the new, aggressive style? The New Deal fundamentally altered the role of the government in managing the economy, giving labor an incentive to lobby the federal government for social and economic change. As Lewis argued:

> With the guarantee of "the right to organize," such industries may be unionized, but, on the other hand, better living standards, shorter working hours, and improved employment conditions for their members cannot be hoped for unless legislative or other provisions be made for economic planning and for price, production, and profit controls. Because of these fundamental conditions, it is obvious to industrial workers that the labor movement must organize and exert itself not only in the economic field but also in the political arena.[77]

This anticipates the role that organized labor would take in politics from 1936 forward. Not only would it push for changes to labor law to facilitate organizing; it would also be an advocate for ever-expanding social welfare benefits. Thus, labor would back Harry Truman's Fair Deal, Lyndon Johnson's Great Society, and Barack Obama's health care package. The union view was that government policies that aided social welfare in general would enable workers to bargain more effectively for higher wages, and thus blue-collar workers became eager allies of liberal intellectuals.

And so a sturdy clientelistic relationship has evolved between labor and the Democrats over the years. Labor provides the party with needed votes and campaign services and generally lobbies for an ever-larger liberal welfare state. In return, the Democrats do two big things for labor: first, when they have a majority, they try for labor law reforms and push aggressively for increased social welfare spending; second, when they lack a majority, they still protect labor unions from Republican efforts to alter existing labor laws. The deep GOP connection to business has long pitted the GOP against the labor unions on a variety of issues, and when the Republican congressional majority grows large enough, it can still be counted on to try to restrict labor, as it did with 1947's Taft-Hartley Act, discussed in Chapter 4. The constant threat of Republicanism is sufficient to keep labor voting Democratic even when the party does not control the government.

This is not to say that organized labor can run the table on the Democratic party. The latter is, after all, a majority-seeking organization that ultimately must balance competing claims from many groups. Labor can expect many of its concerns to be addressed, but it cannot get everything it wants. For instance, the Little Steel Strike of 1937 pitted the CIO against smaller steel manufacturers like Republic Steel, which resisted the Steelworkers Organizing Committee. Lewis asked FDR to support the CIO, but the president refused. The economy was in recession, and FDR did not want to disrupt business further. Lewis angrily responded by denouncing FDR in strident terms:

> *It ill behooves one who has supped at labor's table and who has been sheltered in labor's house to curse with equal fervor and fine impartiality both labor and its adversaries when they become locked in deadly embrace.*[78]

By Lewis's logic, organized labor had delivered Roosevelt success in 1936, so FDR owed labor. But that wasn't how the evolving clientelistic relationship between the two groups would work, as Lewis would learn to his own chagrin. He warned the Democrats not to renominate FDR in 1940, but they did so anyway. Lewis responded by backing the Republican nominee, Wendell Willkie, threatening to take his union members with him, but workers backed FDR overwhelmingly that year, and Philip Murray of the Steelworkers Organizing Committee replaced him as the head of the CIO in 1940.[79]

By the same token, the unions would retain a modicum of independence from the Democratic party, as evidenced in 1939 when FDR asked the AFL and the CIO to reunite. The dueling groups engaged in peace talks, but ultimately Green and Lewis could not resolve the long-standing divide over how workers should be organized. This frustrated

FDR, who hoped that merging with the staunchly anti-Communist AFL would temper the Communist influences within the CIO in advance of the 1940 campaign. Even so, he could not force labor's hand.

Still, these examples merely delineate the boundaries of what has evolved into a decidedly clientelistic relationship between labor and the Democratic party. It is, in the words of political scientist Taylor Dark, an "enduring alliance," in which the party provides unions with substantial benefits in return for labor's continued electoral support.[80]

The party's first and most significant chance to repay labor came at the beginning of FDR's second term. The congressional elections of 1936 produced the largest Democratic majority in the country's history, with the party controlling better than 75 percent of all seats in the House of Representatives; importantly, northern Democrats constituted the lion's share, making up 193 seats, just 25 short of a full majority all by themselves.[81] Not since 1832 have northern Democrats held so much political power in Congress, and they were forceful in their use of it, pushing the Fair Labor Standards Act (FLSA) in 1937–38 to protect the gains unions had secured through collective bargaining. For FDR, the FLSA was to be the next item in what he hoped would be a continuing series of New Deal reforms. Little did he know that the bill would mark the conclusion of the legislative phase of the New Deal, split his party in two, and contribute to a nearly sixty-year stalemate in the Democratic party.

As mentioned earlier, Dixie had for a long time trailed far behind the North on most measures of social and economic well-being, and southerners had tried hard to attract northern capital southward. One way it could do that was through low wages: northern businesses could come to Dixie and pay southern workers less than what they had to pay northerners for the same day's work. Southern boosters also promoted the region as a non-union region full of "real" Americans, promising investors that they need not worry about the headaches created by unionization and "troublesome" ethnic workers. Obviously, northern pro-union Democrats did not like this one bit. After all, the NLRA had not actually given workers any direct benefits; it merely empowered workers to fight collectively for them. With the hard battles finally won against corporate giants like GM and U.S. Steel, pro-union Democrats did not want to see jobs migrate to the anti-union South.

And so was born the FLSA, a measure that phased in minimum wages and maximum hours over the course of several years. Importantly, the wage floor was set so low that it disproportionately affected the South, so much so that southern Democrats in Congress viewed the legislation as a direct attack on their region's interests. "Cotton Ed" Smith, a senator from South Carolina, articulated the southern position bluntly from the Senate floor: "Any man on this floor who has sense enough to read the English language knows that the main objective of this bill is, by human legislation, to overcome the splendid gifts of God to the South."[82] In the end, the FLSA passed over the objections of southern Democrats, but its path to becoming law took more than a year and seriously degraded FDR's political capital in Congress.

The fight within the party over the FLSA was the first signal of a divide that would grow larger over the next couple of decades. Typically, historians and political scientists identify regional and ideological factors in the split: the old southern Democrats were much more conservative than the new northern Democrats, so it was only a matter of time until they would begin battling one another. This is accurate but incomplete; after all, southern Democrats had been strong advocates of progressivism during the Wilson era and had been generally solid supporters of FDR during his first term. Why would they now begin voting like Republicans?

The missing piece of the puzzle is the dynamics of clientelism within the party. The South was the Democratic party's oldest, most loyal client, and its place in the party had its roots in the need for protection against activist, presumably Republican northerners who threatened to intervene in southern affairs. The dramatic increase in union membership, combined with a shift in its policy goals away from the voluntarism of Gompers, meant that there were now northern *Democrats* like Senator Wagner who were empowered to do just what the South had so long feared from the Republicans: meddle in the affairs of Dixie. In other words, it was not just ideological differences that rent the party in two; it was also that these party clients had mutually exclusive demands, requiring the national party to choose one side or the other.

FDR had given the southern conservatives what they wanted in his first term, but after the rise of the labor/liberal coalition in 1936, he began to take sides against Dixie. His promotion of the FLSA is one such example, and there were others. Senate Majority Leader Joseph Taylor Robinson of Arkansas died early in the Seventy-fifth Congress, and the battle to replace him came down to Alben Barkley of Kentucky and Pat Harrison of Mississippi. Though both had generally been New Deal supporters, FDR believed that Barkley had been an ally out of genuine ideological sympathy, while Harrison's support had been due to political calculation. So Roosevelt made his partiality to Barkley known, and the latter squeaked out a narrow 40–39 victory. When Barkley faced a stiff primary battle against Kentucky governor Albert "Happy" Chandler in 1938, FDR instructed James Farley to use the WPA to boost Barkley over Chandler. Barkley won, but the WPA's intercession ultimately prompted a Senate investigation and passage of the Hatch Act, which strictly curtailed political activity by federal employees.[83] Buoyed by his success in the Barkley-Harrison battle, FDR targeted three incumbent Democratic senators for defeat: Walter F. George of Georgia, "Cotton Ed" Smith of South Carolina, and Millard Tydings of Maryland. Roosevelt also targeted three House members, all from the Rules Committee: John J. O'Connor of New York, Howard Smith of Virginia, and Eugene Cox of Georgia. With the exception of O'Connor, Roosevelt was thwarted; every time, the southern conservatives held the line.[84]

This failed purge of the southern conservatives would be a critical moment for the party. Northern Democrats were moving leftward, thanks to the rise of the labor/liberal alliance, and FDR had facilitated it by kneecapping the urban machines in New York, Philadelphia, and Pittsburgh. He similarly believed that southern progressives—in the mold of Senators Hugo Black of Alabama and Claude Pepper of Florida—could become a regional majority, but his efforts to assist its growth backfired. The conservatives consolidated their position and would thereafter oppose the New Deal with more regularity.[85] Dixie's opposition was not born of mere political pique, a lasting grudge against FDR for daring to oust their leaders; rather, it was due to the shift in the political alignment within the country. Southern Democrats had happily supported the progressivism of Wilson and the early New Deal insofar as it left their home region alone, which it usually did. But with the rise of organized labor, an enduring bloc of congressional liberals, and, as we shall see in the next chapter, a growing urban black vote, the northern wing of the Democratic party was no longer content to let the southern wing manage Dixie. Having violated the clientelistic relationship that had bound the two regions together for generations, northern Democrats could no longer expect their southern allies to help turn their agenda into law, and southern intransigence would not end with FDR but rather continue under the tenures of Truman, JFK, and LBJ.

The first half of FDR's tenure is the closest this country has ever come to the reign of Britain's William the Conqueror. The 1920s had reduced his Democratic party to a rump faction, and the Great Depression had thoroughly discredited his Republican opponents. Thus, FDR largely had a free hand for six years to remake American society as he saw fit, without having to worry about a powerful rival faction within his own party or a resurgent GOP. This freedom sets him apart from other presidential greats like George Washington, who had to deal with the Jeffersonian Republican alliance early in his term, as well as from Abraham Lincoln, who had to balance a multitude of factions and personalities in his heterogeneous Republican coalition. Thus, it was FDR's unique privilege to set the precedents in policy and politics that subsequent leaders would be obliged to follow.

FDR would follow in the footsteps of Wilson and Bryan, using an active and vigorous federal government to help "the humble members of society"; however, Roosevelt also borrowed a page from the urban patronage machines and transformed the national Democratic party into a kind of Tammany on the Potomac, with the clients of the post–New Deal party resembling the long-gone Shiny Hat Brigade of Tammany Hall. The new urban machines, the southern conservatives, and even organized labor were wedded to the Democratic party not because of its vision for a more perfect union but because of the private benefits they enjoyed from the party's benevolent protections. Yet instead of merely using the spoils system or public works patronage to pay off these massive client groups, FDR gave them access to the vast powers of the regulatory and welfare state, which they were allowed to use for their own advancement.

Once the party was opened to the client groups in this fashion, it could not be closed. They were an integral part of the coalition from that point on, and their newfound dominance meant a shift in the task confronting party leaders. From the New Deal forward, leaders would have to advance the progressive agenda and tend to the party's clients simultaneously. In the early years of FDR's term, that task was relatively easy, but it grew substantially harder when the sense of economic emergency passed and labor became a party client. The difficulty in passing the FLSA in 1937–38 was a direct result of the conflicting demands of the party clients, and a harbinger of the deadlock to come. From 1937 onward, the party's northern and southern clients would largely be unable to agree on a reform agenda, so little of the progressive program would be enacted for the rest of FDR's term. After World War II, Truman would find it just as difficult to break this persistent stalemate; his Fair Deal would essentially go nowhere because of dissension among the Democratic party's clientele.

CHAPTER FOUR

He Just Dropped into the Slot

Harry Truman and the Consolidation of the New Deal Order

It is all too easy to look upon past events as the necessary result of undeniable social, economic, or spiritual forces. From this perspective, we are bound to conclude that we are here today because—somehow, some way—we were meant to be. This view of the world is quite widespread if not explicitly acknowledged in the discourse about American history, especially in the political realm. In the case of the Democratic party, it's tempting to view the party as it is today—mainly northern and liberal—as the inevitable working out of Franklin Roosevelt's New Deal.

Yet, as is often the case with such arguments about political inevitability, this conclusion is simplistic. Following FDR's death in 1945, there was genuine uncertainty about the future of both party coalitions. In fact, it might have seemed to many contemporary observers that the conservatives had finally regained the upper hand in the Democratic party. The Republican rebound of 1938, discussed in the previous chapter, was not a one-off fluke. Instead, GOP strength expanded slowly but surely through the rest of FDR's term, almost entirely at the expense of the northern, liberal wing of the party. By the time of Roosevelt's death, southern and border-state Democrats actually outnumbered northern Democrats in the House of Representatives, and their numbers were augmented by a congressional seniority system that systematically favored southern conservatives, who had not yet given the slightest hint of a bolt to the Republican party.[1]

Thus, it was not destiny that the postwar Democratic party would take on the liberal form that it possesses today. Instead, contingency played an important role time and again—and most immediately after FDR's death, in the form of an unprepossessing haberdasher turned president from Missouri named Harry S. Truman. The future of the party would depend not only on the choices Truman made, but also on the political successes or failures that followed from them. The election of 1948—much like those in 1896, 1912, and 1968—thus appears in retrospect to be one of those crucial moments in American history when the switch of just a few thousand votes here or there could have substantially altered the course of subsequent events. If Thomas Dewey had indeed defeated Truman and brought to Washington a Republican congressional majority, as most pundits expected that year, who knows what would have happened to the Democratic party thereafter?

And so, while FDR still stands atop the modern Democratic party, his continued supremacy is due in large part to the actions of Harry Truman, who would eventually pursue the same liberal course that Roosevelt had set. In so doing, Truman would help update American liberalism for the post–World War II era. The New Deal would become the Fair Deal, and Truman would be for FDR what John Adams had been for George Washington, and Martin Van Buren for Andrew Jackson: a resourceful yet underappreciated successor who consolidated his predecessor's gains even as contemporaries complained about how he just wasn't good enough.

Not only did Truman point the Democratic party to the same Rooseveltian ends, he also would pursue the same means. His Fair Deal gave the party a liberal raison d'être after the Depression and World War II, and it also enshrined FDR's practice of political clientelism. We will see time and again how Truman tried to balance the pursuit of a greater national purpose with particularistic payoffs to key factions. In this way, he would follow in the footsteps of FDR, who also balanced national policy making with special deals for loyal Democratic groups. What's more, by renewing the national Democratic party's commitment to liberalism, Truman guaranteed a perpetuation of the stalemate that characterized the latter half of FDR's term, meaning that his tenure would essentially be bereft of significant domestic reforms, save for the Taft-Hartley labor bill, which the conservatives would pass over his veto.

In 1944, Franklin Roosevelt was the undisputed champion of the Democratic party, but Senator Harry Truman of Missouri, then still mostly unknown except to those in his home state and the clubby United States Senate, was a symbol of what the party itself had become, possessing many of the characteristics of the old and new factions of the party. Hailing from Jackson County, Truman could trace his family's allegiance to the party of Jackson back to the nineteenth century, a time when most New Deal liberals would have been voting Republican. What's more, Truman got his political start in another mainstay of the old Democratic party, the urban political machine—in his case, the Pendergast machine of Kansas City, which had tapped him to run for the Senate in 1934.[2]

Yet it would be grossly unfair to characterize Truman as some hack machine pol whose loyalties stretched back to the unreconstructed South. While he was not your standard-issue New Deal liberal, Truman was nevertheless a reliable ally of the Roosevelt program during his tenure in Congress, supporting the Wagner Act, Social Security, and the Fair Labor Standards Act. And while Truman came into Washington derisively referred to as "the Senator from Pendergast," his hard, quiet efforts in the unglamorous setting of committee hearings, as well as his amiable manner, eventually made him a favorite in the Democratic caucus. When World War II broke out, Truman solidified this reputation through his diligent work on the Senate Special Committee to Investigate the National Defense Program, popularly known as the "Truman Committee." As the head of this committee, he went after waste, fraud, and abuse in the war industries, relentlessly dogging big business for not doing everything it could to help the fight, though—ever the party loyalist—he was always careful not to make the Roosevelt administration look bad.[3]

All of this helps explain why Truman became president of the United States. He did not want the job by a long shot, and he certainly wasn't the flashiest Democrat in the country, but a scan of the potential ascendants in the mid-1940s suggests that, practically speaking, it could have been nobody else. Franklin Roosevelt might have been the leader of his party, but in a sense Harry Truman *was* the Democratic party.

This was critically important as the Democrats prepared to meet in Chicago in 1944 to nominate Franklin Roosevelt for an unprecedented fourth term. Professional Democrats by that point generally believed two things to be true: first, the party would be gravely disadvantaged if Roosevelt declined a run for another term; second, the chances that the ailing FDR would survive the rigors of another four years in office were not good. This made the stakes for selecting a vice-presidential nominee incredibly high, as the pick was quite likely to become the next president.[4] The behind-the-scenes battle to choose the heir to Roosevelt would be yet another glimpse of the ideological and cultural divides that had appeared during the legislative fights of 1937–38, as party liberals and conservatives would use the vice-presidential pick as a proxy fight for the soul of the party itself. Truman won the nomination because all sides found him acceptable, but his eventual embrace of liberalism would ensure the long-term victory of the party's left wing.

For many party regulars, the high stakes in 1944 meant that incumbent vice president Henry A. Wallace absolutely, positively had to be ousted from the job. As secretary of agriculture during FDR's first and second terms, he had been an integral part of one of the liberals' favorite New Deal programs, the Agricultural Adjustment Administration, and this made him beloved by the party's intellectual base. Wallace's staunch liberalism also made him the first choice of American labor, a key party client in the North but an enemy of the southern Democracy. Yet the vice president had significant drawbacks that nullified his renomination prospects. He was not your typical politician; his wonky approach turned off many party regulars, and so did his interest in mysticism and the affection that the radical fringe had for him.[5]

Another Democrat in the running was former senator Jimmy Byrnes, a South Carolinian whom FDR had named to the Supreme Court in 1941. However, Byrnes was not on the high court for long, as Roosevelt quickly tapped him to be a high-level administrator of the war effort. Soon he had become an extremely close adviser to the president, and by 1944 he was actively angling for the vice-presidential spot.

But like Wallace, Byrnes had significant liabilities. First, he was from the South, and northern political bosses like Ed Flynn of the Bronx predicted that Byrnes might cost the Democratic ticket hundreds of thousands of African American votes in the big cities. What's more, Byrnes was born a Catholic but had converted to Episcopalianism when he married his wife. In this day and age, one's religious beliefs are normally considered outside the bounds of appropriate political discourse, but smart politicos in 1944 knew that Byrnes could hurt the Democrats with the Catholic vote, a bloc whose loyalty could not be taken for granted. Finally, Byrnes was anathema to organized labor, having voted against the Fair Labor Standards Act in 1937 and, later on, resisted efforts by labor to secure pay increases during the war.[6]

A handful of minor contenders were also considered—Senator Alben Barkley of Kentucky, Supreme Court Justice William O. Douglas, and House Speaker Sam Rayburn of Texas—but all of them were found wanting in some way. Ultimately, this was why the party establishment wound its way over to Truman. The process was slow and tortuous, in no small part because FDR didn't like to approach difficult problems head-on, but the selection of Truman in 1944 was the only sensible choice to unify the party.[7] As Flynn said later, "He just dropped into the slot."[8]

The only problem was that Truman did not want the job! He, too, knew how important the vice-presidential nomination would be, and the stubborn Truman resisted multiple entreaties to accept. In fact, he was planning to give the nomination speech for Byrnes at the convention. But ultimately not even Harry Truman could resist the will of Franklin Roosevelt. When FDR finally applied pressure—during the convention itself—Truman relented.[9] Ten months later, he would be president.

Though he left office with an approval rating of just 32 percent, a recent poll of historians by Siena College ranked Truman as the ninth-best president in the nation's history.[10] Today he is commonly thought of in the ways that hit the highlights of David McCullough's influential biography—a straight shooter who told it like it was even when the truth was inconvenient, who came into office amid terribly difficult times and upon the death of a political legend, but who nevertheless managed to forge a broad consensus in the realm of U.S. foreign policy that lasted for a generation.

Yet Dwight Eisenhower, one of the least partisan presidents in American history, thought very little of Harry Truman. He considered his predecessor to be a hyper-partisan, and he detested the Fair Deal.[11] The two men had begun their relationship on a good footing, but by the end of Truman's presidency they were barely on speaking terms. Eisenhower, like Truman, has been remembered very well by subsequent generations (like Truman, he has enjoyed significant and upward revisions to his reputation), so it would be hasty to dismiss his opinion out of hand. What to make of this?

While the revisionist take on Truman has a great deal of merit, so also does Ike's critique. In terms of domestic politics, Truman's "Fair Deal" program became the blueprint for postwar Democratic liberalism, and one of its most notable characteristics was a special policy mix designed to secure the support of union workers, farmers, African Americans, urban dwellers—basically any faction the Democrats thought could be persuaded to vote for them. This wasn't the whole of the Fair Deal—not by any stretch—but the point is that the Truman program not only would try to improve the nation as a whole but also would take special care of the voters who had put him into power. Thanks to Truman and the Fair Deal, postwar American liberalism would look much more like the Fair Labor Standards Act, which combined a national minimum wage program with payoffs to certain client groups, than the NIRA, which sought to build a broad coalition of the whole community to tackle a national problem.

Truman did not find this political posture right away, much to his chagrin. His early tenure was marked by failed attempts to build a nationwide consensus to deal with the demobilization of the war effort. The chief domestic problem for Truman when he assumed the presidency in April 1945 was reconversion from a wartime economy to a peacetime one, particularly as it held the potential for runaway, crippling inflation. Government controls had kept prices in check during the war, but with the mandate of the Office of Price Administration (OPA) due to expire early in Truman's term, the question was: what to do next? The president was squeezed on multiple sides. Liberals in his coalition preferred the maintenance of price controls, with an eye to managing reconversion just as the first New Deal had managed the Great Depression. On the other hand, the conservative coalition of Republicans and southern Democrats—by this point the dominant faction in Congress—had grown tired of such intense governmental regulation of the economy, and they signaled their intention to give Truman only a modest reauthorization of the OPA.[12]

The biggest headache, however, was organized labor. Labor leaders agreed with the liberals on the need to maintain price controls, but they also were preparing to push for major increases in wages. They had in mind a fundamental restructuring of American economic life—a new political equilibrium in which government, business, and labor would work together to develop a fair distribution of the national wealth, one in which prices were kept low and wages were increased.[13] So for instance Walter Reuther of the United Auto Workers had demanded that GM raise wages by 30 percent *without* increasing the price of its product, and he demanded that the car company "open the books" to prove it could pay.[14] Unfortunately for President Truman, many union leaders were prepared to put their money where their mouths were. By the beginning of 1946, some 4.6 million workers were striking, and Truman eventually seized the coal, oil, and meatpacking industries.[15]

When the railway workers threatened to strike, enough was enough for President Truman. He had long been sympathetic to labor, but he had also long been offended by private interests that acted against the general welfare. His immediate attitude toward the unions in this case was similar; after all, a railway strike would shut down the entire economy. In a national address, Truman stated, "I am a friend of labor . . . [but] it is inconceivable that in our democracy [union leaders] should be placed in a position where they can completely stifle our economy and ultimately destroy our country."[16] The next day, before a joint session of Congress, Truman called for having the army take over the railroads, and for drafting strikers into the armed forces. In a moment of high political drama, he received a note in mid-speech that the trainmen had agreed to a settlement; his abrupt announcement of the news was greeted with raucous applause.[17]

Yet when push came to shove, Truman signed no major labor reforms during his tenure, despite the dramatic posture he took on behalf of the national interest in his address to Congress. In fact, Truman vetoed the Case bill, which provided for a sixty-day cooling-off period before a strike, permitted injunctions against certain union activities, made unions liable to suits for breach of labor contracts, and prohibited secondary boycotts.[18] Broadly speaking, it would have accomplished many of the goals that Truman had outlined in his dramatic address, limiting the power of organized labor to hold the economy hostage, although it was tougher in some respects. The bill passed overwhelmingly (49–29 in the Senate and 320–106 in the House); organized labor feverishly petitioned Truman to veto it, and that is what he finally did.[19]

At the Gridiron Dinner in December 1945, Truman had joked that General Sherman was wrong: "I'm telling you I find peace is hell!"[20] This was only a partial exaggeration for the beleaguered president, who was taking it from all sides. When he entered office in the spring of 1945, the Gallup Poll found his job approval at 86 percent, but by the time of the 1946 midterms, just 27 percent of his fellow citizens approved of his performance as president.[21] The Republicans campaigned on a simple slogan—"Had enough? Vote Republican"—and the voters surely did.[22] The 1946 election was a complete and total rout, the worst beating the Democrats would take between 1928 and 2010. For the first time in sixteen years, they found themselves in the minority in both chambers of Congress. The GOP picked up fifty-five seats in the House,[23] and Democratic losses were heavy among liberal Democrats; of the seventy-seven Democrats the New Republic labeled at or above "80 percent liberal," forty-one were defeated. Labor also suffered heavy losses; of the seventy-eight candidates the CIO PAC rated at 100 percent, forty-two were defeated, and 108 of the 132 candidates the CIO PAC stumped against won election.[24] All in all, the Democratic defeat was so broad that Senator William Fulbright, Democrat from Arkansas, suggested that Truman nominate a Republican secretary of state, then resign so that the public mandate could be fully implemented.[25]

However, Truman—the "contrariest goddamn mule from Missouri," as DNC chair Robert Hannegan had once characterized him—would do no such thing. Instead he stood his ground and fought, and it was by way of his battle against the congressional Republicans that the Democratic party would discover its postwar, liberal identity.

The conventional wisdom among the pundits of the day was that 1946 was the moment when the political scales had come back into balance. Franklin Roosevelt, the maestro, had gone to meet his maker, and thus it was destiny for the Republican party to return to a share of political power. What's more, the breadth and depth of the 1946 electoral rebuke—combined with Truman's anemic poll numbers—suggested that the country had made up its mind about the thirty-third president, and the verdict was not positive.[26] Even in his own party, Truman lacked strong support. Already mentioned was how he had aggravated the labor unions, and his troubles extended beyond labor to the liberals. Early in his term, he had submitted a large list of very liberal policy requests to Congress, one that prompted conservatives to suggest that he was trying to out–New Deal the New Deal. And yet this bought him very little credibility with the liberals themselves, who were disheartened by his apparent unwillingness to fight for the proposals. What's more, liberals were generally upset that his "Missouri Gang"—Truman cronies like Harry Vaughan, Ed McKim, and Jake Vardaman—were moving into positions of power as Harold Ickes, one of the first and most iconic New Dealers, resigned from the cabinet and Henry Wallace was sacked after giving a speech at Madison Square Garden urging a soft approach in dealing with the Soviets.[27]

All in all, the cards were totally stacked against Truman by the time the Eightieth Congress came into session in January 1947. The Republicans smelled blood in the water, the American people were skeptical at best, and labor and the liberals wanted to be rid of him. Even so, just two years later, he would be inaugurated to a term of his own. How did this old political hand from Missouri manage such an incredible feat?

To begin with, he got a little lucky. By the time of the 1948 convention, a wide swath of Democratic party leaders—from liberals in the Americans for Democratic Action (ADA) to urban machine pols—wanted to dump Truman for Dwight D. Eisenhower, or "Ike" for short, the commanding general in the country's victory in Europe in World War II. However, Ike unequivocally declared himself not to be a candidate, and there was nobody else of sufficient stature to push aside an incumbent president.[28] Yet luck was only part of Truman's success—the rest of it was careful political positioning by the president, who pursued two strategies simultaneously. On the one hand, he forged a bipartisan foreign policy that emphasized anti-Communism as well as internationalism. Ultimately, this divided the Republicans between their isolationist and internationalist wings while inoculating the Democrats against conservative attacks by pushing the Communists and their sympathizers beyond the boundaries of mainstream political discourse.[29] On the other hand, he set about fighting the Republicans at virtually every turn on the domestic front, and in so doing he articulated a new version of postwar liberalism, one that would hold the core New Deal coalition together for the next twenty years. It is this latter strategy that will occupy our attention here.

After the midterm debacle, a group of Truman's advisers—led by Clark Clifford and known informally as the Monday-Night Group— began meeting regularly to plot how the president might secure re-election despite the stiff political winds he faced. In November 1947, Clifford passed on to Truman a memo written by James Rowe, a political adviser to FDR and one of the first members of the ADA.[30] Truman read the memo carefully, discussed it with his advisers, and eventually followed its recommendations almost to the letter, though it's unclear to what extent Rowe's memo influenced or simply reinforced his thinking.[31] And because Rowe's analysis of the impending political alignment was so piercingly accurate, these steps helped secure Truman a term in his own right.

In the memo, Rowe accurately predicted that the Republicans would renominate Governor Thomas Dewey of New York and that he would be "even more difficult to defeat than in 1944." Rowe also predicted—accurately, again—that Henry Wallace would mount a third-party, progressive challenge, even though at the time "the majority of informed opinion does not favor this particular hypothesis." Rowe then outlined what would become the fundamental political strategy of the Democratic party for the next half century. Both parties, he asserted, "have a minimum, a residue, of voters whose loyalty almost nothing can shake." What was needed, then, was an appeal to the "independent voter," but the old nineteenth-century approach of "party organization" was no longer sufficient to win election. "Better education, the rise of the mass pressure group, the economic growth of government functions—all these have contributed to the downfall of 'the organization.' They have been supplanted in large measure by the pressure groups—and the support of these must be wooed since they really control the 1948 election." The main groups up for grabs in Rowe's view were: the farm vote, essential to "winning of the West—the number one priority"; "organized labor," whose *active* support" was essential to avoid another 1946 defeat; the liberals, who, while numerically small, were similar to "manufacturers and financiers of the Republican Party" in that they were "far more influential than mere numbers entitle them to be"; the African American vote in northern cities, which might hold "the balance of power in Presidential elections for the simple arithmetical reason that [they] not only vote in a bloc but are geographically concentrated in the pivotal, large and closely contested electoral states"; and the ethnic vote, especially the Catholic vote, "traditionally Democratic but there have been disturbingly consistent and fairly well documented rumors that the Catholic fear of Communism is grown so great that it is actively distrustful and suspicious today of any group which gives even an appearance of neutrality towards foreign or domestic Communists." Rowe went on to predict that the Republicans, with their conservative base satisfied, would move to the left to pick up these groups; accordingly, he advised that Truman "swing *further* 'left' than they do," at least on domestic policy. On foreign policy, the major task was to push Wallace to the margins as quickly as possible, "to identify him and isolate him in the public mind with the Communists."[32]

That is exactly what Truman did. On issue after issue in the famed battles between the president and the Eightieth Congress of 1947–48, Truman established positions to the left of the congressional Republicans and often tailored them with an eye to winning the support of particular interests within the country. Two notable fights with congressional Republicans, on labor and civil rights, are worth special attention, as they underscore Truman and the Democrats' relentless focus on particular factions within society. With organized labor, his desire to keep it in his coalition meant that he all but abandoned his earlier calls for reforms in labor relations, and on civil rights Truman played a double game in hopes of winning black votes in the northern cities without alienating the white South.

On the labor issue, the Eightieth Congress was easily the least well disposed toward the unions as any since the 1929–30 session. Combine the 245 House Republicans with the 103 southern Democrats, neither of which had been very supportive of labor for well over a decade, and the conservatives had not just a majority but a *veto-proof majority* in the House to pass laws curbing the power of organized labor.[33] The Senate was more moderate, but still very conservative. What's more, the strikes of 1946 had given the conservatives political cover to roll back labor's gains. The result was the Taft-Hartley Act of 1947, the most important piece of labor legislation since the National Labor Relations Act of 1935. Most notably, Taft-Hartley banned secondary boycotts and blackmail strikes (wherein union workers strike at a non-unionized shop to force it to recognize the union) and gave states the right to outlaw the closed shop. This last item led to the creation of so-called right-to-work states and gave the South a legal basis to continue its anti-union activity, which in the previous decades had often been extralegal. Taft-Hartley also extended the "cooling-off" periods for strikes, and it gave the president the power to investigate strikes that endangered national health and safety, and potentially to ask the attorney general to seek a court injunction.[34]

Truman, the same president who just a few months earlier had called for drafting striking workers into the armed services, denounced Taft-Hartley in unequivocal terms:

> *[It will] reverse the basic direction of our national labor policy, inject the government into private economic affairs on an unprecedented scale, and conflict with important principles of our democratic society. Its provisions would cause more strikes, not fewer. It would contribute neither to industrial peace nor to economic stability and progress. . . . It contains seeds of discord which would plague this nation for years to come.*[35]

The president dutifully vetoed it, but Congress overwhelmingly voted to override the veto.[36] The result was bad policy for labor, but good politics for the Democrats. Whatever enthusiasm gap existed among labor for the Democrats in 1946 was good and gone by the 1948 presidential election.

Meanwhile, civil rights had been an issue that Franklin Roosevelt was generally content to avoid; after all, African Americans were not a significant part of his political coalition, and southern Democrats were. However, the African American vote in the northern cities was growing in size, thanks to the decades-long migration of southern blacks to northern cities, which had a profound effect on political calculations in the North. In 1900, African Americans made up just 1.4 percent of the total population in New York state; forty years later their numbers had grown to 4.2 percent. This was a small change from an absolute perspective, but the Empire State—and its forty-seven electoral votes in 1948—remained the quintessential toss-up state, and the black vote would be critical. Similarly, the African American population in Illinois had grown from 1.8 percent in 1900 to 4.9 percent in 1940—another small difference, but a vital one.[37]

Prior to the New Deal, northern African Americans had been staunchly loyal to the party of Lincoln, yet while the New Deal rarely if ever targeted poor African Americans in particular, it would have been virtually impossible to design such a massive government aid program in a way that did not benefit them, at least a little bit. In response, African Americans flocked to the Democratic banner, but Republicans still believed that they could win them back, considering the Democrats' dependence on the segregationist vote. Dewey, the Republican nominee in 1948, had developed a fairly strong civil rights record in the Empire State, including a state-based fair employment practices commission;[38] he had carried Harlem in his 1942 gubernatorial campaign, and the GOP platform on civil rights in 1944 was stronger than the Democratic platform.[39] Without the maestro FDR at the top of the ticket, the black vote was a real concern for Truman and his political advisers. A swing in the black vote, if it occurred systematically, could be enough to tip key northern states like Illinois, New Jersey, New York, Ohio, and Pennsylvania.

Early in his term, Truman—whose voting coalition in Missouri included African Americans as well as Ku Klux Klan members—did not make much headway with black voters, instead opting to split the difference between them and southern conservatives. A case in point was the battle over FDR's Fair Employment Practices Committee (FEPC), which was meant to end racial discrimination in the war industries and was in part a nod to growing black political power in the North. Truman called for a permanent FEPC—the existing committee was set to expire in June 1946—but he did not push the issue very hard, and he had even eliminated the FEPC's power to issue cease-and-desist warrants the previous December.[40]

But after his midterm drubbing, Truman began pushing for civil rights more than any previous Democrat, and indeed *any* president in more than fifty years. Shortly after the midterms, he signed Executive Order 9808, which established a multiracial Committee on Civil Rights meant to offer "recommendations with respect to the adoption or establishment, by legislation or otherwise, of more adequate and effective means and procedures for the protection of the civil rights of the people of the United States."[41] In October 1947, Truman's commission released its findings, promoting thirty-five recommendations that included a civil rights division at the Justice Department, a permanent commission on civil rights, a federal antilynching law, the end of poll taxes, legislation to secure the voting rights of all citizens, and more.[42] In February 1948, Truman sent a special message to Congress calling for the enactment of his commission's recommendations.[43]

And yet Truman, for all his lofty rhetoric in the prior months, balked at pushing this agenda through the Democratic party itself. The reason was the South, which was quickly becoming a problem.[44] The one glaring mistake in the Rowe memo was the false assumption that the South would stick with the Democratic party. In fairness to Rowe, there were good historical reasons to believe this. FDR had carried about 75 percent of the southern vote all four times, and Harry Truman was a border-state Democrat, only the second to win a major party presidential nomination since the Civil War.[45] Of course, following the argument we are making here, there were also good reasons to expect the South to buck decades of loyalty to the Democratic party. After all, the foundation of the South's relationship with the Democratic party depended on protection from northern, Republican incursions into the racist system of social control in the South; if the northern Democrats violated that, why wouldn't the South defect?

By the time of the convention in Philadelphia, there was growing awareness that a southern political rebellion was indeed brewing. Thus, Truman and his allies fought hard in the platform committee to scotch the liberal civil rights plank that would embody the very proposals the president had promoted. Like John F. Kennedy after him, Truman was playing a double game, representing to northern blacks that he supported civil rights while trying to reassure southern Democrats that they had nothing to worry about. The Truman forces won the battle in the platform committee, but when it came to the floor fight, they were no match for the eloquence of Hubert Humphrey, the mayor of Minneapolis and the chief liberal advocate at the convention for a progressive plank.[46] In one of the most important addresses in convention history, Humphrey pleaded with his fellow Democrats:

> My friends, to those who say that we are rushing this issue of civil rights, I say to them we are 172 years late. To those who say that this civil-rights program is an infringement on states' rights, I say this: The time has arrived in America for the Democratic Party to get out of the shadow of states' rights and to walk forthrightly into the bright sunshine of human rights.[47]

In the end, the liberals carried the day, albeit narrowly: 651½ delegates voted in favor, while 582½ voted against what Truman privately called a "crackpot" civil rights plank.[48] In response, representatives from southern states walked out of the convention, to a chorus of boos and catcalls.

All in all, the 1948 Democratic National Convention was an unpleasant one for many in the party. Much of the tension had to do with the civil rights plank, but there was also a pall hanging over the proceedings, a gloomy sense that the Democratic party had lost its governing mandate, had worn out its welcome with the electorate, and was fracturing internally. Truman would not take the stage to give his acceptance address until the early-morning hours of July 15. Most radio listeners were in bed, which is a shame, as they missed one of the most electrifying convention addresses in American history. Truman's fiery speech to the convention revived the delegates' flagging spirits and hinted at the aggressive reelection campaign the president would wage:

> *[Vice presidential nominee] Senator Barkley and I will win this election and make these Republicans like it—don't you forget that! . . .*
>
> *The reason is that the people know that the Democratic Party is the people's party, and the Republican Party is the party of special interest, and it always has been and always will be. . . .*
>
> *Farm income has increased from less than $2 billion in 1932 to more than $18 billion in 1947. Never in the world were the farmers of any republic or any kingdom or any other country as prosperous as the farmers of the United States; and if they don't do their duty by the Democratic Party, they are the most ungrateful people in the world!*
>
> *Wages and salaries in this country have increased from $29 billion in 1933 to more than $128 billion in 1947. That's labor, and labor never had but one friend in politics, and that is the Democratic Party and Franklin D. Roosevelt.*
>
> *And I say to labor what I have said to the farmers: they are the most ungrateful people in the world if they pass the Democratic Party by this year.*[49]

Truman's speech to the Philadelphia convention is probably the most nakedly partisan of any acceptance address in the postwar era, and it set the tone for the flagrant pressure-group politicking that characterized his fall campaign. The president crisscrossed the country, telling farmers, laborers, westerners—basically any faction that would listen—a story of how the Republicans had hurt their interests during the "Do-Nothing" Eightieth Congress; if they didn't do their duty to the Democratic party in 1948, an even worse fate would await them.[50]

Our argument in this book is that the Democratic party has since been ruined by the kind of factional appeals that Truman made that year—and the thirty-third president deserves a good measure of the blame, because this strategy worked like a charm in 1948; though seemingly the entire country had counted him out, on Election Day it was Truman who defeated Dewey. Following the Rowe memo, his campaign ingeniously broke the country down into factions, to whom the president made blatantly narrow appeals. Labor, farmers, urban ethnics, African Americans, Catholics—everybody was offered something if they voted for Truman; and the result was an electoral coalition that included disparate and diverse places such as the farms of California's Central Valley and the tenement housing on the South Side of Chicago. What was particularly impressive about Truman's win was that he pulled it off even with Henry Wallace on the Progressive ticket and South Carolina governor Strom Thurmond on the States' Rights Democrats (or "Dixiecrats") ticket playing spoiler in several states. Thurmond carried much of the Deep South, and Wallace peeled off enough liberal votes to swing Maryland, Michigan, and New York.[51]

In his State of the Union message in January 1949, Truman, now president in his own right, declared:

> *The strength of our Nation must continue to be used in the interest of all our people rather than a privileged few. It must continue to be used unselfishly in the struggle for world peace and the betterment of mankind the world over.*
>
> *This is the task before us.*
>
> *It is not an easy one. It has many complications, and there will be strong opposition from selfish interests.*
>
> *I hope for cooperation from farmers, from labor, and from business. Every segment of our population and every individual has a right to expect from our Government a fair deal.*[52]

The phrase "Fair Deal" would come to define the domestic agenda of Truman's second term, and it is indicative of the Democratic party's approach to politics through the present day. Its core ideas— aid for housing, education, medical care, farm subsidies, and labor protections—laid the foundation for the postwar Democratic agenda, at least the northern, liberal version of it. Like the New Deal, the

Fair Deal was also a mix of national policy making and clientelism. It combined broad proposals that would benefit the country at large, like universal health insurance, with special payoffs to the groups that had backed the Democrats in 1948, like a repeal of Taft-Hartley and generous subsidies for midwestern farmers. In that sense, there was more than a whiff of unfairness to the Fair Deal, for these special benefits belied the rhetoric of unity that Truman had enunciated at the start of 1949.

Unfortunately for the president, congressional cooperation would largely not be forthcoming, despite the fact that the Democrats had recaptured control of the House and Senate. In the end, the same problem that had stymied the New Deal after 1938 would scuttle much of the Fair Deal: the yawning divide between the northern and southern factions of the party. The party's principal client group in the North, organized labor, thrilled at the prospect of the Fair Deal—and after the debacle of the Eightieth Congress, organized labor's connection to the Democratic party was tighter than ever. Yet the white South was a client as well, and it understood that many of the Fair Deal proposals—on labor, health care, civil rights, and more—would fundamentally alter Dixie's way of life, the protection of which was the reason southerners had joined the Democratic party in the first place.

As we saw in Chapter 3, this divide in the party had first appeared as early as FDR's second term, but by 1948 it had grown into a dangerously wide intraparty schism. Whereas this split had once been limited to legislative battles, southern voters were starting to defect from the party banner. Southern Democrats were returned to Congress in their typically solid numbers, but Truman won just 50.5 percent of the vote in the old Confederacy, the worst for any Democrat since the end of Reconstruction.[53] What makes this especially notable is that Truman and his running mate, Alben Barkley, were both border-state Democrats; in terms of simple geography, not since the Civil War had there been a major-party presidential ticket so close to Dixie.

In Congress, Dixie would align with conservative Republicans time and again to stop the Fair Deal. Southern Democrats in the Senate predictably filibustered Truman's effort to establish a permanent FEPC.[54] Also, Truman's demand for substantial modifications to Taft-Hartley went nowhere fast, as a majority of legislators in the Eighty-first Congress had voted for it during the Eightieth Congress, and pro-labor reform efforts in both chambers were watered down by conservative amendments.[55] Truman's proposals to raise income taxes and expand federal support for education also fell by the wayside.[56]

Truman's farm plan—known as the Brannan Plan—was one of the most blatant political payoffs devised in the postwar era. The old AAA had reduced acreage in hopes of driving up farm prices, and therefore farm income. The Brannan Plan would essentially have put farmers on welfare, subsidizing them to achieve high farm wages and lower farm prices simultaneously. It attracted liberals who had studied the 1948 results carefully and noticed Truman's increased support in the farming areas of the Midwest—their hope was that such a plan could solidify a political union between labor in the cities and farmers in the Great Plains. Republicans and southern Democrats attacked the Brannan Plan with aggression, and in the end it died in the House of Representatives.[57]

Truman was also the first of several Democratic presidents to push for a national health insurance plan. The idea was to raise the Social Security tax to fund insurance for all Americans. The American Medical Association went after the plan ferociously, labeling it socialistic, but Truman would not compromise on a more modest measure. Ultimately, like his plan to repeal Taft-Hartley, his plan for national health insurance lacked nationwide political support, and it fell far short of the necessary votes in the Congress. The House tabled it without taking a vote.[58]

The only major provision of the Fair Deal to make it through Congress was the Housing Act of 1949, which was largely an extension of the Housing Act of 1937.[59] This, plus a modest increase in the minimum wage, was about all that Truman could boast in terms of domestic policy output. All in all, these successes amounted to the most liberal legislation since 1938, but that is not saying very much, and the Republican rebound in the 1950 midterm election solidified the conservative coalition, bringing progressive domestic reforms to a halt.[60]

The final years of Truman's tenure similarly lacked much in the way of domestic policy reforms, and the administration was tied up in the Korean War. The war, plus growing fears of an internal Communist threat from within the government itself as well as stories of crooked administration officials—that old Missouri gang—contributed to a slow but steady decline in President Truman's public standing. When he fired General Douglas MacArthur in the spring of 1951, fewer than one in four Americans approved of him, and when he left office in early 1953, his approval rating stood at just 32 percent.[61]

It's often been said that Harry Truman was an old Jacksonian Democrat, and for good reasons. Both came from humble backgrounds, and their political programs were rooted in personal identification with those who had not gotten a fair deal in life. Truman's pugilistic campaign style was also reminiscent of Jackson. Presidential candidates usually throw some rough elbows during campaign season, but few have gone as far as Truman did in Philadelphia in 1948 when he declared that the GOP "always has been and always will be" the party of special interests, an extraordinary statement about the party that had won the Civil War and found common ground with Truman on foreign policy. It was the sort of thing Jackson might have said about the Whigs in 1832.

But on an ideological level, there is a large gulf between Jackson and Truman. One of Jackson's first acts as president was to veto a spending bill for infrastructure improvement in Kentucky. This marked a consistent theme for Jackson, one that he articulated in his veto message for the Bank of the United States: a powerful government was one that inevitably played favorites and threatened the humble members of society, so the best defense for the common man was a government that stayed out of the way. As noted in Chapter 2, the Democratic party had long subscribed to this Jacksonian faith, but political necessity and socioeconomic changes in the early twentieth century challenged the old order. Under the leadership of Bryan, Wilson, and above all FDR, the party embraced the big-government ethos of progressivism. Harry Truman was perhaps the last Democratic leader who met with a crossroads: he could have gone back to the old Jacksonian way or continued down the progressive path. His Fair Deal unabashedly endorsed the latter course, and in doing so it updated Democratic liberalism for the postwar age.

Yet Jackson's old warnings remained true: a federal government that claimed the power to do big things was also one with the power to play favorites. And by the time of Harry Truman, the Democratic party—now undeniably the party of big government—was indeed prepared to play favorites. The Fair Deal, as we saw, combined big national reforms with special payoffs to the groups that had backed Truman in 1948. What's more, organized labor enjoyed special treatment all through the Truman years; despite all his tough rhetoric about unions early in his term, the president did not sign a single piece of significant labor reform legislation during his eight years in office. Instead, he vetoed the Case bill and Taft-Hartley, and later pledged to water down the latter. In so doing, he helped secure labor's support in the 1948 campaign, but he also demonstrated the dangers that Jackson foresaw in the kind of clientelism that big government breeds: organized labor had acted irresponsibly after World War II, but Truman offered it nothing but harsh words.

Still, by the end of Truman's term, the Fair Deal remained more an idea than an actuality. The burr in the saddle at this point in our story remains the American South, whose view of governmental activism was much more conservative than that embodied by the Fair Deal. Indeed, though Truman managed a narrow electoral victory in 1948, his congressional majority depended far too heavily on the southern Democrats, which meant that for all of his political successes, he would enact few policy reforms. This would be the way of the world through the 1950s, and it was only after the assassination of John F. Kennedy that the next round of bold liberal policy making would begin.

CHAPTER FIVE

Let Us Continue

JFK, LBJ, and the Apogee of American Liberalism

No other period is more important in the development of the modern Democratic party than the 1960s. By the end of the decade, the party would be fundamentally different from what it was at the beginning of the decade. Yet for all the changes of those ten consequential years, the process of change was strangely reminiscent of the 1930s: a national catastrophe inaugurates a brief period of liberal policy making that would transform not only the country but the Democratic party itself. In the 1960s, the catastrophe was not a Great Depression but the assassination of President John F. Kennedy. The reform program of the 1930s was called the New Deal; in the 1960s it would be christened the Great Society. In both cases, we see party leaders pursuing two purposes simultaneously: policy making to reform the whole nation *and* to build the Democratic party by nurturing and growing its client base.

The next five chapters will tell the tale of the Democratic party through the 1960s. Chapter 5 will analyze the events that led up to the monumental policy breakthroughs and outline the national reforms of the Great Society. Chapter 6 will discuss the long-term effects of bringing millions of previously disenfranchised African Americans into the Democratic coalition. Chapter 7 will consider the growth and development of organized labor through the 1960s. Chapter 8 will review the splintering of the Democratic party in the election of 1968. And Chapter 9 will examine the effects of the New Politics left on the Democratic party.

• • •

Truman's unyielding partisan approach to the 1948 presidential campaign helped the Democrats pull out a fifth straight victory, but a sixth
would not be forthcoming. Everybody knew Eisenhower was a sure
winner, so much so that both liberals and conservatives in the Democratic party had tried to draft him four years prior. Yet Ike aligned himself with the moderate, northeastern faction of the Republican party,
with leaders like New York governor Thomas Dewey and Massachusetts senator Henry Cabot Lodge Jr. He cruised to his party's nomination in 1952, beating "Mr. Republican," conservative senator Robert
Taft of Ohio, on the first ballot. As a sop to the conservatives, Ike nominated California senator Richard Nixon for the vice-presidential position; Nixon had been moderate on domestic affairs, but his unyielding
anti-Communism had made him a favorite among the right wing of the
party.[1]

Meanwhile, Democrats were stuck with a version of the same
problem they faced in 1944: how to find a candidate who could appease
all factions. Harry Truman had early on been eyeing Illinois governor
Adlai Stevenson, who was perhaps the only good fit for the party's nod.
He was the sole established Democratic politician in one of the big
states who wasn't either Catholic or Jewish, and while he had a liberal,
reformist record in the Land of Lincoln, he had not fought very hard
for civil rights.[2] The trouble was that the Hamlet-like Stevenson played
it coy, waving away encouragement to toss his hat into the ring until the
very last minute. He finally acceded, and won nomination on the third
ballot, outlasting Tennessee senator Estes Kefauver, Georgia senator
Richard Russell, and the former ambassador to the USSR W. Averell
Harriman. The convention was the longest in the post–World War II
era as southern and northern factions squabbled over delegate creden-
tials and a loyalty pledge.[3]

The 1952 general election campaign was a nonevent. Eisenhower
ran on Korea, Communism, and corruption, though he was careful
not to attack Truman or Stevenson by name. Stevenson's eloquent
campaign addresses moved few voters, but they did make him the new
object of the American left's affections. Though Stevenson himself was

not really much of an intellectual, his speechifying made the liberal elite believe that he was indeed one of their own, which was good enough for him to win the nomination again in 1956. Still, the love of the left couldn't prevent Eisenhower from winning in a walk in 1952, and Stevenson's share of the Electoral College vote that year was the second worst for any Democrat to date since the Civil War.[4]

In the end, Eisenhower's broad personal appeal was more than enough to get a Democratic-leaning country to vote Republican once again. Polling data suggest that Ike cut heavily into Democratic strongholds, winning 18 percent of the black vote, 49 percent of the Catholic vote, and 28 percent of the Jewish vote; all in all, about 30 percent of self-identified Democrats voted for Eisenhower.[5] His coattails were enough to sweep in a Republican congressional majority, albeit barely: the Eighty-third Congress opened with the GOP enjoying an eight-seat majority in the House and a one-seat majority in the Senate. Eisenhower won 55 percent of the presidential vote while Republicans carried just 49 percent of the House vote. For the rest of the decade, the congressional GOP would consistently underperform Eisenhower, and the Republican majority would be lost in 1954, not to return for another twenty-six years in the Senate and forty in the House.[6]

In historical retrospect, Eisenhower's presidency was significant and beneficial for the country at large, but its long-term effect on the American party alignment was modest. A major reason is that Eisenhower's domestic program—dubbed "Modern Republicanism"—was squeezed from both ends, by conservatives in his own party who did not think it went far enough in rolling back the excesses of the New Deal and the Fair Deal, and by liberal Democrats who thought it went too far. So while the country "liked Ike," his administration was a resting period in domestic affairs, at the end of which the old party squabbles would pick up where they had left off.[7]

To appreciate this, we need look no further than the 1960 presidential election, whose top-line similarity to 1948 is striking. Truman managed 49.6 percent of the vote, while Massachusetts senator John F. Kennedy won 49.7 percent. Both won 303 electoral votes. What's more, Kennedy would have to wind his way along a similarly byzantine path for the party's nomination, carefully modulating his public pronouncements to ensure that he did not offend one key constituent group or another. Twelve years on, very little had changed.[8]

Kennedy's tenure in government prior to 1960 was marked by mediocrity in the field of public policy yet great successes in image making and political positioning. Though JFK was witty and charming, he accomplished very little during his fourteen years in Congress, as he was usually preoccupied with running for the next office.[9] On domestic affairs, he was a moderate liberal, a friend to labor who nevertheless voted for the Landrum-Griffin Act, which restricted the freedom of unions. He also kept the Americans for Democratic Action (ADA) at arm's length, despite the fact that he was sympathetic to many of its goals. What's more, his votes on civil rights legislation in the Senate were cynically crafted to appease all factions in the party.[10] JFK's policy goal was to make a name for himself in foreign affairs rather than wade into the messy, divisive domestic policy waters. And for Kennedy, that meant staunch anti-Communism and full-throated advocacy of increased military spending. Political calculations surely played a part in this—the Catholic vote in Massachusetts was intensely anti-Communist—but so also might his father's politically costly flirtation with British appeasers during the 1930s. Regardless of the motives, Kennedy was notably quiet when it came to denouncing Republican bomb thrower Joe McCarthy. In fact, he was the one Democrat not to vote to condemn the Wisconsin senator in 1953 (he didn't vote at all, being in the hospital for surgery).[11] All in all, this meant that the liberals who by this point were the spiritual core of the Democratic party were not huge fans of Jack Kennedy. As historian Robert Dallek has noted:

> *Most liberals subscribed to the view of Kennedy as an ambitious but superficial playboy with little more to recommend him than his good looks and charm. On none of the issues most important to them—McCarthyism, civil rights, and labor unions—had Jack been an outspoken advocate.*[12]

This, of course, stands in stark contrast to the popular liberal memory of JFK nowadays, but it should not come as a huge surprise that the Kennedy legend bears only a superficial relation to the Kennedy record. After all, the Kennedys were supremely good at mythmaking, which was a crucial element in JFK's presidential run. His incredibly wealthy father was known to grease the wheels with important newspaper editors, and JFK himself was a former newspaperman who understood what journalists needed to get their jobs done. So, throughout the 1950s, this handsome, undistinguished senator from Massachusetts could often be found on the covers of publications like *Life* magazine, with probing titles such as "Senator Kennedy Goes A-Courting!"[13] The Kennedys' masterful manipulation of the press later caused Hubert Humphrey to exclaim after the 1960 Wisconsin primary, "Does he own all the newspapers or does he have something on every publisher?"[14]

Of course, the fawning media coverage and careful political triangulation were not ends in themselves. Instead, they were part of a careful strategy that laid the groundwork for what the Kennedys expected to be a bruising presidential nomination battle in 1960. The principal concern, they figured, was JFK's Catholicism, and their solution was to run him aggressively in the primary battles.[15] Back then, unlike today, the primaries did not offer much by way of convention delegates, and in fact presidential contenders who had run well in the primaries—Teddy Roosevelt and Estes Kefauver, for instance—usually did not persuade the delegates to nominate them. Even so, the Kennedys figured that if JFK did well in the primaries, he would signal to the party establishment that his Catholicism would not effectively disqualify him with the voters. With Joe Kennedy's seemingly endless supply of money, JFK's charisma, and younger brother Robert Kennedy's preternatural knack for political organization, the Kennedy team went "a-courting" with the voters. JFK won every primary battle he entered, fending off Humphrey in Wisconsin and West Virginia, where the Minnesota senator was outspent by a very wide margin.

And so, when the party elite gathered for the Democratic convention in Los Angeles in July 1960, Kennedy was the front-runner, and he would win the nomination on the first ballot, despite a last-minute campaign by Adlai Stevenson to swing the convention to him for a third straight time. Nobody within the Democratic party desperately wanted JFK for president, but nobody was offended by him, either. That, plus his strong showings in the primaries, which had eased concerns about his electability, made it a relatively easy convention victory for him.

Of course, the Kennedys still faced general election troubles, particularly with the South. Though JFK had not been terribly liberal on civil rights, he still expected to have problems in Dixie, especially vote-rich Texas. As an urban, Catholic Democrat, Kennedy did not really expect to re-create the old Democratic alliance of the South and West, which were rural and Protestant. Instead, he planned to carry the big states in the Northeast and Industrial Midwest, where the Catholic vote would give him an added boost. But any way JFK figured it, victory could not be secured without Texas. What to do?

The solution was to create one of the more peculiar tickets in recent political history by tapping Texas senator Lyndon Baines Johnson, the Senate majority leader, as his vice-presidential nominee.[16] The Kennedy-Johnson team made a strange pair, to say the least, with the backbench senator in the presidential spot and the outspoken, larger-than-life majority leader in the number-two position. It was a Democratic version of The Odd Couple, dictated largely by electoral expediency.

The stories about Kennedy's offer and Johnson's acceptance of the running-mate slot remain confusing and contradictory even to this day, but one thing is clear: most of organized labor was quite displeased.[17] Johnson had voted for Taft-Hartley in 1947 (Kennedy had voted against it), and this made him persona non grata on the left flank of the party. On top of that, his tenure as Senate majority leader overlapped with the high-water mark of the conservative coalition, and there was very little legislation Johnson could point to as proof that he was a genuine liberal. Yet in the end, labor swallowed hard and accepted LBJ; the electoral arithmetic was simply undeniable, and the alternative, a President Richard Nixon, was simply unacceptable.

What followed next was a down-to-the-wire general election campaign that was basically devoid of significant debate about America's future. A lot of this had to do with the candidates themselves, for both Kennedy and Nixon were young moderates with slender records of accomplishment. Their most notable traits were all-consuming ambitions to occupy the White House, though not to enact any grand vision of a postwar America; they both just wanted the job. And so, during the campaign, they disagreed on practically nothing in terms of domestic policy, and it was only Kennedy's exaggerated charge of a "missile gap" with the Soviets that created any policy space between the two nominees at all. Public opinion hardly moved during the electoral battle, as Nixon campaigned on the vague theme of experience while Kennedy campaigned on the equally vague theme of moving the country forward, gauzily packaged as the "New Frontier."[18] It's a testimony to the emptiness of this campaign that many still believe that Nixon's five o'clock shadow in the televised presidential debate—the first of its kind—might actually have cost him the election.[19]

The final results that year were extremely close. JFK's popular-vote margin was a scant 122,000 out of more than 65 million total ballots cast, and his Electoral College victory was tighter still. A shift of just 30,000 votes in Illinois, Missouri, and New Jersey would have swung the election to Nixon; thus, the rampant vote stealing by the Daley machine in Chicago on behalf of Kennedy was a significant factor, as was the presence of LBJ on the Democratic ticket. Kennedy won the Lone Star State by just 2 percent, and it's an easy bet that with any other vice-presidential nominee, he would have lost Texas and maybe North and South Carolina as well.[20] Nationwide, polling indicated that JFK's victory depended heavily upon reuniting the old FDR coalition that had been broken up temporarily by Eisenhower; he dominated among urban dwellers, those without college degrees, those who called themselves "working class," union workers, and especially Catholics, of whom Kennedy carried an amazing 82 percent.[21]

John F. Kennedy had won the White House by consolidating the core Democratic vote, which still amounted to a plurality of the total public by the time of the 1960 election. However, that does not mean that Kennedy was elected by a liberal electorate. He simply was not. While the Gallup poll at the time of his inauguration showed some 50 percent of Americans calling themselves "Democrats," compared with just 25 percent "Republicans," Gallup also found just 23 percent of Americans urging Kennedy to "go more to the left, by following more of the views of labor and other liberal groups."[22] Most Americans wanted Kennedy either to go to the right or to stay in the political center. JFK's legislative majority in the Eighty-seventh Congress was ideologically similar to the broader public. In the House, the Democrats held a 262–175 majority, which is quite large by contemporary standards; however, it depended entirely upon the 99 southern Democrats, who remained conservative not only on civil rights issues but on economic matters as well.[23] In the Senate, the liberal faction enjoyed a boost thanks to the 1958 midterms, as future leaders Eugene McCarthy and Edmund Muskie were elected that year, but the balance of power still rested with conservative southern Democrats like Harry Byrd of Virginia and Richard Russell of Georgia.

Thus, Kennedy simply lacked a popular or legislative mandate to push for bold, liberal reforms. He also lacked the temperament of a progressive crusader. That was clear enough to anybody who knew him from his time in Congress, as well as from his cabinet appointments, which studiously balanced the major political factions of the age. He kept Allen Dulles at the CIA and J. Edgar Hoover at the FBI, and while he gave ADA-style liberals John Kenneth Galbraith and Arthur Schlesinger top appointments, he also doled out critical nominations to Republicans, installing Douglas Dillon as secretary of the treasury and Robert McNamara as secretary of defense.

In fact, JFK's number-one domestic policy resembles Ronald Reagan's 1981 across-the-board tax cut. Kennedy and his economic advisers were concerned about the "performance gap" in the economy, a difference they perceived was costing the country about five million jobs. Liberals like Galbraith and Leon Keyserling proposed an increase in domestic spending in the public sector, but Walter Heller of the Council of Economic Advisers and Dillon advocated tax cuts for businesses and individuals. Kennedy went for the tax cuts, and his famous address to the Economic Club of New York in December 1962, which Galbraith called "the most Republican speech since McKinley," has been echoed by conservative Republicans for decades.

> [T]he most direct and significant kind of federal action aiding economic growth is to make possible an increase in private consumption and investment demand—to cut the fetters which hold back private spending. . . .

The . . . best means of strengthening demand among consum-
ers and business is to reduce the burden on private income and the
deterrents to private initiative which are imposed by our present
tax system—and this administration pledged itself last summer to
an across-the-board, top-to-bottom cut in personal and corporate
income taxes to be enacted and become effective in 1963.[24]

In general, it's fair to say that JFK was the most pro-business Democrat the country would see between Grover Cleveland and Bill Clinton. In presenting such an economically conservative posture, Kennedy
had set himself up well for his 1964 reelection, as he had undermined
the GOP's standing with the party's traditional, establishment backers
in the Northeast.

Beyond this, the domestic agenda items he offered were generally
in line with the Fair Deal proposals once put forward by Truman, but
Kennedy simply didn't push very hard for them. His proposal for Medicare went nowhere fast, as House Ways and Means Chairman Wilbur
Mills was concerned about its impact on the budget.[25] His proposal to
aid public education was undermined by continuing divisions over race
and religion—namely, whether segregated and parochial schools would
be given aid.[26] His farm bill, originally designed to impose mandatory
controls on agricultural output, passed through Congress in a highly
adulterated form; only controls on wheat were included, and these
were dependent on the voluntary agreement of wheat farmers, which
was not forthcoming.[27] Kennedy also failed to push through legislation
creating a Department of Urban Affairs and Housing. Just as with Truman, most of Kennedy's domestic policy achievements were extensions
of previous enactments. He signed an expansion of Social Security, an
increase in the minimum wage, an expansion of public housing funding, the continuation of Eisenhower's interstate highway program, and
so on.[28]

Regarding civil rights, Kennedy pushed for them harder than Truman or Eisenhower, though he was very hesitant at first. Political concerns were a major factor—specifically, how could he simultaneously
hold African Americans and southern Democrats in his coalition? Both
were critical voting blocs. African Americans had given Kennedy an es-

timated 71 percent of the vote in 1960, and they were a vital bloc in the Industrial Midwest.[29] Meanwhile, the southern white vote still spelled the difference between victory and defeat for the Democrats, and the Republicans had recently been gaining ground in Dixie. Thus, early in his term, Kennedy pursued a highly cautious approach. He refused, for instance, to sign an executive order desegregating federal housing until after the 1962 midterms, despite having blasted Eisenhower for not signing such a rule.[30] On judicial nominations, while he gave Thurgood Marshall a federal court appointment, he also stocked the southern benches with notable racists who would drag their heels on desegregation for decades.[31] It was only after the steady drumbeat of civil rights conflicts in the South—the Freedom Rides, the racial violence in Birmingham, George Wallace's symbolic stand against integrating the University of Alabama—that JFK decided to stop worrying so much about southern sentiment and instead advocate a strong civil rights bill. It's unclear whether or not, had JFK survived, the Civil Rights Act would have passed the Senate. In a Gallup poll taken in early November 1963, a few weeks before his assassination, 46 percent of respondents said that the Kennedy administration was "pushing racial integration too fast," compared with just 31 percent who said the speed was "about right" and 11 percent who claimed it was "not fast enough." It was only after Kennedy's assassination and LBJ's stirring call to continue the work he had started that public opinion shifted substantially.[32]

Kennedy's lasting achievements came mostly in the field of foreign policy and included, particularly, the president's highly regarded handling of episodic crises in Berlin and Cuba.[33] He was also a great success at building and maintaining his public image. For instance, even as his domestic policy agenda was to varying degrees cautious and conservative, his inaugural address seemed like a bold call for liberal reform; Kennedy summoned the country to rally "against the common enemies of man: tyranny, poverty, disease and war itself."[34] Similarly, the Kennedy media machine continued to churn out good publicity for the president and his family, who still appeared often on the covers of magazines like *Life*.[35] This successful public relations strategy, combined with the studious avoidance of divisive domestic policy positions, and with foreign policy triumphs and economic prosperity, meant that Kennedy was an extremely popular president for his entire term. The lowest his job approval number ever fell in the Gallup poll was 56 percent, and his approval averaged 70 percent for his time in office.[36]

In part thanks to JFK's public appeal, the Democrats greatly out-performed historical expectations in the 1962 midterms. While the party of the president usually suffers heavy losses in such elections, the Democrats shed just three seats in the House and picked up two seats in the Senate.[37] Considering that economic growth increased to 5.8 percent in 1964, and the United States enjoyed domestic tranquillity that year, it is quite probable that JFK, had he lived, would have been overwhelm-ingly reelected.[38] Ironically, then, it was worries about reelection that brought JFK to Dallas in November 1963; Lone Star Democrats had become badly fractured, and the president wanted to give them a pep talk in advance of the 1964 election.[39]

With Kennedy's assassination, the nation was plunged into deep grief, and LBJ became the first southern politician since Andrew John-son, nearly a hundred years earlier, to assume the presidency of the United States.

James Rowe appeared in our story in Chapter 4 as the man who out-lined to Truman the political strategy he would use to win reelection in 1948. And he appears again now, for he offered a terrific summary of why the unlikely presidency of Lyndon Johnson was so successful at reshaping American public policy:

> I used to say my boss Roosevelt had both style and substance. And Kennedy had style. And this fellow Johnson has substance. . . . Kennedy looked fine, made nice speeches, but he didn't get much done. . . . A senator would come to Kennedy and say, "I'd love to go along with you, Mr. President, but it would give me serious trouble back home." Kennedy would always say, "I understand." Now Johnson knew damn well that the senator was going to tell him that, and he never let the senator get to the point of his troubles back home. He would tell him about the flag, and by God, the story of the country, and he'd get them by the lapels and they were out the door.[40]

In this quotation lies the key to understanding the unprecedented policy breakthroughs of the Johnson administration. LBJ, like FDR before him, had what Rowe called "substance." He viewed the presidency as an opportunity to do big things, and he knew how to do them, so that's exactly what he did. Yet Rowe is being unfair to JFK here. There is no way that the substantive LBJ could have accomplished what he did without the memory of the slain president to spur the nation to action. If it takes style and substance to do big things, then FDR could do it all by himself, but LBJ needed JFK—just as JFK needed LBJ to win election in the first place.

Johnson had long wanted to be president, having sought the office himself in 1960, and he quickly grasped the challenge—and the opportunity—that the nation's grief presented him with. He had to give meaning to the meaningless assassination of Kennedy, and the way he would do that was by convincing Congress to pass Kennedy's domestic program. In a pitch-perfect performance to a joint session, just a few days after the tragic events in Dallas, Johnson intoned:

> On the twentieth day of January, in 1961, John F. Kennedy told his countrymen that our national work would not be finished "in the first thousand days, nor in the life of this administration, nor even perhaps in our lifetime on this planet. But," he said, "let us begin."
>
> Today, in this moment of new resolve, I would say to all my fellow Americans, let us continue.
>
> This is our challenge—not to hesitate, not to pause, not to turn about and linger over this evil moment, but to continue on our course so that we may fulfill the destiny that history has set for us. . . .
>
> We meet in grief, but let us also meet in renewed dedication and renewed vigor. Let us meet in action, in tolerance, and in mutual understanding. John Kennedy's death commands what his life conveyed—that America must move forward.[41]

With the possible exception of Teddy Roosevelt, no accidental president has ever performed as well out of the gate as Lyndon Johnson did with this speech. Indeed, it is a rare event in the history of the country when the man and the moment meet so perfectly. Johnson felt the grief of the nation and intuited the momentous political opportunity, and he ingeniously connected the two. As he later told historian Doris Kearns Goodwin: "Everything I had ever learned in the history books taught me that martyrs have to die for causes. John Kennedy had died. But his 'cause' was not really clear. That was my job. I had to take the dead man's program and turn it into a martyr's cause. That way Kennedy would live forever and so would I."[42]

This meant forgetting his hesitations about the tax-cut bill, which LBJ had initially disliked as vice president, in part because it closed loopholes for the Texas oil industry.[43] Upon assuming the presidency, Johnson pushed it through Congress with characteristic vigor, and the Revenue Act of 1964 passed overwhelmingly in both chambers, notably by a 77–21 margin in the Senate. The bill cut individual and corporate income tax rates, and has often been credited for facilitating the extraordinary growth of the mid-1960s.[44]

LBJ also defied his sectional roots by throwing his full weight behind the landmark Civil Rights Act of 1964, which outlawed discrimination in public accommodations like hotels and movie theaters, mandated the desegregation of public facilities as well as public schools, expanded the powers of the U.S. Commission on Civil Rights, and made it easier to move civil rights cases from state to federal court. LBJ's strong advocacy of the bill—the first real assault on the southern system of segregation in seventy-five years—came as a surprise to many. After all, Johnson had represented the interests of southern segregationists while in the Congress and, as Senate majority leader, had seen to it that the 1957 Civil Rights Act was substantially watered down.[45] But now, as president, he felt freed from the southern political bonds that had tied his hands, and accurately anticipated that the bill's passage would go a long way toward liberating his home region from this backward system of social arrangements.[46]

The bill passed easily through the House on a bipartisan basis.[47] The Senate was the key challenge; Johnson knew a vigorous filibuster from southern Democrats would be forthcoming there. Even so, the southerners were in a vulnerable position; sustaining a filibuster required the support of one-third of the Senate, and the states of the old Confederacy amounted to a little better than one-fifth.[48] Historically, the South had aligned with western senators in an informal deal wherein the West would support segregation while the South would back western development projects. LBJ, of course, knew full well the nature of this southern/western alliance, as it had been the backbone of his power as Senate majority leader, and he went to work to break it apart, promising senators all sorts of pork barrel goodies to get them to support the measure.[49] In the end, just two of the nine Democrats from the Mountain West region stuck with the southern filibuster.

Of course, LBJ still had to deal with the Republicans, whose concern with the bill had not as much to do with the maintenance of segregation or the preservation of an age-old Democratic alliance as with the issue of federal authority over private establishments. However, Johnson scored a coup by enlisting the support of Senate Minority Leader Everett Dirksen, who ended up bringing in a substantial majority of the caucus, with just a handful of Mountain West Republicans (as well as Texas Republican John Tower) voting against cloture.[50] With overwhelming support from Republicans, and the South/West alliance broken, the Senate voted to invoke cloture by a margin of 71–29 on June 10, 1964, ending a seventy-five-day filibuster by the southern Democrats.[51]

LBJ would pass one more significant piece of legislation before the 1964 election: the Economic Opportunity Act (EOA), which launched the famed "War on Poverty." The problem of persistent poverty as a structural feature of American society had been gaining increased attention in liberal circles, thanks to books like *The Other America*, by Michael Harrington, and *The Affluent Society*, by Galbraith.[52] Kennedy himself had taken an interest in the subject during his extensive campaigning in West Virginia, and he had instructed his Council of Economic Advisers (CEA) to begin formulating antipoverty programs. When Heller, the chair of the CEA, reviewed with Johnson what his team had been working on at the end of the Kennedy tenure, LBJ took an immediate interest in the poverty initiatives, which would become the first major element of his Great Society agenda.[53] By an overwhelming margin, Congress passed the EOA in the spring of 1964.[54]

As we shall see in Chapter 9, the EOA would have an important effect on the structure of the Democratic coalition in the major urban centers, one that was often unintended. For now, it's worth noting simply that passage of the bill contributed to LBJ's political momentum heading into the fall campaign. Johnson boasted a job approval rating of nearly 75 percent in the summer of 1964, and it seemed quite unlikely that any Republican could mount an effective challenge. Still, LBJ would take no risks when it came to securing a term in his own right.

There was not a shred of doubt as to whether Johnson would be nominated at the Democratic convention in Atlantic City, which LBJ micromanaged to an unprecedented degree for a sitting president.[55] The only question on the Democratic side of the ledger in the 1964 election was whom he would pick for vice president. In the end, LBJ's personal dislike of the slain president's younger brother Robert Kennedy, who surely was the favorite candidate of Democrats nationwide, induced him to pass over RFK for the exuberant Hubert Humphrey, the Minnesota senator who some sixteen years earlier had persuaded the Democratic convention in Philadelphia to adopt a liberal civil rights plank.[56]

The LBJ campaign pitch that year was explicitly referred to as the "frontlash" strategy. The conventional wisdom was that a backlash against the Civil Rights Act would peel off conservative Democrats from the Johnson coalition, but LBJ, in turn, set about taking away typically Republican voters by campaigning against GOP extremism—hence frontlash.[57] In this effort, LBJ was greatly aided by the ineffectual candidacy of Senator Barry Goldwater of Arizona, whose campaign has accurately been referred to as a "glorious disaster."[58] Goldwater became the first bona fide conservative in forty years to win the Republican nomination for president. Previous party nominees had been avowedly moderate on domestic policy, usually disagreeing with the means of liberal reform programs rather than the ends, but not Goldwater. He was an unabashed conservative who opposed the liberalism of the post-FDR Democratic party as well as the "me-tooism" of the Republican establishment. To win the nomination, Goldwater put together a political coalition that joined small-town midwestern conservatives—the kind that had vaulted Robert Taft to the big leagues in the 1950s—with the growing Sunbelt region of the South and West, about which we shall have more to say in Chapter 8. In doing so, he transformed the Republican coalition in enduring ways, shifting the balance of power out of the northeastern, moderate establishment into the grassroots conservatives of the modern age, and thus laying the groundwork for the conservative majorities of Ronald Reagan and beyond.[59]

Yet the conservative movement was still in a state of infancy at this point and lacked a viable set of issue positions sufficient to win national office. What's more, Goldwater was not a good presidential candidate, lacking an intuitive feel for the kind of rhetoric needed to win a broad majority. He was gaffe-prone, blithely commenting at one point about how the United States could always "lob [a nuclear weapon] into the men's room at the Kremlin."[60] Worse for the reputation of the Republican party, he allowed his principled stand against the Civil Rights Act, which he opposed not because he was a racist but because of its extensive regulation of private enterprises, to be captured by (largely Democratic) southern segregationists.[61]

All of this played right into the crafty hands of Lyndon Johnson, whose frontlash campaign transformed Goldwater from a principled conservative into a threat to human civilization itself. The Democratic ad hominem attacks are a big reason why 1964 was the first election in the TV age to emphasize negative campaigning. More than 40 percent of Johnson's ads during that cycle were negative,[62] and the Johnson campaign ran one of the most controversial ads in television history: the "Daisy" television ad ran just one time, in early September on NBC, but that was all it took to get people talking.[63]

Johnson's goal was not just reelection, but the largest reelection in history. And that's exactly what he accomplished. He won 61 percent of the vote, more than any popularly elected presidential candidate before or since. Goldwater carried just 52 electoral votes—the states of the Deep South plus his home state of Arizona—as most of the historically Republican parts of the country slipped into the Democratic column.[64] The frontlash strategy was an unequivocal triumph; LBJ successfully painted Goldwater as an extremist, established himself as the candidate of the sensible center, and in so doing picked up 77 percent of independent voters and 23 percent of Republicans.[65] Johnson's presidential victory also had long congressional coattails. The Democratic House delegation increased to 295 members, including 205 Democrats from outside the old Confederacy.[66]

Thus, the way was paved for the "Great Society" Congress of 1965–66. The conservative coalition that had blocked progressive legislation was swept aside—and in its place the country installed the most liberal national legislature since 1936. LBJ would become the master of this Eighty-ninth meeting of the United States Congress, talking to as many as thirty members of Congress a day as he guided one reform after another through the legislature.[67] By the time of the 1966 midterms, Johnson had been so successful that it's fair to say he had outpaced his idol, Franklin Roosevelt. At the very least, the Great Society has had a more lasting effect than the New Deal, which early on was necessarily focused on staving off the Great Depression. The Great Society, on the other hand, sought to reform a country that was enjoying unprecedented domestic prosperity. Without a great economic crisis to address, LBJ could dedicate his efforts to making more lasting reforms than anything Roosevelt could ever do.

The Great Society amounted to hundreds of pieces of legislation, large and small. LBJ enacted new environmental and consumer safety regulations; he established the Department of Housing and Urban Development; he set up the National Endowments for the Arts and for the Humanities; he created the Public Broadcasting Corporation; he expanded the minimum wage provisions and increased Social Security; on and on it went, and each of these provisions could merit an extensive review. To get a fair sense of the scope of national policy making under the Great Society, it's worth looking at three major proposals: aid to education, Medicare, and the Voting Rights Act. Chapter 6 will examine voting rights in detail, so here we will concern ourselves with education and Medicare. On both of these proposals, the size of the liberal majority in Congress enabled Johnson to overcome age-old objections that had stymied previous reform efforts.

Federal aid to education had been on the Democratic agenda for decades, yet reformers had consistently failed to push through significant reforms time and time again because of ancient grievances: the Protestant-Catholic divide over parochial schools and the North-South split over whether segregated schools could get funding. With *Brown*

v. *Board of Education* as well as the Civil Rights Act bringing an end to segregation as a legal social arrangement, the remaining barrier in 1965 was whether parochial schools could receive federal funds.

To get around this dilemma, LBJ employed his outsize liberal majority in Congress as well as the Supreme Court's 1947 ruling in *Everson v. Board of Education of Ewing Township*, which held that federal funds could go to children of parochial schools, just not the schools themselves.[68] Accordingly, the Elementary and Secondary Education Act supported Catholic schools indirectly, by offering funds for items like textbooks and school equipment. The bill passed overwhelmingly, with seventy-three senators in favor and just eighteen opposed.[69] Additionally, the Eighty-ninth Congress enacted the Higher Education Act, which provided money to colleges and universities, funds to train librarians and information specialists, special grants for "developing institutions" like black colleges, and low-interest loans for students.[70] Combined, the effect of these two laws was extraordinary. Prior to the Great Society, education had largely been up to either private institutions or state and local governments. Liberals had tried for decades to involve the federal government, but with no great success until the Eighty-ninth Congress. From that point forward, federal funding would be a key resource for public and private educational institutions.[71]

The passage of the Social Security Amendments of 1965, which instituted the Medicare and Medicaid programs, was another policy achievement that liberals had struggled to implement for decades. Harry Truman, as we saw in the previous chapter, pushed for an expansion of the Social Security payroll tax to subsidize universal health care, and the Kennedy administration had proposed a new entitlement for elderly people's medical care that also depended on an expanded payroll tax. One big thorn in the side of the liberals had long been the House Ways and Means Committee, which since 1957 had been chaired by Wilbur Mills, a conservative Democrat from Arkansas who was keenly worried about budget deficits. However, by 1965 Mills understood the magnitude of the liberal tide that was sweeping through Congress, and he was ready to make a deal.

There were several significant proposals working their way through the legislative process by that point. LBJ had backed a program that would use Social Security revenues to pay for hospital and nursing care, as well as outpatient services. The Republican alternative, offered by Congressman John Byrnes and called Bettercare, would provide federal payments of insurance premiums for the elderly. Additionally, the American Medical Association had pushed Eldercare, which would have expanded existing welfare programs to cover the indigent elderly. Mills's politically ingenious idea was to combine all these programs into a "three-layer cake": Social Security would cover hospital bills, a voluntary insurance program would cover doctors' bills, and an expanded welfare program managed by the states, called Medicaid, would provide care for the poor. In the end, the bill passed overwhelmingly in both chambers.[72]

By the 1966 midterms, the impetus for reform had finally petered out as the divisive issues of Vietnam, crime, and race that would bring an end to the Johnson presidency were already starting to dominate the popular consciousness. Johnson's job approval hit 51 percent in the Gallup Poll in August 1966—the last time in his term that he would register support from more than half of Americans. In the November midterms, the Republicans picked up forty-six House seats, the party's largest victory in twenty years and more than enough to return the bipartisan conservative coalition to political dominance.[73]

The legislative phase of the Great Society was thus finished. Yet in just three brief years—from the assassination of John F. Kennedy to the 1966 midterms—Lyndon Johnson had accomplished as much in the way of domestic reforms as arguably any president, even Franklin Roosevelt himself. What's more, Great Society reforms like the Civil Rights Act, the Voting Rights Act, Medicare, and aid to education would transform American society in more durable ways than many of the key New Deal provisions. As Senate Majority Leader Mike Mansfield would tell historian William Leuchtenburg, "Johnson has outstripped Roosevelt, no doubt about that. He has done more than FDR ever did or ever thought of doing."[74]

The Democratic coalition that FDR created during the Great Depression was a very strange one. As James Rowe put it in 1947, it was an "unhappy alliance of Southern conservatives, Western progressives and

Big City labor."[75] This alliance was large enough to deliver Roosevelt an unprecedented third and fourth term, but it was too "unhappy" to unite around a set of policy initiatives after the initial crisis had passed, meaning that the New Deal was effectively over by 1938. What's more, the tensions between the factions were so great that, as early as 1944, the task of settling upon a national leader would be a quadrennial problem of existential proportions.

As we saw in Chapter 4, the demands of FDR's bizarre coalition were such that Harry Truman really had to be named vice president in 1944. There was no other politician of sufficient credibility who could keep all sides happy. And so it was again in 1960. After the Eisenhower administration, this "unhappy alliance" had another shot at the presidency—if it could somehow find a way to unite its disparate elements. Yet this time there was no Harry Truman available to run—no single candidate whom all of the party's various elements found acceptable. The Democratic solution for that cycle was to run a most improbable pair of politicians who, together, could unite all of the incongruent factions. Kennedy played the part of the debonair northeasterner who sure seemed liberal but was actually conservative enough to hold the Catholic vote. And for the southern conservatives and rural westerners who felt little connection to the Harvard-educated JFK, the Democrats offered the Southwest Texas State Teachers College–educated Lyndon Baines Johnson, the southern Democrat who dressed and spoke like a cowboy.

It is in this unlikely political union of Kennedy and Johnson that we see all the peculiarities and possibilities of Roosevelt's Democratic coalition. Neither Kennedy nor Johnson could have brought about the changes of the 1960s by himself: Kennedy lacked the legislative skills that Johnson had gleaned from his years in the congressional trenches; Johnson lacked the force of Kennedy's larger-than-life persona, carefully cultivated over the years by his media-conscious family. Together, however, the two would transform the country. Johnson, the adroit manipulator of the legislative process, used the grandiose image of the slain Kennedy to push the nation and Congress to adopt his "Great Society." And thus, for a very brief period in the mid-1960s, the dominant conservative coalition of Republicans and southern Democrats fell out of power, and northern liberals enjoyed a three-year window to implement another round of sweeping national reforms.

The effects of this strange-bedfellows ticket are still reverberating to this day. Medicare, civil rights, voting rights, federal aid to education, environmental regulations—the list of reforms from the mid-sixties goes on and on. By and large, these were national policies intended to make the liberals' dream of a "more perfect union" a reality. However, as has always been the case whenever activists expand the power of government to accomplish big, national goals, there was also a sustained effort to nurture and grow the Democratic party itself. Just as FDR's New Deal was simultaneously a project of both national and partisan ends, so also was the Great Society. In this chapter we have reviewed the national purposes of the Kennedy/Johnson administrations. In the next four chapters, we shall examine how these two men used the power of the federal government to grow their party's base of client groups.

CHAPTER SIX

They Can Count

Civil Rights and the Development of Black Politics

In "Federalist" Number 78, Alexander Hamilton praised the independent judiciary, arguing that it would "guard the Constitution and the rights of individuals from the effects of those ill humors, which the arts of designing men, or the influence of particular conjectures, sometimes disseminate among the people themselves."[1] Tragically, African Americans would be systematically denied the remedy offered by this nation's court system for nearly a century after the end of the Civil War. In 1876, a year before President Rutherford Hayes agreed to end the military reconstruction of the South, the Supreme Court, in *United States* v. *Reese,* defined the Fifteenth Amendment in very limited terms, rejecting the claim that it conferred upon citizens a right to vote.[2] Twenty years later, in *Plessy* v. *Ferguson*, the court would sanction the "separate but equal" system that characterized the social and economic norms that governed race relations in the South for the next half century and beyond.[3]

It would be nearly a hundred years before African Americans finally enjoyed the full rights of American citizenship, and by the time the Civil Rights Act and Voting Rights Act were signed into law in the mid-1960s, this once safely Republican bloc of voters had become safely Democratic. And after the 1982 amendments to the Voting Rights Act, they would enjoy guaranteed representation in Congress; forty or so "majority-minority" districts would henceforth elect black members to the House of Representatives, in turn enhancing the power and importance of the Congressional Black Caucus (CBC).

It was in this way that African Americans would go from having no voice in the political process to having a place akin to other Democratic client groups like organized labor and the old South. There is no electoral competition for the black vote today, at least not outside Democratic primaries. Thus, African Americans do not leverage their votes by forcing the parties to craft competing policy programs for them. Instead, they exercise political clout primarily via the CBC, whose members are tightly aligned and in good positions to advance black interests in Congress. In the end, the "deal" between black voters and the Democratic party is similar to that which the party has carved out for organized labor: in exchange for support of the party's agenda, African Americans in Congress have a special opportunity to bend the policy needle in ways that favor their constituents' unique interests.

Without the military or the courts to protect black rights, the only defender that African Americans had against the "ill humors" of southern whites was the Republican party; as Frederick Douglass said, "The Republican Party is the deck, all else is the sea."[4] This was an unfortunate predicament for black America, as the nation's political parties are majority-seeking institutions, not arbiters of justice, and African Americans after the Civil War could expect the GOP to come to their aid only insofar as the party believed they would help it win elections. Sadly, the GOP never really expected that. The result was, as historian Vincent DeSantis explained, one in which GOP rhetoric did not meet reality:

> [W]hile Republicans talked much about safeguarding the vote of the colored man and loudly lamented the state of political affairs in the South, they took few steps to remedy the situation or to meet their obligations to the freedman. Instead of protecting the Negro and looking after him as the ward of the nation, they deserted him and left him as the ward of the dominant race in the South.[5]

The most substantial constraint on Republican intervention on behalf of African Americans was northern public opinion. The GOP had developed as a strictly northern coalition in the 1850s, and party leaders were understandably sensitive to the mood of their home region. Whatever drive there might have been in the North to impose "Radical Reconstruction" on the South in the 1860s had petered out by the 1870s, and by that point northerners were in general agreement that the South should be allowed to deal with racial problems however it chose. Continued focus on this issue would only impede the rebirth of national solidarity, not to mention the development of trade relations between the two sections.[6]

This created an electoral quandary for the Republican party. Because it lacked the public mandate to safeguard black voters' rights, it could no longer use military Reconstruction to keep the southern states from falling under white Democratic control, one after another. With the South becoming uniformly Democratic after the election of 1876, the Republicans would have to pull off a near-sweep of the northern states to win the presidency. This was a substantial hurdle, as the party was the majority coalition in the North but not an overwhelming one. Lincoln and Grant each won two majority victories in the North from 1860 through 1872, but neither could carry 60 percent of the region's popular vote. Worse for the Republicans, the Democratic dominance of New York City meant that the Empire State, far and away the single greatest electoral prize, was closely divided.[7]

Thus, the GOP could not turn its back on the South altogether, and while there were factions within the party that thought the GOP's best bet was to force strict Reconstruction on Dixie, a moderate wing came to dominate by the middle of the 1870s. It would look to crack the region not by military occupation but by forging political alliances with various elements of the white South. Rutherford Hayes, Grant's successor in the White House, tried to win over the conservative, "Bourbon" wing of the southern party, the same one that had backed the Whigs prior to the Civil War.[8] This endeavor proved fruitless, and Presidents James Garfield and Chester Arthur switched gears, instead appealing to the more radical elements of the white South, such as the hardscrabble farmers whose political interests were not represented by the conservative Democratic party.[9] But this, too, proved unsuccessful, and as the nineteenth century wore on, the GOP's position in Dixie only declined.

The final effort by the GOP to crack the Solid South in the nineteenth century came during the Harrison administration of 1889–93. The beginning of Harrison's term was the first time in more than a decade that the Republicans had solid control of the federal government, and the new president had big plans for this restored majority. With regard to the South, Harrison believed that the Republicans already had enough African American supporters in the region to give the party an opportunity there, if only they could be brought into the electorate. Thus, he threw his weight behind a voting rights bill drafted by Representative Henry Cabot Lodge of Massachusetts. This "Force Bill"—as the Democrats denounced it—would have initiated federal supervision of voting in the South, including independent counts of contested returns. The bill passed narrowly in the House, but it failed in the Senate twice—first when northeastern Republicans tabled it to focus on their omnibus tariff bill, and second when Mountain West Republicans aligned with southern Democrats in a deal to kill it in exchange for pro-silver votes on currency legislation.[10]

As we saw in Chapters 1 and 2, the election of 1896 brought about thirty years of virtually uninterrupted Republican dominance of the government. Ironically, this would be bad news for African Americans in the South, as whatever political leverage they once had in the party was now gone. In the thirty years between Lincoln and McKinley, the Republicans averaged 54 percent of the northern presidential vote and 53 percent of the northern House vote. This made breaking through in the South—and, at least for the Harrison administration, enfranchising African Americans—a priority for the party. However, in the thirty years between McKinley and FDR, the Republicans averaged 59 percent of the northern presidential vote and 58 percent of the northern House vote.[11] This small shift in the electorate elevated the Republicans to a national majority regardless of Dixie. Thus, the GOP simply had no political need for the South, or, by extension, for the disenfranchised African Americans who lived there. Unsurprisingly, then, the southern policies of William McKinley, Teddy Roosevelt, William Howard Taft, Warren Harding, Calvin Coolidge, and Herbert Hoover were amorphous and neglectful of black interests. Insofar as any of these Republican leaders took an interest in the South, it was usually only to secure southern delegates to the Republican National Convention or promote interregional harmony.[12]

Despite all this, those African Americans who were able to vote supported Republicans overwhelmingly at the ballot box. After the rise of Jim Crow in the late nineteenth century, African Americans' electoral influence was limited mostly to the North, where they constituted a small but growing minority by the early part of the twentieth century. They had begun moving northward after the Civil War, and a trickle of migrants became a stream by the 1920s; during that decade alone, 90,000 African Americans moved to Ohio, 102,000 to Illinois, and 173,000 to New York.[13] By 1928, African Americans were populous enough to elect the first black congressman from the North, Oscar De Priest of Chicago's South Side. The fact that De Priest was a Republican was a testimony to the fact that, despite nearly a century of neglect from the GOP, African Americans were still loyal to the heirs of Lincoln.[14] Indeed, Herbert Hoover—who presided over the start of the Great Depression and had actively courted southern whites—still won overwhelming victories among black voters in 1932 in Chicago, Cincinnati, Cleveland, Detroit, and Philadelphia.[15]

The New Deal efforts to combat the Great Depression fundamentally changed the American electoral alignment, as we detailed in Chapter 3. It also transformed black political preferences: FDR made dramatic gains in northern black precincts in 1936, and by 1940 he carried better than two-thirds of the black vote.

What brought about this shift? It wasn't civil rights; as we saw in Chapter 3, Roosevelt's need to placate southern Democrats ensured virtually no movement on this issue. Instead, the shift in the black vote was due to African Americans' enjoying material benefits from the array of New Deal alphabet programs. Without doubt, these programs were discriminatory as well; however, African Americans still got something, which was a first since Reconstruction. For instance, in Jacksonville, Florida, the Federal Emergency Relief Act distributed 45 percent of its funds to fifteen thousand black families, and 55 percent to five thousand white families.[16] Viewed from today's perspective, this is fundamentally unjust, but for contemporary black families who had long been totally ignored, it was a revolutionary change.

As a policy, this marked quite a difference from the last Democratic administration, that of Woodrow Wilson, which had gone out of its way to discriminate against African Americans (including in the Navy Department, where FDR had been assistant secretary).[17] Some of this change was due to liberals like Eleanor Roosevelt and Harold Ickes, who were highly sympathetic to the black condition and had the power to do something about it. Of course, politics was also in play; the black vote was a nonfactor in the South, but it was growing in the North, where FDR was trying to create a progressive majority. Increasingly, that meant courting the northern black vote, which would grow in size for twenty years after World War II and even become decisive in swing states like Illinois, New York, and Pennsylvania.

The Republicans were also aware of this trend, and for the first time in nearly a century started taking the black vote seriously. In 1940 they offered the most direct, sweeping, and forceful statement on civil rights to appear in a party platform for generations.[18] As we saw in Chapter 4, the Democrats would offer their own progressive civil rights plank in 1948. With Harry Truman becoming the first president since Benjamin Harrison to make civil rights a part of the national political discussion, it might have seemed as though African Americans were ready to leverage their (northern) votes for real gains.

Alas, it was not to be. Instead, the next decade would witness a return to the kind of politics seen during the decades following the Civil War: lots of rhetoric in party platforms about civil rights, but very little action on the policy front.[19] Our review of Truman's civil rights record in Chapter 4 was a great example of this, and so was the record of his successor, Dwight Eisenhower. Ike tried for some real policy gains on civil rights, though the final results were mostly symbolic in nature. He completed the desegregation of the armed forces, begun under Truman, as well as of public facilities in the District of Columbia.[20] He also threw his weight behind a tough civil rights bill that focused mostly on voting issues, an area where he believed he was on firm constitutional ground. Lyndon Johnson—then Senate majority leader and an aspirant to the White House—recognized correctly that a full-blown southern filibuster would be a political disaster, so he conspired to water the bill down enough that Dixie would accept it. Eisenhower's original proposal would have given the attorney general the right to sue in civil court for preventive relief against discriminatory actions, but Johnson and his southern allies speciously claimed that this would deny southerners the right to trial by jury. Of course, no southern jury was ever going to convict a white official for denying the franchise to a black voter, and that was exactly the point. In the end, the southerners got their way on this matter, thanks in part to support from the junior senator from Massachusetts, John F. Kennedy, and Congress passed the relatively toothless Civil Rights Act of 1957.[21]

In 1960, the Democrats nominated Kennedy and Johnson to the presidential ticket, and without a hint of irony they endorsed a seven-hundred-word plank on civil rights that promised to use the presidency's "full powers—legal and moral—to create an affirmative new atmosphere in which to deal with racial divisions and inequalities."[22] The juxtaposition of the Kennedy-Johnson ticket with this plank starkly illustrates the strategy that both parties had by and large adopted since civil rights had become an issue: strong rhetoric with very little action. The impetus for the dramatic reforms of the 1960s thus did not, could not, come from above, in the halls of Congress or the Oval Office. Instead it came from below: from the growing civil rights movement, which had been developing for decades by the time the Civil Rights Act passed in 1964.[23]

The civil rights movement as a mass form of protest really got its inspiration, according to sociologist Aldon Morris, from the March on Washington Movement of the early 1940s. The march's purpose was to pressure the government to desegregate the defense industries and the armed forces and, according to historian Hugh Davis Graham, this organization "first forced a reluctant black establishment led by the NAACP to go along, then finally forced the embarrassed and irritated President [Roosevelt] to issue his pathbreaking executive order [for the creation of a wartime Fair Employment Practices Committee (FEPC)] on June 25, 1941."[24] The FEPC had little actual power, but it was a symbolic win for civil rights activists, and the march spurred the creation of the Congress of Racial Equality (CORE) in 1942.[25]

The civil rights movement reached a watershed moment with the

Montgomery Bus Boycott of 1955–56. Touched off by Rosa Parks's refusal to move to the back of the bus—she was a member of the local NAACP who had taken training courses in nonviolent resistance—it was spearheaded by the Montgomery Improvement Association, headed by Martin Luther King Jr. and E. D. Nixon. It lasted more than a year and resulted in a Supreme Court decision in 1960 declaring the segregation of buses to be unconstitutional. It was after the Montgomery Bus Boycott that the Southern Christian Leadership Conference (SCLC) was founded, with an office in Atlanta and King as its first president. Nonviolent activities, like the sit-in at the Woolworth's in Greensboro, North Carolina in 1960, started cropping up all over the South, inspired by the success in Montgomery.

In 1961, CORE and the Student Nonviolent Coordinating Committee (SNCC) worked together to test the limits of the Supreme Court's ruling on public transportation with the "Freedom Rides," during which civil rights activists rode interstate buses through the Deep South. This nonviolent demonstration provoked a violent response from whites in Birmingham and worried the new Kennedy administration. As James Farmer, a Freedom Rider who was jailed for his activities, explained:

> [Attorney General Robert] Kennedy called a meeting of CORE and SNCC, in his office. . . . And at that meeting, what Bobby said to them according to the reports, he said, "Why don't you guys cut out all that shit, Freedom Riding and sitting-in shit, and concentrate on voter education." Says, "If you do that I'll get you a tax exemption." That cold-blooded. This was Bobby Kennedy.[26]

Meanwhile, President Kennedy was still playing the same old double game on civil rights. He had run on a platform that backed strong reforms, but he appointed southern racists to the federal bench, and they ultimately impeded the movement.[27]

The civil rights activists would not back down from their aggressive approach; instead, organizers planned a big demonstration for the spring of 1963 in Birmingham. When city officials discovered that a big protest was in the works, they appealed to the Kennedy administration to convince the protesters to back down. The administration in turn reached out to King, who hammered out an agreement with the business committee on discrimination on May 10. But the next day, King's hotel was bombed, as was his brother's house; a riot started, and the egregious overreach of Birmingham public safety commissioner Bull Connor's forces was televised all across the nation. The events in Birmingham set off a mass wave of protests—some 758 demonstrations in 186 cities all across the South. In all, nearly fifteen thousand people were arrested.[28]

Like Rosa Parks's sit-in some seven years earlier, what might have appeared on TV to have been an out-of-the-blue event was in fact the product of calculated planning by the civil rights movement. As Graham argues, the Birmingham activism was designed to draw out the most racist elements in Birmingham into violence. The thinking was that Middle America would be horrified, and the administration would have to respond.[29] The plan worked. In a televised address just a few weeks later, President Kennedy said:

> One hundred years of delay have passed since President Lincoln freed the slaves, yet their heirs, their grandsons, are not fully free. They are not yet freed from the bonds of injustice. They are not yet freed from social and economic oppression. And this nation, for all its hopes and all its boasts, will not be fully free until all its citizens are free. . . .
>
> Now the time has come for this nation to fulfill its promise. The events in Birmingham and elsewhere have so increased the cries for equality that no city or state or legislative body can prudently choose to ignore them.[30]

Kennedy submitted the Civil Rights Act to the House later in June.

The high-water mark of the civil rights movement was the August 1963 March on Washington, timed to coincide with the hundredth anniversary of the signing of the Emancipation Proclamation. Not only was this a sign of the grassroots strength of the movement (with the crowd numbering between 200,000 and 300,000); it was also an organizational coup, the product of a coordinated effort between CORE, the NAACP, the National Urban League, the SCLC, and the SNCC. For his part, the ever-cautious Kennedy tried to prevent it from happening, fearing that it would move public opinion in the wrong direction and derail the efforts to pass the bill. When he realized he couldn't stop the march, he changed tactics and brought organized labor in to beef up its numbers and give it a biracial cast.[31]

The Civil Rights Act, passed after JFK's assassination, did not substantially move the needle on black enfranchisement in the South. And so civil rights agitation would continue into 1965, with the focus shifting to Selma, Alabama. Dallas County (of which Selma is the county seat) was home to some of the worst voting rights abuses: it was 58 percent African American, and yet Republican Barry Goldwater, who had opposed the Civil Rights Act in the Senate, won 89 percent of the vote there in 1964.[32] The plan—organized by the Dallas County Voters League, the SCLC, and the SNCC—was to march from Selma to Montgomery, but on the first day of the march, police attacked the six hundred protesters. Just as in Birmingham, the defenders of the racial status quo badly miscalculated, and people all across the nation witnessed the result. As Selma mayor Joseph Smitherman later said, "When that beating happened at the foot of the bridge, it looked like war. That went all over the country, and the people, the wrath of the nation, came down on us."[33] This is precisely what the civil rights movement's leaders had intended. The Voting Rights Act, discussed below, was a result of this national backlash.

As we saw in Chapter 5, Kennedy's tragic demise in Dallas created an opening to get the Civil Rights and Voting Rights acts passed. However, the assassination was not a sufficient condition. Neither bill would have passed without the rise of the civil rights movement, as well as the careful planning and tactics of its brilliant leadership. In the end, the movement's great success was in putting its issues on the national agenda. That is a critically important, yet often overlooked, form of political power—the power to decide what the country discusses. For years, the political parties had conspired with one another not to talk about civil rights, at least not in any kind of substantive way. Instead, their strategy had been to push symbolic gestures that did little to improve the lot of African Americans. The civil rights movement short-circuited this loop by means of peaceful activism that drew out the worst elements in the South, focused the nation's attention on the deprivations that African Americans had long suffered, and forced the political class in Washington to respond.

Early in 1965, LBJ instructed his attorney general, Nicholas Katzenbach, "to write me the goddamn best, toughest voting rights act that you can devise."[34] That was exactly what he did. The Voting Rights Act of 1965 was a vast departure from the 1957 Civil Rights Act; what it did that its predecessor failed to do was invert the burden of proof. Previously, it had been up to local residents to bring discrimination suits to court and to prove their cases to a local jury, standards that had helped the South play defense against voting rights for years. The Voting Rights Act *assumed* that its targeted jurisdictions were suppressing African American turnout, authorized the federal government to intervene directly, and left it to local jurisdictions to prove that they had acted properly.

Section 2 of the original Voting Rights Act outlawed any device or qualifying mechanism (like a literacy test) that had the intent of denying minorities the right to vote. Section 4 singled out for special supervision any jurisdictions where such mechanisms had been in place and where turnout in 1964 had been less than 50 percent—the overwhelming majority of which were in the states of the old Confederacy.[35] In these locales, all ballot qualifications were henceforth prohibited. Section 5 was the main enforcement mechanism of the bill, and it had the teeth that the previous civil rights act simply lacked. Rather than the federal government pursuing local election officials in southern courts, Section 5 mandated that covered jurisdictions come to Washington to prove that any proposed changes to their registration or election rules would not suppress the minority vote.[36]

The second section of the Fifteenth Amendment had given Congress the "power to enforce this article by appropriate legislation." It had been ninety-five years since that amendment was ratified, and the Voting Rights Act was the first "appropriate" piece of legislation put into place to achieve equal access to the ballot box, regardless of race.

The results were dramatic. In the Deep South states where the African American population was the largest, the number of voters in the 1966 midterm election increased by 60 percent over the 1962 midterms, compared with just a 3 percent increase in the rest of the country. In the presidential election of 1968, turnout increased about 30 percent in the Deep South states, compared with just a 4 percent increase nationwide, and in the Deep South counties where African Americans constituted a majority, turnout in the 1968 presidential election marked a 58 percent increase over 1964.[37]

This new black electorate was overwhelmingly Democratic. African Americans gave Democrat Hubert Humphrey an estimated 97 percent of their vote in 1968, according to the American National Election Studies. In presidential elections since then, black support for Democratic candidates for president has never dropped below 88 percent. By comparison, JFK won about 71 percent of the black vote in 1960 and Adlai Stevenson carried 64 percent in 1956. Thus, an already Democratic constituency became substantially more so after the enactment of the Voting Rights Act.[38]

The addition of African Americans into the electorate would have two profound effects on the Democratic party. Almost immediately, it shifted southern Democrats noticeably to the left, effectively ending the region's unique clientelistic relationship with the national party, as there was no more discriminatory regime to protect. Second, after the 1982 amendments to the Voting Rights Act, African Americans were clustered into forty or so "majority-minority" districts, guaranteeing black representation in Congress and transforming them into a de facto client group. Let's examine both developments in greater detail.

The rise of the black vote would make for a peculiar coalition among Dixie Democrats. As we shall discuss in Chapter 8, southern whites had begun migrating to the Republican party as early as 1952, and after 1968 Republican presidential candidates regularly defeated Democrats in the battle for the southern white vote. However, the battle for Congress was substantially different. Democratic strength among southern whites in the battle for Congress held firm through the 1960s and '70s. Democrats began to decline with this historic constituency only in the 1980s, and they were still able to hold a majority among this bloc through the elections of 1992. Thus, for a quarter century after the passage of the Voting Rights Act, southern Democrats in Congress put together biracial voting coalitions, made up of African Americans and lower-income whites.

Maintaining such a diverse coalition required a significant change in the legislative behavior of southern Democrats. As John Lewis—civil rights legend and currently a congressman from Atlanta—has noted:

> *One thing about white southerners is that they can count, and after the Voting Rights Act, they learned to count very well. . . . More and more black and white politicians get elected by biracial coalitions. You can no longer go into the black community and say one thing and then say something else to the white community if you are going to be elected and provide leadership.*[39]

Appealing to black voters required white Democrats to shed much of their historical distinctiveness. For nearly thirty years after the New Deal, southern Democrats were very much like a third congressional party, aligning with northern Democrats to organize the chamber yet often voting with Republicans on policy matters. After the Voting Rights Act, the old conservative coalition still manifested itself from time to time, but less frequently. According to political scientist Nicol Rae, southern Democrats aligned with northern Republicans 25 percent of the time in the House in 1973; fifteen years later, in 1988, the proportion of times that this coalition appeared was down to just 8 percent. By contrast, southern Democrats voted with a majority of their own party just 55 percent of the time in 1973, and 81 percent in 1988.[40]

We see a similar picture when we look at particular issues. On civil rights, a mere 33 percent of southern Democrats voted for the Voting Rights Act in 1965, but when the law came up for renewal in 1981, an impressive 91 percent supported it.[41] On economic matters, southern Democrats remained much more conservative than northern Democrats, but research by political scientists Keith Poole and Howard Rosenthal persuasively demonstrates that they began moving to the left starting in the late 1960s, right around the time that scores of African

Americans entered their voting coalitions.[42] Of course, southern Democrats remained a reliable vote for key conservative proposals—like
Ronald Reagan's 1981 tax cut and the passage of NAFTA in 1993—yet
by and large they began behaving much more like northern, liberal
Democrats.

This shift was a direct result of the necessary balancing act that
southern Democrats had to make after 1965. White voters invariably
retained the balance of power in a general election, but moving too far
to the right could lead to a primary challenger who, with a significantly
large number of black votes, could steal the nomination from an incumbent, conservative Democrat. As Virginia congressman Lewis Payne
put it:

> We all share a pretty large black constituency, and we're inter-
> ested in trying to do the right things to accommodate black views,
> on issues like the recent civil rights bill. In the first race I ran, blacks
> were very mobilized and were the reason I won. As long as they're
> all with me, it's hard for anyone else to win.[43]

Thus, the Voting Rights Act had the effect of "northernizing" the
southern Democrats. Because new black voters in the South identified
most closely with the liberal wing of the Democratic party, they pushed
southern Democrats toward the national center.

We shall have a lot more to say about this subject in Chapter 8, but
in many respects, the Voting Rights Act was the final nail in the coffin
of the clientelistic relationship the party had long had with southern
segregationists. For more than a century, conservative southerners had
aligned with ethnics in the big cities to protect their region's economic
and social arrangements. Northern liberals in the Democratic party had
started intimating as early as the Wagner-Costigan Anti-Lynching Bill
of 1935 that they were unhappy with this arrangement, and with the
1948 convention they shifted the party's official posture on civil rights.
Now, with the passage of the Civil Rights and Voting Rights acts, the
ancient clientelistic relationship was well and truly finished, which
meant that slowly but surely the white South would leave the liberal
Democratic party for a new alliance with northern Republicans, built

not on racial discrimination but on a shared belief in limited governmental interference in the private economy.

The "Second Reconstruction" of the mid-1960s had secured for African Americans the right to vote, but there was still much left unresolved. Specifically, when were black voting rights violated: was it only when local officials intended to abridge them or when seemingly innocuous rules had the effect of diluting their political power?

In 1973, the Supreme Court declared that vote dilution—not just intent—was the standard to apply. In *White* v. *Regester,* the court ruled that the apportionment plan for the Texas House of Representatives violated the Fourteenth Amendment's guarantee of equal protection because it limited the ability of minority groups to elect candidates of their choice. The court pointed to the context of electoral politics in Texas to conclude that there was an "enhanced . . . opportunity for racial discrimination" for African Americans and Hispanics. Several months later, the Fifth Circuit Court of Appeals tried to specify this ruling in *Zimmer* v. *McKeithen,* which laid down a "totality of circumstances" test for determining when a voting system is discriminatory against minority groups.[44]

This expansive notion of voting rights appealed to activists because intent to discriminate can be notoriously difficult to prove, especially when local officials know they're being watched closely; however, the "totality of circumstances" concept created problems of its own. While the so-called *White-Zimmer* test had an objective gloss, it was at its core subjective; two judges could look at the same situation and use the test to reach two different conclusions.[45] By 1980 the Supreme Court had had enough of the confusion, and in *Bolden* v. *City of Mobile* it did away with it, holding instead that plaintiffs indeed had to establish the *intent* to dilute minority votes. The case revolved around the question of whether the form of government in Mobile, Alabama, was legal under the Voting Rights Act. City commissioners had long been elected at-large in nonpartisan contests, meaning that Mobile did not create this system with the intent to suppress the black vote; nevertheless, no African American had ever been elected to the commission, despite the fact that blacks accounted for a third of the city's population. The

Fifth Circuit struck down the voting system, per *White-Zimmer,* but the Supreme Court reversed the ruling, holding that intent to discriminate must be established.[46]

When the Voting Rights Act came up for renewal in 1982, liberal Democrats were determined to amend it to restore the *White-Zimmer* test. In the Senate, Utah Republican Orrin Hatch was the point man on the Voting Rights Act for the conservative side, but he faced highly organized opposition from the Leadership Council on Civil Rights, a broad coalition that included traditional civil rights groups like the National Urban League and the NAACP, as well as typically nonpartisan civic outfits like the YMCA and the YWCA. There was no organization on the other side to counter effectively the proposed changes to Section 2, and a serious policy debate was preempted by the false assumption that this was a morally simple issue of "voting rights." Meanwhile, the Reagan White House, with its sagging poll numbers and a tough midterm election coming up, chose not to engage in a fight over Section 2, so the law was amended to embody the *White-Zimmer* standard that effective discrimination was a violation of voting rights.[47]

Thus, with virtually no debate on the merits, the Voting Rights Act was transformed from a bill that protected the franchise against efforts to squash it into a legal guarantor of electoral affirmative action. By inserting the *White-Zimmer* test into the law, the Congress gave African Americans something that no other minority group has ever enjoyed: the right to have its preferred representatives in the government. For centuries, partisans have endeavored to draw district lines in such a way that the voting force of their opposition would be diluted; this practice dates back to the eighteenth century, when Patrick Henry persuaded the state legislature to draw the Virginia district lines to thwart his rival James Madison's efforts to win the Fifth Congressional District.[48] However, the Voting Rights Act as amended in 1982 would now exempt racial minorities from this ancient form of gamesmanship. To appreciate the signifance of this for reapportionment, consider that Republicans in New York City are a minority if there ever was one—John McCain received just 21 percent of the vote there in 2008—yet New York Republicans do not enjoy 21 percent of the city's total political representation.[49] Far from it. That same year, the GOP won exactly zero of the more than a dozen House seats from the city. However, thanks to the amended Section 2 of the Voting Rights Act, African Americans (and other racial and ethnic minorities) are entitled to precisely that kind of protection. So while Barack Obama won just 38 percent of the vote in Alabama, the majority-minority Seventh District gave him 72 percent of its vote and accordingly elected an African American to Congress.[50]

This 1982 revision of the Voting Rights Act forced the Supreme Court into what Justice Felix Frankfurter once called the "political thicket" of reapportionment disputes.[51] Because blacks and whites in the South would come to vote for different parties, the court now had the burden of deciding what was an acceptable partisan gerrymander and what was a violation of the law. In *Thornburg* v. *Gingles* (1986), the court created a three-pronged test: a gerrymander runs afoul of Section 2 if (a) the aggrieved minority group is sufficiently large and compact to form a majority in a single-member district that could be created, (b) the minority group normally unites around the same candidate, and (c) the white majority would respond by uniting around an opposing candidate. When those conditions are met, the group is legally entitled to have a district created just for them. In the *Shaw-Cromartie* cases of the 1990s, a more conservative court pulled back on *Gingles* by mandating that race alone could not be the only factor in drawing a district, but that it could be one of multiple, more traditional factors.[52]

The new rules governing racial apportionment would again revolutionize American electoral politics, inducing profound though often overlooked transformations in the Democratic party. Ironically, these changes would be spearheaded by a Republican administration: following the 1990 census, lawyers in the Bush Justice Department pushed aggressively for the creation of scores of new "majority-minority districts," and not just in the South. Section 5 of the Voting Rights Act applies only to targeted jurisdictions, mostly in Dixie, but the newly amended Section 2 affects the nation at large, meaning that if California could draw a "max black" district, the Bush Justice Department pushed it to do precisely that.

The consequences of this aggressive redistricting were extraordinary. In the South alone, thirteen new majority black districts were created in 1992, and all of them, unsurprisingly, elected Democrats. To draw these new districts, Democratic-controlled state legislatures tended to "bleach" districts already held by Republicans, but their ability to do this was not unlimited. And so the Republicans managed to pick up many seats that had been held by white Democrats for generations, because their districts had lost a critical mass of black voters. For instance, redrawing the lines in Alabama resulted in the new majority-minority Seventh District that elected the very liberal Earl Hilliard in 1992; it also led to the "bleaching" of the neighboring Sixth District, where moderate Democrat Ben Erdreich lost to conservative Republican Spencer Bachus in 1992. Thus, the old southern Democratic faction actually lost *two* seats in Alabama—one to a liberal Democrat and the other to a Republican.[53]

Not surprisingly, political scientists have debated just which party has benefited because of this race-based redistricting in the South. Most believe that "bleaching" cost the Democrats dozens of House seats, while others suggest that party losses were fairly minimal. One thing that is certain is that the changes in election law contributed significantly to the size of the Congressional Black Caucus (CBC), a relative newcomer to Democratic power politics.[54]

Founded during the Ninety-second Congress of 1971–72, the CBC had been, for most of its early history, a small group with little influence in the legislative process. The caucus was far to the left of the rest of Congress, and rather than "play the game" to influence public policy through traditional channels, it fancied itself the "conscience of the House" and focused on writing an annual alternative budget.[55] During the 1970s and '80s, growth in the size of the caucus was relatively slow but steady, and by the 102nd Congress of 1991–92 the CBC had a total membership of twenty-five. But after the redistricting that came in the 1990s, the caucus's ranks increased to thirty-eight members, where it has more or less remained ever since.[56]

We shall have more to say about the power of the CBC in Chapters 11 and 12, as it is a major player in the legislative battles of the Clinton and Obama tenures. For now, a few general points about it will suffice. First, the addition of new, mostly southern, and frequently rural black Democrats to the caucus had the effect of moderating it, albeit slightly.

All through the 1990s and 2000s, the caucus was more moderate than it had been in the 1970s and '80s, but it was still more liberal than white northern and especially southern Democrats. Second, the CBC's greater numbers and more mainstream liberal approach made it a significant factor in the legislative battles in Democratic-controlled Congresses. So also did its tight, bloc-style voting. Despite the increase in numbers, the diversity of its membership, and its relatively loose organizational structure, the caucus remained one of the most internally cohesive groups in the entire Congress. Another source of strength for the caucus comes from its well-positioned membership—the third salient point. Because black members of Congress come from very safe districts, they have earned the seniority to advance to prominent leadership posts. In the 111th Congress of 2009–10, CBC members chaired the committees on Homeland Security, Judiciary, Oversight and Government Reform, and Ways and Means.

Fourth, as regards the interests of the CBC, political scientist David T. Canon's analysis suggests that while black members have in recent years aligned more tightly with the northern flank of the Democratic party, they continue to advance the unique concerns of their constituents through all phases of the legislative process.[57] African Americans are substantially more liberal than whites on issues of social welfare; according to the 2004 National Election Study, black voters are more likely than whites to support spending increases for child care (79 percent to 47 percent), public schools (84 percent to 60 percent), financial aid for higher education (78 percent to 43 percent), Social Security (80 percent to 48 percent), the poor in general (85 percent to 47 percent), and food stamps programs (35 percent to 12 percent). The two sides also disagree strongly on issues of race-based income redistribution: 37 percent of blacks thought that the federal government should help minority groups, while just 16 percent of whites thought the same; 43 percent of black voters voiced support for affirmative action, while just 11 percent of whites did; 60 percent of black voters thought that the government should "see to it that black people get fair treatment in jobs," compared with just 26 percent of whites.[58] All in all, this makes black members of Congress substantially more eager to push for redistributive policies, especially those that benefit the African American population in particular.

This is an exceptional way for any group to exercise power in the American political process. African Americans have become over-whelmingly Democratic, so much so that their influence is exercised entirely within the party. Black voters have very low opinions of the Grand Old Party, which they say makes little more than symbolic ef-forts to appeal to them. For the same reason, they have relatively little pull among Democratic presidential and senatorial candidates, at least during the general election. Their vote is perennially built into the party's calculations, meaning that candidates for those offices spend the bulk of their efforts wooing (mostly white) swing voters. Instead, black voting power is felt in the Democratic nomination battle and, more important, in the House of Representatives, where African Americans usually make up about 17 percent of all House Democrats and occupy vital positions in the committee system.

What does all this mean for the story we are telling here? Unlike the other client groups we have reviewed so far—namely, white south-erners, big city machines, and organized labor—African Americans are not in the party primarily for the special benefits they enjoy from membership. Since the Democratic party began embracing wealth re-distribution, starting with the New Deal, it has by and large dominated among African Americans, even when it was giving them substantially less than white voters. That makes black voters different from union voters and southern plantation owners, whose roles in the party were not due necessarily to ideological synchronicity so much as to special carve-outs. Nevertheless, black members of Congress function very much *as if* they are the leaders of a client group, much like organized labor. CBC Democrats are active participants in swinging the policy needle in Congress as far to the left as possible, and on large and small agenda items alike, they *also* make sure that Democratic policy ad-dresses the particular concerns of their constituents. Additionally, the special status of African Americans in Congress—where they are legally guaranteed immunity from the typical partisan gerrymander—has another similarity to that of organized labor in that it is a creation of Democratic-sponsored public policy, in this case the 1982 amendments to the Voting Rights Act.

As we shall see, the presence of African Americans as a kind of client group within the party has created substantial challenges for party leaders ever since the 1980s. The forty or so House votes of the CBC are a virtual necessity for any Democratic president looking to craft a legislative majority, which means that black demands must be met—if not on the bill in question, then somewhere else down the line. Organized labor has long enjoyed this kind of special role in the party, and from this point forward so would African Americans. And so if we think of the job of leading the Democratic party as akin to being a juggler, we might say that the amended Voting Rights Act had the effect of adding yet another ball into the act.

CHAPTER SEVEN

There's No Party That Can Match Us

George Meany and the Evolution of Organized Labor

No economic event in the history of the United States can compare to the Great Depression. Between 1929 and 1933, the real wealth of the United States—measured by gross domestic product—declined by 27 percent.[1] Not until 1939, a full decade after the beginning of the collapse, would the private economy fill in this gaping hole that was dug by the Depression.

Yet those who suffered through the Depression were rewarded with more than a quarter century of economic expansion as the United States rose to become the undisputed industrial powerhouse of the world. Between 1939 and 1969, the country created nine million manufacturing jobs, eight million transportation jobs, and 2.5 million construction jobs.[2] Seeing as how most of these industries were dominated by labor unions like the Teamsters, the United Auto Workers (UAW), and the United Steelworkers (USW), the massive growth in the economy led to a corresponding spike in the percentage of workers who were part of a labor union. The peak for union workers came in 1954, when they amounted to 34.7 percent of the nonagricultural workforce.[3]

Just as labor leaders in 1935 sensed the organizing opportunities that stemmed from the National Labor Relations Act (NLRA), they understood in the 1950s and 1960s the political possibilities for an interest group that represented nearly one in three workers. And so, following World War II, labor moved to resolve the lingering disputes between the American Federation of Labor (AFL, or simply "the Federation") and the Congress of Industrial Organizations (CIO), put to-gether a highly advanced and devastatingly efficient political operation, and sealed its alliance with the Democratic party. The apex of labor's political clout came during the Great Society period of the mid-sixties, when President Lyndon Johnson—who had once regularly voted against labor interests in Congress—worked closely with the union leaders to pass an array of social and economic reforms.

Yet even as the sun broke through the clouds that always seemed to darken labor's outlook, the most perceptive observers understood at the time that those bright days were to be short-lived. The amaz-ing growth of the industrial economy in the postwar years ultimately yielded major breakthroughs in mechanization and automation, leaving manpower less necessary and diminishing the organized workforce. Indeed, after 1953 organized labor would see its share of the workforce slowly decline, so that by 2010 it would account for just 11.9 percent of all workers.[4] What's more, the anti-labor coalition that had formed after the passage of the NLRA was still in place, and even with huge Demo-cratic majorities during the Great Society, it was still powerful enough to prevent labor from achieving its primary goal: the repeal of Section 14(b) of the Taft-Hartley Act, which had given states the right to outlaw union-only shops (a.k.a. the "right to work" provision). Additionally, the old craft and industrial unions, which by this point had anchored the labor movement for a half century, were forced to give way to white-collar, government unions that, as we shall see, have fundamentally different goals.

This chapter tells the tale of organized labor's rapid rise after World War II and its transformation in the 1960s and beyond. Today, orga-nized labor remains a powerful client of the Democratic party, though its role in the coalition has changed notably over the years. In the pages that follow, we will come to understand just how labor's role in Ameri-can politics has evolved.

Prior to the New Deal, unions had been studiously nonpartisan. The legendary Samuel Gompers, founder and head of the AFL, cultivated this approach to politics, backing those candidates in either party who were labor's friends. In a nod to the old Jacksonian view of big government, Gompers actually feared government efforts to intervene in the economy, believing that they would ultimately be anti-union.[5]

As we saw in Chapter 3, this changed after FDR came into office and pushed through the New Deal, in particular the NLRA. Certain unions within the AFL—the United Mine Workers (UMW) and the International Ladies' Garment Workers' Union (ILGWU)—saw the law for what it was: a fundamental realignment of labor relations law and a significant opportunity to expand labor's position in the American economy. Traditional craft unions balked at this, objecting to the notion of organizing workers by industry rather than by craft, and so the activist unions split off to form the CIO, which joined the political fray without hesitation.[6] It founded the deceptively named Non-Partisan League, whose sole purpose was to reelect Franklin Roosevelt in 1936.[7] As George Meany, eventual head of the merged AFL-CIO and previously a major player in the New York AFL, put it:

> I think [UMW president John] Lewis set up the CIO strictly as a basis for a political machine. I don't think there's any question about it. . . . When Lewis and Sidney Hillman [president of the ILGWU] created CIO, I think that's what they had in mind—political power. I have no hard evidence, but it was pretty well known around that forming the CIO had a political side: that Roosevelt wanted to be assured of labor support and felt that he could never get it out of the conservative AFL.[8]

As we saw in Chapter 3, the CIO's push for FDR helped realign the major urban centers of the United States, which remain overwhelmingly Democratic to this day. By the end of FDR's third term, in 1944, it was Hillman who was in on the highest level of talks about who would become vice president.

Meanwhile, the AFL remained largely on the political sidelines. The types of unions in the Federation were mostly the old-time craft unions like the United Association of Plumbers and Pipefitters (UA) and the United Brotherhood of Carpenters and Joiners of America (UBC). These groups had long eschewed political action, instead following a voluntaristic model; they would negotiate contract by contract to improve their wages and working conditions, rather than pursue federal legislation.[9] Federation unions were dominated by skilled crafts-men while the CIO unions often had unskilled or low-skilled workers; this left Federation workers more economically and socially comfortable than their CIO counterparts, and thus less inclined toward activism.

Even so, the separation between these two groups was not all that great, at least in philosophical terms. For starters, businesses viewed both groups skeptically, which meant that, as the party of business, the Republicans were bound not to have a cozy relationship even with the AFL. Additionally, while the Federation had originally been opposed to social welfare legislation like minimum wage laws, which Gompers believed would actually hold down wages, its position evolved so that the AFL was basically split on the issue by the time of the Fair Labor Standards Act of 1937, and by the time of the merger it had come out in favor of a minimum wage hike.[10]

As for the CIO, the common accusation that it was a "radical" outfit is vastly overstated. Of course, the CIO did have a healthy num-ber of communists within it, but it nevertheless gave its full effort to Franklin Roosevelt, who was not a socialist or a communist but a pro-gressive Democrat.[11] In fact, one could argue that the CIO ultimately de-radicalized organized labor by choosing to play within the existing political process rather than pushing for root-and-branch reform. After all, the CIO could, at least in theory, have joined up with the Socialist party, which garnered a not insignificant 2.2 percent of the vote in 1932. However, its leadership went all out for FDR, and as a consequence the Socialist party had all but disappeared by the end of the 1930s.[12]

Ultimately, the differences between the AFL and the CIO had more to do with political strategy than anything else. This meant that, given a change in political circumstances, the AFL and CIO might eventually find it in their interests to join forces. Such circumstances began to develop in the postwar years, and they pushed the AFL and the CIO closer together.

For the AFL, Taft-Hartley served as the wake-up call.[13] Its major provisions—the required oath against communism, the right-to-work allowance, and the limitations on strikes—seemed to the Federation to be an attack on unionism itself. Worse, the fact that it passed over

President Truman's veto proved that there was an active and powerful anti-labor movement in the country. So the Federation realized that it needed to become more involved in politics. As Meany put it:

> *Before Taft-Hartley was put on the statute books over Truman's veto, I didn't push for what you might call a political machine. Like everyone else, I was content to have the national AFL stay more or less neutral. . . . It wasn't until Taft-Hartley in 1947 that the AFL really went into the business of working at elections. We set up Labor's League for Political Education.*[14]

As for the CIO, it had long been politically active, but it was suffering from economic ailments in the early postwar years. The first ten years of its existence, 1937–1946, saw it nearly double in membership rolls—from about 3.7 million workers to 6 million workers.[15] However, that would be the high-water mark; over the next ten years, union membership in the CIO would actually decline. It had organized most of the major industries—auto, steel, and rubber, to name just a few— but after that it had hit a wall and found itself with diminished influence in the postwar economy. Worse, Lewis and the UMW had bailed out of the CIO in 1940, and in the early 1950s Walter Reuther—head of the UAW and second in command at the CIO—found himself in a fight with David McDonald of the United Steelworkers (USW), who was threatening to leave as well.[16] A merger with the AFL, whose membership continued to grow during this period, seemed to be the right medicine to cure what ailed the CIO.[17]

The impetus for unification talks was the deaths of the heads of the AFL and the CIO—William Green and Philip Murray, respectively—in November 1952. Their replacements, Meany in the AFL and Reuther in the CIO, were much more amenable to the idea of joining forces. Meany was above all else a pragmatist, and while Reuther was a political activist with a history of sympathies for socialism, he also recognized that the key to labor's success was to work within existing structures like the Democratic party.[18]

Even so, the unification was not finalized until 1955, in large part because moderate Republicans were still actively wooing the AFL.

In the 1952 GOP nomination battle, Dwight Eisenhower enjoyed the backing of the northeastern wing of the Republican party, which had long been more open to labor's political demands than the conservative base in the Midwest. When Ike became president, he made good faith gestures toward the AFL by naming Martin Durkin of the plumbers' and pipefitters' union as secretary of labor and Lloyd Mashburn of the Los Angeles Building Trades Council as undersecretary. What's more, in his 1953 State of the Union message, Eisenhower hinted at a desire for peace between labor and the Grand Old Party:

> *The determination of labor policy must be governed not by the vagaries of political expediency but by the firmest principles and convictions. Slanted partisan appeals to American workers, spoken as if they were a group apart, necessitating a special language and treatment, are an affront to the fullness of their dignity as American citizens. . . .*
>
> *In the field of labor legislation, only a law that merits the respect and support of both labor and management can help reduce the loss of wages and of production through strikes and stoppages, and thus add to the total economic strength of our Nation.*
>
> *We have now had 5 years' experience with the Labor Management Act of 1947, commonly known as the Taft-Hartley Act. That experience has shown the need for some corrective action, and we should promptly proceed to amend that act.*[19]

Nice words for labor aside, the détente between the GOP and the AFL was short-lived. Durkin felt betrayed by Eisenhower when the administration refused to support his recommendations on how Taft-Hartley could be modified, and he resigned his post in protest in September 1953. From that point forward, the Eisenhower administration took a more aggressive posture toward organized labor, eventually signing on to the restrictive Landrum-Griffin Act at the end of the decade. And so the final reservations of the AFL were swept aside, and it joined formally with the CIO in 1955.[20]

With the AFL and CIO joining forces, it's appropriate to ask: What were the political objectives of this new entity? And why would it bind

itself so tightly to the Democratic party? We already answered part of
the question in Chapter 3: organized labor would work actively for the
northern, liberal wing of the party in the electoral arena, and the liberals would do what they could for organized labor in Congress and the
White House. But what exactly did labor want? On the one hand, it
had direct interests at stake, like the repeal of Taft-Hartley, but labor
was also after indirect benefits. As Meany put it:

> We do not seek to recast American society in any particular
> doctrinaire or ideological image. We seek an ever-rising standard of
> living. Sam Gompers once put the matter succinctly. When asked
> what the labor movement wanted, he answered, "More." If by a
> better standard of living we mean not only more money but more
> leisure and richer cultural life, the answer remains, "More."[21]

In other words, labor saw gains for its members through the kind
of broad social welfare programs liberal Democrats advocated. For
instance, if the government enacted legislation on minimum wages,
maximum hours, and good working conditions, it would put all laborers, including the organized, in a better bargaining position vis-à-vis
their employers. Similarly, federal programs like Medicare and aid for
education would improve the working class's position, enabling labor
to deal more aggressively for better wages. Additionally, labor also
pushed Keynesian economic policies, including the Kennedy/Johnson
tax cut, because it believed that the government should take an active
role in using up the excess capacity in the economy to generate full
employment—a major goal of organized labor.[22] What's more, labor
was an early advocate of the civil rights movement, and its Committee
on Political Education (COPE) even developed a "Southern Strategy"
to aid African Americans in the segregated South. Labor's interests
on this front were not simply wrapped up in social justice, but also included a raw political calculus: the southern delegation in Congress was
dominated by anti-union, conservative Democrats; bringing African
Americans into the electorate would weaken the conservatives' position
and give labor an opportunity to forge an alliance with newly registered
blacks.[23]

As mentioned above, many unions in the AFL came relatively late to this view, but with the merger and the installation of Meany as the head of the new AFL-CIO, labor became a politically potent force for this liberal agenda. Meany's approach to politics emphasized lobbying in Washington, D.C., over organizing the unaffiliated sectors of the economy; the stately AFL-CIO offices in Washington, just a few blocks away from the White House itself and virtually next door to that bastion of economic conservatism, the Chamber of Commerce, are a lasting testament to Meany's emphasis. The political culture of Washington in the 1950s and '60s was perfect for a consummate insider like Meany, who had cut his teeth as a lobbyist in Albany for the AFL. The president and his top advisers, as well as the barons who sat atop the key congressional committees, ruled the nation's capital—all of which made Meany, who had developed friendships with all the big players, a key power broker.[24]

Another major focal point of the new AFL-CIO was an active role in political campaigns. Both groups had had campaign organizations in place before the merger—the CIO PAC and AFL's League for Political Education—and Meany transformed these into a single campaign/lobbying outfit known as COPE, which functioned very similarly to modern-day interest groups, issuing legislative scores to members of Congress, contributing to presidential and congressional campaigns, and working to get out the labor vote. While COPE was nominally nonpartisan, almost all of its campaign contributions went to Democrats, who almost always were the ones to receive the top legislative scores. In the 1964 election, COPE spent about $950,000 on the Democrats' behalf, a princely sum for the period, and this figure excludes in-kind contributions like pamphlets and volunteers. What's more, COPE would increase its participation in subsequent elections—presidential and congressional—through the rest of the decade.[25] All in all, it was a real force to be reckoned with. As COPE director Al Barkan put it in 1970:

> *We're kind of proud of our organization. We've got organizations in 50 damn states and it goes right down from the states to the cities. . . . There's no party that can match us. Give us ten years*

or fifteen years and we'll have the best political organization in the
history of this country.[26]

A great indication of labor's clout can be seen in the "evolution" of
LBJ's attitude toward labor. Johnson had been anti-labor as a member
of Congress, and key members of labor had even opposed Kennedy's
decision to make him vice president. Yet when he became president,
he made earnest appeals to Meany, Reuther, and other labor leaders
pledging that he would be a friend to them. While LBJ exaggerated or
flat-out lied about many things during his tenure, his promise to labor
turned out to be the truth.[27] The AFL-CIO, in turn, became a key ally
of LBJ in his push for the Great Society, and it was critical in helping
Johnson pass new public works, public housing and hospital construction, Medicare, job training, Head Start, the Kennedy tax cut, and
more.

Unfortunately for labor, its moment in the sun was relatively short-lived,
as it faced a declining presence in the labor force: between 1956 and
1976, the number of manufacturing workers affiliated with a union
declined by 250,000, mining and quarry workers declined by 120,000,
transportation workers declined by 400,000, and electric, gas, and sani-
tary workers declined by 10,000.[28]
    Social scientists have offered many reasons to explain this decline.
The largest factor is, without doubt, the mechanization and automation
of the industrial economy. Organized labor's response to this change
was to protect existing workers instead of making sure the next generation of workers enjoyed the same protections. Unions like the long-
shoremen, railway workers, and printers all negotiated contracts that
protected the incomes of redundant workers and paid relatively little
attention to future jobs or wages. Historian Melvyn Dubofsky offers a
telling anecdote about the unionized printers at the *New York Times*:
"Having become superfluous, the remaining printers could sit around
the . . . plant cutting out paper dolls, playing cards or otherwise wasting
time until they chose to retire or accept a cash payment for quitting."[29]
    Other factors were also at play. The proliferation of air-conditioning,
the growing energy sector, and generous government subsidies increas-

ingly made the Sunbelt an attractive place for businesses to relocate to. This region was dominated by right-to-work states that outlawed closed shops, meaning that industrial workers in Texas were much less likely to be unionized than those in New York. Another contributor was the rise of the white-collar, service economy. Between 1956 and 1976, the U.S. economy added just 2.4 million jobs in the goods-producing side of the economy, where the unions had long been a dominant factor; meanwhile, the service-producing side of the economy saw an enormous 26 million jobs created during this period. Jobs in sectors like finance, banking, retail trade, and information services were not a good fit for the old union model, as white-collar workers often were in a better position because they had more transferrable skills. What's more, these workers generally viewed organized labor skeptically, adding an extra hurdle to unionization of these sectors.

There were also undeniable signs of labor's weak political position, despite its superior campaign and lobbying operations. While organized labor was very successful in facilitating the general social welfare breakthroughs of this period, it suffered big disappointments in advancing reforms that would directly aid unions. Its first notable failure after the merger was the enactment of the Landrum-Griffin Act of 1959. Adopted in response to labor corruption trials in the 1950s, the act mandated that a union had to hold secret-ballot elections (which would free the rank and file from pressure from the bosses), submit annual reports to the Department of Labor, and limit the disciplinary actions that it could take against its members. The act also barred members of the Communist party from holding office in unions, guaranteed a "bill of rights" to members that included regular elections of officers, and limited the powers of unions to place subordinate organizations in trusteeship. Landrum-Griffin passed through Congress with overwhelming bipartisan support, thanks to the outcry over criminality in unions like the Teamsters.[30] This did not surprise labor, but what did surprise and offend it was the unwillingness of Congress to allow the newly merged AFL-CIO to root out the corruption for itself. After the merger, the AFL-CIO established an Ethical Practices Committee to promote proper behavior among workers, but this was not enough for the Congresses of the late 1950s, which, even though they had Democratic majorities, still were dominated by the conservative coalition.[31]

After the 1964 election, organized labor was hopeful that it could finally repeal Section 14(b) of Taft-Hartley, which allowed states to outlaw the closed shop. As noted above, COPE went all out for LBJ in 1964, in hopes that he and a new, liberal Congress could muster enough votes to get this reviled law changed. Though Johnson had voted for Taft-Hartley in 1947, he was happy to help organized labor in its push for revision in the Eighty-ninth Congress of 1965–66. The president correctly recognized that this was a highly controversial piece of legislation, and LBJ, always the master of congressional psychology, sensed that it was best to save this item until after the major parts of the Great Society had passed. The AFL-CIO went along with this out of deference to LBJ as well as its general commitment to his social welfare agenda,[32] and the bill did not come up for final passage in the House until late July 1965. In an ominous sign, it limped through with a final vote of 221–203; even though the liberals dominated the lower chamber, the coalition of southern Democrats (78 against) and Republicans (117 against) remained a formidable threat to labor.[33]

The Senate would be an even greater challenge, as southern Democrats and Republicans actually amounted to a small majority of 52 votes. Beyond this group, LBJ also had reason to worry about the dozen or so Democratic senators from the Farm Belt, who were afraid of being rebuked by agribusinesses that did not want their workers to join unions. So LBJ leaned on urban liberals to back a hefty farm bill that would raise the price of wheat, and in return Farm Belt Democrats supported labor's bill. Even with all this, Johnson and Meany still could not get the bill through. The conservative coalition had generally been content not to block the major provisions of the Great Society using the Senate filibuster, but Taft-Hartley's restrictions on the closed shop were too sacrosanct for Republicans and southern Democrats. Senate Minority Leader Everett Dirksen had entered the chamber just a few years before his hero and one of the bill's namesakes, Robert Taft, passed away, and he simply would not allow a straight up-or-down vote on the bill. He was prepared to couple a repeal of 14(b) with a constitutional amendment that would have overturned the "one man, one vote" rulings of the Supreme Court of Chief Justice Earl Warren, which had redistributed legislative power from the rural areas to the cities, but Meany flatly refused. Without a deal, Senate Majority Leader Mike Mansfield was not willing to subject the Senate to a lengthy filibuster, so that was that. To this day, 14(b) remains the law of the land.[34]

Despite these setbacks, labor did not walk away totally empty-handed. It won multiple expansions to the Fair Labor Standards Act during the Kennedy/Johnson years, as well as the Contract Work Hours and Safety Standards Act, which clarified the rules governing maximum hours, and the Manpower Development and Training Act, which appropriated $35 million to help workers displaced by automation and technological advance. Yet all in all, it's fair to say that labor gave more than it received during this period: while it offered vital assistance to elect Kennedy, Johnson, and Democratic Congresses, it failed to secure its major goal of repealing 14(b).

Like so many other aspects of American life, organized labor was greatly influenced by the social and cultural tumult of the late 1960s. As we shall see, the result would be a labor movement fundamentally different from previous incarnations, as well as one that was almost as divided as it had been before the merger.

The most notable change that came about in the 1960s was the rise of public sector unions. The NLRA, which the CIO had used to such great effect, offered no privileges to government workers, so by the time of the Kennedy administration the public sector was governed by a patchwork of different labor rules and regulations. For instance, workers for the Tennessee Valley Authority were basically allowed all the same privileges that private workers had under the NLRA; the Interior Department gave its workers the right to bargain collectively; and the Post Office had no formal policy, generating a hodgepodge of rules across the country. On the citywide level, New York City and Philadelphia adopted collective-bargaining provisions during the 1950s, but other cities resisted such pressures.[35]

One problem that public sector unions had was a bad reputation in many quarters. Firefighters and policemen had tried to unionize in the early part of the century, and this eventually resulted in the infamous Boston Police Strike of 1919, which Massachusetts governor (and future president) Calvin Coolidge had to put down.[36] As late as 1959, even the AFL-CIO Executive Council was lukewarm at best on public sector unions, declaring this about federal workers: "[I]n terms of accepted collective bargaining procedures, government workers have no right beyond the authority to petition Congress—a right available to every citizen."[37]

Yet there was something almost irresistible about public sector unionism. The rise of the modern welfare state after the Great Depression had vastly increased the number of governmental employees—from four million in 1939 to more than eight million in 1959, roughly the time when public sector unionism begins to take off.[38] Additionally, most states outside the South had strong pro-labor political factions eager to aid their allies, and the 1958 midterms saw a new generation of pro-labor Democrats elected all across the North. The major breakthrough for government workers came in 1959 in progressive Wisconsin, where the American Federation of State, County and Municipal Employees (AFSCME) had been founded in 1932. The Democratic wave of 1958 had swept in a new Democratic governor as well as the first Democratic majority in the statehouse since 1936. AFSCME saw an opportunity, and was able to push through the first public sector collective-bargaining law of any state in the union.[39] Other states soon followed suit, and by the end of the century almost all states offered collective bargaining to at least some of their workers, and a majority of states (mostly in the Northeast and Midwest) offered it to all state employees.[40]

On the federal level, President Kennedy realized that aiding federal government unions could be an easy way to pay back organized labor for all of its efforts on his behalf in the 1960 presidential election. JFK named Arthur Goldberg—a key behind-the-scenes player in the AFL-CIO merger and future Supreme Court justice—to head a committee to investigate how best to go about unionizing federal workers, and its recommendation was for an executive order that recognized federal unions. In January 1962, Kennedy signed Executive Order 10988, which stated: "Employees of the Federal Government shall have, and shall be protected in the exercise of, the right, freely and without fear of penalty or reprisal, to form, join and assist any employee organization or to refrain from any such activity."[41] Of course, there were important limitations in this new allowance; unions were not allowed to bargain collectively for wages, to strike, or to force employees who refused to join to pay union dues anyway.[42] Even so, it was a landmark victory for public workers.

All in all, changes in state and federal laws in the early 1960s helped bring about massive growth in public sector unionism. While industrial labor declined between 1956 and 1976, government unions saw a better than 200 percent expansion, from fewer than a million to more than three million members.[43] Included in these numbers is the National Education Association (NEA), the nation's largest teachers' union, which transitioned in the 1960s from a professional association into a more activist union prepared to organize new school districts, strike for higher wages, and align with other unions like AFSCME in pursuit of shared political goals.[44]

The rise of government unions was, in many respects, a godsend for the existing craft and industrial unions. Even though they were in decline—both in real terms and as a share of the workforce—the addition of public workers mitigated the AFL-CIO's eroding position in the workforce. In 1956, union workers made up 33.4 percent of the total nonagricultural workforce, and in 1976 they still accounted for 27.4 percent, a notable decrease but not as bad as it would have been without government unions.[45] Importantly for the union organizations, member dues did not decline (in fact, they went up as unions charged their workers more) and unions had just as strong a grassroots presence in the political realm.

However, public workers would bring about a major restructuring in the values and interests of organized labor. The merged AFL-CIO of the 1950s and '60s—dominated by private sector labor—originally proffered what economist Leo Troy has called "neo-mercantilism"; its agenda was to work with the government and business to maximize the share of the private sector's pie that private workers received. Government employees have absolutely no interest in such an arrangement, as their pay comes entirely from the government. Instead, according to Troy, they are interested in the socialization of private income—the collection of taxes from the private sector to be redistributed by a government staffed with well-paid union workers.[46]

This difference became more salient as government workers eventually came to dominate organized labor. By 1993, government workers made up 47 percent of the nationwide union membership, and by 2009 they constituted a majority of union workers.[47] There are two major implications in this change. First, as we shall discuss in later chapters, government workers would find natural allies in the African American electorate, as well as in the New Politics left, in that all these groups are extremely interested in the socialization of private income, albeit for different reasons. This would help bring about changes in the Democratic party that would become evident in the 1990s and beyond. Second, as we shall see below, the rise of government unions contributed to increasing tensions within the labor coalition as the old divisions that had separated the AFL and the CIO began to reemerge.

The merged AFL-CIO that was formed in 1955 was to last little more than a decade before it was torn apart by the social and cultural divides of the late 1960s. Walter Reuther of the UAW had been a key player in the unification of the AFL and CIO in the mid-1950s, yet in a testament to the superiority of the AFL by that point, the presidency of the new organization went to Meany. At first, Reuther was happy to work with Meany, but he was fed up by 1967, pulling his UAW out of the AFL-CIO and offering this stinging rebuke:

> The AFL-CIO, in policy and program, too often continues to live with the past. It advances few new ideas and lacks the necessary vitality, vision and imagination and social invention to make it equal to the challenging problems of a changing world. It is sad but nevertheless true that the AFL-CIO is becoming increasingly the comfortable, complacent custodian of the status quo.[48]

What accounts for this new divide? Some of it was wrapped up in personality; Reuther and Meany just were not meant to be friends. Strategy was also a factor; Reuther was much more interested in building union strength from the grass roots and did not like the fact that Meany had concentrated most political power around himself.[49] Much of the tension could be traced back to the social, cultural, and political views of the various unions: while virtually every union was to the left of the Republican party, the growing rifts in the Democratic party—which we shall discuss in detail in Chapters 8 and 9—were nevertheless mimicked in the AFL-CIO. A left-right split on the Vietnam War was the most notable philosophical difference, and the urban crisis was another big divide. Liberal leaders like Reuther were strong advocates of urban-renewal programs such as Model Cities, while many conservative workers were drawn to the George Wallace campaign of 1968, which played on white anger over the urban unrest.[50]

There was also a split on the nomination rules in the Democratic party. As we shall see in Chapter 9, the AFL-CIO was invited to participate in the reform process that followed the disastrous 1968 convention, but the old rules favored Meany and the power brokers in the AFL-CIO, so they encouraged a boycott. However, the more liberal unions—AFSCME, the Communications Workers of America (CWA), the International Association of Machinists (IAM), the NEA, the Oil, Chemical and Atomic Workers Union (OCAW), and the UAW—favored party reform.[51] When liberal George McGovern won the nomination in 1972 via the new rules, the AFL-CIO voted overwhelmingly not to endorse him. Again, however, a group of dissident unions—notably AFSCME, CWA, IAM, the Service Employees International Union (SEIU), and UAW—disagreed. Those still affiliated with the AFL-CIO pulled back from participating in COPE in 1972 and began operating an independent political arm designed to help McGovern.

As we shall see in later chapters, these internal divisions persisted through the 1970s and beyond as labor squabbled over the 1976 and 1980 presidential elections. It was only in the 1980s, with the resurgence of conservative Republicanism, that labor reunited in shared opposition to Ronald Reagan. Even then, however, tensions remained as a group of eight splinter unions—the Hotel Employees and Restaurant Employees Union (HERE), the Union of Needletrades, Industrial and Textile Employees (UNITE), the SEIU, the Teamsters, the UBC, United Farm Workers (UFW), and the United Food and Commercial Workers—pulled out of the AFL-CIO in 1995 to form Change to

Win, a more leftist federation committed to increasing labor's organizing activity.

We shall continue to revisit organized labor in the chapters to come, but it's appropriate to conclude this chapter with a general statement about its enduring relationship with the Democratic party. Labor is a client of the Democratic party, fully committed to its platform—not just the planks that benefit organized labor but also those that advance larger redistributive goals. In return, labor continues to expect that Democratic leaders do what they can, when they can, to advance labor's particular interests. Unfortunately for the unions, the durability of the conservative coalition has basically meant that they have made precious few union-specific gains since the NLRA. To this day, the reviled Section 14(b) remains the law of the land and has kept organized labor effectively out of the South.[52] The unions would love nothing more than to have this law repealed, especially as industrial jobs have migrated to Dixie, but they simply lack the political clout to make it happen. Despite these limitations, organized labor remains powerful enough that national Democratic leaders are obliged to do everything within the realm of political possibility for it, which means that the policy needle will inevitably bend to the interests of labor whenever the conservative coalition cannot block those pro-labor initiatives.

CHAPTER EIGHT

The Share-Out Runs Its Course

*The Election of 1968 and the
Splintering of the Democratic Party*

Political alignments in this country are notoriously sticky, enduring for decades after the initial shocks that created them fade away. Plenty of examples illustrate this point. In Chapter 1, we saw that Americans were still divided along North-South lines for decades after the Civil War. Over the past few chapters, we've seen the enduring quality of the New Deal realignment, shades of which have lasted even to the present day. Today, conservative Republicans—as well as many liberal Democrats—aver that Ronald Reagan's influence has stretched decades beyond his actual administration to affect the two major parties in fundamental ways.[1]

And so it was with the Great Society. The reforms of the Eighty-ninth Congress of 1965–66 would permanently restructure the electoral alignment in this country; the Voting Rights Act alone stands as a significant milestone in our nation's political history, as millions of previously disenfranchised African Americans and poor southern whites were brought into the southern electorate.[2] But there is an important difference between the Great Society and other alignments. The Civil War helped transform the Republican party into a national majority coalition that more or less dominated the political process until the Great Depression. Similarly, the New Deal established the Democrats as the majority coalition in the United States for many decades, even if they were incapable of pushing through progressive reforms after FDR's initial legislative triumphs. The Great Society is unique in that it had the *opposite* effect on the standing of both major parties. Ironically, it was a liberal, Democratic reform program that helped create a conservative, Republican majority.

Why did things turn out this way? Several reasons stand out, some involving the choices of the political leaders of the age, and others involving long-term trends beyond anybody's control. When it came to leadership, the Democrats were in many ways poorly served by Lyndon Johnson, a man with personal limitations that kept him from securing his party's long-term position, despite his many strengths. Without doubt, he was a master of the legislative game, and he brought to the White House a progressive vision that surprised and impressed many northern liberals who had long thought of him as a tool of the oil and gas industries.[3] Yet he was unwilling to deal openly and honestly with his fellow citizens, he was consumed by an egotistical drive to outdo FDR, inducing him to push for too much too fast, and he had a persistent tendency to promise more than he could possibly deliver. These flaws help account for his administration's failure to resolve the key issues of the late 1960s: Vietnam, crime and urban decay, and racial tensions. Over time, the country lost faith in the president and, more broadly, in the capacity of the federal government to solve public problems.

Beyond the failures of LBJ, there were larger forces at work to constrict the Democratic coalition. In both the North and the South, there was a revolution in race relations after the "Second Reconstruction" of the mid-1960s that would reshape the party system. With the landmark civil rights laws now securely on the books, the political debate over race in America was transformed; whereas once it had been a conversation about the legal rights of African Americans, it became a discussion about the extent to which the federal government was responsible for their social and economic welfare. In the North, this new debate slowly pushed many old New Deal voters, especially white ethnics, out of the Democratic party. This process began in 1968 when George Wallace performed strongly with this group and picked up speed thereafter, only temporarily slowed down by the Watergate scandal. In the South, a similar process occurred: white suburbanites in "New South" metropolitan areas, who were already basically voting Republican by that point, solidified their relationship with the Grand Old Party because of the new racial divide.

Thus, the Great Society period is another demarcation in the history of the Democratic coalition—the party at the end of LBJ's administration was substantially different from the one at the beginning. As we shall see, it had become more black, more northern, and more liberal than ever before—but with its ethnic vote in the North less secure and its white base in the South all but gone, it was substantially less able to win a nationwide majority to govern. Lyndon Johnson—the ardent New Dealer and faithful disciple of Franklin Roosevelt—had followed in his idol's footsteps by fundamentally transforming American society, but in so doing he had undermined the political position of his cherished Democratic party.

Far and away, the number-one concern of voters in the 1968 presidential election was the war in Vietnam; though Americans had been actively fighting for only three years, this tiny country in Southeast Asia had been of interest to the foreign policy establishment for more than a decade.[4] Presidents Eisenhower and Kennedy had both been involved in Vietnam, signifying the broad, bipartisan foreign policy consensus that a Communist-free Vietnam was essential to the United States' regional security interests. Accordingly, long before the arrival of the Johnson administration, the United States had been supporting the anti-Communist government in South Vietnam with military and economic aid—more than a billion dollars during Eisenhower's second term alone.[5] Unfortunately, financial aid could not make up for the fact that the United States lacked an honest and effective partner in the South Vietnamese government, and the assassination of President Ngo Dinh Diem in late 1963 left the regime highly unstable.

The coup that killed Diem took place just a few weeks before Lee Harvey Oswald assassinated John F. Kennedy, and thus it was almost entirely up to the LBJ administration to figure out what to do next. Johnson faced a difficult situation; with South Vietnam on the brink of collapse, it appeared increasingly likely that continuing the U.S. commitment would require active military engagement against the North Vietnamese. LBJ, who had been in Congress when China fell to the Communists during the Truman administration, knew all too well the kind of pressure that Republicans and southern Democrats could apply against liberal administrations perceived to be weak against the Communists, and he was not prepared to lose Vietnam. Nevertheless, his initial response to the deteriorating situation there was to do more of the same—more military advisers, more aid, etc.—while his advisers quietly developed a plan to apply direct pressure on the North via air strikes.

In August 1964, when the North Vietnamese supposedly attacked American vessels in the Gulf of Tonkin, Johnson received from Congress a resolution approving the use of military force to take "all necessary measures to repel any armed attacks against the forces of the United States and to prevent further aggression."[6] However, Johnson's initial response to this resolution was one of restraint. The campaign of 1964 was heating up, and the president's frontlash strategy, as outlined in Chapter 5, demanded a muted approach that would attract moderate Republicans and independents. In his public report on the Gulf of Tonkin incident, Johnson promised: "[O]ur response, for the present, will be limited and fitting. We Americans know, although others appear to forget, the risks of spreading conflict. We still seek no wider war."[7]

It was only after his historic triumph over Republican Barry Goldwater in the election of 1964 that Johnson initiated a bombing campaign against the North Vietnamese, and by March 1965 "Operation Rolling Thunder" was under way. This led, in turn, to the injection of U.S. ground forces—first to protect key air bases, then to take the fight directly to the Vietcong. Unfortunately, the early assessments of American commanders about the military's ability to repel the North Vietnamese turned out to be far too optimistic. As a consequence, the country poured more and more resources into the fight against an enemy that proved stubbornly resistant to the supposed irresistibility of America's military power. In December 1964, the United States had a total force of 23,300 personnel in South Vietnam; by December 1965, it had increased to 184,000; by December 1966 it stood at 385,000.[8]

The approach of the Johnson administration to the war was political in many respects. The president was acutely concerned about public opinion, and how the loss of popular support for the war would endanger his cherished Great Society reforms. Thus, he typically refused to give the generals on the ground everything they wanted, took great pains to justify the enhanced involvement as a response to the actions of the Vietcong, buried the true costs of the war deep in the Pentagon's budget, understated the full scope of U.S. involvement, and overstated the progress being made. Slowly but surely, political insiders, journalists, and eventually the public at large became aware of the difference between what the Johnson administration was saying and what was really happening—and the phrase "credibility gap" entered the lexicon to describe this divide.[9]

Even so, the public's reaction to U.S. involvement was initially positive. A Gallup poll taken in August 1964 found that fewer than 16 percent of Americans disapproved of America's role in the conflict. It was the rising casualty count that slowly eroded the president's standing. By the end of 1967, with American casualties in the conflict now topping 69,000 (16,000 killed plus 53,000 wounded), 46 percent viewed the war as a mistake, compared with just 44 percent, who still supported it.[10]

The bottom fell out on the administration on January 30, 1968, when the North Vietnamese launched a surprise attack on the South during the annual Tet holiday, including a dramatic assault on the U.S. embassy in Saigon. Although the United States and the South Vietnamese were caught off guard, they quickly gained the initiative and thoroughly repulsed the Communist attack. The North Vietnamese suffered a stinging defeat, failing to deliver a knockout punch against the South and losing as many as 40,000 soldiers in the process.[11] Yet it was the United States that lost the crucial public relations battle as Americans all across the country saw news footage of the carnage that seemed to give the lie to the optimistic assessments of LBJ and his commander in the field, William Westmoreland.[12] In February 1968, those disapproving of LBJ's handling of the war amounted to a majority for the first time in the Gallup poll, and his overall approval rating fell to just 40 percent. The credibility gap had grown to a chasm.

The effects of the so-called Tet Offensive on domestic politics were significant. Even though "hawks" still outnumbered "doves" by nearly two to one in the broader public, Tet seemed to galvanize antiwar sentiment on the American left—and its full effects were felt in the New Hampshire Democratic primary, held on March 12, 1968. At this point, the only challenge to LBJ's renomination was from Minnesota Democrat Eugene McCarthy, who did not actually expect to defeat Johnson at the party convention but was simply making a statement.[13] After Tet, McCarthy's campaign caught fire, and he surprised the political world by scoring 42 percent of the vote in the New Hampshire primary, holding LBJ to less than half of the primary electorate.[14]

Johnson's anemic showing in the Granite State induced Robert F. Kennedy—the president's longtime adversary—to "actively rethink" his prior commitment not to enter the nominating battle.[15] The thought of losing the nomination to RFK was just too much for LBJ, whose political advisers told him he would lose resoundingly in Wisconsin's primary. At the end of March, Johnson took to the national airwaves to announce a new peace initiative, and he surprised the country with this concluding announcement.

> *With America's sons in the fields far away, with America's future under challenge right here at home, with our hopes and the world's hopes for peace in the balance every day, I do not believe that I should devote an hour or a day of my time to any personal partisan causes or to any duties other than the awesome duties of this office—the presidency of your country.*
>
> *Accordingly, I shall not seek, and I will not accept, the nomination of my party for another term as your President.*[16]

Of course, Vietnam was not the only issue that was polarizing the country by the end of the 1960s. Americans were also growing increasingly anxious about the rising crime rate. The statistics are startling; from 1960 to 1969, the violent crime rate rose by 126 percent, the murder rate by 55 percent, the robbery rate by 186 percent, and the motor vehicle theft rate by 150 percent. Most categories for which the FBI has kept crime statistics show year-over-year increases of 5 percent or more through the whole decade, and 1968 was the worst year for the spread of crime in the entire decade as most categories posted higher than 15 percent jumps in reported crimes.[17]

The crime issue tied into a sense that the great American cities were in precipitous decline. *Time* magazine's preelection edition in 1968 featured a cover story on the social breakdown of New York City that focused on the political failures of Republican mayor John V. Lindsay, who had actually been in the running for the GOP's vice-presidential spot in the summer. Yet now *Time,* reviewing the seemingly innumerable list of civic problems plaguing the Big Apple—ethnic and racial strife, inflation, crime, "militant" civil service unions, traffic, and rapidly expanding welfare rolls—was forced to conclude of Lindsay's city: "No other metropolis in the world offered its inhabitants greater hope of material success or a wider variety of cultural rewards. Yet for all its dynamism and glamour, New York City, day by day, little by little, was sliding toward chaos."[18]

The story of urban decline cannot be told without detailing the growing, racially tinged violence of the decade. By 1968, race riots had become all too common in the United States, yet their locus was largely not in the Deep South, where African Americans had been denied voting and civil rights for generations. Violence had begun there early in the decade as civil rights demonstrators had clashed with racist police forces; as we saw in Chapter 6, these conflicts were a key factor in finally pushing the Kennedy administration to propose a civil rights bill. Yet the unrest would continue after the bill's passage, spreading beyond the Deep South; the summers of 1964 through 1967 would see significant rioting all across the country, in Cincinnati, Detroit, Los Angeles, Newark, Philadelphia, and Tampa. Dozens of people were killed, thousands were arrested, and the cost of property damages ran into the tens of millions.[19]

In response to the wave of violence during the long, hot summer of 1967, LBJ established the Kerner Commission, chaired by Illinois governor Otto Kerner, to investigate the reasons for the disturbances and suggest ways to deal with it. The commission found that the violence had its roots in racial tensions; most incidents were the result of young African Americans lashing out at "symbols of white American society—authority and property," due to "an increasingly disturbed atmosphere, in which typically a series of tension heightening incidents over a period of weeks or months became linked in the minds of many in the Negro community with a shared reservoir of underlying grievances." The ultimate causes, according to the Kerner Commission, were "the severely disadvantaged social and economic conditions of many Negroes compared with those of whites in the same city and, more particularly, in the predominantly white suburbs." The commission's report ominously concluded that "our nation is moving toward two societies, one black, one white—separate and unequal," and that to avoid "the continuing polarization of the American community and, ultimately, the destruction of basic democratic values," the nation had to implement a "compassionate, massive, and sustained" social effort, "backed by the resources of the most powerful and the richest nation on this earth."[20]

Yet the political situation kept LBJ from following through on the commission's recommendation for "unprecedented levels of funding." His biggest problem had to do with money, which is to say that he was out of it; the growing cost of the Vietnam War had forced him to trim his precious Great Society programs by 1967, and there was nowhere near the revenue needed for the kind of domestic Marshall Plan that Governor Kerner and his colleagues had in mind. Even if Johnson had the money to pour into urban programs, he lacked the public support to do it anyway. On the issue of how to deal with the problem of crime in general, Americans were simply not well disposed to the suggestions of the Kerner Commission. In February 1968, the Gallup Poll asked people "what steps . . . should be taken to reduce crime," and an overwhelming majority listed conservative solutions like "more law enforcement," "increase the police force," and so on. Just 18 percent called for "correct[ing] social conditions which cause crime."[21] Unfortunately, 1968 would see a continuation of the previous years of violence. The April assassination of Martin Luther King Jr. in Memphis brought a wave of riots in Baltimore, Chicago, Washington, D.C., and other places.[22]

Adding to racial tensions were the growing calls for school desegregation, which had been on the national agenda since the Supreme Court's historic ruling in *Brown* v. *Board of Education* in 1954. The South had been dragging its heels on the issue for more than a decade, and by 1968 the court had grown impatient with Dixie's intransigence.

In *Green* v. *County School Board,* an obviously exasperated Justice William Brennan wrote: "The burden is on a school board to provide a plan that promises realistically to work now, and a plan that at this late date fails to provide meaningful assurance of prompt and effective disestablishment of a dual system is intolerable."[23]

Desegregation of the public schools was not, however, a strictly southern matter. Northern schools often exhibited de facto segregation; that is, race was not the primary factor in determining who went to which school, but the ultimate result was essentially the same: white students in one school, black students in another. By 1968, this situation had become a salient issue in the North as a number of northern school districts had already had court-mandated desegregation imposed on them—notably Grand Rapids, Hartford, Newark, Oakland, and Tacoma. Other communities, like Berkeley, acceded to pressure from the NAACP to desegregate, over the objections of local residents.[24] Still others, like Boston, saw ongoing battles between civil rights groups and anti-integrationists.[25]

The Johnson administration had initially been hesitant to use the heavy hand of government to move the process of northern school desegregation along, in large part because it counted on the support of majority white machine governments in major American cities like Chicago.[26] However, by 1968 the Department of Health, Education and Welfare (HEW) was more willing to use the powers granted it under the 1964 Civil Rights Act—such as withholding federal funds for public schools—to speed up northern integration. HEW did not go so far as to outlaw de facto segregation, but it did denounce differences between white and black schools; call for an equalization in the quality of teachers, facilities, and textbooks; and require the eventual elimination of de facto segregation by redrawing district lines and school bus routes.[27] These policy changes corresponded with a noticeable decline in public support for school integration. In 1962, the American National Election Studies found that 45 percent of whites agreed that the federal government should ensure school desegregation, yet by 1968 that number had fallen to just 33 percent. Meanwhile, the proportion that thought the federal government should not be involved had risen from 34 percent to 45 percent.[28]

Another racially tinged issue that continued to influence the debate
was the question of "open housing," or whether and to what extent federally subsidized housing would have to promote integration. The issue
was such a hot potato that John F. Kennedy refused to sign an executive
order curtailing discrimination until after the 1962 midterm elections,
even though during the 1960 campaign he had chided Ike for not signing such an order.[29] The next year, California passed Proposition 13,
which nullified a state anti-discriminatory housing law.[30] As a mayoral
candidate in 1966, Republican John V. Lindsay had promised to build
160,000 new apartments to address the housing problem in New York
City—but by the early 1970s he was locked in a battle with Jewish home
owners in Queens over whether a new project would be built in the
middle-class neighborhood of Forest Hills.[31] In all of these cases, the essential question boiled down to the same issue that made school integration so contentious: would middle-class whites in the northern cities and
suburbs be required to share their neighborhoods with lower-income African Americans? The 1964 Civil Rights Act had little to say about the
issue, but after the assassination of Martin Luther King Jr., the Ninetieth
Congress passed the Fair Housing Act as an amendment to the original
bill. The new law gave the federal government real regulatory power to
prevent discrimination in selling or renting housing to minority groups,
ensuring that the issue would be on the agenda in the 1968 election.[32]

The issues of war, crime, and race combined to smash the Democratic coalition into pieces in the 1968 presidential election. The party's
crackup would be dramatically symbolized during the national convention in Chicago in August, when antiwar activists clashed with police
in a violent confrontation on the streets of the Windy City. Inside the
convention hall, the party regulars—typified by Chicago mayor Richard J. Daley—would square off against the more youthful antiwar left
wing, which had been internally fractured, dividing its support during
the primaries between McCarthy and Robert F. Kennedy. After RFK's
assassination in June, the left remained divided, with the doves split between McCarthy, South Dakota senator George McGovern, and Massachusetts senator Ted Kennedy. Yet even if RFK had lived and united
the antiwar left, his prospects for nomination would probably have
been dim; after all, presidential nominating politics in 1968 were still

basically governed by very old rules in which operatives from the state parties controlled the show. That year, the party bosses nominated Vice President Hubert Humphrey on the first ballot, even though he had not won, or campaigned actively in, primaries.[33]

As we shall see in the next chapter, the events in Chicago would have long-term implications for the Democratic party, pushing it to reform its nomination process in ways that privileged its liberal, activist base over the regulars. Yet Chicago's effect on the actual election in 1968 was quite limited. The antiwar faction, of course, lost the nomination battle to Humphrey, but in November most liberals would nevertheless wind their way back to supporting the Democratic ticket.[34] Their problem was that they simply had nowhere else to go: Humphrey's two major opponents—Richard Nixon, the Republican nominee, and George Wallace, the Alabama governor running with the American Independent party—were to the right of the Democratic nominee on the war issue. So, in the end, most liberals came home to Humphrey, who toward the conclusion of the campaign hinted that his terms for peace in Vietnam would be more dovish than LBJ's.[35]

The country narrowly elected Nixon to the presidency that year; the Republican's margin over Humphrey was just half a million votes out of more than seventy-two million cast, making it the closest presidential contest between 1960 and 2000. From a certain standpoint, Democrats might have had reasons to cheer about this. It is historically very difficult to hold the White House for three consecutive terms; President Johnson's popularity was anemic at best, making him a drag on the Democratic ticket; the Republicans had nominated a known quantity in Nixon, who over the years had carved out for himself a moderate and respectable image; and even so, the Democrats still almost captured a third consecutive term.

Still, the 1968 result was indeed an ominous sign for the Democratic party, for a few reasons. In the North, Wallace had peeled off urban ethnic voters who had been some of the most loyal supporters of the post–New Deal Democrats. Meanwhile in the South, the rising suburbs of the Sunbelt cities had brought to life a new political animal, southern Republicanism, which in turn would contribute to the end of Democratic hegemony over the region.

These changes in the North and South were evident in 1968, and they would continue over the next several decades and have a lasting effect on the composition of the Democratic party, so they are worth a detailed examination.

Wallace had risen to national attention by the middle of the decade, thanks to his highly dramatic stands against civil rights, which had caught the eye of the national media. In his 1963 inaugural address as Alabama's governor, he promised "segregation today, segregation tomorrow, segregation forever."[36] A few months later, he again garnered national attention with his infamous stand at the schoolhouse door, symbolically blocking the integration of the University of Alabama. The ambitious Wallace would parlay these hyperbolic demonstrations against integration into four consecutive campaigns for the White House. In 1964, he stuck his toe in the water of presidential politics and discovered an impressive level of support in the North. Running against stand-ins for LBJ in the various primary battles that year, he managed to pull 33 percent of the vote in Wisconsin, 43 percent in Maryland, and 30 percent in Indiana, including an outright victory of 1,300 votes in Lake County, the home of industrialized Gary.[37] Opposition to the civil rights reforms on the agenda in Congress was the key to Wallace's northern strength, as he swayed many urban ethnic whites who had been longtime Democratic loyalists.[38] With racial issues still on the front burner in 1968, it came as no surprise when the ambitious governor launched an independent bid.

What is most significant about the Wallace candidacy in 1968 is that it was substantially broader than Strom Thurmond's Dixiecrat campaign of twenty years prior. At first glance, this might seem surprising, as the two had quite a bit in common: both were governors from states in the Deep South; both were former Democrats and would return to the party after their unsuccessful challenges; and both had taken hardline stances against civil rights. Yet crucial differences stand out. For starters, Wallace won 13.5 percent of the nationwide popular vote, while Thurmond carried just 2.4 percent; what's more, Wallace won 8 percent of the vote outside the states of the old Confederacy, while Thurmond's non-South vote was negligible.[39] In particular, Wallace was relatively strong in the metropolitan areas of the Midwest, running well ahead of his average share of the northern vote in Cincinnati, Cleveland, Detroit, Flint, Gary, Pittsburgh, and Toledo. Detailed survey data taken of voters in Pennsylvania and Ohio suggest that his voters were non-college-educated white men—often of Irish or Polish descent—who had attained a middle-class life as skilled laborers or craftsmen in the cities or inner suburbs. In other words, these were precisely the kinds of voters that had backed the Democratic party since 1932.[40]

Wallace was able to break through with these voters in ways that Thurmond never could, by exploiting the issues mentioned above—Vietnam, crime, and race. A notable Wallace ad from 1968 serves as a good example of the nature of his appeal:

MALE NARRATOR: *Why are more and more millions of Americans turning to Governor Wallace?*

[Sound of school bus engine]

Follow as your children are bused across town.

WALLACE: *As President, I shall—within the law—turn back the absolute control of the public school systems to the people of the respective states.*

[Footsteps]

MALE NARRATOR: *Why are more and more millions of Americans turning to Governor Wallace? Take a walk in your street or park tonight.*

[Gunshot, glass breaking]

WALLACE: *As President, I shall help make it possible for you and your families to walk the streets of our cities in safety.*

[Ship engine/horn, seagulls]

MALE NARRATOR: *Why are more and more millions of Americans turning to Governor Wallace? Watch your hard-earned tax dollars sail away to anti-American countries.*

WALLACE: *As President, I will halt the giveaway of your American dollars and products to those nations that aid our enemies.*

[Applause]

MALE NARRATOR: *Wallace has the courage to stand up for America. Give him your support.*[41]

Wallace drew huge crowds in areas that were hundreds, sometimes thousands, of miles from the Deep South: 5,000 in Milwaukee and Canton, 6,000 in Indianapolis, 7,000 in Toledo and the suburban Chicago city of Cicero.[42] During his raucous campaign rallies, he would berate liberals in both parties who intended to use the federal government to impose national solutions on local communities.[43] Offering himself as an alternative, he promised to require federal district judges to stand for election, repeal the sections of the Civil Rights Act that barred discrimination in private establishments, and beef up crime-control measures (excluding gun control). Yet Wallace was no libertarian; he pledged to expand Social Security and Medicare, as well as promote a tax code that would treat lower-income earners more fairly. On the Vietnam War, he averred that if diplomatic negotiations failed, he would pursue "military defeat of the Vietcong in the South and the destruction of the will to fight or resist on the part of the government of North Vietnam."[44]

Why would this populist pitch find such traction in the North? It had to do with a subtle but significant shift in the debate over civil rights. In the early 1960s, when somebody was liberal on civil rights issues, that usually meant that he supported antilynching laws, opposed Jim Crow and legal segregation, and favored federal guarantee of voting rights. In other words, the civil rights conversation largely focused on the extent to which African Americans should be brought into civil society in the states of the old Confederacy. Yet by the end of the decade, practices in the northern cities were brought under closer scrutiny, and, what's more, the debate came to focus increasingly on the distribution of economic and social resources. This made a huge difference when it came to northern public opinion; after all, school integration, unlike voting rights, required whites to share their wealth with African Americans, which in this case meant their children's schools. Similarly, the question of open housing could not be fully understood without reference to property values, and thus the economic standing of white voters. Ditto the question of race-based violence, which urban whites saw as a threat to their families' safety and home property values. And, of course, the Kerner Commission's call for a kind of domestic Marshall Plan would inevitably be paid for by taxes on the white middle class.

In other words, the debate on civil rights had become a question of how much whites, southern and northern, would be asked to pay to equalize the status of African Americans. This amounted to a fundamental threat to the old Democratic coalition, a challenge that has found no better expression than in Theodore White's masterful *The Making of the President 1968*. According to White, the essential premise of the New Deal Democratic party had been one in which voters on the lower end of the socioeconomic scale supported the party of Roosevelt, which in turn would see to it that they enjoyed an equitable share of the national prosperity, a political transaction that White labels the "share-out." Yet by 1968, he explains:

> [I]n pursuit of the philosophy of share-out, the Johnson administration had come to consideration of that last group still clamoring for its share—the unfortunate and underprivileged black population of America. Here, however, was a faultline that the old philosophy of share-out could not straddle; for what the blacks clamored to share was not only money, jobs and material things but such intangibles as dignity and equality. And the sharing that was demanded in this quest was demanded not from the affluent so much as from white workingmen, who were asked also to share their schools, neighborhoods and places of amusement with the blacks. All through 1968 the working-class base of the Democratic coalition was to be torn almost as if by civil war, as white workingmen questioned the risk and the pace imposed on them in the adventure. The philosophy of the share-out . . . was to run its course in 1968.[45]

It's worth mentioning just how affluent "white workingmen" had become by 1968. As noted above, most Wallace supporters in Ohio were actually middle-income voters.[46] The great postwar prosperity that the nation enjoyed had elevated much of the working class into the middle class, and the "share-out" provisions of the New Deal and the Great Society—highly popular reforms like Social Security, Medicare, aid to public education, and government-subsidized student loans for college—had helped secure their long-term interests. With the emergence of African Americans as active partners in the Democratic coalition, working-class whites were suddenly asked to pay a price they had never paid before.

This would permanently alter the Democratic coalition in the North. The New Deal divide in northern politics was mostly class-based, a battle between the haves and the have-nots. Compared with the Yankee middle class and small-town conservatives in the Midwest, white working-class voters in and around the big industrial cities saw themselves as the have-nots, and accordingly voted Democratic in most elections. Yet the civil rights agenda, as it evolved to focus increasingly on the welfare of African Americans, shifted the partisan divide. By the end of the 1960s, white working-class voters were more inclined to view themselves as the haves vis-à-vis their African American neighbors, which in time would make them more well disposed to the Republican party, the historic home of the haves.

The Wallace candidacy was an early way station on the white working class's journey to becoming a core Republican bloc. Wallace essentially promised a return to the old white Democratic coalition: a more expansive social safety net, a more progressive tax code, and a civil rights policy that would let white ethnics determine the racial balance in their own communities. Of course, his appeal was unsuccessful, and the white ethnic vote would begin its movement toward the GOP after 1972. While the Republicans in Congress had overwhelmingly supported the Civil Rights and Voting Rights acts, the party was philosophically indisposed to the federally mandated redistribution of wealth; whereas this position had once been a liability in picking up the votes of the white working class, it would now become an asset. By 2008, when Barack Obama won the nationwide popular vote by 7 points, whites without a college education backed John McCain over Obama by 18 points.[47]

After the Civil Rights Act passed in July 1964, LBJ reportedly told his aide and fellow Texan Bill Moyers, "We have lost the South for a generation."[48] In the decades since, this idea has become an article of faith among liberal Democrats, who have developed an elaborate story about how the party's stand on civil rights permanently undermined its position in Dixie. Meanwhile, the Republican party—in pursuit of a "Southern Strategy"—embraced the politics of racism in a dirty deal with southern bigots, forever tarnishing the party of Abraham Lincoln.[49] Of course, the real story is much more complicated. In fact, the South had begun abandoning the Democratic party more than a decade before the passage of the Civil Rights Act, and the reasons had more to do with economics than racism.

We argued in Chapter 1 that there was no great ideological thread that connected northern to southern Democrats in the decades after the Civil War. There was, instead, an alliance that depended upon a political exchange: the South would support northern Democrats for president—usually, but not always, politicians from New York who had no direct ties to Tammany Hall—and in return Dixie would receive protection from federal incursions into its social and economic systems. That last phrase—social *and* economic systems—is crucially important in understanding the end of Democratic hegemony in the South. The deal between the regional factions of the Democratic party was not strictly about the South's racial status quo. Jim Crow was one, highly execrable, aspect of a broader system of economic, political, and social repression that preserved the position of the regional elites—the land-owners, country store merchants, lawyers, doctors, etc.—at the expense of laborers and small farmers, black and white. This was what southern Democrats in Congress were bound to protect. They were happy to vote for legislation that funneled money into their impoverished region, but they consistently opposed any federal reforms that seemed to challenge the southern elites.

As we noted in Chapter 3, the region's dependence on cotton was the principal factor in the peculiar shape that southern society and politics would take after the Civil War. Yet by the end of World War II, the hegemony of cotton was finally coming to an end in Dixie, thanks in part to the unintentional side effects of the New Deal. The Agricultural Adjustment Act subsidized the mechanization of southern cotton production, making it less labor intensive and thus displacing millions of farmers. In fact, the number of people living on farms in the South fell dramatically in the postwar years—from 12.7 million in 1945 to just 4.1 million in 1969.[50] An enormous throng of humanity was forced out of the southern countryside and into the major cities, North and South, contributing significantly to the urban unrest of the 1960s. African Americans constituted a disproportionately large share of the migrants, and the net result was a mass exodus of blacks out of Dixie.[51]

Just as significant as the migration of African Americans from the South was the migration of whites *into* the region. Between 1940 and 1970, a net 3.1 million whites would move into the old Confederacy.[52] This figure surely understates the total number of whites who traveled south, as poor white farmers displaced from their tenant plots often moved out of Dixie just as black farmers did. This growth in the white population was concentrated largely in the rising metropolitan centers of the South—Atlanta, Charlotte, Dallas, Houston, Miami, Tampa, and Washington, D.C.

What brought these white transplants to Dixie? In the 1880s, Henry Grady of the *Atlanta Constitution* had advertised a "New South," which was mostly hot air back then, but was not anymore.[53] The postwar economic boom produced a monumental transformation in the southern economy. Whereas once the region depended largely upon cotton, it would now rely upon a multifaceted economic base that was made up of six pillars: agribusiness, defense, advanced technology, oil and natural gas, real estate, and tourism.[54] Much of this regional development was due to the adept use of congressional power by senior southern Democrats, who expertly worked the committee system to deliver the South many more federal dollars than it paid in taxes. As Earl and Merle Black argue in *Politics and Society in the South*:

> *Federal programs and policies stimulated the growth of southern defense industries (both production plants and military bases) during World War II; helped finance the infrastructure (highways, airports, water and sewage systems) needed for economic expansion; and then pumped more money into the region in the form of subsidies for agricultural products, defense installations, contracts for the electronics and aerospace industries, subsidies for oil and natural gas producers, encouragement of real estate speculation and construction through tax laws; and finally, through social security, facilitated retirement to warmer climates.[55]*

This new southern economy required above all else a new, professional class of workers to animate it. Thus, a modern southern middle class—made up of technicians, managers, administrators, salespersons, clerks, and secretaries—grew very quickly in the postwar years, accounting for nearly 50 percent of all southern whites by 1970.[56]

These new middle-class voters posed a fundamental challenge to the old clientelistic relationship between Dixie and the Democratic party, for several reasons. First, as we noted, that old relationship had been rooted in the regional elite's need to protect its cotton-based economy, which these new voters had virtually nothing to do with. Unlike wealthy white landowners in the Mississippi Delta, bank managers in Tampa or insurance executives in Dallas had little to gain socially or economically from the old Jim Crow system. Relatedly, consisting as it did of such a large number of northern transplants, this new middle class did not possess the strong familial and regional traditions that had tied the old South to the Democratic party.

Most important, if clientelism and tradition did not link these new voters to the Democratic party, then neither did ideology. From 1932 forward, the Democratic party had carved out an identity for itself as a liberal or progressive faction. Yet the rising middle class of the South was decidedly conservative. In a survey of political attitudes in 1968, 47 percent of middle-class whites in the South labeled themselves conservative, compared with 38 percent who were moderate and just 14 percent who were liberal.[57] These middle-class, southern conservatives found natural allies in a fast-changing postwar Republican party. After the Great Depression, the GOP had tacked to the center in hopes of holding on to the Northeast and the Industrial Midwest. Thus, Republican presidential nominees had been moderate, even liberal Republicans who offered what Arizona senator Barry Goldwater had derided as a "dime-store New Deal." However, the rise of the Sunbelt gave western Republicanism—for decades on the progressive end of the party—a new, conservative flair. These new right-wingers were based not in the Great Plains or the Mountain West, but rather in fast-growing urban centers like Phoenix, Arizona, and Orange County, California, which both grew by nearly 1,000 percent between 1940 and 1970, due to the same kinds of forces that were driving growth in the

South.[58] Western suburbanites would align with southern suburbanites and the conservatives of the small towns in the Midwest to seize control of the Grand Old Party from the northeastern establishment by the end of the 1960s.[59]

And so these middle-class suburbanites would come to form the backbone of southern Republicanism. Contrary to the contemporary narrative of the Democratic left, this new GOP would begin to grow more than a decade prior to the passage of the Civil Rights Act and the Voting Rights Act. In fact, the growth was evident as early as 1952, when Dwight Eisenhower won 48 percent of the two-party vote in the South, based largely on big hauls in the major metropolitan centers of Dallas, Houston, Miami, and Tampa.[60] The rise of the GOP's electoral power in the South would continue for the next half century on the presidential level, and the Republicans would cut into the Democratic congressional majority in the South in fits and starts over the years, winning a majority of southern Senate seats in 1980 and a majority of House seats in 1994.[61]

All in all, it's fair to call this process a nationalization of southern politics, as the class-based divisions that had dominated in the North since the New Deal had finally come to Dixie. By the dawn of the twenty-first century, the pattern was basically the same, north and south. Conservatives and upper-income voters were more likely to support Republicans, while liberals and lower-income voters were not.[62]

To what extent did race relations play a role in this development? Listening to liberal commentators of today, you'd think that the Southern Strategy was a secret deal between Richard Nixon, Strom Thurmond, and John Tower to repeal the Voting Rights and Civil Rights acts, which of course the congressional Republicans had strongly supported.[63] If that were the case, Thurmond and Tower would have to go down as the all-time suckers of southern politics, as Nixon, Ronald Reagan, and George W. Bush all approved extensions (and, in the case of Reagan and Bush, *expansions*) of the Voting Rights Act. Still, as with everything else in the South, issues of race are inescapable in considering the southern Republicans.

In fact, the role of race in southern politics would come to resemble the dynamic in the North—one where the shift in the politics of "share-out" strengthened the GOP's hold over the new suburbs. According to historian Matthew Lassiter, the federal government's involvement in the regional development of Dixie was a major factor in this transformation. The availability of federally sponsored home loans, federally funded highway construction projects, and new industries backed by federal investments helped create the new middle-class suburbs. Meanwhile, thanks to the federal sponsorship of public housing, the central cities became home to large numbers of poor African Americans, who had been displaced from their farms in part because of New Deal agricultural subsidies. In response to this imbalance, as noted above, liberals in the mid-1960s began to emphasize new "share-out" programs for African Americans that required new burdens on the white middle and working classes. Suburban whites in the Sunbelt reacted negatively to this demand for resources, embracing a "color-blind" ethos that stressed individual merit and local control of problems and increasingly finding a voice for their grievances in the Republican party.[64]

This is why the importance of the Goldwater candidacy of 1964 in the rise of southern Republicanism is so often misunderstood. Goldwater, as we saw in Chapter 5, facilitated the transformation of the Republican party into a conservative coalition with an electoral base outside the Northeast. However, his southern appeal—based on opposition to the Civil Rights Act—was highly counterproductive. It gravely damaged his standing in the North, where he carried a smaller share of votes than any Republican nominee since Taft in 1912; what's more, it did not aid him substantially in Dixie, where he still ran behind Eisenhower (in 1956) and lost the region to LBJ.[65] And so the party's strategy in 1968 and beyond was to build a transregional coalition positioned between Wallace on the right and Humphrey on the left, working to maximize the party's vote haul in the growing metropolises of the New South. Thus, Republicans would continue to support the "Second Reconstruction" while opposing race-based measures of wealth redistribution, like busing and, in later decades, affirmative action.[66]

The combination of newly enfranchised African Americans and the drift of whites toward the GOP would have profound effects on the Democratic party. First, the ancient clientelistc relationship between the region and the national party was finished. Jimmy Carter would be the last Democrat to win a majority of the presidential vote in the old Confederacy, in 1976; congressional Democrats would continue to retain a majority position in the region for some time longer, based largely on the power of incumbency, familial ties to the party, and populist appeals, but without the need to suppress blacks' voting rights, the South was free to vote its conservative ideology, and that meant it would eventually become solidly Republican by 1994. Second, the Southern Democrats who survived this shift would be largely integrated into the liberal, northern wing of the party, owing in large part to the fact that many had large numbers of black, liberal constituents. This meant that the intraparty ideological schism that had characterized Democratic politics since 1937 would effectively be brought to an end, and future Democratic majorities in the government would invariably be very liberal ones, as we shall see in Chapters 11 and 12.

One of the most amazing, albeit subtle, trends in contemporary elections is how the descendants of Franklin Roosevelt's voters now generally support conservative Republicans like George W. Bush.[67] Indeed, the Democratic coalition is fundamentally different today from what it was in the 1930s, '40s, or '50s, which is why we have dedicated as much effort as we have to the policy and politics of the Great Society period, for it amounts to another great shift in the party's coalition.

This chapter has tried to account for this change, which was well under way by the end of the 1960s. Part of the explanation for this trend lies in LBJ's mismanagement of public affairs during his term. He was a master of the legislative process, but his approach to Vietnam, crime, urban problems, and racial tensions polarized the American electorate and led to his renunciation of the Democratic nomination in 1968. Ultimately, the country turned for leadership to Richard Nixon, the man they had rejected just eight years earlier. But even if LBJ had been more cautious and forthright in his approach to public problems, the new divide of the late 1960s was in certain respects inescapable. After all, it revolved around the redistribution of resources—not just tax dollars but also communities and schools—from the white working and middle classes to African Americans in the cities. There was only so much that even the most able politician could do to bridge this new gap.

As it turned out, LBJ failed miserably in holding the country together, and 1968 saw the splintering of his coalition over these hot-button issues. In the North, the Democratic decline worked largely to the benefit of George Wallace, whose support in the Industrial Midwest was surprisingly strong; in time, the white working class that was drawn to Wallace would eventually back the GOP. In the South, the politics of Jim Crow were replaced by a politics similar to that of the North, one that mixed class and race in a battle for scarce resources between white suburb and black city. The new middle class of the South had already been partial to the Republican party, and this new racialized divide only made it more so.

The result for the national Democratic party was one of stinging defeat. Humphrey would lose in 1968, and the party's nominee in 1972, George McGovern, would be defeated by the largest margin of any Democrat since 1924. Yet as we shall see in the next chapter, the defeat in 1972 would prompt root-and-branch reforms that, along with similar changes in the organization of Congress, would fundamentally alter the way the party did business in the future.

CHAPTER NINE

Too Much Hair and Not Enough Cigars

The New Politics and Party Reform

A cornerstone of American liberal philosophy is the concept of pluralism: in a democratic society such as ours, power is widely dispersed, no single entity dominates the process, and all individuals or groups have an opportunity to shape public policy.

This was a view that many liberal scholars began to expand upon in the 1950s and '60s. For instance, Louis Hartz's *The Liberal Tradition in America* argues that the political theory of John Locke was not so much an abstract philosophy for Americans but an accurate depiction of their world. Americans had settled a virgin continent, free of social structures like feudalism, owing obligation to no other man but rather to a government of limited powers designed to protect their liberty.[1] In *Who Governs?* political scientist Robert Dahl moves from theory to reality in his study of New Haven, Connecticut, where he finds a political system dominated by shifting coalitions, giving all participants an opportunity to influence the government.[2] In *Community Power and Political Theory*, Dahl's student Nelson Polsby offers a trenchant summary of the pluralist view, arguing that "[pluralists] see American society as fractured into a congeries of hundreds of small special interest groups, with incompletely overlapping memberships, widely different power bases, and a multitude of techniques for exercising influence on decisions salient to them."[3] Thus, no group dominates the body politic.

This view of the American polity was not limited to the ivory tower; it has long animated progressive/liberal political action. The process-oriented reforms of the early twentieth century—items like the ballot initiative, recall petitions, and the direct election of senators—were all designed to curb bossism and patronage and open the political process up to average people. Similarly, Teddy Roosevelt's Square Deal was about bringing all concerned parties to the bargaining table, so that each got what was coming to them. Pluralism was also a key component of the New Deal—programs like the AAA and the NIRA were designed to bring in a diverse array of actors to solve the economic crisis of the 1930s.

Yet despite the liberal commitment to open politics, the liberal party—which, after the 1930s, was without question the Democratic party—was still fairly closed. FDR managed some basic changes in the party structure: he destroyed the reviled Tammany Hall, ended the convention rule that nominees had to win two-thirds of all delegates (which had effectively granted the segregationist South a veto), and brought organized labor into the coalition. However, the power structure of the party at the start of the 1960s was still essentially the same as it had been fifty years prior: dominated by big-city bosses, segregationist southern Democrats, and party regulars. By and large, they decided who would win the party nomination at the quadrennial convention and—with the exception of rare liberal triumphs in the 1930s and 1960s—kept Congress from enacting the liberal agenda the party offered in the platform. On the nomination front, the early attempts of progressives to use primaries to select convention delegates turned out to be a dismal failure. In 1916—the high tide of progressivism—more than half of the delegates to the Democratic National Convention were selected in primaries. However, by 1960 that number had fallen to less than 40 percent. The party regulars were firmly in control of the nomination process, and JFK's use of the primaries that year was mostly to signal to the establishment that he was electable.[4]

The turmoil of the next decade would accomplish what generations of reformers could not: fundamental, pluralistic changes to the Democratic party structure. As a consequence, new groups would enter the coalition to take a share of power, and the balance within the party would be permanently altered. As we shall see, the result was an ironic one: the party would be more "open" in the pluralist sense, but now so dominated by clients that it became virtually impossible for it to govern for the public at large. In other words, opening up the party had the effect of narrowing its appeal.

Such pluralistic changes to the party would not arrive out of thin air. Instead, the party establishment was forced to mend its ways in the face of strong challenges from different factions within the "New Politics" left that emerged during the 1960s. That phrase is a commonly used one, so we'll need to specify exactly who threatened the party status quo during that tumultuous decade.

The first and most significant players to challenge the regulars were what political scientist James Q. Wilson has called the amateur Democrats:

> *For the most part, they are young, well-educated professional people, including a large number of women. In style of life, they are distinctly middle- and upper-middle class; in mood and outlook, they are products of the generation which came of age after the Second World War and particularly after the Korean conflict; in political beliefs, they are almost entirely among the liberals of the left. They bring to politics a concern for ideas and ideals.*[5]

Adlai Stevenson was the "patron saint" of these young liberals, who got involved in politics not because they wanted patronage, or even new social networks; they were there to change the world. And we should not be fooled by the adjective "amateur": these new liberals learned well how to play the game of politics early on. Even before the 1960s, they carved out a niche in the political system, thanks largely to the 1958 midterm elections. The recession of that year hardly damaged Dwight Eisenhower's standing with the country at large, but the Republicans lost forty-eight House seats. In the place of the vanquished Republicans arose a new, young class of liberals who were highly dissatisfied with the status quo in Congress and in response formed the liberal Democratic Study Group in 1959, which shall factor into our story later on.

These amateur Democrats represented a liberalism that was geared less toward the working class and instead focused more on civil rights—as many had been inspired by the struggle of southern blacks in the 1950s and '60s—as well as middle-class concerns. As political scientist Byron Shafer put it, these amateur Democrats concerned themselves with "the quality of life in general and with the state of the natural environment in particular, in the same way that their counterparts from the orthodox Democratic coalition had been concerned with economic welfare in general and with economic progress and growth in particular."[6] They also had views of organized labor that ranged from indifference to outright contempt of its leaders, who were increasingly viewed as part of the "bossism" problem in the party itself.[7]

These young liberals animated the 1968 Eugene McCarthy campaign—"Get Clean for Gene" was the slogan that encouraged young college students to shave their beards, cut their hair, and go door-to-door for the Minnesota senator.[8] They formed the backbone of Bobby Kennedy's campaign in 1968, which was tragically cut short by his assassination, as well as of George McGovern's 1972 quest for the nomination, which we shall discuss below. What's more, these new liberals also were the prime movers behind three interests that continue into the present day: the feminist, environmental, and consumer rights movements.

The modern feminist movement has its origin in Betty Friedan's *The Feminine Mystique.* First published in 1963, it argues that despite the material comfort of middle-class suburban women, there is a spiritual and personal emptiness that plagues them. Friedan rails against the way modern culture reinforces the idea that the woman's place is in the home, and she encourages "every woman . . . [to] create, out of her own needs and abilities, a new life plan, fitting in the love and children and home that have defined femininity in the past with the work toward a greater purpose that shapes the future."[9] Three years later, Friedan and a group made up mostly of middle-class white women founded the National Organization for Women (NOW). Originally a nonpartisan outfit, NOW was nevertheless an activist group often aligned with more radical New Politics factions for the purpose of promoting social and economic equality. Eventually, NOW would embrace the causes of abortion rights and lesbian rights, and move fully into the constellation of Democratic groups.

Just as the suffragette movement predated modern feminism, the environmentalist movement has roots that stretch back to the beginning of the twentieth century—to Teddy Roosevelt, Gifford Pinchot, and the U.S. Forest Service in 1905. Yet both movements began anew in the 1960s with the publication of wildly popular books. For the feminists, it was *The Feminine Mystique*. For the environmentalists, the book was *Silent Spring*, by Rachel Carson, which first appeared in 1962. Carson's emphasis was on the dangers of pesticides, and she helped shift the focus of environmentalists from conservation in general to the unique dangers of industrial pollution. New environmental groups like the Union of Concerned Scientists and the National Resources Defense Council sprang up in the 1960s, and older groups like the Audubon Society and the Sierra Club both enjoyed a nearly 1,000 percent increase in membership between 1960 and 1980. They all quickly gained political power thanks to the environmental laws passed during the Great Society period, as well as the creation of the Environmental Protection Agency, in 1970.[10]

The consumer rights movement is another powerful interest to emerge during this period, and it sprang up almost entirely because of the tireless efforts of one man—Ralph Nader. Much like *The Feminine Mystique* and *Silent Spring*, Nader's *Unsafe at Any Speed*—a scathing critique of the safety protocols of car manufacturers, published in 1965—garnered attention outside policy circles and transformed Nader into a bona fide political celebrity. Over the next two decades, Nader would create scores of watchdog groups that relentlessly lobbied Congres and the public for increased governmental regulations on consumer products. While his influence would wane after the election of Ronald Reagan, he will come to play an important role later in our story, in Chapter 11.

These three sets of interests were the ones from the New Politics left that eventually became enduring Democratic clients. Their privileged role in the party is not due to the fact that they had many voters behind them, as organized labor and African Americans do. Their numbers are in fact small, at least when viewed from the perspective of the whole electorate. Instead, their power is due to the development of highly sophisticated lobbying and campaign operations to push their agenda, and the employment of effective public relations strategies to rally public opinion. Northern Democrats in Congress have thus become highly dependent upon their support, and in turn are extremely responsive to their agendas.

It's worth noting that these groups are public spirited; for instance, a cleaner environment would not be a private benefit accruing only to members of the NRDC, but rather a public good that all could enjoy. This stands in contrast to some of the interests of other clients, e.g., the desire of organized labor for a repeal of Taft-Hartley, which would be a benefit accruing to labor alone. Regardless, these New Politics groups still have a clientelistic relationship with the Democratic party. The reason is that their policy preferences, while public spirited, are narrow in focus. In other words, a broadly liberal voter would weigh the interests of environmentalism against the need for economic growth, but a lobbyist for the NRDC makes no such calculation. His group is instead solely focused on its environmental agenda, without regard for the broader set of interests that public institutions must consider and balance, and it supports the party insofar as the party supports its agenda. We will see an excellent example of this in Chapter 12: the Pro-Choice Caucus in the House of Representatives threatened to vote en masse against health care reform in 2010 if the final bill included a pro-life provision. This kind of limited focus, which placed the greater political and policy goals of the party a distant second behind abortion rights, is the key to understanding why these groups are party clients, despite their public-spiritedness.

All of these groups eventually came to work within the existing political establishment, but the 1960s also saw the rise of genuinely radical groups that felt that the political system was fundamentally corrupt and that extra-systemic agitation was the only way to achieve progress. The forebears of these far-leftists had once been part of the Communist movement in America, which had all but disappeared after the rise of McCarthyism and the disclosure of Stalin's atrocities.[11] With the growth of the postwar middle class, a radical leftist critique of American pluralism reemerged on two distinct fronts.

There was the New Left, centered in the academy, particularly in student groups, which offer a stinging critique of the old pluralist outlook. To begin, scholars Peter Bachrach and Morton Baratz argue that Dahl and Polsby fail to account for how powerful elites control the political agenda, deciding what policies will and will not be considered before the multiplicity of groups get a chance to speak.[12] This kind of critique echoes through the works of academics like C. Wright Mills and Michael Harrington, who assert that power is fundamentally mal-distributed within the American system.[13] Additionally, radical power theorists like Steven Lukes and John Gaventa argue that the operations of the power elite are even subtler than what Bachrach and Baratz had theorized; the elites manipulate social structures to influence the thoughts and feelings of average people to ensure that the final political outcomes are always to their liking.[14] This radical notion is also articu-lated by neo-Marxist thinkers like Herbert Marcuse, who argue that the problem with the system of American capitalism is "cultural, aesthetic, and psychosexual," causing suffering that middle-class Americans were not even aware of.[15]

These theoretical critiques of pluralism quickly found student ad-vocates who were ready to act on them through extra-systemic means. Students for a Democratic Society (SDS) was founded in 1959, and while its famous mission statement, dubbed the "Port Huron State-ment," was mostly a rehash of post–New Deal liberalism, the burgeon-ing student movement was radicalized in relatively short order. The Berkeley Free Speech Movement culminated with a massive student revolt in the middle of the decade, and in 1968 student radicals seized buildings at Columbia University. The Vietnam War, which was mas-sively unpopular on the left and particularly in the student left, was the impetus for this radicalization, which was not limited merely to student groups. Civil rights groups like CORE and SNCC moved far to the left in the mid-1960s as they begin to push black power.[16]

The second front of radicalism to emerge during this period was the welfare rights movement, which often received the support of far-left thinkers and activists. In fact, this movement can in many respects be traced back to a controversial article in the *Nation* by radical Colum-bia sociologists Frances Fox Piven and Richard Cloward. Arguing that the economic resources in the country were unjustly distributed, Piven and Cloward suggested squeezing state and local Democratic officials by registering poor people en masse for welfare. This would strain state and local budgets, and in turn force national party leaders to address the needy with a massive new entitlement program.[17] Ultimately, such a strategy was never instituted on a grand scale, but a version of it was. George A. Wiley, a former official of CORE and longtime friend of Piven and Cloward, helped form the National Welfare Rights Organization (NWRO) in 1966. The goal of the NWRO was to function as a kind of interest-group lobby for the indigent; poor people would join a local chapter of the NWRO, paying a fee to support the group, which in turn would lobby on behalf of its constituents to secure special assistance grants from state and local welfare agencies.[18]

More broadly, radical advocates for the poor became adept at navigating the byzantine process of governmental bureaucracies to secure resources for the indigent while simultaneously putting pressure on state and local Democratic leaders. One crucial pathway was the Office of Economic Opportunity (OEO), a cornerstone of LBJ's War on Poverty. The empowering law called for the "maximum feasible participation of the residents of the areas and the members of the [Community Action Programs, or CAPs]" that were sponsored by the government. The OEO took this clause to mean that local people had to have a sizable say in the process. The result of this interpretation was totally unanticipated by policy makers, as many OEO-backed groups became radicalized and began to put pressure on establishment politicians.

For instance, the Mobilization for Youth movement in New York City was supposed to be the shining star of the War on Poverty, but instead it became an organizer of rent strikes.[19] In Syracuse, Crusade for Opportunity was taken over by black radicals who argued that "no ends are accomplished without the use of force."[20] In Milwaukee, the OEO-sponsored Inner City Development Project hosted classes on how to start up welfare rights organizations, and generally backed protests all throughout the Milwaukee area.[21] Meanwhile, the Organization for Organizations, another OEO-funded group in Milwaukee, sponsored trips to Chicago to meet with famous radical organizer Saul Alinsky, whose *Rules for Radicals* was a manual to educate organizers on "how to create mass organizations to seize power."[22]

LBJ, of course, had no interest in this kind of partisan fratricide, and he responded to complaints by party dons like Chicago mayor Richard J. Daley by tamping down the program.[23] As LBJ's director of the Bureau of the Budget, Charles Schultze, put it:

> [O]ne of the characteristics of the Johnson administration . . . [is that] on the one hand you might say he is the last New Dealer. . . . Food, education, social security. On civil rights, in terms of clearing away the legal obstacles, he was also sincere, clearly and deeply, although realistic.
>
> At the same time, however, you get into the much more complex problem of a redistribution of political power, and the relationship of the Negro in the ghetto to the established political machine, and the fact—right or wrong—that the black community and Mexican American community felt that the established mechanism channels wouldn't do it. They wanted extra political channels through community action programs, community organizations, picketing. . . . [T]his he found much more difficult to accept. He found it much more difficult to accept a broadened welfare program, particularly where it was broadened to cover those who might be doing something for themselves.
>
> A mayor Daley would come in and complain about the Community Action Program; and he was intuitively and basically on Mayor Daley's side, on [the] grounds—trying to express it his way, I guess—[that] "here's a good mayor who is trying to do something for his community. Why can't these people operate and gain power politically?" I think that explains part of his complex reaction: this combination of passionate conviction, on one hand, but a deep devotion to the existing political structure and order, on the other hand.[24]

LBJ was largely able to ease the political tension over the OEO in 1967, when Congress voted to give local governments the option of taking over the CAPs. However, as we shall see, this would be insufficient to stem the growing discontent that was brewing within the leftist quarters of the Democratic party. More and more factions in the country felt that the pluralists were dead wrong: the existing political process systematically excluded them from participating, and increasingly they would focus their ire on the Democratic party. This growing conflict between the old-guard New Dealers and the New Left would explode into violence during the party's 1968 Chicago convention, and the aftermath of that great conflict would forever transform the Democratic party.

If these groups were the fuel and the Vietnam War was the spark, then the Democratic convention in Chicago was the fire pit, the place where the old guard of the Democratic party finally clashed with the New Politics left.

The conflagration occurred both outside and inside the convention. On the streets of Chicago, radicals like the SDS and the Youth International Party (the "Yippies") got into an open conflict with the Chicago Police Department, which was run by Daley, a symbol of the party establishment.[25] Meanwhile, in the convention hall, the traditional power brokers closed ranks around the candidacy of Vice President Hubert Humphrey, who—despite not having won any primaries—won the nomination on the first ballot. Humphrey managed this feat because of his connections to the traditional party, particularly organized labor, which enabled him to line up convention supporters months before the meeting in Chicago. The Humphrey backers on the local level, in turn, were highly effective at strong-arming the McCarthy supporters, making sure that the latter's strength at the Chicago convention was much less than what he was pulling from the grassroots. And of course a big factor in Humphrey's easy win was the assassination of Robert Kennedy in June. Unlike McCarthy, RFK was prepared to make an aggressive push with the party regulars to win the nomination, and his death scattered his supporters across the Democratic spectrum.[26]

All told, the Chicago convention was an ugly spectacle. The police forces of the old guard used violence to shut down the protesters outside, while the political forces used strong-arm tactics to squash debate inside. The insurgents could not even get a peace plank written into the platform, as LBJ—intimately involved in the convention despite being in Washington, D.C.—squashed it.

Yet, as has been the case so often in our story of this peculiar political party, the seeds of major changes were sown in Chicago with nary a second thought—by the establishment itself. The grand pooh-bahs of the convention thought it necessary to toss the losers some kind of bone: they had lost the nomination; they had lost the fight for an antiwar plank; they had to get *something* in this pluralistic system, right? As it turned out, the establishment shortsightedly granted the insurgents the keys to the whole kingdom. The form this gift took was the adoption of a resolution calling for major changes in the delegate nomination process, specifically an end to the unit rule (wherein states had to vote as a bloc on the convention floor) and the opening up of the process to grassroots participants. The idea drew on the work of the Hughes Commission, an ad hoc study group led by Iowa governor Harold Hughes, which had cataloged all the unfair practices in delegate selections leading up to Chicago. The convention endorsed this idea without much debate, and in so doing set about a major reform initiative with virtually no consideration. As political scientist William Crotty put it:

> *At no point did the convention in any way actively debate or intensively review the major issues associated with commencing a reform initiative, the rationale for creating reform commissions, the reality of the need for reform commissions, the jurisdiction of reform commissions, or the obligations and potential consequences of the actions of reform commissions.*[27]

As with the National Labor Relations Act of 1935—a hastily considered piece of legislation passed overwhelmingly by friend and foe alike—the 1968 convention's endorsement of a reform initiative would set the stage for a kind of political revolution.

Much like the CIO in the 1930s, the New Politics left saw an incredible opportunity in this reform process, and it dominated the subsequent proceedings. Meanwhile, the old guard—most notably the AFL-CIO—declined the invitation to participate. And because there was no incumbent Democratic president, who surely would have influenced the process to ease his path to renomination in 1972, the New Politics crowd basically had a free hand to reform the system as it liked.

Leading the charge was Senator George McGovern of South Dakota, who was installed on the Commission on Party Structure and Delegate Selection (a.k.a. the McGovern-Fraser Commission). McGovern was a symbol for the New Politics left in many respects. Growing up in solidly Republican South Dakota, McGovern became a devotee of Adlai Stevenson when he heard a speech of his one day in the summer of 1952.[28] He also had earned a PhD in history, had been one of the leading doves in the United States Senate, and had received the support of many former RFK backers during the 1968 convention, where he finished third behind Humphrey and McCarthy.[29]

The belief of McGovern and his New Politics allies was that opening up the process to "the people" was not simply normatively superior; it would also guarantee the triumph of their worldview. Yet they did not want to take any unnecessary chances, so they pushed for the creation of participatory caucuses all across the nation, where political amateurs with New Politics sympathies could dominate the selection process. They didn't want primaries, which might be dominated by the "reactionary" forces of the old guard. As commission member Austin Ranney commented:

> [W]e did not want a national presidential primary or any great increase in the number of state primaries. Indeed, we hoped to prevent any such development by reforming the delegate-selection rules so that the party's nonprimary process would be open and fair, participation in them would greatly increase, and consequently the demand for more primaries would fade away.[30]

In other words, the hope of the reformers was not to destroy the basic party structure, but to shift the balance of power within that structure from the regulars to the New Politics movement. And so the reformers banned the closed party caucus, sanctioned participatory conventions, mandated that women and minorities should be included in the process "in reasonable relationship to their presence in the population of the state," eliminated the unit rule, outlawed participation fees, and even banned ex officio delegates (i.e., party officials like senators and congressmen, who had previously enjoyed automatic delegate status).[31]

In some ways, the reformers were successful. The process was opened up, the power of the bosses and party regulars was greatly diminished, and a broader base of Democrats could now participate in the selection of the party nominee. (The Republicans would follow suit over the course of the 1970s.) What's more, the reformers nationalized the nomination process—the state parties, and even the state legislatures, had to recognize the supremacy of the Democratic National Committee in setting the rules for delegate selection.[32]

However, rather than strengthen the party as an organization, the reforms utterly decimated it. Despite the intentions of Ranney and the rest of the liberals on the reform commission, party primaries soon became the way of the nominating world. By 1980, 71 percent of Democratic delegates would be selected by party primaries.

Why did this happen? As is so often the case with such sweeping reforms, their architects failed to consider how strategic actors would respond to their well-intentioned changes to the rules. As it turned out, the regulars figured out that primaries would solve a number of problems the new rules created for them. First, they had been confused by the complex nature of the changes that had been demanded, yet they knew that candidate primaries were acceptable according to the new rules, and delegates selected from a primary could thus survive a challenge at the convention. Second, primaries had the advantage of diminishing the influence of ideological zealots. The New Politics left fashioned itself a majority of the party, but that was quite far from reality, as party regulars all across the country knew. Opening the party up to a wide array of Democrats—as would happen in primaries, which have much higher turnout than caucuses—would dilute the power of the purists. Third, primaries protected normal party business from interference from the New Politics groups. The regulars were concerned that caucuses would draw ideological true believers into the more mundane operations of the party, so segregating the presidential nominating process from regular business would protect the party organization from being overrun.

And so we can thank George McGovern and his Commission on Party Structure and Delegate Selection for the mess that is the modern nomination process. The rise of candidate primaries has led to the permanent presidential campaign, in which would-be presidents have to campaign around the country for two years or even more, raising money to compete not just in the general election but now in the dozens of primary battles that mostly occur more than six months prior. That kind of full-scale operation helped create the cottage industry of the campaign professional: the pollster, the media consultant, the television adman, the direct mail specialist, and so on.[33]

The new system would also have a profound effect on the balance of power within the Democratic party, for the reforms bolstered the standing of interest groups, including those on the New Politics left. The reason had to do with the changing strategy of contenders for the nomination. In the old system, their goal was to unite a majority (and, before 1936, a supermajority) of delegates behind their candidacies. In the new system, their goal is something similar to the slogan of the television show *Survivor*: "Outwit, Outplay, Outlast." They don't have to forge broad majorities of diverse party delegates; they simply need to win more primary voters than all their competitors. That means, in turn, an emphasis on mobilizing the groups thought to be most amenable to a candidate's message or background.

Of particular interest to such candidates are the factions with deep pockets and relatively broad bases of support—like the teachers' unions, the trial lawyers, the environmental left, feminist groups, and so on. These groups can provide the money, and in many cases the boots on the ground, to help their favored candidates win victory. And so the reforms ensured the New Politics interest groups a seat at the table, though they did not come to dominate, as many of the reformers had originally hoped. African Americans and other minority groups also gained power because of the reforms, which required that delegates reflect the racial and ethnic diversity of the country.[34]

The losers in all this were the traditional bases of party power—in particular the machine bosses like Mayor Daley (whose delegates were actually turned away at the 1972 Democratic National Convention), the conservative South, and the traditional unions in the AFL-CIO.[35] For decades, they had controlled the nomination process in ways that were similar to what we saw in 1944, when they came together around the choice of Truman for vice president, and in 1960, when they balanced the ticket between JFK and LBJ. Those days were now long gone.[36] Of course, these older groups were not pushed out of the process, though that was basically the case in 1972 (as we shall discuss below). Subsequent reforms in the early 1980s returned to the old guard a portion of the power they had lost, but in the end they would be forced to share power with the new groups.[37]

The biggest winners under the new rules were the presidential candidates. With so many different groups now participating in the nomination process, and the threshold for victory a mere plurality of the vote, candidates became relatively free to build coalitions that contain only a subset of the total party. This means that winning coalitions can and do vary from cycle to cycle. For instance, Jimmy Carter and Bill Clinton won the party nomination thanks to strong hauls from the South, where they enjoyed the support of African Americans and working-class whites. On the other hand, Michael Dukakis won in 1988 in large measure because the southern vote split along racial lines, with African Americans going to Jesse Jackson and whites going to Gore. Walter Mondale won in 1984 owing to organized labor's backing, but in 1992 labor's preferred candidate, Tom Harkin of Iowa, turned out to be a dud.

The new nomination rules can thus produce general election candidates who owe the party's major clients virtually nothing, and who often have very little background in catering to their interests. Meanwhile, as we shall see later in this chapter, the power of the party's clients has only grown in Congress, so that there is the potential for interbranch, intraparty conflict: on the one hand, a chief executive with relatively little sympathy for the party clients; on the other, a congressional caucus that is deeply in hock to them. As discussed in Chapters 11 and 12, this would be the experience of both Carter and Clinton.

The nomination battle in 1972 was the first under the new rules, and it was an unmitigated disaster for the Democratic party. South Dakota senator George McGovern, a staunch liberal who vehemently opposed the Vietnam War, won primarily by mobilizing the various groups of the New Politics left—the National Welfare Rights Organization, feminist groups, and environmentalists—all of whom were attracted to his strong antiwar position and his promises to slash the defense budget and greatly expand social welfare. In winning the nomination, McGovern bested Maine senator Edmund Muskie, who largely received the support of the party establishment, as well as former vice president Hubert Humphrey, who was bankrolled by organized labor. Amazingly, McGovern captured the nomination despite the fact that he won an outright majority in just two contested states, Massachusetts and Oregon. For the South Dakota senator, the path to nomination relied on winning pluralities in the primaries and caucuses based on support from a die-hard group of New Politics loyalists, whom journalist Theodore White described in these terms:

> As the Democratic primaries . . . in the early spring of 1972 moved on from Florida to Wisconsin, the Democratic regulars discovered a . . . guerrilla presence too late. No other metaphor but that of a guerrilla army on the move can describe the upheaval that was to shake and change the entire Democratic Party in the next ten weeks, for the march of George McGovern in those ten weeks would go down as a classic in American political history.[38]

Unfortunately for the Democrats, these groups were not nearly the political force they thought they were. In fact, they were far to the left of the mainstream American voter—as was reflected in the ultra-liberalism of their candidate as well as the 1972 Democratic platform, one of the most radical documents ever produced by a major political party. What's more, their ideal of "participatory democracy" made the 1972 convention in Miami Beach a ridiculous spectacle, as time had to be granted to every group to have its say on this or that particular item. In the end, McGovern wasn't able to give his nomination address until three o'clock in the morning, when the television audience was a small fraction of what it had been for the prime-time show.[39] As one labor representative succinctly summarized the whole carnival: "There is too much hair and not enough cigars at this convention."[40]

In the general election, McGovern suffered the greatest loss of any Democrat since 1924. He carried less than 38 percent of the vote and won only Massachusetts and the District of Columbia. According to the exit polls, he held fewer than one in three white voters and barely two in five Catholic voters; this meant that he failed to carry the white working class, which for forty years had been the backbone of the Democratic coalition.

The McGovern debacle of 1972 demonstrated to all who cared to see that if these New Politics groups in the Democratic party were allowed to dominate the process, the result would be a permanent Republican majority. The New Politics liberals were simply too far outside the mainstream and unable to appeal to the traditional working-class base of the old Roosevelt coalition. As we shall see moving forward, after 1972 the goal of national party leaders would be to balance the demands of this New Left with the need to hold the political center, which the party had until this point essentially dominated. This task would be easier said than done.

The changes in the presidential nominating system between 1968 and 1972 were the most sweeping and consequential reforms since the Democrats and the Whigs had destroyed the legislative caucus system some 140 years prior. Yet this would not be the end of the reformist spirit of the period. Big changes were coming to the United States Congress, and they would forever shift the balance of power.

Since 1910, when progressive Republicans joined with Democrats in a revolt against Joe Cannon, the dictatorial Speaker of the House, political power in the House of Representatives had been broadly distributed across the committees, especially to the chairmen, who had in the following years carved out their own personal fiefdoms where they were free to operate as they pleased. Because seniority was the method by which chairmen were selected, and southern Democrats came from the safest seats in the country, the South dominated the most powerful positions in the congressional party. We saw in Chapter 3, for instance, that these southerners were a major reason why FDR chose not to throw his weight behind the Wagner-Costigan Anti-Lynching bill: Roosevelt was afraid that the southern chairmen would retaliate by blocking the New Deal. Eventually, southern Democrats did come to oppose FDR's reform initiatives, starting with the Fair Labor Standards Act, and from 1938 onward southern Democrats used their prime positions to join with Republicans in a "conservative coalition" that blocked liberal reforms. The only time after FDR that the left was really able to push through its agenda was following the 1964 election, when a wave of northern, liberal Democrats swept into Congress.

The 1964 surge aside, this stultification left the northern liberals unhappy. Their feeling was that the Democratic party was the majority, and they represented the dominant sentiment in the party, so they should have the power to enact their agenda; instead, they were the junior partners in a coalition dominated by conservatives.[41] This was soon to change, as the liberals' presence in Congress was growing, in a "two steps forward, one step back" fashion. Two big "wave" elections, in 1958 and 1964, brought in scores of northern liberals, many of whom lost their seats in subsequent elections. But not all of them lost, and those who survived joined a growing faction of young, restless liberals in Congress who were unhappy with the way the institution was functioning.

They would finally have their moment in the 1970s, after a series of events tipped the balance of power toward the reformers. The first sign of change was the retirement of House Speaker John McCormack, who had come into the House all the way back in 1928. With this guardian of the old regime now gone, there seemed to be an opening for reform, one that widened considerably after a number of scandals came to light. Several members of Congress went to jail for taking bribes in the early years of the decade, and Wilbur Mills—the legendary chairman of the House Ways and Means Committee, who was the decisive congressional actor in getting Medicare enacted—was impelled to resign in disgrace for publicly cavorting with a stripper.[42] The coup de grâce for the old regime came with the resignations of both Richard Nixon and Vice President Spiro Agnew. Nixon's fall from grace, combined with the bad recession of 1974–75, brought into Congress the third northern, liberal wave in just sixteen years. In the Ninety-fourth Congress of 1975–76, there were a total of 181 Democrats from the North and the West, more than at any time since 1936, and the liberals finally had the numbers to shake things up.

Their reforms would take three shapes. First, they decreased the power of committee chairs by giving the Democratic caucus a vote (by secret ballot) on each chairman; related to this, they also empowered subcommittee chairs by guaranteeing them their own staffers and clearly specified jurisdictions. Second, they increased the power of the party leadership, which up to that point could do little more than apply moral suasion to win over the committee barons.[43] After the reforms, the Speaker had the power to appoint the majority members of the all-important House Rules Committee; he also gained the power to send bills to multiple committees, and thus to bypass truculent committee chairmen. Additionally, the "whip system" was greatly expanded, giving the Speaker more lieutenants in the battle to round up supporters for major roll calls. Third, the reforms made all the leaders of the party—be it the Speaker or committee chairmen—answerable to the caucus itself. The House Democratic Steering and Policy Committee—which functioned like an executive council for the whole caucus—gained the power to make committee assignments, which had previously been left up to the Ways and Means Committee. What's more, the caucus was empowered to vote by secret ballot on the subcommittee chairmen of the Appropriations Committee, to ratify the Speaker's selection for the Rules Committee, and to make alternative nominations to the Appropriations, Budget, and Ways and Means committees.[44]

The sum total of these reforms effectively centralized power in the House Democratic caucus. Previously, seniority meant that southern Democrats were basically free to do what they wanted, but after the reforms, the caucus took control of the House power centers. The winners in this shift were the northern and western Democrats, who, after 1958, had amounted to a majority of the Democratic caucus. The losers were the southern conservatives, who were forced to move to the left in order to retain the leadership positions. The net effect was to increase dramatically the ideological homogeneity of the House Democrats: in 1965, for instance, southern Democrats voted with the rest of the party just 55 percent of the time; by 1985, that number had risen to 76 percent.[45]

The reform era that followed the 1968 election produced one final, lasting change in the way politics functions, even to this day; the Federal Election Campaign Act (FECA) of 1971, and its amendments in 1974, still govern the way political campaigns for national office are run. The FECA has its roots in a problem that organized labor faced after the passage of Taft-Hartley, which outlawed political contributions directly from labor unions. Organized labor had gotten around this restriction by creating the Committee on Political Education (COPE), which accepted voluntary contributions from union members and gave them to candidates. However, a federal court in 1968 ruled that COPE was illegal, and it sentenced union officials to jail time. Hoping to avoid a showdown in the Supreme Court, the AFL-CIO persuaded its congressional allies to include in the FECA a provision to make political action committees (PACs) like COPE legal. Of course, in doing that, the FECA also showed businesses an easy way around the Tillman Act of 1907, which had outlawed corporate contributions.[46] In 1974, in the wake of the Watergate scandal, Congress amended the FECA to place fairly strict restrictions on campaign contributions; PACs and individuals could give just $5,000 to any given candidate per election and faced caps on total contributions in any given political cycle.

This would combine with changes in the media environment to create a new type of political campaign. Since the Eisenhower victory in 1952, television advertising and mass media had become an increasingly important factor in the campaign for federal office—not just for the presidency but for the Senate and even the House. Television ads cost lots of money to produce and air, which meant that loads of campaign dollars were needed to hire admen and buy space and time in the media. Plus, as congressional districts grew in size, it became harder for members of Congress to keep tabs on their constituents, and this difficulty created a need for public opinion pollsters, image consultants, and so on. In other words, Congress put strict limitations on how campaigns could be funded just as the cost of running a campaign was skyrocketing.

This opened the door for those New Politics interest groups discussed above. Candidates had to go searching high and low for campaign dollars from multiple sources. It was no longer sufficient to lean on a handful of wealthy contributors or COPE, so environmental, feminist, and consumer advocacy groups suddenly had a tremendous opportunity to fund Democratic candidates, as did business and pro-

fessional groups. All told, the number of PACs whose purpose was to
fund the campaigns of like-minded candidates increased greatly in the
years following the FECA—from about 1,700 in 1978 to 4,200 in 2004.
And PAC support never comes cheap; a PAC usually supports incumbent members of Congress situated in key committees to get them to
focus committee attention on proposals that help it, and table those that
harm it.[47]

Nobody has been better than the New Politics left at using PACs
and sophisticated lobbying operations to set the congressional agenda.
Political scientist Jeffrey Berry has found that, even though they make
up a relatively small share of the total lobbying industry in Washington,
they have had tremendous influence in getting Congress to focus on
their issues. In 1964, for instance, 64 percent of the congressional agenda
focused on material issues like wages and work standards, which were
of top concern to organized labor; in 1991 it was the "post-material"
concerns of environmentalists, feminists, and consumer groups that
dominated the scene, accounting for 71 percent of the congressional
agenda that year.[48] These New Politics groups became so effective not
simply by giving money to the right members of this or that committee;
they also created a full-fledged program to "educate" members about
how they should vote. Members of Congress loathe uncertainty; they
want to know the effect a policy proposal will have on the economy and
society, and above all they want to know how it will affect their chances
for reelection.[49] Lobbying groups from the New Politics left have a keen
understanding of these needs, and they have become extremely effective
at supplying members with policy and political information that cuts
down on this uncertainty, and of course helps them get the legislation
they want.[50]

Once again, the losers in this were the old groups of the Democratic
party—especially the old craft and industrial unions, whose interests
now figure less prominently in the congressional agenda. One of the
most limited resources of any Congress is its time. It's in session for only
a portion of the year, and the New Politics' domination of that portion
has left the party's traditional partners with less time to press their demands.[51]

All told, the reforms in Congress—not just in the House leadership structure but also in campaign finance and lobbying—reinforced the reforms of the party nomination process. They all facilitated the New Politics' left's rise from marginal or radical groups to a place of prominence in the political realm, an ascent that has often come at the expense of the traditional power brokers of the party. Conservative southern Democrats, industrial labor Democrats, and big-city machine Democrats all saw their positions diminished as these new Democrats came into their own.

The result of these reforms of the nomination process, campaigns, and Congress was that the Democratic party—which since its beginning in the 1820s had had a working-class ethos, be it agricultural or industrial—became substantially more attuned to the middle class. For generations, it was the Whig/Republican coalition that had dominated this group, but after the cultural and political upheavals of the 1960s, middle-class voters would have two parties from which to choose. The Republicans, as they long had been, remained the party of business-centered economic growth, the "full dinner pail," as Republican president William McKinley called it. But by the end of the 1960s, the Democratic party's image as the party of the farmer or workingman began to fade, and instead it would come more and more to represent the values and priorities of these middle-class leftists who had fallen in love with Adlai Stevenson, shaved their beards for Gene McCarthy, and fought like hell for George McGovern. None of these leaders ever became president of the United States, but in time their followers would take a seat in the Democratic party, forever altering its basic character.

It's appropriate here to pause and reflect on the big picture. In the preceding five chapters, we have seen the modernization of organized labor, the rise of the African American vote, the demise of the Solid South, the growth of government unions, and now the emergence of the New Politics left. Taken together, the 1960s would perhaps be the most transformative period in the history of the Democratic party, arguably more so even than the 1930s, when FDR enacted the New Deal. What does all of this mean in the broader historical context?

James Madison's insights in "Federalist" Number 10 remain as true in our day as they were in his—American politics is dominated by *factions*. Sometimes these factions are highly organized interests, like the AFL-CIO. Sometimes they are disorganized, like those who oppose federal funding of fetal stem cell research. Sometimes they're geographical in nature, as people who live near each other tend to have the same outlook on life and thus the same preferences for government policy, and so on. The great task of republican government is, as Madison noted, translating the selfish interests of these factions into policies that are in the public interest.

Because political conflict invariably finds expression through the two major parties, it is the job of the Democratic and Republican parties to accomplish this essential task of republicanism. This means in practice that parties have to be responsive to their loyal factions without forsaking the national interest; it's one thing for party supporters to enjoy a few fringe benefits, quite another for them to dominate a party so thoroughly that it ignores the public good. This has long been a tricky balancing act; and as we saw in Chapter 1, during the Gilded Age the parties were miserable failures at it, existing only to scrape out narrow victories so they could distribute the spoils of victory to their voters, who were loyal because of ancient prejudices rather than because of support for any forward-looking vision of a better society.

Beginning with Franklin Roosevelt, the Democratic party adopted a new approach to this challenge. To hold its base groups and simultaneously secure the public good, the party would use the vast regulatory and redistributive powers of the federal government. For decades, this method brought the Democrats great political success; while it was regularly unable to continue FDR's progressive program after 1938, the party nevertheless controlled Congress from 1932 through 1968 for all but four years, and the presidency for all but eight. The Great Society of Lyndon Johnson can be seen as the culmination of the Rooseveltian project.

The factions that came to depend on the largesse of Democratic-run governments became clients of the national party, much as the Irish in New York City were clients of their patrons in Tammany Hall. They would vote for the party in every election, and the party in turn would see to it that their interests were well represented in Washington. In many instances these factions were committed to the grand ideological project of the progressive wing of the party, but they also had narrower priorities to which the party was obliged to respond, as payment for their electoral support.

In time, these groups would overwhelm the party. As we shall see, it would become nearly impossible for party leaders to keep this diverse group of clients happy while simultaneously governing in the public interest. After the 1960s, there were just too many mouths to feed. The environmentalists want something. So do the feminists. So do the consumer advocates. So do the miscellaneous well-heeled groups in the New Politics left. So do industrial and craft labor unions. So do government labor unions. So do African Americans.

After you satisfy all of these groups, how can you advance the public interest? Where will you find the time in the relatively short legislative sessions? After all that effort to appease your clients, how do you muster the political capital to do anything else? Considering how far the interests of some of these groups are from those of middle-of-the-road voters, it's all but inevitable that at least one group will demand an item that comes at the expense of almost everybody else. What do you do then? What do you do when the country genuinely wants a break from liberal reforms, but your clients demand that these reforms continue unabated? What do you do when the country requires reform of the government, but your clients depend on the programs in question? What do you do when the middle class has had enough income redistribution, but your clients need more dollars transferred from taxpayers to them?

As we shall see, these questions really have no good answers, and the Democratic leaders who followed LBJ—Carter, Clinton, and Barack Obama—would all struggle with the inherent tension in the post-FDR mission of the Democratic party, for Roosevelt's old balancing act is no longer possible.

CHAPTER TEN

Hard Choices and Scarce Resources

Jimmy Carter and the Rebellion of the Clients

———————

Writing at the end of the Great Society period, political scientist Theodore Lowi observed the emergence of "interest-group liberalism":

> *It may be called liberalism because it expects to use govern-*
> *ment in a positive and expansive role, it is motivated by the high-*
> *est sentiments, and it possesses strong faith that what is good for*
> *government is good for the society. It is "interest-group liberalism"*
> *because it sees as both necessary and good that the policy agenda*
> *and the public interest be defined in terms of the organized interests*
> *in society. . . . The most important difference between liberals and*
> *conservatives, Republicans and Democrats—however they define*
> *themselves—is to be found in the interest groups they identify*
> *with.*[1]

Over the past nine chapters, we have told the story of how the Democratic party created, then nurtured such groups. The first such client was the southern segregationist wing of the party, which depended upon the national Democrats to protect it from Republican incursions into the region's illiberal way of life; this wing would all but disappear by the late 1970s, but as we have seen, many others appeared. In the 1930s, Franklin Roosevelt transformed urban politics and expanded the ranks of organized labor, bringing both labor leaders and rank-and-file workers into the party as dependents that rely upon it to maintain their legal status as well as to elevate living conditions through government intervention. In the 1960s, John F. Kennedy and Lyndon Johnson brought in new clients—namely, public sector labor unions and African Americans. These groups now depend upon the Democratic party for their own reasons—public sector labor demands an increased socialization of the national wealth, and African Americans request more social welfare provisions. Finally, the social changes of the 1960s generated organized interests on the American left—most notably the feminist, environmental, and consumer movements. While relatively small in number, these well-heeled interests, as we have seen, have become extremely skilled in pushing their legislative agenda through Democratic-controlled Congresses.

Lowi's "interest-group liberalism," when defined in terms of the Democratic party, suggests a political coalition that uses the powers of the government to protect and expand the interests of these varied clients, whose only overlapping interest is, to borrow a concept from Samuel Gompers, *more*. They require more social welfare benefits, more taxes taken from other groups, more regulation, and more government involvement in previously private spheres of activity.

The challenge for Democratic presidents following LBJ would thus be monumental. Since John Adams, American presidents have played a dual role: as leaders of their political party as well as of the nation. That has long meant tending to both the interests of the party clients (be they Republican or Democratic) *and* the national interest. Always a delicate balancing act, the management of party and nation became practically impossible for Democratic leaders following Lyndon Johnson, who was himself a victim of intraparty dissension in 1968. The demands of the Democratic party's clients have become too varied and too burdensome for a president to satisfy them while at the same time promoting the national good. And so, as we shall see, Presidents Jimmy Carter, Bill Clinton, and Barack Obama have all been failures in one way or another, for they have been unable to juggle both their party clients and the public interest at the same time.

Carter's failure was the first and, to date, most spectacular. He approached the presidency with a kind of studied aloofness, placing himself above the petty politics of client management, yet ironically it would be his own party's clients that would undermine his administration. Carter faced the impossible task of tending to the national interest, which required fiscal retrenchment to control inflation, and satisfying his party's clients, who demanded an ever-expanding array of government benefits. His efforts to balance these contradictory demands were totally unsuccessful, and he failed miserably in both duties.

Jimmy Carter—a single-term governor from the state of Georgia—made for an unlikely presidential nominee in 1976, and the origins of his peculiar rise from obscurity can be traced to the failures of the Nixon presidency. Richard Nixon had entered office in January 1969 intent upon shaping a new Republican majority out of the broken pieces of the New Deal coalition, and he pursued that goal from four often contradictory directions: ending the war in Vietnam, cracking down on crime, giving symbolic recognition to the South, and consolidating the liberal gains of the Great Society period.

Nixon's civil rights record best exemplifies the ideological incoherence of this strategy. During his tenure, the integration of public schools continued apace, but Nixon took pains to deflect political credit for this achievement, moving the enforcement of integration out of the Department of Health, Education and Welfare and into the Department of Justice. Thus, Nixon could move integration along while claiming that he was merely doing the bidding of the Supreme Court. Similarly, Nixon offered an expansive new welfare entitlement (the "Family Assistance Plan"), pushed for affirmative action in the construction industry, and created the Office of Minority Business Enterprise while simultaneously nominating conservative, southern judges to the Supreme Court and publicly opposing busing.[2]

In the end, the strategy failed to create a new Republican majority in the nation. While Nixon won an overwhelming victory over George McGovern in 1972, Republicans picked up just twelve House seats, leaving the party far short of a majority.[3] Less than two years later, Nixon would resign in disgrace because of his role in the cover-up of the Watergate burglary, making Gerald Ford the thirty-eighth president of the United States. Ford—a Republican insider who had served as House minority leader prior to his elevation to the vice presidency—had to contend with an economic slowdown in 1974–75 as well as a resurgent Democratic party. Running on recession and Watergate, the Democrats picked up forty-eight seats in the House in the 1974 midterms. The new freshman class of Democrats—dubbed the "Watergate Babies"— gave President Ford a headache as he tried to hold the line on spending during his brief tenure. During his term, Ford vetoed sixty-six bills, the most frequent use of the veto pen since Harry Truman, rejecting Democratic efforts to increase farm price supports, housing subsidies, public sector jobs, and more.[4]

At no point during any of these events—Nixon's smashing re-election in 1972, his disgraced exit in 1974, and Ford's battle with the Ninety-fourth Congress—was any serious political observer predicting that Carter would be the next president of the United States. Yet that was exactly what Carter and his people were planning, and as early as November 1972 his wunderkind political adviser, Hamilton Jordan, outlined a strategy by which Carter could snatch his party's nomination and then the presidency. Jordan argued to Carter that "[p]erhaps the strongest feeling in this country today is the general distrust and disillusionment of government and politicians at all levels."[5] With the Watergate imbroglio, the "desire and thirst for strong moral leadership" would only increase, and that would be Carter's entry point into the national political discourse.

Carter would offer himself as such a reform candidate, promising not another New Deal or New Frontier, but moral revival. As Iowa State Democratic chairman Tom Whitney put it: "[Carter] said there was a real need in America for a candidate who would respond to the kind of doubts people have not only about government but about themselves and where they were going. The quality that was most important [according to Carter] was believability—not in terms of a single issue but in terms of human life."[6] Thus, Carter would run what political scientist Stephen Skowronek has called an "autobiographical campaign," emphasizing how he himself was a good, moral person who would never lie to the people.[7]

Though he was a governor from the Deep South, from which no president had ever been elected, Carter had carved out for himself a reputation as a leader of the "New South." In May 1971, *Time* magazine featured a story on the New South, with Carter on the cover, and it opened with a stirring line from his inaugural address as governor of Georgia: "I say to you quite frankly that the time for racial discrimination is over. Our people have already made this major and difficult decision. No poor, rural, weak or black person should ever have to bear the additional burden of being deprived of the opportunity of an education, a job or simple justice."[8] This made for another core element of the Carter campaign pitch: he would be the representative of a reformed, socially progressive southern Democratic party, one that stood in contrast to the segregationist wing led by George Wallace, who would again run for president (his fourth attempt) in 1976.

Longtime observers of Georgia politics surely noted the irony of Carter's reinvention as the paragon of the New South. After all, in his 1970 campaign for the governor's mansion, Carter positioned himself as the Wallace sympathizer in the race. He criticized his main opponent, former governor Carl Sanders, a racial moderate, for having refused to allow Wallace to speak in Georgia, and Carter promised to invite him to speak in the state.[9] Carter was advantaged by an attack on Sanders that featured a picture of the former governor with an African American basketball player from the Atlanta Hawks (of which Sanders was a co-owner) pouring champagne on him. Carter's people denied any involvement with the racist smear campaign, but some sources did link it to the Carter team.[10] In the runoff against Sanders, Carter won just 7 percent of the African American vote;[11] nevertheless, as governor he earned a reputation as a racial moderate, hiring a record number of African Americans for state government jobs as well as hanging a picture of Martin Luther King Jr. in the Georgia statehouse.[12] He also became known as a reformer, instituting "zero-based budgeting" as a way to get the state's finances in order. Yet his moralistic approach to governance—wherein simple political matters often became pitched battles of good versus evil (with himself, naturally, on the side of the good)—turned off many Georgia politicos, and in fact one aide suggested that if Carter were eligible to run for reelection in 1974, he would have lost.[13]

Regardless, Carter was term-limited in the Peach State, and he committed to a presidential run, carefully positioning himself as one of the only centrists in a field dominated by liberals like Morris Udall and

Sargent Shriver.[14] The other candidates expected a "brokered" convention in which no clear winner emerged from the long stretch of primaries and caucuses; the Carter team, on the other hand, correctly sensed that a candidate could win the nomination outright, and they crafted an ingenious strategy built on this assumption.[15] The plan was to compete everywhere, win early contests to gain name recognition, defeat Wallace in the South, and win as many delegates as possible in the northern states.[16]

His campaign coffers through 1975 were mostly empty, and Carter was outspent by both Henry "Scoop" Jackson and Wallace. Even so, a smart grassroots campaign operation combined with Carter's personal magnetism in small-group meetings, not to mention his indefatigable energy, led to a major coup in January 1976, when he finished in front of all other candidates in the Iowa caucuses.[17] He followed that up with a win in the New Hampshire primary on February 24 and the Vermont primary on March 2. A week later, he won a fifty-thousand-vote victory over Wallace in the Florida primary, effectively ending the Alabama demagogue's dream of forging a national coalition of angry, disaffected whites. Carter then dominated the spring primaries, winning Illinois, North Carolina, Wisconsin, Pennsylvania, Indiana, Michigan, and New Jersey. By the time of the Ohio primary on June 8, he had the nomination sewn up.

Carter managed such an amazing feat because the liberal vote was split in multiple ways, enabling him to carry the nomination based upon middle-of-the-road Democrats. In the more liberal states, Carter outflanked Udall by winning the moderate and conservative vote, and in the more conservative southern states, he placed himself to the left of George Wallace. In a divided field, this was sufficient to sweep him to victory.[18] Also of help to Carter was his strong support among African Americans. Though he had campaigned as a kind of Wallaceite in 1970, his performance in office had convinced high-profile African Americans like Andrew Young and Martin Luther King Sr. to get behind his candidacy.[19] The decisive factor in the nomination of Carter, however, was momentum, the strange phenomenon in American primary battles whereby doing well in yesterday's contest improves a candidate's standing in today's battle. Every week in the spring of 1976, the major news networks featured at least one story about Carter winning a primary battle somewhere, and no amount of campaign money can buy that kind of positive attention.

In the end, Carter's victory, while surprising and impressive, did not come because the party was united behind him. In fact, Carter won just 39 percent of all the primary votes during that period,[20] and according to political scientist Larry Bartels, he would have lost "almost every one of his crucial primary victories" if all of the contests had been held on the same day.[21] What's more, the party's major interest groups, like organized labor, had been somewhat cool to Carter, fully getting behind his candidacy only after he won the Ohio primary in June.[22] One reason for labor's hesitancy was the nature of the Carter campaign, which often left no clear idea of where the candidate stood on the issues. At times, this obfuscation earned Carter bad press. For instance, writing in *Harper's,* Steven Brill criticized Carter's flip-flops, which he said "span the range of basic national issues and correspond with the constituency he seeks."[23]

As suggested in Chapter 9, Carter's victory was a consequence of the new primary system, in particular how it enabled a savvy candidate like Carter to seize the nomination without the backing of most of the party's clients. Under the old system, he would never have captured the nomination, since his appeal was largely regional, his political outlook placed him squarely to the right of the liberal wing of the party, and he had virtually no ties to organized labor. But the new rules favored the candidate with ingenious campaign strategies and an engaging persona, which were precisely what Carter possessed.

Of course, Carter systematically moved to the left after the primaries because he needed the help of the party's liberal interests for the general election. So, for instance, he endorsed a plan of the United Auto Workers for national health insurance in April to alleviate labor's concerns.[24] He also secured the endorsement of the National Education Association (NEA), whose grassroots members had been initial backers of Carter, after he endorsed the idea of a Department of Education.[25] Organized labor tossed in fully for Carter in the general election, contributing upwards of $11 million that year, or about half of what the Carter campaign spent.[26] It really had no choice, as Ford, who had

vetoed a pro-labor common-site picketing bill, was persona non grata to
union leaders.

At the start of the general election campaign, Carter had a twenty-
point lead over Ford, but that gap closed to a dead heat by November.[27]
On Election Day, Carter won a narrow, two-point victory over Ford
that depended heavily upon a near sweep of Dixie. Ford actually outpolled Carter outside the region, and if it were not for the South, which
had not supported a Democratic candidate so heavily since 1944, Ford
would have won. What's more, turnout that year was the lowest it had
been for a presidential contest in nearly thirty years. All in all, the results suggested that the country did not much care for Ford *or* Carter.[28]

As Carter assumed office in January 1977, he faced serious challenges on
multiple fronts. For starters, he was far from a consensus choice of his own
party. The most powerful interests within it—notably organized labor—
had swung behind him only after his nomination was secured, and they
remained deeply skeptical of him. Carter, as a governor from a state with
an insignificant labor movement, had little experience in placating union
bosses. Plus, he had a disdain for interest group liberalism, bringing to the
White House a notion that political scientist Charles O. Jones has called
a "trusteeship" vision of the presidency. Carter felt that his job was to
defend the national interest *against* clients like organized labor, and time
and again he would mismanage relations with the unions.[29]

In addition, Carter faced a political economy different from any
that his Democratic predecessors had faced. Between the end of the
Great Depression and Carter's inauguration, the American economy
had increased by more than 600 percent.[30] This unprecedented expansion helped bankroll the social welfare ambitions of Democratic leaders
(and Republican ones, for that matter), who were able to tap into the
growing national income and redistribute portions of it to the party clients that demanded full employment and generous social welfare provisions, all without slowing down the great American growth machine.[31]
Yet starting in the 1970s, the economic engine began to sputter. In
particular, the growth rate of American productivity began to slow, and
with it so did the American economy's ability to generate ever-higher
standards of living for American workers.[32]

Thanks to a series of supply shocks in oil and food, as well as Keynesian stimuli pushed by Nixon, Ford, and Carter, the average American faced this economic hardship primarily in terms of rampant inflation. In the 1960s, the Consumer Price Index increased by an average of just 2.3 percent per year, but in the 1970s the annual rate of growth was 7.1 percent, and during Carter's tenure it reached a frightening 9.7 percent per year.[33] The necessary cure for this kind of runaway inflation is tight monetary policy plus fiscal retrenchment—in other words, a scaling back of federal activity. To Carter's credit, he realized just how dire was the threat of inflation before most of his advisers did, and early on he committed himself to budgetary restraint as well as interventions in the economy to stop the wage-price spiral.

This put Carter on a collision course with the clients in his own party. Labor, African American groups, feminists, and others demanded what they had always demanded: an active federal government that did more for their interests. Yet with the country reeling from runaway inflation, Carter simply could not provide that to his clients.[34] Instead, he tried to forge a new identity for his political party, one that dealt with this age of limits. As he said at the dedication of the JFK Presidential Library in October 1979:

> After a decade of high inflation and growing oil imports, our economic cup no longer overflows. Because of inflation, fiscal restraint has become a matter of simple public duty. We can no longer rely on a rising economic tide to lift the boats of the poorest in our society. We must focus our attention and our care and our love and concern directly on them.
>
> We have a keener appreciation of limits now—the limits of government, limits on the use of military power abroad, the limits of manipulating, without harm to ourselves, a delicate and a balanced natural environment . . .
>
> And we face these times when centrifugal forces in our society and in our political system as well—forces of regionalism, forces of ethnicity, of narrow economic interests, of single-issue politics—are testing the resiliency of American pluralism and of our ability to govern. But we can and we will prevail.

The problems are different; the solutions, none of them easy, are also different. But in this age of hard choices and scarce resources, the essence of President Kennedy's message—the appeal for unselfish dedication to the common good—is more urgent than it ever was. The spirit that he evoked—the spirit of sacrifice, of patriotism, of unstinting dedication—is the same spirit that will bring us safely through the adversities that we face today. The overarching purpose of this Nation remains the same: to build a just society in a secure America living at peace with the other nations of the world.[35]

For Carter, this reinvention of the Democratic ideology meant comprehensive reform—of the tax code, of the welfare system, of the energy grid—to make government work better at the tasks it had already set for itself, rather than expanding the size and scope of Washington's agenda. For the party's clients that did indeed want more, he usually tried to offer them half a loaf, trying to meet them halfway while also fighting inflation.

As we shall see, Carter's efforts were a disaster. He failed to reform government, he failed to control inflation, and he alienated many powerful Democratic clients, many of whom eventually backed Ted Kennedy's candidacy in 1980.

Carter ran into early trouble with the clients within his own party over his proposed economic stimulus. When he took office, the unemployment rate was still at a higher-than-average 7.5 percent, and the economic growth rate in the second half of 1976 had averaged less than 3 percent.[36] So Carter offered a package that called for $900 million in corporate tax cuts, a $50 tax rebate to all Americans, and a modest increase in public works programs, totaling $31.2 billion over two years. Overall, the Carter stimulus was not that large by historical standards—coming in at less than 1 percent of GDP, compared with Ford's proposed stimulus of 1.5 percent.[37] The AFL-CIO and the U.S. Conference of Mayors were not happy with the size or the emphasis on tax cuts, feeling as though it did not do enough for traditional Democratic constituencies. The AFL-CIO called for $30 billion in one year on public works alone, and blasted Carter's proposal as "a retreat from the goals we understand President-elect Carter to have set during last year's election campaign."[38]

The president and the AFL-CIO also butted heads early on over the minimum wage. Presidents Nixon and Ford had agreed to minimum wage hikes during their eight years in office, but because of inflation, the real buying power of the minimum wage by the time Carter took office was the weakest it had been since the 1950s.[39] With a Democratic Congress and president, the AFL-CIO, which had an interest in the issue because the minimum wage set the floor from which labor negotiated for its workers, hoped for a significant increase of 70 cents, bringing the minimum from $2.30 to $3.00. Yet Carter's growing concern about inflation gave him pause; worried about a wage-price spiral, the president did not think it prudent to give organized labor everything it was asking for. Instead Carter proposed a 20-cent increase, which AFL-CIO president George Meany called "a bitter disappointment to everyone who looked to the administration for economic justice."[40]

So Carter's early efforts to meet his party's clients halfway—on the stimulus and the minimum wage—won him few friends. The same is true of his reform efforts, particularly regarding welfare reform. The federal welfare system was a vast, complicated array of ad hoc programs created over the years—and comprehensive reform of the system fitted nicely with his campaign pledge to make the government work better. Yet, again, Carter would run into conflict with the AFL-CIO. Welfare included jobs programs, which influenced the labor market and thus drew the attention of the Federation.[41] The AFL-CIO wanted any welfare reform proposal to include a full employment program, full federal financing, and guaranteed, inflation-adjusted incomes that corresponded with the poverty level.[42] The issue also attracted the interests of welfare rights groups that—in contrast to organized labor—did not much care for make-work jobs and instead preferred direct, inflation-indexed subsidies.

As a testimony to Carter's naïveté about the ways of Washington, he failed to bring these groups into the policy-making process early on. Instead, he tasked Joseph Califano, secretary of Housing, Education, and Welfare (HEW), to design a proposal within the executive branch. Califano, who had worked under LBJ in constructing the Great Society, naturally assumed that Carter was prepared to spend more money on welfare, so he was surprised later on to learn that Carter's intention was to spend no additional money; instead, Carter felt that the system could be made more efficient. After months of contentious debate within the executive branch, Carter eventually proposed the Program for Better Jobs and Income (PBJI) in August 1977, which included a very modest increase in total spending (just $2.8 billion).[43]

Initially, politicos in Washington received PBJI favorably, but soon enough Carter paid the price for his lack of consultation with the party's clients. Welfare rights groups blasted the plan because they found the benefits too measly and the system too complicated, and they caustically renamed the program "JIP." Organized labor disliked it because the public works jobs would merely pay the minimum wage, a standard that would damage union members' position in local labor markets.[44] Meanwhile, fiscal conservatives—most notably Senate Finance Committee chairman Russell Long of Louisiana—simply did not believe that the program would be as inexpensive as Carter advertised, and they claimed vindication when the Congressional Budget Office estimated that the true cost would be five times what the administration had projected.[45]

In the end, Carter's proposal was done in by this left-right cross fire. Organized labor persuaded liberals on the public assistance subcommittee of the House Ways and Means Committee to expand the bill in many ways, including the indexing of benefits. When it got to the full committee, run by conservative Al Ullman, it was a dead letter. Carter's administration quietly dropped the proposal from its 1978 agenda.[46]

Just as organized labor checked Carter's ambitions on health care, the president checked labor's dream of comprehensive health care reform. Again, the AFL-CIO had a "selfish" reason to support an enhanced federal role in health care: if the burden was lifted from employers, labor leaders would have more room to negotiate for higher wages.[47] As noted above, Carter had signed on to the UAW's universal health care plan during the campaign, but with inflation now so high, he was hesitant to enact a sweeping new entitlement. Instead he offered a piecemeal program that would be phased in as the economy permitted it, beginning with an effort to cap hospital costs, which were rising at roughly double the inflation rate. No new money would be spent prior to 1983 under the Carter plan.[48] Yet organized labor had no interest in anything less than comprehensive reform, as only that would take the pressure off employers and free up unions to negotiate for higher wages. Just as with welfare reform, there was no middle ground between Carter and the unions, so in the end nothing happened at all.[49]

Even Carter's legislative successes were caught up in intraparty squabbles. During the campaign, he had backed a separate cabinet-level department for education, which won him the endorsement of the NEA. However, the American Federation of Teachers (AFT), the NEA's much smaller rival and an affiliate of the AFL-CIO, opposed the creation of a department solely for education, fearing that breaking up HEW would endanger the cooperation among administrators of various programs. In the end, Carter and Congress created a separate department for education, and on the same day he signed the bill, the NEA endorsed his reelection.[50]

Carter was also an early victim of the culture war. His electoral coalition in 1976 was a strange combination that included pro-choice feminists like Betty Friedan and Bella Abzug as well as evangelical Christians, an increasingly active political bloc staunchly opposed to abortion. During the campaign, Carter held these strange bedfellows together with a highly nuanced position on abortion—he was person-ally opposed to it but would not support national legislation overturning *Roe* v. *Wade*—thus leaving all parties thinking that he would be mostly sympathetic to their views. Once in office, Carter ended up infuriat-ing all sides on the issue. To satisfy pro-lifers, he supported the Hyde Amendment, which prohibited federal funds from being used to pay for abortions. When feminist leaders protested that it was unfair that poor women could not receive abortions, Carter responded flatly that "many things in life . . . are not fair." Also infuriating to feminist leaders was his decision to force out two high-profile female advisers—Abzug and Midge Costanza—when they protested his anti-inflation policies. Yet all this effort bought him very little with the pro-life movement, which was attracted to Republican Ronald Reagan's unequivocal stand against *Roe* in the 1980 campaign.[51]

• • •

The most contentious battle between Carter and the Democratic party's clients involved the government's efforts to control inflation. Specifically, the labor, minority, urban, and New Politics groups that now dominated the party all balked at Carter's anti-inflation program, yet offered little by way of substantive alternatives. How could they do otherwise? Their fundamental demand was for more, always more: more social welfare programs, more efforts to generate full employment, and more investment in decaying urban areas. Runaway inflation required *less* of all these things, which the large and vociferous clients within the party simply would not accept.

Carter's principal tool in fighting the menace of inflation was the federal budget, and the battles within his own party over government spending were monumental. By the time Cartter offered the FY 1979 budget, in early 1978, inflation was already increasing by more than half a percent per month, so Carter offered a budget that he advertised as "tight and lean" but "compassionate." The claim was not without merit; for instance, Carter kept public service jobs under the Comprehensive Employment and Training Act at FY 1978 levels and actually added funding for youth employment meant to train more than 150,000 kids.[52] Yet the president turned down the recommendations of Housing and Urban Development Secretary Patricia Harris to initiate a major new funding initiative for urban centers, which prompted the U.S. Conference of Mayors to call Carter a "traitor to urban America."[53] The budget was voted down in the House, with nearly three-quarters of northern Democrats going against the president.[54]

The inflation fight also caused a breakdown in relations between Carter and Meany; after the administration had negotiated a deal with the postal workers to keep wage increases in line with the government's wage and price guidelines, Meany publicly denounced the agreement—and in August 1978 Carter actually banished Meany from the White House. For a while, the head of the Democratic party and the head of organized labor were actually not on speaking terms.[55]

Frustration with the president's anti-inflation efforts boiled over at the party's 1978 midterm convention in Memphis, Tennessee. At that meeting, the UAW proposed a "dissident" budget that was voted down, though not overwhelmingly; nearly 40 percent of the attendees voted with the union and against their own president.[56] *Time* caught the mood of the meeting well when it noted:

> [T]here was an undercurrent of feeling among many Democratic factions that Carter is not really their President. Black leaders have been particularly vocal in their discontent, but it is shared by others: labor, Jews, intellectuals, farmers, urban leaders and old-line machine politicians feel a wariness about the man.[57]

The politician who *did* seem as if he could be "their President" was Edward M. Kennedy, and in a speech at the gathering, Kennedy indirectly blasted the administration's anti-inflation efforts:

> I support the fight against inflation. But no fight against inflation can be effective or successful unless the fight is fair. The party that tore itself apart over Vietnam in the 1960's cannot afford to tear itself apart today over budget cuts in basic social programs. . . .
> There must be sacrifice if we are to bring the economy back to health. But the burden must be fairly shared by all. We cannot accept a policy that asks greater sacrifice from labor than from business. We cannot accept a policy that cuts spending to the bone in areas like jobs and health, but allows billions of dollars in wasteful spending for tax subsidies to continue, and adds even greater fat and waste through inflationary spending for defense.[58]

Yet what else was the president to do? The year-over-year inflation rate at the time of Kennedy's speech was a shocking 9 percent. Carter simply did not have the luxury of increasing social welfare spending in a way that would satisfy organized labor, African American groups, feminists, and the rest of his party's clients. The national good required the very sort of retrenchment that Carter was proposing.

Conflict between the two sides would only grow more intense during the second half of Carter's tenure. In October 1978, he announced a new anti-inflation program that set a wage increase target of 7 percent—the hope was that restraining wages would also hold prices down, and thus check inflation. To give the goal some real teeth, Carter pledged a new procurement policy wherein any business that contracted with the government would have to follow the guidelines. Not only did the AFL-CIO denounce this action; it also challenged the policy in federal court.[59] Labor's resistance to such guidelines was due to its belief that union workers would often bear most of the burden, and companies would find ways around price restrictions.[60] After high-stakes negotiating between the White House and the AFL-CIO, both sides eventually worked out a "National Accord" in which labor agreed in principle to the restraint of wages and Carter upped the target from 7 percent to 9.5 percent, which many of the president's advisers thought made the whole concept of wage control worthless.[61]

Any sort of détente between Carter and the party's clients was totally undermined as 1978 gave way to 1979 and the *monthly* inflation rate began to exceed 1 percent, forcing Carter to exercise even more fiscal restraint. Because the president had committed himself to a 3 percent real increase in defense spending, domestic spending had to be trimmed, including housing, job training, and even Medicare and Social Security. In response to these cuts, Ted Kennedy accused Carter of being "insensitive" to the poor.[62] Meanwhile, Louis Martin, the president's assistant for minority affairs, warned Carter that the Congressional Black Caucus did "not buy the linkage between the battle on inflation and the need to cut job programs."[63] The budget battle for FY 1981 was just as contentious, and in his final budget proposal, Carter expressed his exasperation with his own political coalition by stating:

> We can no longer, as individuals or groups, make special pleas for exceptions to budget discipline. Too often we have taken the attitude that there must be alternative sources for reduction in programs that benefit our particular group. That attitude is in part responsible for the rapid budget growth . . . [which] we can no longer afford.[64]

Sadly for Carter's tenure, this was a lesson that the clients within his own party had not learned. The president had entered office hoping to reshape the New Deal political coalition to handle this new age of "hard choices and scarce resources," but his efforts failed in two ways: he did not retain the support of his own coalition, and he could not curb runaway inflation. As the election season began in early 1980, the monthly inflation rate hit an unbelievable 1.4 percent, the likes of which had not been seen since the end of price controls after World War II.

Ted Kennedy had been unhappy with the Carter administration almost from the get-go, and had been mulling over a challenge to the president as early as 1978, when he hired a political organizer who was familiar with Iowa.[65] Though he had been highly critical of Carter, he waited until after the dedication of the JFK Presidential Library, in October 1979, finally declaring his candidacy in early November.[66] According to political scientist Andrew Busch, Kennedy "was pro-busing, pro-racial preferences, pro-abortion, pro-judicial liberalism, pro-welfare, pro–War on Poverty, and anti-anticommunist. It was not at all clear whether the Ted Kennedy of 1979 would have supported the John Kennedy of 1962 on Cuba or tax cuts."[67] His goal was to rally the long list of Democratic clients that had grown disenchanted with the Carter administration— union workers, urbanites, African Americans, and feminists—and seize the nomination from an incumbent president, something that had not happened in one hundred years.

The Gallup Poll all through 1979 had Kennedy far ahead of Carter among self-identified Democrats—by 30 points or more.[68] However, that lead suddenly disappeared late in the year, thanks to the Iran hostage crisis. Carter's job approval numbers with the entire electorate jumped from 31 percent to 57 percent in the Gallup Poll, and he took a commanding lead over Kennedy among Democrats.[69] Kennedy also did himself no favors with a disastrous performance in an interview with Roger Mudd of CBS—when Mudd asked him why he wanted to be president, Kennedy stammered his way through an incoherent answer. Though Kennedy was an early favorite in the first three primaries—in New Hampshire, Massachusetts, and Vermont—Carter won two of the three, leaving Kennedy with a victory only in his home state.[70] Through the early phase of the primary season, Carter employed an effective "Rose Garden Strategy," wherein he would make seemingly important announcements about the crisis from the White House, thus playing up his role as commander in chief during a time of crisis. This helped him win the primaries not only in Florida and Georgia but also in Illinois, where he carried 65 percent of the vote.[71]

Kennedy finally caught a break on March 25, when he defeated Carter in Connecticut and New York. The victory in the Empire State was quite impressive: Kennedy bested the president by nearly 200,000 votes; he won all sixteen congressional districts in New York City; and he carried all five boroughs by a two-to-one margin or better.[72] A month later, Kennedy won a narrow victory in Pennsylvania; then he carried Maryland in May and finished up the primary season with wins in California, New Jersey, and New Mexico.

The epic battle between Carter and Kennedy rent the Democratic party in two. Organized labor was particularly split. Twenty-five AFL-CIO unions—including the International Association of Machinists, the International Chemical Workers, and the United Mine Workers—backed Kennedy. Meanwhile, Carter won the support of the independent NEA as well as twenty AFL-CIO unions, including the International Ladies' Garment Workers' Union, the Seafarers International Union, and the Communications Workers of America.[73] One reason Carter managed to pull in decent union backing, despite his anti-inflation efforts, was his support over the years for legislation that appealed to particular unions. For instance, the seafarers union backed Carter in part because of his support for cargo-preference legislation.[74]

In general, Kennedy's voting coalition was made up of liberals, minorities (Hispanics in the West as well as African Americans, who started out with Carter but wound their way over to Kennedy in large numbers), as well as blue-collar workers.[75] Carter, meanwhile, dominated the South and ran very strongly in rural, agricultural areas like upstate New York. At the end of the primary season, Carter had outpolled Kennedy by nearly three million votes, yet he had carried only 51 percent of the total Democratic electorate, a dismal performance for an incumbent president. What's more, Kennedy had surged later in the primary season, after the "rally 'round the flag" effect of the hostage crisis began to fade. If a one-day primary had been held in April, it's not at all clear that Carter would have defeated Kennedy.

Trying to play off his late-stage momentum, Kennedy sought to unbind delegates from their primary electorates, but his quest for an "open convention" failed narrowly on the floor, with 1,936 delegates backing Carter to 1,391 supporting Kennedy.[76] As a final act in this unprecedented internecine battle, Kennedy stirred the party faithful with his famous "Dream Will Never Die" address, but in it he endorsed only the party platform, not Carter himself.[77] That platform turned out to be a major headache for the Carter team as the Kennedy forces pushed through a series of minority planks that, according to Carter's adviser Stuart Eizenstat, "took little cognizance of the roaring inflation, high interest rates, and ballooning federal deficit of the time and pushed instead for a huge domestic spending package."[78] In its sprawling, 36,000-word platform, the party promised a whole host of new, liberal initiatives: a $12 billion jobs program, a national health insurance program, comprehensive child care entitlements, public works spending, new jobs training, and more. Plus, in a not so subtle rebuke to Carter, it also declared:

> [F]or the sole and primary purpose of fiscal restraint alone, we will not support reductions in the funding of any program whose purpose is to serve the basic human needs of the most needy in our society—programs such as unemployment, income maintenance, food stamps, and efforts to enhance the educational, nutritional or health needs of children.[79]

If a convention platform is the voice of a political party, then in 1980 the Democratic party soundly rejected Carter's call to reframe New Deal/Great Society liberalism for this new "age of limits."

So Jimmy Carter limped into the general election campaign against Ronald Reagan, who had finally won the Republican nomination in his third attempt. Though the Gallup Poll showed a tight race all the way through, Carter averaged just 40 percent support from August through November.[80] In the end, that was all he received; this was the worst showing by an incumbent president since Herbert Hoover in 1932. Reagan won 50 percent of the vote in a three-way contest (with Republican congressman John Anderson running as an independent) and carried forty-four states. Polling data showed a complete collapse in the traditional New Deal coalition as Reagan won 54 percent of the white working class, 51 percent of white Catholics, and 47 percent of union members. In an unprecedented shift, the South gave a Republican 51 percent of the vote, to just 44.5 percent for Carter, the southern Democrat; white southerners supported Reagan by a 59–36 margin.[81]

Much to the dismay of liberal Democrats, the age of Reagan had begun.

Today's Democratic party has largely forgotten the Carter term. For evidence of this, one need only recall the 2008 Democratic National Convention. Carter was given a brief window to address the convention on Monday, outside prime time and sandwiched between Margie Perez, a jazz singer, and Maya Soetoro-Ng, Barack Obama's half sister. Insofar as Carter's tenure is remembered at all today, it is usually by conservative Republicans, who find the Georgian a useful foil for lavishing praise upon Ronald Reagan.

Much of the blame for Carter's failure must be placed at the feet of the president himself. As former adviser James Fallows argued in a scathing critique in the *Atlantic Monthly* in 1979, Carter was a good man, but as a president he was insular, arrogant, moralistic, ignorant of history, too focused on the details and not enough on the big picture. He alienated many of his would-be allies in Washington, D.C., just as he had as governor of Georgia, with needless fights over trivialities as well as an incessant moralizing that always featured him as the avatar of the good, the true, and the right.[82] What's more, Carter had the misfortune of taking office at a time when the great American prosperity machine was grinding to a halt, forcing him to deal with the politics of decline; whereas presidents since FDR got to decide how the surplus bounty of America would be distributed, Carter had to decide how to spread the pain of an economic contraction. As Herbert Hoover had learned before him, it's virtually impossible to be politically successful in that kind of environment.

Yet we cannot ignore the story of this chapter—of how Jimmy Carter, time and again, tried unsuccessfully to force his party to face the new "age of limits," tried to redesign the old liberal program for the

future, and tried to tackle the danger of inflation. We might contrast
Carter's speech at the dedication of the JFK Presidential Library with
the 1980 Democratic platform, and in that case we would have to conclude that though Carter won the nomination that year, Kennedy had
won the soul of the party.

The argument of this book is that, after four decades of adding
clients, the Democratic party is no longer capable of governing for
the public good and holding its coalition together—as somewhere,
somehow, these two goals will conflict with one another, forcing party
leaders to face a political dilemma with no solution. This contributed
significantly to the failure of the Carter presidency. He tried to tackle
the problem of runaway inflation, but the demands of the clients within
the party undermined his efforts and eventually brought about the challenge from Kennedy. In other words, Carter failed at both serving the
public good and keeping the party united.

Jimmy Carter would return to Plains, Georgia, in the winter of
1981, and so he fades from our story. Yet these clients within the Democratic party would persist, and continue to hamper the efforts of Democratic leaders for the next thirty years.

CHAPTER ELEVEN

A Temporary Triangle

Bill Clinton and the Circumvention of the Clients

When President Bill Clinton took office in January 1993, the Democrats had a reputation as a fractious group of rent seekers, more interested in maximizing government benefits for their clients than expanding the economy or standing up to the Soviet Union. When he left in 2001, the "New Democrats" seemed triumphant, with the party now focused relentlessly on growing the American economy for the middle class. This new reputation helped Democrats capitalize on public discontent with the Bush administration, and the party took control of Congress in 2006, and then the White House in 2008.

There is no doubt that Clinton was a different kind of Democrat. In 1992, he took the party's nomination not by appealing to the particular interests of African Americans, consumer rights advocates, environmentalists, feminists, and union workers, but instead by speaking to the middle class. Indeed, candidate Clinton at times openly broke with his party's clients—for example, when he denounced rapper Sister Souljah at a Rainbow Coalition event sponsored by Jesse Jackson and when he endorsed the North American Free Trade Agreement (NAFTA), which organized labor vehemently opposed.[1]

Like Carter before him, Clinton could win without the once dominant party clients because of the McGovern-Fraser reforms of the early 1970s, which had taken the nominating power from the delegates at the quadrennial convention and given it directly to the people. Candidates ever since have been able to bypass the client leaders who had previously served as gatekeepers to the party nomination and form their own voting coalitions. So whereas Jimmy Byrnes was denied the vice-presidential nomination in 1944 because labor leaders wanted nothing to do with him, Carter and Clinton could win the presidential nomination on the first ballot in 1992 and there was nothing that the AFL-CIO could do about it. In fact, given the alternative—four more years of the anti-union Republicans—they were duty-bound to give Carter and Clinton an all-out effort.

But while Democratic presidential candidates had found paths to the nomination independent of the clients, members of Congress, especially the House, were more dependent than ever. As we saw in Chapter 9, the New Politics lobbying groups—consumer rights, environmentalist, and feminist—had all put together impressive lobbying and PAC operations, guaranteeing that Democrats in Congress would be responsive to their interests. As for African Americans, as we noted in Chapter 6, the 103rd Congress, seated in 1993, was the first to feature federally mandated "majority-minority districts," which had swelled the ranks of the Congressional Black Caucus to some forty members. And even though organized labor was on the decline in the broader economy, it still had many friends in Congress. If anything, labor's congressional allies had only grown over the years. In 1955, 116 House Democrats received better than a 90 percent score from the CIO's Committee on Political Education (COPE). In 1975, 158 Democrats received such a score. And in 1993, the first year of the Clinton tenure, 199 Democrats had higher than a 90 percent score from COPE. Meanwhile, campaign donations from labor PACs had become extremely important for the war chests of incumbent Democrats—between 1986 and 1996, labor contributions to House candidates nearly doubled, with the extra funds flowing overwhelmingly to Democrats.[2]

The added importance of labor money could be traced to the campaign finance reforms of the 1970s, which tightly restricted contributions at the same time that candidates began spending exorbitant sums on television ads. The new campaign finance laws had another important consequence, for they brought corporate America into electoral campaigns lock, stock, and barrel. Prior to the 1970s, corporate campaign contributions were limited, but the new laws permitted businesses to form corporate and professional PACs, which collect voluntary contributions from employees, then distribute them to friendly legislators.

While the Republican party has long been known as the party of businesses, corporate PACs were usually non-ideological, searching above all for access to the policy-making process. In the 1980s, House Democrats were quite adept at using their majority status to attract as much corporate money as possible; between 1978 and 1994, Democrats usually collected about half of all corporate and trade association PAC contributions, and the dollars almost always went to incumbents placed on whatever committee a corporate group was looking to influence.[3] While it would be inaccurate to say that corporations had become clients like unions or African Americans—after all, corporate PACs flocked to the GOP after it won the majority in 1994—they nevertheless had an impressive amount of leverage over the party that still claimed to represent the people over the powerful.

Thus, while Clinton might have won the nomination without the party clients, he could not escape their influence in Washington. This created substantial trouble for him early in his term. In the instances when he tried to work with them—as on deficit reduction and crime control—his centrist intentions were lost to the liberal clientelism of the Democratic Congress, undermining public support for the finished products. And in the instances when he tried to govern without the clients, he was met with either legislative gridlock (as on health care) or a bill that created a political headache for him (as on NAFTA).

In reality, Clinton found his stride—and began building his reputation for effective, centrist governance—only after the Democrats lost Congress. The sizable GOP majorities in the 104th Congress of 1995–96 meant that Clinton was finally free of his fellow Democrats, and could craft popular compromises with Republicans. The left wing of his party, meanwhile, was caught between a rock and a hard place, gravely disappointed with Clinton but too fearful of the Republicans to defy him. It was during this period that Clinton enacted his most lasting reforms—a balanced budget, health care portability, tax cuts, and welfare reform.

Like Eisenhower before him, Clinton hoped that his brand of centrism would redefine his party, helping it forge a lasting majority coalition. But, just as with Ike, it was not to be for Clinton. Ralph Nader—a consumer advocate and sometime client of the Democratic party—launched a third-party challenge against Vice President Al Gore, Clinton's heir apparent, in 2000. The result was a split in the Democratic vote that, while not very large, was nevertheless substantial enough to hand the presidency to Republican George W. Bush.

The Clinton era can thus be divided into two segments—during the first, from 1993 to 1995, Clinton was held captive by his party clients just as Carter had been; during the second, from 1995 to 2000, Republican control of Congress liberated Clinton, enabling him to govern as a true New Democrat. Unfortunately for the reformist Democrats, this second segment did not evolve into a lasting change in the structure of the party. Instead, it was merely a brief moment when a centrist president suddenly found himself free of his liberal clients.

The election of Ronald Reagan in 1980 marked a low point in the Democratic party's postwar history. While not nearly as badly off as it had been in 1904 or 1924, the party was nevertheless in dire straits. The Republicans had taken the Senate for the first time since 1954, and as for the House of Representatives, Reagan had a working conservative majority on the floor for his first year in office, as a combination of Republicans and southern Democrats coordinated to pass large tax cuts and significant reductions in domestic spending. Democrats enjoyed a rebound of sorts in 1982, picking up twenty-six seats in the House, though the GOP extended its Senate majority, making this the first time in more than fifty years that Republicans controlled the Senate for two terms in a row.

By the beginning of 1984, Democrats were in the midst of another knock-down, drag-out contest for the nomination. The early front-runner was Walter Mondale, the Minnesota liberal who had been vice president under Jimmy Carter. Early on, Mondale had secured the support of the groups that had come to dominate the party—the AFL-CIO, the National Education Association, and the National Organization for Women.[4] Mondale's principal opponent was Gary Hart, former campaign manager for George McGovern and now a U.S. senator from Colorado, who promised to replace "tired assumptions with fresh ideas," suggesting that there was something wrong with the party's clientele liberalism.[5] Mondale and Hart sparred all through the primary season, and it was not until the California primary, in June, that the former vice president could declare victory. In the general election, Mondale ran a traditional Democratic campaign meant to rouse the old New Deal coalition.[6] The result was an electoral debacle: Reagan won 59 percent of the vote, took every state except Minnesota, and made serious inroads into the traditional Democratic coalition. He carried 70 percent of the southern white vote, 52 percent of working-class Catholics, and even 47 percent of the labor vote. African Americans were the only group to remain wholly loyal to the Democrats in 1984.[7]

The Hart challenge to Mondale during the primaries was the first sign of a new reformist movement within the Democratic party, and after the crushing defeat of 1984, the ranks of Democratic reformers would only grow. In particular, a group of "New Democrats" began to argue that the party had to craft a political message for a wider audience than the special interests within it.[8] The vehicle for the New Democrats was the Democratic Leadership Council (DLC), which attracted many notable, mostly southern political leaders like Bill Clinton of Arkansas, Al Gore Jr. of Tennessee, and Sam Nunn of Georgia.[9]

The DLC tried to swing the 1988 nomination by expanding the Super Tuesday primary; its hope was that by encouraging southern states to hold their primaries on the same day, they could provide a moderate Democrat with much-needed momentum. However, the plan backfired in 1988 when Gore split the southern vote with civil rights activist Jesse Jackson; the southern stalemate handed the nomination to Michael Dukakis of Massachusetts.[10] Like Hart before him, Dukakis promised "new ideas and new leadership" and emphasized his administrative competence over his liberal ideology.[11] However, in the general election campaign, George H. W. Bush, Reagan's vice president, who had won the GOP nomination with relative ease, recast Dukakis as a typical liberal, thanks in part to the controversial Willie Horton ad. During Dukakis's term as governor, convicted murderer Horton was given a weekend furlough, during which he raped and beat a woman. Dukakis did not design the furlough program, though he did support it, and Bush portrayed Dukakis as just another soft-on-crime liberal.[12]

On Election Day, Bush won an easy victory, carrying 53 percent of the vote and forty states.

By Labor Day 1991, George Bush seemed invincible. He was still riding high off the victory in the Gulf War, and his approval rating was an impressive 68 percent in the Gallup Poll, strong enough to scare off the entire top tier of potential Democratic challengers. All of the party leaders regularly bandied about by Washington pundits and election watchers declined to seek the Democratic nomination, which at that point seemed little more than an invitation to be roadkill on George Bush's triumphal march to a second term.[13] Ultimately, the Democratic challengers in 1992 were a bunch of B-listers: former governor Jerry Brown of California, Clinton, Senator Tom Harkin of Iowa, Senator Bob Kerrey of Nebraska, and former senator Paul Tsongas of Massachusetts.

Clinton was, in many respects, a formidable candidate. He was the chair of the DLC, former chair of the National Governors Association (NGA), and serving his fourth consecutive term as governor of Arkansas. Thanks to his connections with the DLC and the NGA, he raised more money than his opponents and had put in place the best ground operation by the time the primaries began.[14] Yet what kept Clinton from being the runaway front-runner was the widespread rumor that he had a "bimbo problem," and a few weeks prior to the New Hampshire primary, the *Star* tabloid reported that he had carried on an affair with his wife's hairdresser. Later, stories surfaced about the unseemly way that Clinton had avoided being drafted into the Vietnam War.

Had he faced more formidable opponents, such scandals surely would have sunk the Clinton candidacy. Fortunately for him, he really had to reckon with only the dour Tsongas and the quirky Brown. After finishing second in New Hampshire, Clinton triumphed on Super Tuesday—finally, the DLC plan to pack southern primaries on a single day had the desired effect—and he picked up momentum that he carried into the Illinois and Michigan primaries a week later, where he ended the Tsongas candidacy. A brief Brown boomlet in Connecticut was quickly undone when Clinton trounced him in the New York primary the next week, and that was effectively that.

In the general election, Clinton ran as an unabashed, unapologetic centrist; rather than offer a vast constellation of new federal programs for the party's clients, he promised to make government work harder and better for the "forgotten" middle class.[15] He pledged to enact a middle-class tax cut, end welfare as we know it, get tough on crime, and make deadbeat dads pay their fair share.[16] His nomination address was a masterful articulation of the New Democrat philosophy, and he surely raised eyebrows among the liberals when he said:

> *The Republicans have campaigned against big government for a generation, but have you noticed? They've run this big government for a generation and they haven't changed a thing. They don't want to fix government; they still want to campaign against it, and that's all. But, my fellow Democrats, it's time for us to realize we've got some changing to do, too. There is not a program in government for every problem, and if we want to use government to help people, we have got to make it work again.*[17]

One Bush campaign official complained, "I can't figure out a way to run against him from the right!"[18]

Despite his professed centrism, Clinton still enjoyed the backing of the party's traditional clients, including organized labor, which had fallen on hard times. Not only was the percentage of union members in the workforce still in decline, but twelve years of Reagan and Bush had seriously degraded labor's political position, as Republican appointees to the National Labor Relations Board and the federal courts had narrowly interpreted labor laws, thus placing maximum pressure on unions.[19] Though Clinton was a moderate Democrat from a southern state with a minimal union presence, and though he had even fought labor unions during his tenure in Little Rock, organized labor went all out to help the party ticket that year.[20]

For a Democrat, it does not get much better than that: to have the full support of the party's clients while disclaiming any obligation to them. Even with this advantage, Clinton still won only 43 percent of the vote in 1992, less than Michael Dukakis's share. A major reason was the presence of H. Ross Perot, an idiosyncratic Texas businessman turned third-party candidate who won about 19 percent of the vote. The core

Democratic constituencies were about all that Clinton carried, but that was enough to secure victory in 1992.[21]

Our argument across the final three chapters is that the Democratic party's clients have grown so numerous, and their demands so onerous, that the party as a whole is not capable of simultaneously tending to them and governing for the public interest. This requires us, in turn, to identify what the public interest was at the time the Democrats were installed in power; after all, we need to have a standard by which to evaluate the party's performance in office. During the Carter years, the prime objective of public policy should have been dealing with runaway inflation; as we saw, Carter's efforts were a miserable failure, in large part because his own partisans opposed him at almost every turn.

As Clinton was inaugurated in January 1993, the challenges had shifted. Inflation was low and steady while the economy was recovering steadily, if not robustly, from the recession of 1990–91. While prosperity seemed to have returned, the popularity of the Perot candidacy nevertheless suggested there was widespread dissatisfaction with the record of both parties. Indeed, Clinton picked up on this theme himself by promising, during the general election campaign, to be a new kind of Democrat: he would break through the old categories to solve lingering public problems such as crime, welfare dependency, and the deficit. This, then, suggests the challenge demanded by the public good as he took office, and the standard by which we can evaluate him: could he break through the frustrating left-right paradigm to solve problems in a way that again inspired public confidence in the nation's government?

He did not get off to a good start. Almost right away his efforts to appease the party's clientele made this supposed New Democrat suddenly seem like a 1960s-style liberal. An early flap regarded the issue of gays in the military. Homosexuals had been important financial supporters of the Clinton campaign, and the new president sought to lift the ban on their serving in the armed forces.[22] However, his proposal met with opposition from the Joint Chiefs of Staff, as well as from Nunn, a fellow alumnus of the DLC and the chairman of the Senate Armed Services Committee. The ultimate compromise—"Don't ask, don't tell"—did not satisfy gay rights groups, nor did it help reestablish

Clinton's reputation as a moderate.[23] Compounding the flap over gays in the military were controversial executive orders regarding abortion counseling, federal sponsorship of fetal tissue research, the provision of federal funds for UN population programs, the French abortion pill, and abortions performed in overseas military hospitals.[24] What's more, some of Clinton's executive appointments also generated controversy. For instance, he nominated Lani Guinier, of the NAACP Legal Defense and Educational Fund, to be assistant attorney general for civil rights. Guinier had been a longtime friend of both Bill and Hillary Clinton, but her published work suggested that she favored guaranteed proportional representation for minorities, and Clinton eventually had to withdraw her name from consideration.[25]

Clinton's management of Congress also created trouble for the new president. Early in his term, he proposed a $16 billion stimulus bill, full of "investments," which was basically a payoff to the big-city mayors and the Congressional Black Caucus (CBC), who were bound to be resistant to subsequent efforts to balance the budget.[26] The bill passed easily through the House of Representatives, albeit with no GOP support. Republicans, after all, had little incentive to deliver political patronage to Democratic clients under the guise of "stimulus," and Senate Republicans dutifully filibustered it. In the end, only a $4 billion extension in unemployment benefits was put into law.[27]

The stimulus bill was a preview of the bigger fight on the budget deficit, as the congressional GOP in the post-Reagan era had grown confident of its ability to win electoral majorities, and was thus less likely to accede to programs tailored largely to support the Democratic party's client groups. And so the Republicans uniformly balked at Clinton's deficit reduction program, which was an excellent example of the problem that the president encountered when he moved from Little Rock to Washington. Deficit reduction was not a liberal Democratic goal, although liberals had long blasted Reagan and Bush for their outsize deficits. Still, Clinton the New Democrat was serious about deficit reduction, believing that lowering the deficit would free up private capital to invest in the economy, generate confidence in the bond market, and eventually lower interest rates and thus bring about broad, sustained prosperity.[28] This was the kind of view more likely to be espoused by an Eisenhower Republican than a liberal Democrat, and it was a testament to the president's centrist, pro-growth instincts.[29]

Yet to get such a program passed through the 103rd Congress, dominated as it was by liberal Democrats, he had to craft the kind of deficit reduction that the party clients could agree to.[30] Thus, the deficit reduction package consisted of tax hikes on wealthy individuals, small businesses, and energy consumption; military spending cuts; only minor tweaks to the country's vast entitlement system; "investments" in public projects, and other various *increases* in domestic discretionary spending to garner the support of different clients (like an increase in the earned income tax credit, which appealed to the CBC).[31] This was the kind of package that could win liberal Democratic votes, but it turned off Republicans, moderate Democrats, and above all the broad middle of the country. The biggest problem for Clinton was the slow, tortuous process the package took to get passed, as the House liberals and moderate Democrats in the Senate went back and forth debating spending levels and energy taxes. All the while, congressional Republicans blasted Clinton for abandoning his promise to be a new kind of Democrat. In the end, the bill passed by just a single vote in the House, and Vice President Gore had to break a 50–50 tie in the Senate. In a worrisome sign for President Clinton, by August 1993, his approval on the deficit was just 39 percent, on the economy just 38 percent, and on taxes a measly 34 percent.

Crime control was another issue on which Clinton's New Democratic instincts were overwhelmed by the political demands of his congressional allies. Crime had long been a Republican issue—the Democrats were seen as soft on punishment and too willing to throw money at the problem; indeed, this is the exact sentiment to which George Bush's Willie Horton ad spoke. However, Clinton had a good record on crime in Arkansas, and his crime bill included many get-tough provisions that could significantly reform the party's image. He pushed for gun control, an expansion of the death penalty, the institution of a "three strikes and you're out" rule, and a community policing initiative that Clinton claimed would put 100,000 new police officers on the streets.[32]

The problem for Clinton was that crime is an issue that invariably crosses racial, economic, and therefore political lines, especially on the Democratic side of the aisle.[33] Thus, the "get tough" provisions Clinton offered were bound to offend urban liberals, particularly members of the CBC, who believed that the justice system was inherently biased against African Americans. Worse for Clinton, the politically powerful National Rifle Association held great sway with rural, conservative Democrats, meaning that a crime-fighting bill that included gun control measures would have to attract substantial support from liberals. So Clinton had to insert roughly $7 billion worth of new social programs to attract the urban left.[34] This made for about 25 percent of the total cost of the bill, and ultimately it eroded public support.[35]

The process by which the crime bill became law mirrored the process of the deficit reduction package, which is to say that it was drawn out and messy and ultimately undermined public support for the bill. At one point, a strange-bedfellows coalition of Republicans, rural Democrats, and CBC members defeated the House leadership on what should have been a minor procedural vote, forcing Clinton and congressional Democrats to make side deals to attract enough members to get the bill passed. All this deal making, plus the social spending during what was supposedly an age of austerity, took its toll. A Gallup poll taken after the midterm found that just 43 percent approved of the social spending in the bill, that only 42 percent approved of Clinton's handling of crime, and that 52 percent trusted the GOP over the Democrats on the issue.[36]

With several other major policy initiatives, Clinton crafted or supported legislation independent of his congressional allies—and he met with mixed success, at best. Clinton's support of NAFTA ultimately resulted in a legislative victory without the major clients, but that came at a steep political price. NAFTA had been drafted during the Bush administration, and though Clinton supported it, he tried to convince Canada and Mexico to accept more stringent labor and environmental standards.[37] The two countries were not willing to give enough to satisfy the left flank of the Democratic party, and an alliance of labor unions, environmental groups, and consumer rights advocates united against the implementation of the agreement, meaning that the majority of House Democrats would vote against it.[38] With support mostly coming from Republicans, NAFTA passed through Congress, but at great cost for Clinton: the AFL-CIO withheld its full financial support from Democratic incumbents who had backed NAFTA, and a statistical analysis by Professor Gary Jacobson indicates that voters, particularly former Perot supporters, punished pro-NAFTA Democrats in the 1994 midterms.[39]

If open defiance of his clients brought no political success, neither did ignoring them. That's what Clinton tried with his health care reform initiative.[40] He wanted it to be the crown jewel of his domestic policy achievements, and he tasked the First Lady and Ira Magaziner with formulating a proposal. The two created an enormous task force—consisting of some five hundred analysts—to draft a plan from scratch. All deliberations were conducted strictly in private, and though there were open lines of communication between Clinton, Magaziner, and Democratic leaders in Congress, the task force paid little attention to what legislators had to say.[41]

The final product was like Frankenstein's monster, an outrageous proposal stitched together from a series of separate ideas that collectively would reshape one-seventh of the American economy around the principle of "managed competition."[42] The political problem was that a lot of people made a living off the health care system, so the proposal inevitably produced economic losers. In particular, expanding coverage to all persons would raise the cost of health care, as demand for service would go up. To keep costs in line, doctors, nurses, hospitals, old-age homes, drug companies, and so on would have to cut their costs.[43] Additionally, all businesses would now be required to pay a share of the health premiums for employees. Thus, while some groups like the American Medical Association initially sounded some positive signals, many others, like the Chamber of Commerce and the Health Insurance Association of America, were opposed virtually from the get-go.[44] These groups eventually launched a massive advertising blitz against the Clinton proposal, whose public support quickly eroded. The anti-reform coalition even lobbied other lobbying groups, and the AMA ultimately withdrew its support from the employer mandate in December 1993.[45]

In theory, Clinton might have been able to overcome pressure from business and medical interests, much as LBJ had in pushing Medicare through in 1965. However, he had two significant problems keeping him from repeating that success. First, the insurance companies had a lot of friends in Congress, many on the Democratic side of the aisle. Health care had been a hot topic during the 1992 campaign, so the health care industry was careful to increase its contributions to well-placed members of Congress. In fact, the top twenty-four health PACs nearly tripled their contributions between 1990 and 1992, from $5 million to $13 million.[46] Second, the Democratic clients that had traditionally supported universal health reform were only lukewarm about the Clinton proposal, which had largely been drafted without their input. For instance, organized labor had negotiated very expensive health benefit plans for their members, and the Clinton plan to tax such "Cadillac" programs was not welcome. Just as in the late 1970s, organized labor was committed to universal health care insofar as it improved the standing of its members. This was why it was opposed to Carter's phase-in program, and why it did not go all out for the Clinton plan, which never even received an up-or-down vote in Congress.[47]

During his first two years as president, Bill Clinton seemed damned if he did and damned if he didn't. When he worked with his party in Congress, he passed legislation consistent with his broad goals, but he had to tailor it so thoroughly to the needs of the party clients that he lost popular support in the middle of the country. When he ignored his clients, he did not do much better. Their ambivalence on health care undermined the reform effort, and while Clinton won a legislative victory on NAFTA, his client groups responded by withholding funds from pro-NAFTA Democrats, many of whom lost in the 1994 midterms.

All in all, it was a disappointing record, and the judgment of the public—as expressed in the 1994 midterms—was extremely harsh. The GOP picked up a net fifty-two seats in the House, winning control of the lower chamber for the first time in forty years. As mentioned above, support of NAFTA hurt Democrats, and so did support of the deficit reduction package and the crime bill.[48] Polling also indicated that the Perot voters who had supported congressional Democrats in 1992 bolted overwhelmingly to the GOP.[49] All in all, it made for the single worst midterms for any party since 1946.

●   ●   ●

At the beginning of 1995, Bill Clinton found himself in a political fix that no Democrat had experienced since Harry Truman. Both suffered the loss of House and Senate majorities to Republican midterm tsunamis. Additionally, both had a kind of legitimacy problem—Truman because he had not been elected president and Clinton because he won with much less than 50 percent of the vote. Yet Truman and Clinton would respond to these challenges in markedly different ways. Truman became a partisan brawler, denouncing the Republicans as mere tools of the special interests and sending to Capitol Hill very liberal policy proposals that he knew the GOP majority would not accept. Clinton, on the other hand, worked with the congressional Republicans, and, though their relationship was often contentious, together they produced policies more in keeping with Clinton's promise to be a different kind of Democrat.

Amazingly, Clinton was able to accomplish this only because his party lost both chambers of Congress. With the Democrats in control of the legislature, the bonds of partisanship forced Clinton to work with them, and thus be responsive to the party's extensive clientele. But with the Democrats no longer in charge, Clinton could finally operate independent of the clients and—by checking the most conservative elements of the congressional GOP—could finally govern for the broad middle of the country.

The political strategy that Clinton employed would become known as "triangulation." As his top political strategist, Dick Morris, described it:

> *Parroting the rhetoric of the congressional Democrats—who opposed all things Republican—would merely be sharing the storm cellar with them, waiting until the Republican twister passed safely by. Adopting the Republican agenda begged the question, what is the relevance of Clinton? I wanted to suggest that the president take a middle course, but not one that just split the difference between the two parties. The president needed to take a position that not only blended the best of each party's views but also transcended them to constitute a third force in the debate. . . .*
>
> *This [would be] a temporary triangle as the older and less en-*

lightened members of the Democratic Party hang back. But soon it will resolve itself into a new bipolar divide between the two parties with the Republicans back where they have always been and the Democrats fully committed to the new positions you have articulated.[50]

Clinton first initiated his triangulation strategy on the budget. The brash new Speaker of the House, Newt Gingrich of Georgia, demanded a seven-year balanced budget plan, one that would pull resources from Medicare, which had begun growing at an insupportably fast rate.[51] Some of Clinton's advisers—e.g., George Stephanopoulos and Leon Panetta—urged Clinton to hang back and attack the GOP, rather than propose his own balanced budget. However, Morris encouraged Clinton to put forth his own proposal, and Clinton agreed.

In doing so, the president pulled off a substantial political coup. He claimed that the Republican budget unfairly damaged educational and environmental programs, as well as Medicare. The alternative he offered pledged a balanced budget in ten years—not seven—without touching those popular programs.[52] The GOP, naturally, rejected Clinton's counteroffer, and the two sides went back and forth through the winter of 1995–96, with the government shutting down twice because of the impasse. The result was that Clinton agreed to a budget deal over seven years, while the Republicans agreed to scale back their proposed tax cuts and leave Clinton's sacred programs alone.

Largely absent from this deal were House Democrats, who were not at all pleased by the finished product. Donald Payne of New Jersey—the head of the CBC—said that the deal marked "a quantum leap backward for social policy, and it will have long-lasting, explosive results." Patricia Schroeder of Colorado—a high-profile feminist—complained that the Republicans had played Clinton "like a kitten with a string."[53] But in the end, all they could do was gripe. Clinton was free to operate without their input, which was basically what he did.

If Democrats were disgruntled over the budget, they were absolutely apoplectic over Clinton's decision in the summer of 1996 to sign the Republican welfare reform bill. Initially created under the Social Security Act to support widowed women temporarily, Aid to Families

with Dependent Children, the principal welfare program, had bal-
looned into a massive federal entitlement.[54] While the government's
annual expenditure on welfare was much smaller than that for national
defense, Medicare, or Social Security, welfare had become a symbol of
government activism run amok; after all, here was a program with out-
of-control costs that seemed to contribute to a vicious circle of poverty,
the very thing it was created to prevent.

It is little wonder that candidate Clinton—the one who told his
fellow Democrats that they had a special responsibility to "make government work again"—would emphasize welfare reform during his
campaign. Little wonder as well that once Clinton entered the White
House and found himself having to deal with a Democratic congressional coalition dominated by African Americans, feminists, and organized labor, he would blanch. Instead of promoting welfare reform,
Clinton touted health care reform—and submitted a welfare proposal
only halfway through 1994, far too late in the legislative calendar for
Congress to take real action.

Now, with the liberal Democrats pushed to one side, Clinton had
wiggle room to deal with the Republicans. The GOP had included welfare reform in its "Contract with America" and added it to the initial
budget proposal, but Clinton vetoed it in late 1995, and then again in
early 1996.[55] Undeterred, the congressional GOP submitted to Clinton a
third welfare bill, over the objection of House liberals, in the summer of
1996, just a few months from the election.[56] While there were elements
of the package that Clinton did not like—for instance, restrictions on
welfare for legal immigrants—he decided nevertheless to sign the bill,
believing that this would be his last chance to make good on his 1992
campaign promise. Unsurprisingly, liberals were enraged, but once
again, what else could they do but complain?[57]

Clinton's triangulation strategy also included a series of minor
measures designed to help him overcome the reputation for cultural liberalism that he had built in 1993–94. He backed the V-chip and school
uniforms, and signed the Defense of Marriage Act, recasting himself as
the great defender of the middle-class American family. Against these
moves, however, Clinton was careful never to go too far to the right; for
instance, he twice vetoed the Partial-Birth Abortion Ban Act and, in a

speech at the National Archives, defended affirmative action, arguing that it was a noble and useful idea that simply needed reform. "Mend it, don't end it," he said, and most of America seemed to agree.[58] These gestures toward the left helped preempt a challenge from another Democrat in the 1996 primaries.[59]

Another factor that scared off a left-wing challenge was Clinton's massive fund-raising haul. Worried about his prospects through much of 1995, Clinton put together the most impressive campaign money machine to that point in American history. He and the Democrats raised more than $130 million in "soft," unregulated money, nearly three times the amount from 1992. While some of this came from unions like AFSCME and the Communications Workers of America, the Democrats also pulled in tens of millions of dollars from big corporations, like Seagram's and MCI, which by that point had grown quite comfortable with his "New Democratic" brand of governance. This money bankrolled an early ad campaign against Bob Dole, the presumptive Republican nominee, and by the summer Clinton had comfortably pulled ahead in the polls.[60]

Given that the Democrats were about to reelect a president, something that had not happened since 1964, one would think that they would have been happy when they convened in Chicago in late August. Yet they were notably glum, united not out of affection or enthusiasm for Clinton but out of pure fear of the alternative: the first unified Republican control of the government since 1954.[61] As New York Democrat Chuck Schumer put it, "What kept us close to the president was the Republicans. Their extreme nastiness pushed Democrats into Bill Clinton's arms, even those who didn't like him very much."[62] To add insult to injury, Clinton's convention forces made sure the party adopted a decidedly centrist platform—one that emphasized balanced budgets, tax cuts, and welfare reform. If one didn't know better, one might have thought this was actually the Republican convention.[63]

The consequence of triangulation was not only a Democrat who seemed awfully like a Republican, which was bad enough for the liberals, but also a congressional Democratic caucus that was essentially hung out to dry by its own president. Convinced that Dole was about to lose, congressional Republicans moved to the center and sent Clinton a raft of proposals that he could sign, like a minimum wage increase and a health insurance portability law. Combining these acts with the balanced budget and welfare reform, the government looked functional once again, and the congressional Democrats seemed superfluous.[64] Though the congressional Democrats enjoyed unprecedented support from environmental, feminist, and labor groups in 1996, their efforts to retake the majority were in vain.[65]

On Election Day, the voters returned to Washington, D.C., a divided government. Clinton won an easy victory over Bob Dole, but another challenge from Ross Perot kept him under 50 percent of the vote once again.[66] In his second inaugural address, the president acknowledged the split mandate the voters had given on Election Day, interpreting the results as a message that the people wanted Clinton and the congressional GOP "to be repairers of the breach and to move on with America's mission."[67]

To that end, Clinton signed a Republican-backed balanced budget agreement in 1997 that cut taxes and increased certain discretionary spending programs, once again leaving the left out in the cold.[68] As a capstone to Clinton's not insignificant achievements, he hoped in his second term to forge a grand bipartisan compromise on entitlements with his old nemesis Newt Gingrich. The Republican Speaker had taken a beating in the polls and was interested in being remembered as a great statesman, not just a Republican insurgent. And so Clinton and Gingrich, by the end of 1997, had worked out a deal in which Clinton would agree to reform Social Security, by means including the creation of private retirement accounts, and in return Republicans would not use the budget surplus for tax cuts.

And then the Lewinsky scandal hit. News broke that the president had carried on an illicit affair with a young White House intern, had possibly lied about it under oath, and had encouraged Monica Lewinsky, his paramour, to do likewise.[69] The scandal sank any opportunity for a grand compromise; instead, it reignited the old partisan flames as Republicans in the House aggressively investigated the president, then eventually pushed for impeachment. Clinton tacked to the left—at least when it came to the partisan rhetoric—so that the liberals in his caucus could get behind him, if not out of affection, then at least out of the knowledge that, if the scandal pushed Clinton out, it would be only a matter of time before congressional Democrats suffered a fate similar to the GOP in the 1974 midterm elections.[70] After months of sleazy revelations and partisan bickering, the public finally decided that, while Clinton had behaved inappropriately, his actions did not merit removal from office. The House impeached the president, but the Senate did not convict, with the final vote breaking largely along party lines.

With a grand policy breakthrough now out of the cards, the only way Clinton could secure his place in history was by making sure Gore was elected to succeed him. As the heir apparent, the vice president took full advantage of all the political and financial connections that Clinton made available.[71] That, plus the front-loading of the primary calendar, which advantaged front-runners, gave him a substantial edge.[72] Though the AFL-CIO had been displeased by the Clinton tenure, it did not even try to stop the Clinton-Gore juggernaut, instead endorsing the vice president in 1999. In return, Clinton did not push hard for a new World Trade Organization agreement, after poorer nations refused to go along with his labor and environmental proposals.[73]

Still, it was unreasonable for Gore not to expect a challenge from the left, given the Clinton record over the previous five years, as well as his own twenty-year reputation as a moderate. It was former New Jersey senator Bill Bradley who finally tossed his hat into the ring. Though Gore had every conceivable institutional advantage, as well as a healthy lead in the national polls, Bradley put up a robust fight. Powered by the dissatisfaction in the Democratic ranks for what seemed like an opportunity missed during the previous eight years, Bradley collected a substantial amount of money, even outraising Gore on the eve of the New Hampshire primary. Gore's artless response was to get to Bradley's left, going so far as to blast the former senator for retiring in 1996 rather than staying to fight the vicious Republicans.[74]

In the New Hampshire primary, Bradley came within just a few thousand votes of defeating Gore—and his coalition in the Granite State was an early version of Barack Obama's electorate: younger, college-educated liberals who often considered themselves independents. Gore won the state narrowly by carrying regular Democrats and older voters. Unfortunately for Bradley, the primary calendar was a brutal one. There were no major contests for more than a month after New Hampshire, and with the surprise victory of John McCain on the Republican side, Bradley found it virtually impossible to get media attention. In the end, despite Bradley's strong position at the end of 1999, Gore managed to win every primary and caucus in 2000.[75]

The demise of the Bradley challenge did not mean that Gore was free and clear to tack to the center against the GOP nominee, George W. Bush of Texas. Instead, the emergence of the Ralph Nader candidacy in the spring of 2000 forced the vice president to stay on the left.[76]

If the Democratic party is like the sun, then Ralph Nader would have once been Pluto—in the orbit of the party, but on its outer edges. He was a famous New Politics activist in the 1960s—a kind of Great Society muckraker in the tradition of Upton Sinclair and Lincoln Steffens. His high-profile status as a "consumer rights advocate" in the mid-1960s helped bring about a series of major reforms—on highway safety, food safety, energy regulations, and more. By the mid-1970s, Nader was so famous that he actually hosted an episode of *Saturday Night Live*. Regardless of his nonpartisan appearance, he actually was a kind of client within the Democratic party, dependent upon liberal Democrats like Walter Mondale and Abraham Ribicoff having powerful positions within Congress. Democrats, in turn, sought him out to legitimize their own positions: George McGovern, for instance, asked Nader to be his vice-presidential nominee in 1972; Jimmy Carter ostentatiously sought out Nader's counsel during the summer of 1976, then staffed his White House with former "Nader's Raiders" like James Fallows.[77]

However, the Reagan era marked a severe decline in Nader's status. While he had managed to work with LBJ and Nixon, now Nader could not even get face time with the new president.[78] Nader had hoped that Clinton's election would bring him back to influence, but it did not; in fact, Clinton never met with him once during his tenure, and Gore—who had kept communication lines open with Nader during the 1980s—shut him out as well.[79]

Nader connected this personal snub to the exponential rise of corporate political giving, and concluded that the system had been totally corrupted by big business: no longer was the Democratic party the advocate of the people against the powerful; instead, there were no real differences between the Democrats and the Republicans, both being tools of the corporations. And so Nader decided to launch a third-party challenge in 2000, one that unabashedly appealed to the various client groups of the left.[80] His argument was that Clinton had done nothing for the environment, for African Americans, for consumer protection, or for labor—so why should the left reward him by voting for Gore?

The Nader challenge had a significant effect on the Gore campaign. Rather than run as the heir to Clinton in the New Democratic tradition, Gore reinvented himself as a Bryanesque populist. In his nominating address in Los Angeles, Gore solemnly intoned:

> [My] focus is on working families—people trying to make house payments and car payments, working overtime to save for college and do right by their kids. . . . Whether you're in a suburb, or an inner city . . . Whether you raise crops or drive hogs and cattle on a farm, drive a big rig on the interstate, or drive e-commerce on the Internet . . . Whether you're starting out to raise your own family, or getting ready to retire after a lifetime of hard work.
>
> So often, powerful forces and powerful interests stand in your way, and the odds seemed stacked against you—even as you do what's right for you and your family. . . .
>
> I want you to know this: I've taken on the powerful forces. And as President, I'll stand up to them, and I'll stand up for you.[81]

Quite a transformation for the man who had quietly urged Clinton to sign welfare reform.

While Gore reinterpreted his centrist record as the last stand of American populism, his campaign team dispatched the party's old band of client group leaders—from labor to African Americans to feminists and so on—to dissuade rank-and-file Democrats from bolting to Nader.[82] Those same groups also spent a king's ransom to push Gore past the finish line; even the NAACP chipped in to the effort with a vile ad blasting Bush for vetoing a hate crimes law in Texas.[83] The leaders of these groups all knew that, while Clinton might have occasionally ignored them, Bush would be downright hostile, and with a total Republican majority in Congress, they would have nowhere to go.

In the end, the efforts of the clients on behalf of Gore *almost* worked. Though Nader was polling between 5 percent and 8 percent of the vote in the summer, on Election Day he pulled in a little less than 3 percent. Most of the Democratic party came home to Gore—but not all of it. The Nader vote cost Gore the four electoral votes of New Hampshire and, most important, the twenty-five of Florida. And thus Bush—not Gore—became the forty-third president.

In other words, Nader played the spoiler—not just by stealing votes on the left from Gore, but also by forcing him to reinvent himself as a "people versus the powerful" populist, an image that turned off the middle class, which had prospered during the Clinton years.[84] Even though the economy was doing better in 2000 than it had done in more than a decade, and Clinton's job approval rating was higher than ever, Gore could not win election in his own right. Nader snatched votes from the left, and Gore's attempts to head him off lost him votes from the center.

And so Dick Morris's prediction that Clinton's strategy would form a "temporary triangle"—between himself, the Republicans, and the congressional Democrats—was *exactly wrong*. The triangle was indeed a temporary one, but it was not the congressional Democrats who eventually folded into the Clintonian, New Democratic center. Instead, Clinton's inattention to his party's clients brought about the Nader challenge, which was strong enough to place George W. Bush in the White House, so that the Democratic center disappeared from the White House while the clients of the left remained in Congress.

The New Democrats would all but vanish in the years to follow. In the summer of 2008, Barack Obama—the presumptive nominee—refused to attend the DLC convention in Chicago, instead opting to visit the *Daily Kos* gathering across town; in 2010, the DLC would finally shut its doors, having run out of money. However, the liberal clients remained firmly in place in the United States Congress. In fact, their control over the congressional party grew substantially after 1994: the Republican majority depended upon a shift in southern congressional politics toward the GOP, so southern moderates (like Clinton and Carter) were less likely to be elected to Congress, let alone have enough seniority to hold the key leadership posts. Instead, the party leaders would come almost exclusively from the party's left wing and would have strong ties to the same client groups we have discussed so far.

In other words, the Clinton presidency is best viewed not as a great change in the structure or ideological outlook of the Democratic coalition but as a "stitch in time," a brief moment when a centrist Democrat could free himself from the party's clients and govern with the Republicans. The party itself had not really been reformed—Clinton just enjoyed a short window of opportunity to operate independently of it. In 2000, the left wing of the party would reassert itself and make sure that this centrist moment ended when Clinton left town.

CHAPTER TWELVE

You're on the Menu

Barack Obama and the Triumph of the Clients

As we have noted time and time again throughout this work, the challenge in a republican system of government run by political parties is a significant one: the ruling coalition must find a way to balance the particular demands of its partisan loyalists with the broader needs of the public. This is an endemic feature of American politics, and a look at the earliest political history of this nation demonstrates clearly that even John Adams, Thomas Jefferson, and Andrew Jackson all struggled with this.

For the Democrats following the 1960s, this balancing act became particularly difficult, as that tumultuous decade added scores of new party clients to an already substantial list. Now party leaders would have to manage not only industrial and craft labor and urban political bosses, but also public sector labor, African Americans, feminists, environmentalists, consumer rights groups, and more. As we saw in the past two chapters, both Jimmy Carter and Bill Clinton failed to do this—Carter could not get his clients to take on inflation, and Clinton could not coax them into solving the big problems of crime and deficits without payoffs that undermined his political position. In the end, Carter was defeated; Clinton was ultimately successful, but only because congressional Democrats were swept wholly out of power for the first time since the 1950s.

The George W. Bush years saw few changes to the structure of the Democratic party. If anything, the party's antiwar position only strengthened the liberal clientele, as many of the New Democratic, re-formist forces within it ultimately backed the Iraq War and thus fell out of favor. Also aiding the left-wing clients was the continued emigration of southern whites from the party, leaving the liberal client groups the dominant force.

These clients would basically get their first choice for president in 2008 as the party nominated Barack Obama after a protracted and bruis-ing primary battle. With the financial crisis hitting just six weeks before Election Day, it was an easy win for the charismatic young Democrat. What remained to be seen, however, was whether and how Obama would check the party's clients for the sake of the national interest. Could he succeed where Carter and Clinton had failed? Would he even try?

Over this final chapter, we will see that Obama has made no such attempts. Either unaware of or uninterested in the competing demands of Democratic clients and the public good, Obama has let the former dominate the agenda while the nation at large limped through the worst economic recovery in generations. The country responded by sweeping the Democratic majority out of Congress in the 2010 midterms, but by then the party clients had already done quite a bit of damage.

Everybody in the English-speaking world expected Hillary Clinton—the wife of the former president and now a senator from New York—to run for the White House in 2008. The Clintons had obviously been plotting a path back to 1600 Pennsylvania Avenue since they left it in early 2001, and sure enough, Mrs. Clinton tossed her hat into the ring at the beginning of 2007, quickly lining up endorsements and climbing to the top of the polls.

The real surprise on the Democratic side of the ledger was the can-didacy of Barack Obama, the very junior senator from the state of Illi-nois. Though he had served barely two years in the Senate, he declared his candidacy shortly after Clinton, in the winter of 2007. While many other Democrats pursued the presidency that year, it was Obama who would emerge as Clinton's chief rival.

Obama was a politician of odd juxtapositions. For instance, he talked unabashedly about how politics can speak to the most noble and honorable traditions in American society. Yet when he first ran for the state senate in Illinois, his campaign team sponsored a series of legal challenges to get his opponents tossed off the ballot.[1] Similarly, his old political backers were strange bedfellows. He had cut his teeth in Chicago politics in the early 1990s working for Project Vote, which had been sponsored by groups from the far-left side of the aisle—like the Association of Community Organizations for Reform Now (ACORN) and the Service Employees International Union (SEIU) and by radical religious leaders like Father Michael Pfleger and the Reverend Jeremiah Wright. In a crowded field in the 2004 Democratic primary, Obama got a jump start, thanks to an endorsement from the SEIU and other activist unions, which also backed him early on in the 2008 campaign.[2] Yet for all of his far-left connections, Obama also sidled up to establishment interests with relative ease. His top contributors in 2004, for instance, were the University of Chicago and Kirkland & Ellis, a law firm that represented such important clients as the Chicago Board of Trade. And at the start of the 2008 presidential battle, Obama was able to match Hillary Clinton dollar for dollar, in no small part because of his connections to Wall Street and Hollywood.[3]

Indeed, there was something about the junior senator from Illinois that seemed to make everybody on the Democratic side comfortable, Clinton loyalists notwithstanding. Well-heeled establishment Democrats loved his Harvard background and his connections to figures like former secretary of the treasury Robert Rubin. Meanwhile, leftist Democrats adored his early opposition to the Iraq War—he was the only serious candidate in the 2008 field never to have supported it—as well as his ties to the SEIU, which by that point had become perhaps the most important labor group in politics. And Obama's speeches hit all the right rhetorical notes for the diverse Democratic constituencies. He was careful to sound transformational but not radical, vague but not evasive, intellectual but not wonky—and he always cast his candidacy in historic terms: together, he promised, Americans could make history . . . by electing Obama!

At times, the Obama campaign seemed more than a little bit like a cult of personality, with hundreds of thousands of devotees believing in this young senator for no particular reason.[4] He offered no policy-based alternative to his major rivals, nor did he have a record that indicated that he was the transformational figure he claimed to be. But he sure was cool. And Team Obama parlayed his mystique into huge fund-raising hauls. Taking a page out of Ralph Nader's playbook, Obama's campaign gurus had their candidate address stadium-size crowds, but unlike Nader's organizers, they roped attendees into the movement by getting contact info; channeling them to their innovative social networking site My.BarackObama.com; and ultimately collecting hundreds of millions of dollars in small contributions from them.[5]

Meanwhile, Obama and his team plotted a brilliant path to the nomination. They anticipated that, if he were to defeat Clinton, he would do so only through a bruising battle for convention delegates, so Obama's campaign mastered the byzantine rules that the Democratic party uses to select delegates, and took advantage of various opportunities—like the caucuses that select delegates in many western states. Caucuses are low-turnout affairs where intensity of support matters more than anything else, so they were a great place for Obama—having as he did so many die-hard supporters—to outflank Clinton. Additionally, Obama's campaign recognized the potential support to be had among black voters, especially in the South, where African Americans now dominated Democratic primaries. Clinton had an early lead with African Americans, but Team Obama understood that it was very soft support; once Obama demonstrated his electoral viability, black voters would swing his way.[6]

In the end, the nomination battle played out precisely as Obama had hoped. He won a narrow victory in Iowa and, thanks to the nation-wide organization he had created, came out ahead on Super Tuesday. For the next four months, Obama and Clinton battled to a virtual tie in terms of popular support, but Obama won more delegates, thanks to his ingenious planning.[7]

Republican nominee John McCain hoped that he could exploit Obama's weakness with the so-called Clinton Democrats—working-class whites in the Midwest who had not been swept up in Obamamania. Perhaps he could have, but the financial crisis of September 2008 basically cost the Republicans the election. Swing voters swung decisively to Obama and the Democrats, although this was ironic because most of the major financial firms that had contributed to the problems in the first place—AIG, Bank of America, Citigroup, JP Morgan, and Morgan Stanley—gave overwhelmingly to Democrats in general, and to Obama in particular, that year.[8] Yet Obama's coziness with the big financial houses did not stop the typical left-wing groups from pitching in to help the Democratic effort; the SEIU led the way with $75 million in total campaign spending.[9]

On Election Day, Obama scored a comfortable 53 percent of the vote and swept all of the swing states except Arizona and Missouri. The country had elected the first African American president in its history, and handed him huge Democratic margins in the Congress.

Although Obama's victory in 2008 was a milestone in the struggle for racial equality in the United States, the fact of the matter was that the same problems that had afflicted the Democratic party since the 1960s remained. Specifically, the party was still dominated by client groups whose interests often diverged dramatically from the public good. If anything, those groups had only consolidated their positions within the party since the last time a Democrat won the presidency. In the Congress of 2009, a staggering 237 Democrats would score 90 percent or higher with the AFL-CIO, and 239 would score 90 percent or higher with the League of Conservation Voters, compared with 158 and 36, respectively, in 1993. Not only was the new Congress stocked with loyalists to the core Democratic groups, but so also was the House leadership, as Speaker Nancy Pelosi reestablished the old seniority rules for selecting committee chairmen. Fifty years ago, that would have been a boon to southern conservatives who hailed from safe districts; in the twenty-first century, however, the safest Democrats were from union districts, minority districts, and districts full of the New Politics liberals who donate to the Sierra Club or EMILY's List.[10]

Thus, the challenge for a Democratic president was now greater than ever, but if ever there was a moment when a sustained focus on the public good over the demands of the Democratic clients was necessary, 2009 was that moment. The financial crisis that had catapulted Obama into the presidency had spread throughout the economy at large, so that by the first quarter of 2009, GDP was shrinking by an annualized 6.7 percent while the nation shed more than 750,000 jobs per month. The country desperately needed bold, vigorous action to restore economic prosperity.

Was Obama up to the enormous challenges he faced? Could he

succeed where Carter and Clinton had failed, and somehow tame the seemingly wild Democratic Congress? As with everything else about Obama, the signals were decidedly mixed. On the one hand, Bill Clinton had been the only Democrat to win reelection since Franklin Roosevelt, and he did so by pursuing a moderate course and staying independent of his party's clients, yet Obama's campaign for change in the 2008 primaries was a not so subtle critique of Clinton's triangulation. This suggested that maybe Obama was a man of the clients, as did his tight alliance with the SEIU.

On the other hand, Obama seemed to recognize the tensions between the demands of the clients and the public interest. His campaign book, *The Audacity of Hope,* opened with a trenchant summary of the problem. Contrasting the "dirty and nasty" side of politics that generated widespread public cynicism, Obama praised

> *another tradition to politics, a tradition that stretched from the days of the country's founding to the glory of the civil rights movement, a tradition based on the simple idea that we have a stake in one another, and that what binds us together is greater than what drives us apart, and that if enough people believe in the truth of that proposition and act on it, then we might not solve every problem, but we can get something meaningful done.*

Reading this, one gets the impression that Obama might have been the leader who could finally get his party to focus on the public interest, something no Democratic president had done for nearly half a century.

Which way would he go? Unfortunately, the independent thinking of his writing was illusory. For reasons unknown, the forty-fourth president has to date focused relentlessly upon the interests of the party clients over the public good. Whether it was the stimulus, the auto bailout, financial reform, cap and trade, or health care, this president and his allies in Congress have catered solely to the party's sundry client groups and paid only lip service to the public interest, which has suffered great harm during his tenure.

• • •

Identifying the public interest seems like a tricky problem. How do we know if something is good for the whole country or merely the projection of our self-interest onto everybody else? In practice, however, it is often pretty easy to figure out, as some issues are obviously urgent national concerns. During the Carter administration, the top priority of the public was, without doubt, taming inflation. In the first two years of the Clinton tenure, it was about restoring faith that the government could solve big problems that had basically been ignored for twenty years. For the Obama tenure, it all came down to one word: jobs. This gives us an obvious metric against which to evaluate this president: he was pursuing the public interest when he was focusing on job creation, and ignoring it when he wasn't.

To Carter's and Clinton's credit, they tried to govern for the public interest during their tenures, though both essentially failed when the Democrats ran Capitol Hill. Carter could not get the party clients to agree to a robust anti-inflation program, while Clinton was forced to load up his centrist proposals with left-wing agenda items to win over his party clients. Obama, on the other hand, has never really tried. Almost every important program he has endorsed has had as its target some client or interest aligned with the Democratic party, not the public at large.

Obama guaranteed that the party clients would rule when, early on, he chose to delegate most of the policy formation to congressional Democrats. As we noted in the previous chapter, special-interest money has flooded Capitol Hill, sweeping away congressional Democrats and Republicans alike. The Democrats are now dependent upon not only labor unions and New Politics groups like feminists and environmentalists, but also trial lawyers and other professional associations, big financial firms, agribusinesses, the medical industry, and more. Together these groups contribute tens of millions of dollars to the Democratic campaign effort, and it's simply unrealistic to expect that, left to their own devices, congressional Democrats would defy their financial masters for the public good. Yet Obama let them write all the major reforms, ceding them so much ground that at times even congressional leaders, notoriously defensive about presidential incursions, complained that Obama wasn't involved *enough*.[11]

The problems with this approach became clear shortly after he was sworn in, with the American Recovery and Reinvestment Act (ARRA), a stimulus bill that hit all of the erogenous zones of the Democratic party and was the single largest payoff in history to the party's vast clientele. Congressional Democrats, with President Obama's blessing, pumped nearly $1 trillion into the American economy, with loyal Democrats being the point of entry for much of the money.

The single largest category of stimulus funding was what its proponents called "tax *cuts*," which amounted to $288 billion. However, there were no permanent reductions in marginal tax rates in the ARRA. Instead the Democrats actually offered tax *credits*, many to core constituencies. For instance, there was a $3 billion expansion of the earned income tax credit (EITC) and a $9 billion expansion of the child tax credit, both of which benefited the sorts of low-income voters typically represented by the Congressional Black Caucus (CBC). Similarly, the "Making Work Pay" tax credit, which cost $89 billion, cut the Social Security tax for all workers, even those who don't pay income taxes. Environmentalists won big with changes to the tax law as well, as the ARRA offered $9 billion in energy tax credits.[12]

The next-largest category was "contracts, grants, and loans," which amounted to $275 billion. This included $85 billion committed to education, largely meant to keep teachers on state payrolls. The big winners in this, obviously, were the National Education Association and the American Federation of Teachers, both loyal party clients. Industrial and trade unions also won a big payday with the $50 billion committed to transportation and infrastructure improvements, while environmental groups won with $28 billion for clean energy projects and grid enhancements. Ditto the CBC, which saw an additional $16 billion for low-income housing.[13]

Finally, there were large expansions of the entitlement state. The government spent $85 billion to fund state Medicaid programs, a provision that kept state government layoffs low and ensured that members of the American Federation of State, County and Municipal Employees (AFSCME) continued to pay their dues. There was also a $61 billion subsidy for unemployment insurance and a $29 billion grant for family services, which quietly included a major change to the welfare laws: after the 1996 reforms, states would not get more money for enrolling more people in welfare programs, but the stimulus did away with that, promising more money for more enrollees, even if those new enrollments came from loosening the qualifications. Unsurprisingly, in the years following the stimulus, the number of people on food stamps has skyrocketed, exceeding 14 percent of the population as of this writing.[14]

Littered throughout the ARRA were parochial programs that made the final cut because some crucial swing voter in Congress demanded them. There's $30 million for Nebraska hospitals and $50 million for the National Endowment for the Arts. There's an exemption for Florida yacht repair companies from paying the federal workers' compensation insurance. There's a requirement that the Transportation Security Administration buy 100,000 uniforms from American textile plants. There's billions for Amtrak and other public transportation projects that Democrats from big cities love, as well as big subsidies for the agricultural and timber interests that dominate in the West.[15]

Of course, it's unreasonable to expect a political party not to reward its loyal clients after it wins, at least a little bit. As the old saying goes, to the victor go the spoils. So the more relevant question is, whose interests hold sway—those of the public at large or those of the clients? It's hard to fault a party for letting its loyalists "wet their beaks" a little bit here and there, but what is inappropriate is a party clientele that is driving public policy. An examination of the stimulus indicates pretty clearly that too much of the money was either disbursed to party clients (such as through an expansion of the EITC) or disbursed in ways preferred by clients (like the energy tax credits). This would not be a problem from a public-spirited perspective if the ARRA ultimately stimulated the economy to a satisfactory degree. Did it?

It probably helped the economy at least a little bit. For instance, the infrastructure spending was probably stimulative, so that would be an example of a particular party client (trade unions) *and* the broader public benefiting. However, there were major *efficiency* problems with the ARRA—i.e., the package did not do nearly as much for the economy as one would have hoped, and as the Obama administration advertised, given the price tag.

For starters, very little of the money was actually spent in 2009, when the economy was still technically in recession. Just 23 percent of

the total was spent that year, and a paltry 11 percent of the money dedicated to work projects was spent. Most of that money did not actually
get into private hands until 2010 or later.[16]

Second, large portions of the money went to outfits that either could
not spend the money or did not need it. One small example was the
Milwaukee public school system, which received $89 million over two
years for new construction projects, even though the district already has
fifteen vacant school buildings. A larger and more troubling example
was the Department of Energy, which received $40 billion in stimulus
money to distribute in grants and loans, but its loan guarantee office
failed to get the money out the door until the White House applied
pressure late in 2009.

Third, many of the items were clearly non-stimulative. On health
care, the ARRA included a $20 billion "down payment" on an Obama
agenda item: modernizing medical records. That might be a worthwhile
goal, but it is a lousy way to jump-start the economy. Additionally, empirical studies of the package have suggested that restricted grants to
states, such as grants for education programs, did little to stimulate, as
states responded to the free money by reducing their borrowing levels.[17]
Obama and the Democrats also promised a flood of "green jobs" that
would come from the clean energy grants, but three years later they have
largely failed to materialize. For instance, California won a $186 million
grant to weatherize drafty homes but has created only 538 new jobs from
the money as of this writing.[18] What's more, it is quite possible that the
transfer payments worsened the employment situation. Alan Krueger,
now the chairman of President Obama's Council of Economic Advisers, argued in a 2003 article that "unemployment insurance . . . [tends] to
increase the length of time employees spend out of work."[19] Meanwhile,
economists John Taylor of Stanford and Allan Meltzer of Princeton have
argued separately that tax credits like those offered in the stimulus do little to revive the economy. As Metzler put it, "Unless tax cuts are expected
to last, consumers save the proceeds and pay down debt."[20]

When we add up all of these problems, we're now talking about half
or more of the stimulus, suggesting that it did an extremely poor job of
reviving the economy and creating new jobs. Indeed, James Feyrer and
Bruce Sacerdote of the National Bureau of Economic Research have

concluded that the ARRA's "multiplier"—the extent to which a dollar of stimulus money created new economic activity—was very low.[21]

While we must concede that the stimulus had some impact on the economy, it is also apparent that it was grossly inefficient. It was too loaded with payoffs to various party clients to have the bang for the buck that the Obama administration promised. The White House assured the country that if the ARRA became law, the unemployment rate would not exceed 8 percent, but as of this writing it is above 9 percent. Given what was actually in the bill, it is little wonder this prediction was so far off the mark. Maybe a government-designed stimulus program could have revived the economy, but the ARRA was not it.

Organized labor has been in decline for more than fifty years, and today just 12 percent of American workers are part of a union, including just 7 percent of private sector workers.[22] Despite their declining fortunes in the economy, unions are as powerful as ever in the halls of government. As mentioned above, more congressional Democrats than ever are highly loyal to union interests, and organized labor has never had as good a friend as Barack Obama in the White House. Before Obama, every modern Democratic president qualified his support of the unions at some point or other. FDR refused to intervene in the Little Steel Strike, Truman threatened to draft striking workers, Kennedy voted for Landrum-Griffin, LBJ for Taft-Hartley, and Carter and Clinton worked directly against union interests on inflation and trade, respectively. But Obama has never faltered in his support of the unions—not as a U.S. senator, when he voted with the AFL-CIO 96 percent of the time, and certainly not as president of the United States.

A main goal of union lobbyists has always been access—one reason George Meany ran the AFL-CIO for a quarter century was that he had the ears of the power brokers in Washington. In the Obama White House, union allies have better access than ever. Obama named Patrick Gaspard, formerly of the SEIU, as his political director, and he made Hilda Solis, a California Democrat who voted with the AFL-CIO 98 percent of the time while in the House, the secretary of labor. Obama also made strong pro-labor appointments to the Federal Election Commission and the National Labor Relations Board (NLRB), and White House visitor logs have revealed that the most frequent guest at 1600 Pennsylvania Avenue during 2009 was Andrew Stern, who was then the president of the SEIU.[23] Another important symbol of Obama's commitment to unionism was his decision to involve himself in the Wisconsin labor dispute between Republican governor Scott Walker and state government workers. Just a few weeks after Obama bemoaned how heated rhetoric had degraded our politics, he used a martial metaphor to describe the events in the Badger State: "Some of what I've heard coming out of Wisconsin, where they're just making it harder for public employees to collectively bargain generally, seems like more of an *assault on unions*."[24]

With such a staunch friend in the White House, unions were bound to do well, but their gains would not come through Congress. As we noted in Chapter 7, since World War II labor unions have not been able to push through major legislation that benefits their members directly, and they again failed in 2009. Though President Obama endorsed the "card check" provision of the Employee Free Choice Act—which would have required employers to recognize a union once half of the workers had signed cards saying they wanted one—this reform could not secure the filibuster-proof majority needed to pass the Senate.[25] So, without enough support in Congress, most of the benefits that organized labor has won in the past few years have been due to executive action. Obama required that federal contractors post a "balanced notice of their employees' rights" under the National Labor Relations Act; he mandated that, when federal agencies change contractors, the new firm must first offer jobs to the non-supervisory workers who worked at the old firms, thus dictating the kind of seniority-based hiring that unions support;[26] he also forbade contractors from being reimbursed for money they spent to campaign against union formation;[27] finally, he encouraged federal contractors to negotiate project labor agreements, which typically benefit unions.[28]

The president's appointees have also been busy on behalf of the unions. At the Department of Transportation, Secretary Ray LaHood expanded his department's interpretation of the Davis-Bacon Act—a law that requires federal contractors to pay prevailing wages—to apply to the green jobs generated by the ARRA.[29] And the NLRB has been an aggressive advocate of union rights, going so far as to order the Boeing corporation to halt its plans to move part of its Dreamliner production to South Carolina, a right-to-work state.[30] That latter move prompted outrage from the typically centrist editorial page of *USA Today,* which argued, "Boeing tried to do the right thing by keeping jobs in the USA and is getting punished for it. In the legal sense, its 'mistake' appears to have been giving its workers a choice instead of just ignoring them."[31]

Significant as all these enactments were, they pale in comparison with the huge victory the United Auto Workers won in the bailout of General Motors and especially Chrysler. President Obama faced a major dilemma regarding the auto companies when he took office; the Big Three carmakers had been struggling for years as foreign competition had cut into their margins, and the recession of 2008 had put GM and Chrysler on the brink of destruction. Late in 2008, President George W. Bush agreed to offer them about $18 billion from the Troubled Asset Relief Program (TARP), but this was but a temporary measure designed only to get them into the spring, when Obama would have to deal with them.

Conservatives and free-market advocates hated the idea of an auto bailout. Their attitude was that the market had rendered its judgment against these companies, and they should face an orderly liquidation through the bankruptcy courts. Yet like Bush before him, Obama decided to save them both.[32] That was not altogether controversial, considering the importance of the automakers to the economy of the Midwest, but the deals the White House gave the UAW certainly were.

The president and his auto task force—led by investment banker Steve Rattner and former United Steelworkers official Ron Bloom—decided not to let Chrysler fall into bankruptcy, and to instead have the UAW's pension plan take a majority stake in the company, with Italian carmaker Fiat and the government itself owning the rest. This would never have happened in a bankruptcy court, because Chrysler had many secured creditors who otherwise would have been in front of the UAW to take control of the company's assets. When the task force explained its intentions to representatives of those creditors, they were naturally aghast, but Bloom breezily responded, "I need workers to make cars, but I don't need lenders."[33] Many of the secured creditors were the big Wall Street firms, which were in hock to Washington because of the TARP bailout, so they went along with the deal, bad as it was. However, the smaller creditors revolted at first and refused to accept the terms.[34] That was when the president of the United States took to the airwaves to demagogue them:

> While many stakeholders made sacrifices and worked constructively, I have to tell you some did not. In particular, a group of investment firms and hedge funds decided to hold out for the prospect of an unjustified taxpayer-funded bailout. They were hoping that everybody else would make sacrifices, and they would have to make none. Some demanded twice the return that other lenders were getting. I don't stand with them. I stand with Chrysler's employees and their families and communities. I stand with Chrysler's management, its dealers, and its suppliers.[35]

It is telling that the UAW's effective bailout was "justified"; years of loyalty to the Democratic Party had paid off, and the UAW thus took control of Chrysler, including many of the company's bad debts. Normally, a new owner is not allowed to write down the debts of the previous owner for tax purposes, but the ARRA included an oft-overlooked provision that made an exception—but only for companies now owned by union pension plans.[36]

UAW workers also won special consideration when it came to their pensions. Workers at Delphi, which supplied parts to GM, were to have their pensions assumed by the government's Pension Benefit Guaranty Corporation. Normally, this would mean pension cuts ranging between 20 percent and 40 percent, as well as the elimination of health and life insurance benefits. The Obama administration's bailout of GM, however, exempted Delphi's *unionized* employees from the reduction. They won full pension benefits, while Delphi's *non-union management* saw its pension benefits cut dramatically.

Traditionally, we think of business and labor interests as separate and irreconcilable—businesses align with the Republicans and labor with the Democrats. However, as we saw in Chapter 11, big business shifted its political strategies after the passage of the Federal Election Campaign Act in the 1970s—with congressional Democrats now regularly outraising Republicans among corporate groups, which are more interested in government rents than advancing an ideological agenda.

Indeed, by the time he entered the White House, Barack Obama had developed a cozy relationship with the types of interests we usually think of as Republican-dominated. As we noted above, the big financial firms on Wall Street generally backed Obama over McCain by wide margins—and the new president did not disappoint them. He staffed his administration with former Wall Street executives—like Rattner, Larry Summers, and Rahm Emanuel—and though Treasury Secretary Timothy Geithner had spent his career in the government, he was close to Rubin, formerly of Citigroup, and Wall Street was quite comfortable with him.[37] What's more, Obama renominated Ben Bernanke as chairman of the Federal Reserve, a move that the big financial firms cheered, as Bernanke had lowered interest rates to virtually zero, enabling companies like Goldman Sachs to rake in billions of dollars in profits just a few short months after the near collapse of the markets.

And that's not all. Geithner's financial stability plan, released early in 2009, was "strikingly favorable to Wall Street," as *New York* magazine's John Heilemann noted.[38] The Street in particular loved the so-called Public-Private Investment Program, wherein the Treasury Department agreed to go 50–50 with any private investor willing to buy the bad mortgages that had precipitated the panic; additionally, the Federal Deposit Insurance Cooperation (FDIC) would offer a loan for more than 85 percent of the purchase price. In essence, government supports meant that for very little risk to hedge funds, they had an opportunity to walk away with massive profits. What's more, the government supports helped create a market for the bad mortgages, which had been worthless just a few months prior, thus enabling the big banks to unload them from their balance sheets.[39]

As with the auto bailout, it's arguable that all of this, while highly unpalatable, was quite necessary. The argument—and it's a reasonable one—goes like this: the federal government simply could not afford to allow GM to go under, nor could it allow a bunch of "zombie banks" with bad debt on their balance sheets to drag the economy underwater, so it had to take vigorous action. Let's put aside the larger economic and ideological issues about whether this was sound policy and instead ask a more direct political question: did the Obama administration give preferential treatment to its friends as it dealt with this crisis? With the auto bailout, as we saw, the answer was definitely yes. The same goes for the financial bailout. The tycoons of Wall Street contributed tens of millions of dollars to Obama and his congressional allies, and in the end it was money well spent.

There was never really any doubt that the Congress would pass some kind of financial reform after the 2008 election; the question was how significant the new rules would be. At issue in particular were the mega-banks that were created after the Clinton administration, with bipartisan congressional support, did away with the Glass-Steagall Act, which had mandated that investment and commercial banks had to be separate. The Gramm-Leach-Bliley Act of 1999 ended that separation and led to the creation of huge firms like Citigroup, which the government had deemed "too big to fail" after the financial panic in 2008. Now that the dust had settled, would the government allow mega-banks like Citi to persist?

Wall Street fully anticipated the coming reform drive, so it dispatched high-profile lobbyists, many of whom had worked as staffers for the House Financial Services Committee, to Capitol Hill to talk Congress out of stiff reforms. A particular target of the Street was the so-called Volcker rule. Proposed by former chairman of the Federal Reserve Paul Volcker, now an adviser to the Obama administration, this would have kept firms from using federally insured cash to speculate in the financial markets, so it would have spoken directly to the issue of "too big to fail," as the mega-banks had access to the Federal Discount Window as well as the guarantee of the FDIC. The banks, obviously, did not want the Volcker rule, and their friends within the administration were not fans of it, either.

In the end, despite the most liberal Congress in at least forty years, not to mention widespread public revulsion at the excesses of Wall Street over the past decade, the Volcker rule was watered down to essentially nothing. In fact, the major Wall Street firms endorsed the Dodd-Frank financial reform bill because, as Fox Business Network's Charles Gasparino argues:

The trade-off for all this regulation is government protection,
which is what makes the crony capitalism of the modern banking
business really work. . . . [I]mplicit in just about every facet of the
bill was that "too big to fail"—the notion that Citigroup, Bank of
America, Goldman Sachs, J.P. Morgan, and Morgan Stanley are
so large and intertwined in the global economy that they need to
be monitored and propped up no matter how much money they
lose—was here to stay.[40]

"Crony capitalism" is a great way to describe the relationship between big business and today's Democratic party. Well-heeled firms
donate tens of millions to the party for Election Day, and afterward
they can rest assured that, no matter how vociferously party leaders
might rail against million-dollar Wall Street bonuses, they'll get bailed
out whenever they get into trouble. As for the smaller financial outfits
that don't have friends in high places—like those who rebelled against
the Chrysler bailout—they can expect a stern presidential rebuke for
"unjustified taxpayer-funded bailouts."

"Crony capitalism" is also the best way to describe the Democratic party's
efforts on environmental regulations during 2009 and 2010. Obama—
like other national Democratic leaders before him—was deeply indebted
to the environmental movement, which had developed not only a crack-
erjack congressional lobbying effort, but also sophisticated electoral operations. Obama accordingly staffed the executive branch with staunch
environmentalists like Carol Browner and Steven Chu, who once said
that "coal is my worst nightmare." Almost right away, these new overseers
produced big changes in environmental policy, always toward tighter
regulations of business. In 2009, the Environmental Protection Agency
(EPA) ruled that carbon dioxide poses a threat to human welfare and
thus falls under its regulatory umbrella. It also ruled that California could
regulate greenhouse gases on its own, and the Obama administration
took advantage of the auto bailout to raise the Corporate Average Fuel
Economy (CAFE) standards to thirty-five miles per gallon by 2020. In a
great example of Obama-style cronyism, the big automakers also received
billions of dollars in federal grants to develop electric cars.

It was, however, on cap and trade that Obama and the Democratic party shattered all previous records for crony capitalism and corporate welfare. The cap-and-trade program the Democrats advocated in 2009 was basically a scheme to limit the total annual carbon emissions into the environment, then allow private companies to trade carbon credits. The hope was that this would reduce the pollutants released into the air and thus mitigate the dangers from global warming.

The final product—dubbed the Waxman-Markey bill and endorsed by President Obama—was designed with three key Democratic groups in mind. For starters, it limited the total emissions in the United States and thus won the support of groups like the Sierra Club and the Environmental Defense Fund. Second, it doled out $50 billion worth of free carbon credits to private enterprises, making it the single largest corporate welfare payout to big business in American history. Once again, lobbyists for all sorts of industries—ranging from coal to timber to agribusiness—descended upon the House Energy and Commerce Committee to win all sorts of special carve-outs and exemptions. For instance, Waxman-Markey rewarded "no-till" farming with carbon credits because the process traps carbon dioxide in the ground. As it turned out, agribusiness giant Monsanto makes special seeds that are necessary for "no-till," and they had hired Dean Aguillen, a former staffer for Nancy Pelosi, to lobby Congress on its behalf.[41] Other big winners in the cap-and-trade plan were the big Wall Street firms, as Waxman-Markey would create a new carbon marketplace where the mega-banks could win huge commissions for executing carbon credit trades. Third, Waxman-Markey would implement a government rebate program to mitigate the increased energy costs that would go along with the new limits on carbon consumption. Most income groups would still end up paying more out of pocket—*except the lowest quintile,* which happens to be the most loyal Democratic group and where families would see, on average, a net *gain* of $125 per year because of cap and trade.[42]

The cost to the American economy for this nexus of environmental advocacy, corporate welfare, and income redistribution would be significant. According to the Congressional Budget Office, Waxman-Markey would slow the American economy by about 0.5 percent per year in 2020 and by 2.25 percent per year in 2050. It's worth pointing out that economic growth per year over the past decade has averaged just 1.6 percent; this means that if such a cap-and-trade program had been implemented forty years ago, the United States would now be in the midst of a decades-long recession. Fortunately, mining and industrial interests hold more sway in the Senate, where the Waxman-Markey bill died without ever receiving a vote.[43]

The country, it seems, dodged a bullet on cap and trade. Even if we assume that the bill would have been effective at mitigating global warming (a big "if," considering the reluctance of emerging economies like China and India to impose similar regulations), implementing an economy-wide regulation of energy in the midst of the worst contraction since the Great Depression is not really in the public interest. It would have been one thing to implement such a program during the 1960s or the 1990s, amid robust growth, but the sluggish American economy needs all the help it can get at the moment, not a whole new regulatory regime designed to limit energy consumption.[44]

Health care reform was, without doubt, the top priority of the Obama administration in its first two years in office. Never mind that just 9 percent of voters considered it the "most important issue" in 2008, or that the economy was still in a recession when the deliberations on new legislation began.[45] A universal health care bill would, Obama must have hoped, elevate him to the pantheon of great liberal presidents who had expanded the social welfare state: FDR, LBJ, and now Obama. What's more, a universal coverage bill would disproportionately aid Democratic clients, something that was obviously a top concern of this president; for instance, organized labor had been pushing for a universal coverage program for years, believing that federal subsidies for care would strengthen labor's negotiating position with employers. Thus, viewed from within the confines of the Democratic party, a focus on health care reform was a no-brainer for President Obama, regardless of what the broader public wanted.

The president faced two enormous obstacles on the road to reform. First, most people—and above all most voters—already had health insurance, and a redistributive scheme intended to cover the uninsured at the expense of those with coverage would not go over well.

Second, there was a vast constellation of interest groups in the health care universe—hospitals, doctors, nurses, insurers, the drug companies, senior citizen advocates, and so on—all of whom would be greatly affected by reform. If these groups suspected that they would be losers in the final deal, it was an easy bet that they'd take to the airwaves to blast the finished product, just as the insurers had done with their famed "Harry and Louise" ads in 1994.

Thus, the White House implemented a two-tier strategy. First, to sell a public still reeling from the recession on health care reform, Obama argued that such reform was essential to a sustainable economic recovery. Of course, health care had remained largely unreformed in the 1990s, one of the most fantastic periods of economic growth in the country, but this was as good a rhetorical angle as the White House could devise. So to pave the way for the reform efforts, the president told a joint session of Congress in February 2009:

> *Now is the time to act boldly and wisely to not only revive this economy, but to build a new foundation for lasting prosperity. . . .*
>
> *[We] must . . . address the crushing cost of health care. This is a cost that now causes a bankruptcy in America every thirty seconds. By the end of the year, it could cause 1.5 million Americans to lose their homes. In the last eight years, premiums have grown four times faster than wages. And in each of these years, one million more Americans have lost their health insurance. It is one of the major reasons why small businesses close their doors and corporations ship jobs overseas. And it's one of the largest and fastest-growing parts of our budget. Given these facts, we can no longer afford to put health care reform on hold. We can't afford to do it. It's time.*[46]

Notice the emphasis here on cost control—this would be another feature of the president's speeches over the next thirteen months. Yet cost control was always, in fact, a secondary concern—nothing more than a rhetorical smoke screen designed to lull the mass public into acquiescence. As David Bolan, a key aide to the Senate's Health, Education, Labor and Pension (HELP) Committee, would admit after the bill had passed, "This is a coverage bill, not a cost reduction bill. There is stuff here that will begin to address the issue of cost, but this is not a cost reduction bill with a bit of coverage on it—it is really trying to get coverage first."[47]

Second, the White House lured as many interest groups—or, in Washington parlance, "stakeholders"—to the bargaining table as it could. The thinking was that if Obama and congressional Democrats could not get them to endorse specific legislation, at least they could delay the date on which these groups launched their anti-reform advertising blitzes.[48] In fact, Ted Kennedy had been holding informal policy sessions since the fall of 2008, and he invited representatives from such groups as Aetna, the AFL-CIO, the American Association of Retired Persons (AARP), the Chamber of Commerce, and the Pharmaceutical Research and Manufacturers of America (PhRMA) to participate. The meetings were strictly off the record, intended as a venue for policy makers and interest group leaders to hammer out the outlines of a bill.[49]

Industry participation in the Kennedy meetings was just one of many signals from interest groups that they were looking to cut a deal. Many of them increased their campaign contributions during the 2008 cycle, fully expecting that if the Democrats took control, health care would be at the top of the agenda. One of the largest recipients was Senator Max Baucus of Montana, chairman of the supremely powerful Senate Appropriations Committee; since 2005 he had received more than $400,000 from health insurers and drugmakers. Chris Dodd, who would take control of the HELP committee after Ted Kennedy's death, was the beneficiary of a television ad campaign in 2009 in Connecticut—where he faced a tough reelection battle—courtesy of PhRMA. Obama, for his part, received $2 million from these sectors of the health field during 2008 alone.[50] What's more, the health industry employed scores of lobbyists, including many former and prominent House members, like Billy Tauzin, once the chairman of the House Energy and Commerce Committee and now a lobbyist for the pharmaceutical industry. And Tom Daschle, though he had withdrawn as Obama's nominee for Health and Human Services, nevertheless remained a top White House adviser on health care, even as his firm did lobbying work for United Health Group.[51]

Again, contrary to the common conception of a left-right spectrum among interest groups, corporate and union groups teamed up this time around. For instance, large companies like Walmart and AT&T were members of Better Healthcare Together, an advocacy group founded by John Podesta, head of the Obama transition team. Stern's SEIU was also in the group, making for a strange-bedfellows coalition indeed, as Walmart and the SEIU had butted heads many times over the years. However, on this issue, both sides had something to gain. The SEIU would obviously be better off with a national health policy, and Walmart could win as well. If the government mandated that all employers must provide health insurance while allowing the sorts of policies Walmart already offered its employees, the retailing giant could gain an advantage over its competitors, as its buying power in the market would mean lower premiums, and hence lower input costs.[52]

The Walmart example is a great indication of the motivations for interest group participation in the reform process. All of them claimed to be public-spirited, looking out, above all, for the interests of the country, but their interests were far more parochial. They intuited that there were benefits for themselves to be gained by playing along, and Obama sweetened the pot dramatically when he endorsed an individual mandate. Never mind that he had opposed this during the campaign, or that it was massively unpopular with the public; this was a fantastic way to bring the "stakeholders" to the bargaining table. Mandates would essentially force thirty million Americans to become new customers of the health care industry whether they wanted to or not—and the opportunity for massive increases in revenues for doctors, nurses, hospitals, drugmakers, and insurers was an excellent bargaining chip for the White House and congressional Democrats.[53]

The result of the negotiations between Democrats and eager interest groups was a plethora of sweetheart deals. To begin with, most of the industry groups did not want the so-called public option, a government-run insurance plan that would compete with private plans, so the White House backed away from that early on, and the Senate Finance Committee excluded it from its finished product.[54] On top of that, most of the major groups made specific concessions and in exchange had an opportunity to nudge reform in their direction. The most infamous of all such deals was cut between the White House and

Billy Tauzin, representing PhRMA. The drug manufacturers agreed to $80 billion in discounts over the next decade, and promised a $150 million advertising campaign on behalf of reform efforts. In return the White House guaranteed PhRMA new rules protecting them from makers of generic drugs, as well as a continued reimportation ban on drugs from Canada. The cynicism of the deal was astounding. After all, not only had Obama promised to end the reimportation ban during the campaign—he had actually run an ad called "Billy," in which he sanctimoniously bemoaned the fact that PhRMA had gotten a sweetheart deal when Tauzin was in Congress.[55]

Cynicism notwithstanding, the PhRMA deal served as a template for deals with other big stakeholders, most notably the hospitals and the doctors lobby.[56] The administration even came close to a deal with America's Health Insurance Providers (AHIP), even as Obama and his flacks were publicly denouncing the greed of the insurers at every possible opportunity. The negotiations between the two sides ultimately resulted in the Senate Finance Committee's adopting forty-eight amendments favorable to AHIP, prompting Senator Jay Rockefeller to joke that "the insurance industry is not running this markup, but it is running certain people in this markup." In the end, it was only the Finance Committee's decision to water down the mandate penalties that pushed away AHIP, which feared a "death spiral" of ever-increasing premiums resulting from weak mandates.[57]

Industry groups were not the only ones who won special deals. As we noted in Chapter 11, organized labor's tepid support of Bill Clinton's reform efforts in 1994 was a big reason the legislation died in Congress, and labor was so lukewarm because of the taxes on expensive insurance policies. Union representatives had long negotiated for such "Cadillac" policies because they were 100 percent tax deductible, and they did not take kindly to such a change in policy. While moderate Democrats and even Republicans were interested in taxing high-end policies in 2009, liberal Democrats who were closely aligned with organized labor staunchly opposed the idea. In the end, the White House and organized labor cut a deal: there would be a tax on such policies, but it would not take effect until 2019.[58]

Feminists also won a major coup. Since the 1970s, abortion policy in the federal funding of health care had been governed by the Hyde Amendment, named after the late representative Henry Hyde of Illinois. The Hyde Amendment strictly forbade federal dollars from paying for abortion with a very high wall separating the two. Not only could Medicaid recipients not receive coverage for abortion; government employees could not get abortion coverage through their insurance either. The powerful Pro-Choice Caucus in the House was not prepared to allow the Hyde language to enter the final health care bill, and instead offered a "compromise": government-sponsored insurance exchanges would include policies that cover abortion, but no federal funds would be used to pay for that coverage. Pro-life groups, most notably the Catholic Bishops, denounced this as an accounting gimmick; money is fungible, after all, and a dollar that a beneficiary receives for, say, eye care is a dollar that has been freed up for an abortion. A small group of pro-life Democrats led last-minute negotiations with Nancy Pelosi in the hours leading up to final passage of the reform bill, but when the Pro-Choice Caucus told the Speaker that eighty or more of their members would defect from the party line if the pro-lifers got their way, the leadership gave in. When it was all said and done, the pro-life Democrats won nothing more than a meaningless executive order, which essentially repeated the compromise language that they had found so unacceptable in the first place.[59]

As with the stimulus bill, the fact that health care reform—which finally passed in March 2010—catered to so many loyal Democratic clients and health care interests is not, in itself, a problem for republican government. As noted above, practically speaking, clients are always going to get a share of the pie when their party is in charge. The real question is whether the balance of government efforts are on behalf of the public at large. And, as with the stimulus, the answer with the health care reform law is a resounding no.

The Patient Protection and Affordable Care Act (PPACA), as health care reform was ultimately known, was a poorly titled piece of legislation, as it neither protected patients nor got health care costs under control. On the patient protection front, President Obama promised time and again that "if you like your health insurance, you can keep it." However, that was not necessarily true. Because the penalty that will be assessed on employers who refuse coverage is much lower than the cost of insuring workers, companies will have a strong incentive to drop their coverage. The Congressional Budget Office estimates that 7 percent of all employees will lose their employer-sponsored coverage, but consulting firm McKinsey has subsequently polled companies and found that 60 percent of all employers who understand the PPACA intend to drop or substantially alter their health insurance coverage.[60]

As for the exchanges, low- and middle-income people will be eligible for federal insurance subsidies to keep their out-of-pocket costs down, meaning that if employers drop health care at a greater rate than the feds have estimated, the cost of the subsidies will be substantially greater than the Democratic leadership claimed it would be. Worse, individuals who do not qualify for subsidies on the exchanges will see their insurance costs increase by roughly 11 percent, an outcome that would directly contradict the president's promise to keep costs under control. Those who remain in employer-based insurance will, on average, see no substantial change in their insurance costs—and thus no relief from what has been a major drag on wages and incomes over the past twenty years.[61]

What about nationwide health spending? This was a constant rhetorical focus of the president, who toured the country all through 2009 proclaiming that we had to "bend the cost curve" downward. According to Richard Foster, the government's chief actuary for Medicare and Medicaid, total federal health expenditures over the next decade will go up, not down. Worse, many of the cost control provisions within the bill are simply unrealistic, and unlikely to survive subsequent congressional action. For instance, PPACA requires Medicare payment reductions that are in line with economy-wide increases in efficiencies. While this seems sensible at first blush, the fact is that the health industry regularly does not see efficiency improvements that match the rest of the economy—owing to how labor-intensive the industry is and the fact that patient-by-patient care precludes comparable economies of scale. According to Foster, many care providers might very well drop Medicare, as the program simply will not reimburse them for their costs. Congress will never allow this to happen, for obvious political reasons, which means that PPACA will cost substantially more than President Obama has advertised.[62]

So, in the end, the mass public gets a bill that might force people off their current coverage, will not reduce their insurance costs and in many cases will raise these costs substantially, and drives total federal health spending upward, probably by much more than Obama and congressional Democrats would admit. This means that the public at large loses in the deal, while the winners are the usual cast of Democratic constituencies as well as the special interests that dealt with the White House early on.

The astute reader will have already noted the very important word left unmentioned for many pages: *jobs*. As we argued earlier, that had to be the metric by which we would judge the Obama administration's fidelity to the public interest. While the president promised many times to "pivot to jobs" during his first two years in office, he never actually did. The care and feeding of the Democratic base—be it through the stimulus, cap and trade, the auto bailout, financial reform, or health care— took up too much of his time and political capital.

While the president and his allies in Congress were making the world a better place for Democratic clients everywhere, the economy limped through the worst economic recovery in more than fifty years.[63] Real income continued to stagnate, the job market never rebounded, the housing market remained in a depression, businesses sat on capital, and consumers stopped spending. All the while, confidence in the government plummeted to new lows after a temporary uptick following Obama's inauguration.

In November 2010, the voters responded to Democratic mismanagement with righteous anger—not just over the president's inattention to the economy but also over the mess created by the massively unpopular PPACA. In November 2010, the Republicans picked up a net of sixty-three House seats, the single largest midterm gain since 1938.

To put the relentlessly clientelistic policies of the Obama administration into proper perspective, it's necessary to look back some 135 years into history, for it is only during the Gilded Age that we have seen a political party behave with as little regard for the public interest as the Democrats have in the last three years.

Writing in the 1870s, Republican senator James Grimes of Iowa complained that the Republican party had gone "to the dogs. Like all parties that have an undisturbed power for a long time, it has become corrupt, and I believe that it is today the most corrupt and debauched political party that has ever existed."[64] There are a lot of ways to conceive of Republican perfidy during the Gilded Age—the dishonest impeachment of Andrew Johnson, the criminality of the Grant administration, or the blatant election stealing in 1876. But there was something much worse than all of this, for Republican economic policy during the late nineteenth century was deeply anti-republican. The GOP hiked tariff rates to secure the financial support of industrial and agricultural magnates, then handed out the additional tax dollars in generous bonuses to Civil War veterans, the most loyal Republican group. All the while, farmers—especially in the South—suffered because of high prices, and GOP protectionism contributed to the rise of the industrial and financial trusts, which would eventually pose a threat to the republican system of government bequeathed by the Founding Fathers.

While the Obama administration and its Democratic allies in Congress have not committed ethical misdeeds similar to those of Grant's cronies, the Democratic party's modus operandi in government today is nevertheless more than a little bit like that of the Gilded Age Republicans. The Democratic party under Obama is now the faction that robs Peter to pay Paul—with Peter being the fellow smart enough to vote or contribute to the party, and Paul being the guy who didn't have such foresight. As Tom Donohue, the head of the Chamber of Commerce, commented during the health care debate, "If you don't get in this game . . . you're on the menu!"[65]

How do we account for this? After all, it was not long ago that Democratic presidents, namely Carter and Clinton, seemed committed to checking the party's clients, aware that there was tension between their interests and the public good. Why has there been such a marked change between them and Obama?

Part of the answer might simply be Obama's managerial style. Report after report has depicted him as a hands-off executive, one who prefers to "lead from behind," which was the phrase often invoked to explain the administration's role in the Libyan civil war. This makes sense when we think about his role in domestic policy as well; after all, it is a very rare event when congressional leaders complain that the White House is not involved enough in the legislative process.

But there must be something more, and the answer seems to lie in the slow but sure transformation of the Democratic coalition over the last sixty years. As noted in Chapter 8, starting in 1952 we begin to see the steady erosion of the old bonds between the northern and southern Democrats. Carter and Clinton were southern governors who came to power after this process began, but well before it was concluded. We are now in the final stages of the South's political evolution, so nowadays it is difficult for a Democrat to win a gubernatorial or senatorial victory in the South, much less parlay that victory into a national campaign for president. Most Democratic politicians in Dixie now face strong challenges from Republicans that limit their prospects for advancement, and those who do get to the elite tier—like governors and senators—often have to take issue positions that put them too far to the right of the northern wing of the party for them to win a nomination.

This matters because the South is largely bereft of the sort of clients who now dominate the national party (an ironic development, because the white South was once the principal client of the party). Organized labor is a negligible part of the workforce in Dixie. Environmentalists, feminists, and consumer rights activists have virtually no presence in the South, in contrast to their strength on the Pacific Coast and in the Northeast. African Americans are numerous in the South, for sure, but a Democrat who wants to hold a statewide office must become a master of balancing their interests against those of whites. It's only by means of such biracial voting coalitions that southern Democrats can stay in power.

Thus, Carter and Clinton—coming as they did from the South—not only possessed relatively few ties to the party's dominant clients but also understood the dangers of giving in to these clients' every demand. They recognized that failing to attend to the interests of the broader public, including voters who are not loyal Democrats, is politically dangerous. Indeed, Clinton knew this from personal experience; elected governor in 1978, he was voted out of office in 1980 for enacting too liberal a program. He learned the lessons of his defeat quite well; after he won back the governor's mansion in 1982, he was careful never to move too far to the left of his state. This, in turn, explains why Clinton took so naturally to the "triangulation" strategy after the Republican victory in 1994.

Barack Obama has no such experiences in his history. Instead, his political background prior to the White House is one of total immersion in the clientelism of the modern party. He was a state senator from the South Side of Chicago, where African Americans dominate. His particular district was centered on Hyde Park, which is a bastion of the New Politics left. He won the 2004 Senate nomination in large part because he had the support of the SEIU, with which he had worked on voter mobilization projects as early as 1992, and he faced only token opposition in the general election. He never experienced the kind of rebuke that Clinton suffered in 1980, and he never had to learn just how different the interests of the party clientele are from the interests of the broader public. Little wonder that, as president, he has done virtually nothing to check the clients for the sake of the public good.

Unfortunately, it is hard to see Obama as an exception to the rules that now govern the party, at least in the North. It is difficult to imagine a President Mondale, a President Dukakis, or a President Kerry behaving much differently from the way President Obama has actually behaved, when we consider that they all come from the same basic political environment, one where managing the clientele is a top priority.

If southern Democrats cannot win the nomination any more and northern Democrats cannot break free of the clients, then why should we expect another Democratic president whose outlook is similar to Clinton's or Carter's? We shouldn't. Instead, it is more reasonable to anticipate that future Democratic presidents will be highly responsive to the interests of labor, feminists, African Americans, consumer rights groups, environmentalists, and so on, just as Obama has been.

To put matters bluntly: as troubling as the Obama tenure has been, what is even more discouraging is that it is a sign of things to come from the Democratic party.

Conclusion

The story told here has not been a tale of right and wrong. There are no good guys and bad guys, heroes and villains, in this account. American politics is regularly cast in such moralistic terms, but that has not been our approach here. Instead, our focus has been on the factions within American society, and how the Democratic party has transformed the interests of those factions into public policy.

That is the great challenge of a republican system of government such as ours—one in which the people are sovereign and the government operates on their behalf. Such governments are easy to envision in theory but hard to realize in practice. People are fundamentally self-interested, always ready to put themselves over the community, so it is very difficult to devise a government run by people that puts the whole community first. Meeting in Philadelphia in the summer of 1789, the framers struggled with this task, debating for months on end about how a government could represent all the people rather than a privileged few. Their answer was a complicated system of limited government, separation of powers among three coequal branches, a bicameral legislature, and a government for a large geographical area. The hope was that this would be a government powerful enough to do the work of the people and designed in such a way that it would never work against them for the sake of a few.

The republican principles of the framers live on today, in the hearts and minds of conservatives, liberals, and moderates alike. Our two great political parties—the Democrats and the Republicans—regularly offer public-spirited platforms that are in keeping with those principles, at least on the surface. Even a casual observer of the political scene could not fail to note that both sides couch their arguments in communitarian language: what is good for *our* national defense, *our* prosperity, *our* shared sense of justice, and so on. In other words, both sides publicly argue that everybody would benefit from their particular programs.

Unfortunately, the public faces of both parties often mask some decidedly anti-republican tendencies. Governed only by the ambitions of politicians and a slender set of rules, parties are not constrained to act only on behalf of all the people, and they regularly do not. While the rhetoric of both sides may speak to the public good, behind the scenes Democrats and Republicans are often eager to make deals with various factions within society—if that is what it takes to win. We have called this practice clientelism—the exchange of votes for governmental favors between a faction and a party. The great oversight of our Constitution was the framers' failure to anticipate the inevitability of political parties, and thus to provide for better mechanisms to control their behavior. For if a political party is behaving in an anti-republican manner, and it controls the government, then the government—even with all of its checks and balances—will likewise behave in an anti-republican manner.

The fear of anti-republican parties corrupting our government has been a persistent one, dating back to the 1790s. For example, Thomas Jefferson and James Madison opposed Hamilton's banking proposals in part because they thought the plans would benefit Hamilton's friends while harming the farmers of Virginia. What's more, opposition to clientelism brought the Democratic party into existence in the 1820s. Andrew Jackson and his allies formed it as a vehicle for their vengeance against the "corrupt bargain" of John Quincy Adams and Henry Clay, and more generally to fight the public venality of the "Era of Good Feelings," wherein politicians in Washington and moneymen in New York and Philadelphia seemed to conspire for their own benefit rather than doing the work of the people.

As an alternative, Jackson and his Democrats would stand up for the "humble members of society"—the small farmers, the laborers, and the urban ethnics who did not have connections to get a special deal from the government. While the party lost this identity to the sectional grievances of the late nineteenth century, William Jennings Bryan re-ignited the old Jacksonian flame at the dawn of the twentieth century. Later, Woodrow Wilson and Franklin Roosevelt implemented a new philosophy to secure equal treatment for the downtrodden—an active, "progressive" federal government that would reshape society to make it more just. To this day, this remains the public-spirited message of the Democratic party: that the whole country will be better off if all its people are treated equally.

Yet the Democrats wasted little time before committing the very errors they had pledged to rectify. Andrew Jackson's principle of "rotation in office" evolved from a leveling, democratic institution into the crooked "spoils system" of rewarding political cronies. In time, the spoils system became the foundation for morally bankrupt political machines like Tammany Hall, whose only purpose in winning office was to pay off the supporters who had put it there. The nineteenth-century patronage regime was modernized in the twentieth century by the liberal Democrats who expanded the size and scope of the government with the New Deal. The Democratic party would no longer use mere patronage to reward a few thousand loyalists; now it would take advantage of the massive new regulatory and redistributive powers of Washington to reward millions of new party clients—not only with federal jobs but with beneficial laws that reshaped society to advance their particular interests. The party could take care of whole classes in society—farmers, union workers, urban ethnics—with a single stroke of the presidential pen.

Of course, most voters are not clients of the Democratic party, or of the Republican party for that matter. Most voters expect no special favors after Election Day, and the parties compete for their support only by offering broad-based programs ostensibly designed to benefit all (or, at least, most) Americans. It's always been this way—even at the height of the New Deal majority, the Democrats could never claim half-plus-one of the public as their clients. Thus, the political challenge facing modern Democratic leaders is to keep the party clients happy while simultaneously governing for the whole nation.

Franklin Roosevelt was the master of this balancing act. Consider his agricultural policy in particular. Without doubt, the Agricultural Adjustment Act (AAA) aspired to benefit all the country's farmers, who had been hit especially hard by the Great Depression. The AAA offered economic support for farmers who limited their crop output, in the expectation that this would eliminate the agricultural surplus, increase farm income, and thus revitalize this important sector of the national economy. Yet under the surface, the AAA was full of political payoffs, especially to southern plantation owners. As we saw in Chapter 3, AAA payments initially went to the landowners, to be divided up as they pleased among the impoverished sharecroppers, and even after this defect was fixed, much of the federal money found its way not to the poor farmers of the Cotton Belt but to the wealthy landowners who had plenty of friends on the House and Senate agriculture committees.

To varying degrees, FDR's early successors—Harry Truman, John F. Kennedy, and Lyndon Johnson—were more or less able to juggle the party's clients with the public interest in a similar fashion. The only real hiccup during this period was caused by the migration of African Americans into northern swing states, which forced the Democrats to liberalize their civil rights stand at the expense of the southern segregationists who had long been vital to the party. And even then, Truman, JFK, and LBJ all managed electoral victories with a more liberal civil rights plank.

However, the tumult of the 1960s interrupted the party's ability to tend to the clients and the public interest. The major problem was the addition of new clients, all of whom had their own power bases within the party and their own unique set of demands. African Americans entered the electorate as Democrats in the 1960s, demanding increased social welfare spending. Feminist groups demanded regulations to secure equal treatment in the workplace, more generous welfare benefits for poor women, and greater access to abortions. The environmental and consumer rights movements wanted new layers of government regulations to protect the quality of life. Finally, the rise of public sector labor unions consistently pushed the Democrats to expand the scope of government at all levels and inhibited its ability to reform the federal bureaucracy. Add these groups to industrial and craft unions, which had belonged to the party more or less since the 1930s, and the Democrats suddenly had too many clients with too many demands. No longer, it seemed, could Democratic leaders tend to their interests while focusing on public concerns.

Jimmy Carter, as we saw in Chapter 10, tried to please both his clients and the public and failed miserably at both. The great challenge during the Carter tenure was the threat of runaway inflation, and dealing with this economic menace put the president on a collision course with many Democratic clients, especially organized labor, which wanted an ever-expanding social welfare state. Again and again Carter tried to meet the clients halfway, in hopes that a compromise would appease them while also taming inflation. It didn't work; Ted Kennedy launched a challenge to Carter in the 1980 Democratic primary, and inflation helped Ronald Reagan defeat him in the general election.

Elected in 1992, Bill Clinton promised to be a different kind of Democrat, a credible pledge considering that his political background up to that point had little to do with the party clients. As governor of Arkansas, Clinton knew that his electoral success would invariably depend on convincing enough Republican presidential voters to split their ballots; and as the chairman of the Democratic Leadership Council, he advocated reforms that infuriated the party's clients. And yet, during his first two years as president, Clinton found himself unable to break free of the clients, who by then had come to dominate the Democratic congressional caucus. On deficit reduction and crime control, the need to appease the liberals in Congress overwhelmed Clinton's centrist impulses; his health care reform was a failure in part because he could not get buy-in from the clients; and while NAFTA was a legislative victory, the clients responded by withholding support in the 1994 midterms. It was only after that debacle that Clinton was free to govern as a true centrist, as the 1994 elections cleaned the Democratic majorities out of Congress and installed Republicans with whom Clinton could actually work. In the end, however, the clients got the last laugh—with Ralph Nader playing the spoiler in the 2000 election.

Barack Obama has, to date, proved himself to be the anti-Clinton. Running for the Democratic nomination in 2008 on the implicit argument that Clintonism had failed, President Obama has time and again acceded to the demands of the Democratic clientele. The stimulus bill, designed by congressional Democrats with Obama's blessing, pumped $800 billion into the economy, largely through Democratic clients like labor, environmental groups, and African Americans. Obama followed that up with a bailout of the auto industry that gave the United Auto Workers much more than they would have won in bankruptcy court, then proceeded as if the economic crisis had passed. His financial reform legislation was highly preferential to his big-money donors on Wall Street; his cap-and-trade bill tried to award environmentalists, well-heeled businesses, and the poor in one fell swoop; and his health care bill is the apogee of anti-republican, liberal clientelism, a sprawling, trillion-dollar payoff to an array of groups that leaves the average American in no better shape. The 2010 midterms saw the worst drubbing for the Democratic party since 1938 as the GOP won control of the House of Representatives—due punishment for Obama's focus on the party clients at the expense of the national interest.

Having explained what has happened to the Democratic party, I think it's appropriate to close by asking why this has happened.

First, we must acknowledge the role that contingency has played. For instance, as we noted at the beginning of Chapter 4, the election of 1948 seems to have been one moment when the switch of just a few thousand votes, from Harry Truman to Thomas Dewey, might have had an enduring effect on the party, perhaps strengthening the hand of the conservatives in the South. There are other such examples. The Supreme Court's ruling in *Schechter Poultry* v. *U.S.* in 1935 contributed to FDR's push for the National Labor Relations Act (NLRA), which revived organized labor. If the Court had gone the other way, the NLRA and the ensuing revolution in labor relations might never have happened. JFK's decision to select LBJ as vice president had a profound effect on the party; if Kennedy had not made that choice, if he had not been shot, or if LBJ had behaved as president as he had in the Senate, catering to the conservatives in the South and West, the party would probably be different now from what it turned out to be.

There are plenty of other examples because, after all, history as it has come down to us was never inevitable. Even so, the "breaks," such as they were, have tended to favor the northern, liberal wing of the party, which has firmly accepted FDR's model of policy and politics.

As we noted in Chapter 3, the FDR model was to use a large, progressive federal government to advance the public good and to pay off the party's loyal constituencies. The flaw of this approach is the key to understanding why the party is what it is today. Transforming party loyalists into clients, as that model prescribes, is not a one-way street. American political parties are open institutions that anybody is free to join, and the party clients, once they became dependent upon the continuation of their federal benefits, had plenty of incentives to sign up. Over time, they have taken over the party—dominating the congressional caucus and now, it seems, the presidency as well. They have the power to bend the policy needle toward their own ends, leaving the public interest basically unattended to.

The party has thus become a threat to the American republic itself. If we understand a republican government as being "of the people, by the people, for the people," as Abraham Lincoln argued in the Gettysburg Address, then Democratic governance today fails that standard. Instead, the Democrats are the party of, by, and for the politically privileged few, at the expense of everybody else.

This is not the first time in American history that such a fate has befallen a political coalition. We noted at the end of Chapter 12 that today's Democrats look more than a little bit like the Gilded Age Republicans, in that both imposed burdens on their opponents to grant favors to their supporters, with the broader public good left unattended to. And of course Andrew Jackson founded the Democratic party in 1828 to stop exactly this kind of favoritsm. Recall this line from his veto message, which I quoted in the preliminary pages of this book: "There are no necessary evils in government. Its evils exist only in its abuses. If it would confine itself to equal protection, and, as Heaven does its rains, shower its favors alike on the high and the low, the rich and the poor, it would be an unqualified blessing."

It is ironic that Jackson's heirs would come to stand for exactly what he opposed. But above all it is tragic. It is tragic because the United States needs a healthy, two-party system, and more to the point it needs the Democratic party.

There is a reason, after all, that the party survived the disastrous presidencies of Franklin Pierce and James Buchanan, both of which contributed mightily to the onset of the Civil War; survived Grover Cleveland's handling of the Panic of 1893; survived the rebuke suffered by the Woodrow Wilson administration in 1920; survived the "credibility gap" of the LBJ administration; and survived the incompetence of the Carter administration. It is in part because the party's core message—as articulated by Jackson nearly two centuries ago—still resonates to this day. America is a radically egalitarian country, at least in its outlook; the people are inherently skeptical about special privileges and always ready to listen to a political party that promises an equal playing field.

Today's Democratic leaders talk a lot about equality, but their actions speak louder than their words. As we have seen over the past three chapters, the party has come to play a double game—complaining loudly about inequality in society while enacting policies to advance the interests of its own clients. This has created a void in the body politic—one that the Republican party, which has long been the party of economic expansion rather than the ideal of social equality, is simply not able to fill. With the exception of the Tea Party, there is no real faction out there making the Jacksonian case for an end to special privilege.

What prospects are there for reform within the Democratic party today? It is hard to be optimistic. The party has had reform movements in the past—Clinton's New Democrats, for instance, but that effort emanated largely from the South, which has since slipped into the Republican column. What's more, as we noted in Chapter 2, major party reforms usually happen only after electoral defeats that leave a party badly chastened. The Democrats have not suffered such a loss in nearly a quarter century, since the election of 1988.

For now, liberal Democrats seem more inclined to point a finger at the voters when faced with indications of their party's weakness. For instance, it is not uncommon to hear them aver that their agenda is indeed in the best interests of the common people, if only the people could see the truth of the matter. The most recent and noteworthy articulation of this idea came from Barack Obama during the 2008 Democratic nomination battle, when he tried to explain to a crowd of San Francisco liberals why small-town Pennsylvanians were not supporting him:

[O]ur challenge is to get people persuaded that we can make progress when there's not evidence of that in their daily lives. You go into some of these small towns in Pennsylvania, and like a lot of small towns in the Midwest, the jobs have been gone now for twenty-five years and nothing's replaced them. And they fell through the Clinton administration, and the Bush administration, and each successive administration has said that somehow these communities are gonna regenerate and they have not. So it's not surprising, then, that they get bitter, they cling to guns or religion or antipathy to people who aren't like them or anti-immigrant sentiment or anti-trade sentiment as a way to explain their frustrations.[1]

Perhaps tens of millions of voters are indeed so "bitter" that they regularly vote for the wrong party. Perhaps the expressed opinions of these people do not reflect their best interests, and only the party elite can understand what they really need. Perhaps they are suffering from a kind of "false consciousness," similar to what the students and academics of the New Left claimed was ailing Middle America in the 1960s. However, following the argument of this book, we contend that these voters perceive the Democratic party more clearly than its leaders do. As humble as their stations in life may be, they recognize correctly that the Democratic party has become a party of privilege—if not the economically privileged on Wall Street (though they are surely now part of the mix), then the politically privileged clients that have dominated it for more than a generation.

Therefore, liberals who are upset about their political failings should stop pointing at the voters and start asking themselves what is wrong with their own coalition. Put aside the issue of whether liberalism is the best public policy alternative; the real question is whether the Democratic party is still a good vehicle for public-spirited liberalism. The answer is that it is not. The demands of the clients make the result of liberal governance not public policy, but clientelistic policy. Liberalism, as implemented by today's Democratic party, simply does not help the "humble members of society," unless of course they have the right political connections.

What would Old Hickory say about that?

Acknowledgments

This book would not have been possible without the assistance of some very important people, to whom I owe a great deal of thanks.

First and foremost, thanks to my wife, Lindsay Cost. She was a great source of emotional support throughout the writing of this book. She also meticulously read the finished draft, ensuring that it was as refined as possible, and helped me research and organize several sections, especially those regarding civil rights and organized labor. Her generous assistance was indispensable, and I am so very blessed to have her in my life.

Thanks to my editor, Adam Bellow. This is my first book, and it was a huge leap of faith on his part to believe that I was up to the task of writing a work of such scope. Adam also helped me conceptualize the project at its earliest stages; the outline we put together turned out to be a reliable guide for the rest of the process. Thanks as well to Kathryn Whitenight and the editorial team at Broadside Books for doing an exemplary job in refining my raw manuscript for publication.

Thanks to my agent, Byrd Leavell of the Waxman Agency, who stuck with me through thick and thin. For over a year he labored to find me a good project, and though it seemed at times that it would not happen, he never quit.

Thanks to my father, John Cost, and my friend Dan Wilson. Both took a week out of their busy lives to pore over a draft of this book with a fine-tooth comb. Their comments were very helpful as I put the finishing touches on the book.

Thanks to my mother, Lyn Cost, whose generous assistance in taking care of our newborn was vital to the completion of this project. My mother has always been my "number one fan," and her support over the years gave me the confidence I needed to pull this project off.

Thanks to my in-laws, Dan and Kaye McKenzie, who babysat for our little boy all last summer while I labored over this book. Our little fella is a cutie, for sure, but taking care of a baby day-in, day-out is no small favor!

Thanks to my friend and colleague Sean Trende, whose unique insight into the broad themes of American politics and generosity in letting me pick his brain helped me formulate the argument of this book.

Thanks to the editors and staff of the *Weekly Standard*, above all Bill Kristol, Daniel Halper, Mark Hemingway, and John McCormack, who were always gracious and understanding when I had to put blogging aside to meet a deadline. Thanks also to the editors at *RealClear Politics*, especially John McIntyre, who in 2005 offered me, a previously unheard-of blogger, a fantastic platform to develop and refine my analytical skills.

Notes

Introduction

1. Jackson, Andrew, "Veto Message, July 10, 1832," in *American Presidency Project,* ed. John T. Woolley and Gerhard Peters. University of California at Santa Barbara, 2011. http://www.presidency.ucsb.edu. Accessed September 21, 2011.

CHAPTER 1: All the Toiling Masses

1. For a lively review of Garfield's assassination as well as the perfidious politics of the age, see Millard, Candice, *Destiny of the Republic: A Tale of Madness, Medicine and the Murder of a President.* New York: Doubleday, 2011.
2. Adams, Henry, *The Education of Henry Adams.* New York: Barnes and Noble, 2009, 234.
3. See Key, V. O., *Southern Politics in State and Nation: A New Edition.* Knoxville: University of Tennessee Press, 2006, 315–382.
4. For a good consideration of how the German Lutherans factored into political calculations of the day, see Phillips, Kevin, *William McKinley.* New York: Henry Holt and Co., 2003, 80–81.
5. See Burnham, Walter Dean, with Thomas Ferguson and Louis Ferleger, *Voting in American Elections: The Shaping of the American Political Universe Since 1788.* Bethesda, MD: Academica Press, 2010, 80–84 and 158–163.
6. See Hoogenboom, Ari, *Outlawing the Spoils: A History of the Civil Service Reform Movement, 1865–1883.* Urbana: University of Illinois Press, 1968, 5–7.
7. See Mosher, Frederick C., *Democracy and the Public Service,* 2nd ed. New York: Oxford University Press, 1982, 58–64.
8. Bruns, James H., *Great American Post Offices.* Hoboken, NJ: John Wiley & Sons, 1998, 21.
9. Hoogenboom, 6.
10. Bruns, 21–22.
11. See Cashman, Sean Dennis, *America in the Gilded Age: From the Death of Lincoln to the Rise of Theodore Roosevelt,* 3rd ed. New York: New York University Press, 1993, 224–230.
12. Bing, Julius, "Our Civil Service" in *Putnam's Magazine: Original Papers on Literature, Science, Art, and National Interests,* vol. 2. New York: G.P. Putnam & Son, 1868, 236.
13. See *National Party Conventions, 1831–2004.* Washington, DC: Congressional Quarterly Press, 2005, 69–70. See also Boller, Paul F., Jr., *Presidential Campaigns,* revised ed. New York: Oxford University Press, 1996, 142–144.

14. The high point of his résumé to that date was a stint as the collector of the Port of New York. See Karabell, Zachary, *Chester Alan Arthur.* New York: Henry Holt and Co., 2004, 21–28.

15. Ibid., 106–111. To the surprise of many, the transformation of the federal bureaucracy was quite swift. By the end of the second Cleveland administration in 1897, about 87,000 workers, or 43 percent of the total federal labor force, were governed by the civil service system. The main reason for this rapid change was that presidents had the authority to transform patronage jobs into permanent positions. Control of the White House changed hands in every consecutive election from 1884 to 1896; this meant that outgoing presidents would solidify all of their patronage appointments on their way out the door.

16. For a fascinating look at the Philadelphia machine in the postwar era, see McCaffery, Peter, *When Bosses Ruled Philadelphia: The Emergence of the Republican Machine, 1867–1933.* University Park: Pennsylvania State University Press, 1993.

17. See "Historical Census Browser," University of Virginia Library. http://mapserver.lib.virginia.edu. Accessed September 21, 2011.

18. See Erie, Steven P., *Rainbow's End: Irish-Americans and the Dilemma of Urban Machine Politics, 1840–1945.* Berkeley: University of California Press, 1988, 20–21.

19. Ibid., 18.

20. See Glazer, Nathan, and Daniel P. Moynihan, *Beyond the Melting Pot: The Negroes, Puerto Ricans, Jews, Italians, and Irish of New York City.* Cambridge, MA: MIT Press, 1984, 221–229.

21. Riordan, William E., *Plunkitt of Tammany Hall: A Series of Very Plain Talks on Very Practical Politics.* New York: Dutton, 1963, 18–19.

22. Compared with 62 percent in 2008. See Burnham, 81. See also McDonald, Michael, "2008 General Election Turnout Rates," in *The United States Elections Project.* George Mason University, October 6, 2010. http://elections.gmu.edu. Accessed September 21, 2011.

23. See Erie, 53.

24. Ibid., 60.

25. Ibid., 46.

26. Ibid., 86–87.

27. For a scathing contemporary account of the rampant corruption in the machine cities, see Steffens, Lincoln, *The Shame of the Cities.* New York: McClure, Phillips & Co., 1904.

28. Riordan, 9.

29. See Cherney, Robert W., *A Righteous Cause: The Life of William Jennings Bryan.* Norman: University of Oklahoma Press, 1995, 65–67.

30. See Wright, Gavin, *Old South, New South: Revolutions in the Southern Economy Since the Civil War.* Baton Rouge: Louisiana State University Press, 1986, 118.

31. See Morison, Samuel Eliot, Henry Steele Commager, and William E. Leuchtenburg, *The Growth of the American Republic,* vol. 2. New York: Oxford University Press, 1980, 169–180.

32. See Goodwyn, Lawrence, *The Populist Movement: A Short History of the Agrarian Revolt in America.* New York: Oxford University Press, 1978, 25–28.

33. See "1880 Presidential General Election Results," in *Atlas of U.S. Presidential Elections,* David Leip. http://uselectionatlas.org. Accessed September 21, 2011.

34. "Populist Party Platform of 1892," in *The American Presidency Project,* ed. John T. Woolley and Gerhard Peters. University of California at Santa Barbara, 2011. http://presidency.ucsb.edu. Accessed September 21, 2011.

35. See "1892 Presidential General Election Results," in *Atlas of U.S. Presidential Elections.*

36. See Calhoun, Charles W., *Benjamin Harrison.* New York: Henry Holt and Co., 2005, 94–100.

37. See "Cordage Trust Goes Under," *New York Times,* May 5, 1893.

38. See Graff, Henry F., *Grover Cleveland.* New York: Henry Holt and Co., 2002, 114.

39. See Morison et al., 180–186; and Morris, Charles R., *The Tycoons: How Andrew Carnegie, John D. Rockefeller, Jay Gould, and J. P. Morgan Invented the American Supereconomy.* (New York: Times Books/Henry Holt and Co., 2005), 246–248.

40. See Edwards, Rebecca, and Sarah DeFreo, "Ben Tillman's Fiery Tongue," in *1896: A Website of Political Cartoons.* Vassar College, 2000. http://projects.vassar .edu. Accessed September 21, 2011.

41. See Cherney, 54–55.

42. Bryan, William Jennings, *Speeches of William Jennings Bryan,* vol. 1. New York: Funk & Wagnalls Co., 1911, 240 and 249.

43. See "Democratic Party Platform of 1896," in *The American Presidency Project.* There was a noticeable sectional division in the convention roll call vote. Most of Bryan's vote came from the South and the West, with many eastern delegations either voting for Robert Pattison of Pennsylvania or abstaining. See also *National Party Conventions, 1831–2004,* 203.

44. See "1896 Presidential General Election Results," in *Atlas of U.S. Presidential Elections.*

45. See Morison et al., 194–195.

46. Bryan, 248.

47. See Johnston, Louis, and Samuel H. Williamson, "The Annual Real and Nominal GDP for the United States, 1789–Present." National Bureau of Economic Research. http://nber.org. Accessed September 21, 2011.

48. See "1900 Presidential Election Results," in *Atlas of U.S. Presidential Elections*; and Dubin, Michael J., *United States Congressional Elections, 1788–1997: The Official Results of the Elections of the 1st through 105th Congresses* (Jefferson, NC: McFarland & Co., 1998), 313–385.

49. Bryan, 248.

CHAPTER 2: Bryanism with a Princeton Accent

1. This idea of a political party comes from the definition offered by E. E. Schattschneider:

> A party may be defined in terms of its *purpose* and in terms of the *methods* used to attain its purpose. A political party is first of all an organized attempt to get power. Power is here defined as control of the government. That is the objective of the party organization. . . . [T]he bid for power must be made by way of

certain special and characteristic means. . . . First, it is a peaceable method. The parties do not seize power by a coup d'état. They act within the framework of the regime.

    Schattschneider, E. E., *Party Government*. New Brunswick, NJ: Transaction Publishers, 2008, 35–37.

2. To appreciate this, consider how Republicans dominated gubernatorial elections during this period. See *Congressional Quarterly's Guide to U.S. Elections*, 4th ed., vol. 2. Washington, DC: Congressional Quarterly Press, 2001, 1384–1414.

3. "Democratic Platform of 1900," *The American Presidency Project,* ed. John T. Woolley and Gerhard Peters. University of California at Santa Barbara, 2011. http://www.presidency.ucsb.edu. Accessed September 21, 2011.

4. See "1900 Presidential Election Results," in *Atlas of U.S. Presidential Elections,* David Leip. http://uselectionatlas.org. Accessed September 21, 2011.

5. See DeGregorio, William A., *The Complete Book of U.S. Presidents*. Fort Lee, NJ: Barricade Books, 2005, 381–382.

6. See "Telegram Halts Convention," *New York Times,* July 10, 1904.

7. See *National Party Conventions, 1831–2004*. Washington, DC: Congressional Quarterly Press, 2005, 205.

8. See Addams, Jane, *Twenty Years at Hull-House*. New York: Signet Classics, 1981.

9. See Hofstadter, Richard, *The Age of Reform*. New York: Vintage, 1955.

10. See McKenna, Marian C., *Borah*. Ann Arbor: University of Michigan Press, 1961. See also Lower, Richard Coke, *A Bloc of One: The Political Career of Hiram W. Johnson*. Stanford, CA: Stanford University Press, 1993.

11. See Link, William, *The Paradox of Southern Progressivism*. Chapel Hill: University of North Carolina Press, 1992.

12. See Cashman, Sean Dennis, *America in the Gilded Age: From the Death of Lincoln to the Rise of Theodore Roosevelt*, 3rd ed. New York: New York University Press, 1993, 345–380.

13. This theory was best expounded by Herbert Croly, who, in *The Promise of American Life,* promoted Hamiltonian means (big government) to promote Jeffersonian ends (democratic equality). See Croly, Herbert, *The Promise of American Life*. New York: Cosimo Classics, 2005.

14. See Bryan, William Jennings, *Speeches of William Jennings Bryan*, vol. 2. New York: Funk & Wagnalls Co., 1911, 63–91.

15. See *National Party Conventions, 1831–2004*, 86–87.

16. See *Congressional Quarterly's Guide to U.S. Elections,* 1384–1414; and Martis, Kenneth C., *The Historical Atlas of Political Parties in the United States Congress, 1789–1989* (New York: Macmillian Publishing Co., 1989), 157.

17. See *National Party Conventions, 1831–2004,* 206.

18. See "Democratic Party Platform of 1908," in *The American Presidency Project*.

19. See "1908 Presidential Election Results," in *Atlas of U.S. Presidential Elections*.

20. See "Republican Party Platform of 1908," in *The American Presidency Project*.

21. See "U.S. Business Cycle Expansions and Contractions." National Economic Research, September 20, 2011. http://nber.org. Accessed September 24, 2011.

22. Sarasohn, David, *The Party of Reform: Democrats in the Progressive Era*. Jackson: University Press of Mississippi, 1989, 123.

23. See DeGregorio, 389.

24. See Gould, Lewis L., *The William Howard Taft Presidency*. Lawrence: University Press of Kansas, 2009, 51–60.

25. See Burnham, Walter Dean, with Thomas Ferguson and Louis Ferleger, *Voting in American Elections: The Shaping of the American Political Universe Since 1788*. Bethesda, MD: Academica Press, 2010, 168.

26. See *Congressional Quarterly's Guide to U.S. Elections, 1384–1414*; and Martis, 162–165.

27. See Chace, James, *1912: Wilson, Roosevelt, Taft & Debs—The Election That Changed the Country*. New York: Simon & Schuster, 2004, 146–147.

28. See Cherney, Robert W., *A Righteous Cause: The Life of William Jennings Bryan*. Norman: University of Oklahoma Press, 1995, 124–125.

29. See Cooper, John Milton, Jr., *Woodrow Wilson: A Biography*. New York: Alfred A. Knopf, 2009, 73.

30. Clements, Kendrick A., *The Presidency of Woodrow Wilson*. Lawrence: University Press of Kansas, 1992, 10. Fortunately for Wilson, Bryan refused to make any comment when word of the letter got to the press, and ultimately it did not dissuade him from the Wilson candidacy. See "Bryan Has Nothing to Say," *New York Times,* January 8, 1912.

31. See Brands, H. W., *Woodrow Wilson*. New York: Henry Holt and Co., 2003, 16–19.

32. See Cooper, 129–135.

33. See Cherney, 125.

34. Chace, 144

35. Ibid., 155.

36. See *National Party Conventions, 1831–2004*, 89–90 and 209.

37. See "Presidential Primaries, All States, 1912, Summary," in *Voting and Elections Collection*. Congressional Quarterly. http://library.cqpress.com. Accessed September 21, 2011.

38. See *National Party Conventions, 1831–2004*, 88–89 and 90–91.

39. See "Progressive Party Platform of 1912," in *The American Presidency Project*.

40. See Cooper, 355.

41. See Wilson, Woodrow, *The New Freedom: A Call for the Emancipation of the Generous Energies of a People*. Charleston, SC: Nabu Press, 2010.

42. See "1912 Presidential Election Results," in *Atlas of U.S. Presidential Elections*.

43. See Martis, 164–167.

44. For instance, in the three major swing states of the period—Indiana, New York, and Ohio—Wilson's share of the countywide vote was about 94 percent identical to Bryan's share in 1908. See *Atlas of U.S. Presidential Elections*.

45. See Burnham, 88–89.

46. See Clements, 47–52.

47. When Wilson claimed, in November 1914, that the "future is clear and bright with the promise of best things," thanks to his legislative record, many progressives scoffed. In a *New Republic* piece entitled "Presidential Complacency," Croly retorted:

   How can a man of President Wilson's intelligence see in tinkering with the tariff and anti-trust laws, and in a reorganization of the banking system of the country, the causes of a better social order? How many sincere progressives follow him in believing that his legislation has made the future clear and bright with the promise of best things? Where will such leadership finally land the Democratic party and the progressive movement? . . .

President Wilson could not have written his letter unless he had utterly misconceived the meaning and task of American progressivism. . . . He deceives himself with these phrases, but he should not be allowed to deceive progressive popular opinion.

Croly, Herbert, "Presidential Complacency," *The New Republic*, November 21, 1914.

48. See Clements, 41–42.
49. See Cooper, 234–235.
50. Ibid., 234.
51. See Clements, 41–42.
52. Martis, 164–167.
53. His predecessor, William Howard Taft, would say of Wilson: "I regard him as a ruthless hypocrite, and as an opportunist, who has no convictions that he would not barter at once for votes. . . . He surrenders a conviction, previously expressed, without the slightest hesitation, and never even vouchsafes to the public the arguments upon which he was induced to change his mind." DeGregorio, 427.
54. See Clements, 44–51 and 60–61.
55. See Link, Arthur, *Woodrow Wilson and the Progressive Era*. New York: Harper, 1954, 224.
56. See *National Party Conventions, 1831–2004,* 92–93.
57. See Cooper, 350–355. Unfortunately, few books have been written on the close election of 1916. For one of the few serious works on the subject, see Lovell, S. D., *The Presidential Election of 1916*. Carbondale: Southern Illinois University Press, 1980.
58. Ibid., 360.
59. See "1916 Presidential General Election," in *Atlas of U.S. Presidential Elections*.
60. For a full summary of the debacle that was the Hughes campaign in California, see Olin, Spencer C., Jr., "Hiram Johnson, the California Progressives, and the Hughes Campaign of 1916," *Pacific Historical Review*, vol. 31, no. 4 (1962), 403–412.
61. See "1916 Presidential General Election Results," in *Atlas of U.S. Presidential Elections*.
62. Wilson, Woodrow, "Inaugural Address, March 4, 1917," in *The American Presidency Project*.
63. Though the 1920 campaign turned out to be a huge Republican blowout, it nevertheless was a fascinating contest dominated by six former and future presidents. For more, see Pietrusza, David, *1920: The Year of the Six Presidents*. New York: Basic Books, 2009.

CHAPTER 3: A Mediator of Interests

1. See *National Party Conventions, 1831–2004*. Washington, DC: Congressional Quarterly Press, 2005, 98–99. In the face of two conservatives sitting atop the major party tickets, the progressives within both parties split off and sponsored

a third-party ticket with Republican Robert M. La Follette of Wisconsin for president and Democrat Burton K. Wheeler of Montana for vice president. They won endorsements from high-profile progressives like Harold Ickes, Jane Addams, and W. E. B. DuBois, and managed to get 17 percent of the vote, which was the best third-party showing between T.R. in 1912 and Ross Perot in 1992. See Thelan, David P., *Robert M. La Follette and the Insurgent Spirit*. Madison: University of Wisconsin Press, 1976, 179–192.

2. See Burnham, Walter Dean, with Thomas Ferguson and Louis Ferleger, *Voting in American Elections: The Shaping of the American Political Universe Since 1788*. Bethesda, MD: Academica Press, 2010, 93.

3. It's not just the duration of the Depression but the depth of it that plagued the Republicans. According to the Bureau of Economic Analysis, real gross domestic product declined from 1929 to 1932 by 25.7 percent, a loss of wealth the likes of which the country has never experienced before or since. See "Real Gross Domestic Product, Chained Dollars, 1929–2011." Bureau of Economic Analysis, 2011. http://bea.gov. Accessed September 21, 2011. For an excellent (though tilted to the left) account of the crash that precipitated the Depression, see Galbraith, John Kenneth, *The Great Crash, 1929*. Boston: Mariner Books, 2009.

4. For an account of how FDR inspired the country in the midst of the Depression, see Alter, Jonathan, *The Defining Moment: FDR's Hundred Days and the Triumph of Hope*. New York: Simon & Schuster, 2006.

5. See Roosevelt, Franklin D., "Inaugural Address, March 4, 1933," in *The American Presidency Project,* ed. John T. Woolley and Gerhard Peters. University of California at Santa Barbara, 2011. http://presidency.ucsb.edu. Accessed September 21, 2011.

6. The following account of the "First New Deal" comes primarily from Schlesinger, Arthur M., *The Age of Roosevelt, Volume II: The Coming of the New Deal* (New York: Houghton Mifflin, 2003); Leuchtenburg, William E., *Franklin D. Roosevelt and the New Deal, 1932–1940* (New York: HarperCollins, 2009), 41–117; Smith, Jean Edward, *FDR* (New York: Random House, 2008), 278–359; and, to a lesser extent, Conkin, Paul K., *The New Deal*, *Third Edition* (Wheeling, IL: Harlan Davidson, 1992), 21–49. All four works approve highly of the New Deal, so for a contrarian take see Shlaes, Amity, *The Forgotten Man: A New History of the Great Depression* (New York: HarperCollins, 2007); Folsom, Burton W., Jr., *New Deal or Raw Deal? How FDR's Economic Legacy Has Damaged America* (New York: Threshold Editions, 2009); and Fleck, Robert K., "The Marginal Effect of New Deal Relief Work on County-Level Unemployment Statistics," *The Journal of Economic History*, vol. 59, no. 3 (1999), 659–687.

7. Schlesinger, 16.

8. From this point forward, the farm vote plays a greatly diminished role in our story. Considering how important the farmers have been up to this point in our story, an explanation is merited. Two big factors stand out. First, the number of farmers or farmworkers declined by about one million in the forty years that separate William McKinley and Franklin Roosevelt. By 1990, the number of people who made their living from a farm would be just 20 percent of what it was in 1900. Second, the basic structure of the New Deal farm policy—wherein farmers received substantial subsidies—endured long after the end of the Great

Depression, and received support from Democrats and Republicans alike. A significant element of this bipartisan support comes from the large number of senators of both parties who come from the Farm Belt and are able to block legislation that would defund farm subsidies (like the now infamous ethanol subsidy). Subsidies have meant that farm prices are now stable, farm incomes are now stable, and thus farmers are less dependent upon the ebbs and flows of the world economy. See Rasmussen, Wayne D., "The New Deal Farm Programs: What They Were and Why They Survived," *American Journal of Agricultural Economics*, vol. 65, no. 5 (1983), 1158–1162; and Sobeck, Matthew, "Major Occupational Groups—All Persons," in *Historical Statistics of the United States*, ed. Susan B. Carter, Scott Sigmund Gartner, Michael R. Haines, Alan L. Olmstead, Richard Sutch, and Gavin Wright (New York: Cambridge University Press, 2006), 2–133.

9. Leuchtenburg, 84, 88, and 90.

10. Southern Democrats were usually highly supportive of FDR's New Deal during its early phases, defying the president in large numbers (as we shall see) only beginning with the Fair Labor Standards Act. Still, Glass was an early opponent of FDR in the Senate, as were Josiah Bailey of North Carolina and Thomas Gore of Oklahoma. See Poole, Keith, "Roll Call Data," *VoteView*. University of Georgia, 2011. http://voteview.com. Accessed September 21, 2011. What's more, the Virginia state machine run by conservative Democrat Harry Byrd was a constant thorn in the side of the New Dealers. See Koeniger, A. Cash, "The New Deal and the States: Roosevelt Versus the Byrd Organization in Virginia," *The Journal of American History*, vol. 68, no. 4 (1982), 876–896; and Sweeney, James R., "'Sheep Without a Shepherd': The New Deal Faction in the Virginia Democratic Party," *Presidential Studies Quarterly*, vol. 29, no. 2 (1999), 438–459.

11. Interior Secretary Harold Ickes—one of the most important New Dealers—welcomed the American Liberty League. According to the *Washington Post*, Ickes "would like to see political parties 'divided on real issues' with 'all the progressives together and all the conservatives together.'" See "Political Realignment?" *The Washington Post,* August 25, 1934.

12. See Brinkley, Alan, *Huey Long, Father Coughlin & the Great Depression* (New York: Vintage, 1983); and Jeansonne, Glen, "Challenge to the New Deal: Huey P. Long and the Redistribution of National Wealth," *Louisiana History: The Journal of the Louisiana Historical Association*, vol. 21, no. 4 (1980), 331–339.

13. See Martis, Kenneth C., *The Historical Atlas of Political Parties in the United States Congress, 1789–1989*. New York: Macmillian Publishing Co., 1989, 188–189.

14. See "*A.L.A. Schechter Poultry Corporation* v. *United States,* 295 U.S. 495 (1935)," *FindLaw*. Thomson Reuters, 2011. http://findlaw.com. Accessed September 22, 2011.

15. For good summaries of the "Second New Deal," see Smith, 333–359; Leuchtenburg, 143–196; Schlesinger, Arthur M., *The Age of Roosevelt, Volume III: The Politics of Upheaval* (New York: Houghton Mifflin, 2003); and Conkin, 54–82.

16. On the partiality of American business toward the GOP in the 1936 election, see Webber, Michael J., and G. William Domhoff, "Myth and Reality in Business Support for Democrats and Republicans in the 1936 Presidential Election,"

The American Political Science Review, vol. 90, no. 4 (1996), 824–833. See Baum, Matthew A., and Samuel Kernell, "Economic Class and Popular Support for Franklin Roosevelt in War and Peace," *The Public Opinion Quarterly*, vol. 65, no. 2.0 (2001), 198–229.

17. See Weed, Clyde P., *The Nemesis of Reform: The Republican Party During the New Deal*. New York: Columbia University Press, 1994, 93–96. One reason for the GOP's false hope was its victory in a 1935 special election in Rhode Island's First Congressional District, which had previously been held by the Democrats. They also took back control of the New York state assembly in 1935. See Dubin, Michael J., *United States Congressional Elections, 1788–1997: The Official Results of the Elections of the 1st through 105th Congresses* (Jefferson, NC: McFarland & Co., 1998), 508; and Dubin, Michael J., *Party Affiliations in the State Legislatures: A Year by Year Summary, 1796–2006* (Jefferson, NC: McFarland & Co., 2007), 137.

18. See *National Party Conventions, 1831–2004*, 106–107.

19. See "1932 Presidential General Election Results," in *Atlas of U.S. Presidential Elections*, David Leip. http://uselectonatlas.org. Accessed September 21, 2011.

20. See Martis, 190–191.

21. See Leuchtenburg , 132–179.

22. See Smith, 360–415.

23. See Burnham, 178.

24. FDR made sure to use the New Deal to lock down support in the Great Plains and the West, which had long been vital to Democratic electoral prospects. However, much like the South, the West had well-developed Democratic state parties with independent streaks—and western Democrats grew suspicious of the federal regulatory state that the New Deal came to embody. See Anderson, Gary M., and Robert D. Tollinson, "Congressional Influence and Patterns of New Deal Spending, 1933–1939," *Journal of Law and Economics*, vol. 34, no. 1 (1991), 161–175; Arrington, Leonard, "The New Deal in the West: A Preliminary Statistical Inquiry," *Pacific Historical Review*, vol. 38, no. 3 (1969), 311–316; Fleck, Robert K., "Electoral Incentives, Public Policy, and the New Deal Realignment," *Southern Economic Journal*, vol. 65, no. 3 (1999), 377–404; Fleck, Robert K. "Inter-Party Competition, Intra-Party Competition, and Distributive Policy: A Model and Test Using New Deal Data," *Public Choice*, vol. 108, no. 1/2 (2001), 77–100; Patterson, James T., "The New Deal in the West," *Pacific Historical Review,* vol. 38, no. 3 (1969), 317–327; Wallis, John Joseph, "Employment, Politics, and Economic Recovery During the Great Depression," *The Review of Economics and Statistics*, vol. 69, no. 3. (1987), 516–520; Saloutos, Theodore, "The New Deal and Farm Policy in the Great Plains," *Agricultural History*, vol. 43, no. 3 (1969), 345–356; and Wright, Gavin, "The Political Economy of New Deal Spending: An Econometric Analysis," *The Review of Economics and Statistics*, vol. 56, no. 1 (1974), 30–38.

25. A significant tool in his consolidation of power over the urban machines was the WPA. See Erie, Steven P., *Rainbow's End: Irish-Americans and the Dilemma of Urban Machine Politics, 1840–1945*. Berkeley: University of California Press, 1988, 128–139.

26. See LaCerra, Charles, *Franklin Delano Roosevelt and Tammany Hall of New York* (Lanham, MD: University Press of America, 1997), 43–52; and Smith, 70–76.

27. FDR had the support of Pendergast in Kansas City and Crump in Memphis, while Cermak in Chicago was not in favor of Smith, which helped FDR pick up most Illinois delegates on the first ballot. See Dorsett, Lyle W., *Franklin D. Roosevelt and the City Bosses*. Port Washington, NY: Kennikat Press, 1977, 6–20.

28. Ibid., 50.

29. See Allen, Oliver E., *The Tiger: The Rise and Fall of Tammany Hall* (Reading, MA: Addison-Wesley, 1993), 232–254; and Erie, 107–128.

30. See LaCerra, 88–89; and Dorsett, 57–59.

31. See "National Affairs: A New Kind of Tiger," *Time*, August 22, 1955.

32. McCaffery, Peter, "Style, Structure, and Institutionalization of Machine Politics: Philadelphia, 1867–1933," *Journal of Interdisciplinary History*, vol. 22, no. 3. (1992), 435–452; and McCaffery, Peter, *When Bosses Ruled Philadelphia: The Emergence of the Republican Machine, 1867–1933* (University Park: Pennsylvania State University Press), 1993.

33. See "1928 Presidential General Election Results," in *Atlas of U.S. Presidential Elections*.

34. See Dubin, *Party Affiliations in State Legislatures*, 159.

35. See Greenberg, Irwin F., "Philadelphia Democrats Get a New Deal: The Election of 1933," *The Pennsylvania Magazine of History and Biography,* vol. 97, no. 2 (1973), 210–232.

36. Luconi, Stefano. "Bringing Out the Italian-American Vote in Philadelphia," *The Pennsylvania Magazine of History and Biography*, vol. 117, no. 4 (1993), 251–285; Luconi, Stefano, "Machine Politics and the Consolidation of the Roosevelt Majority: The Case of Italian Americans in Pittsburgh and Philadelphia," *Journal of American Ethnic History*, vol. 15, no. 2 (1996), 32–59; and Luconi, Stefano, "The New Deal Realignment and the Italian-American Community of Philadelphia," *Journal of American Studies,* vol. 28, no. 3 (1994), 403–422.

37. See Greenberg.

38. See Dubin, *United States Congressional Elections,* 517; and "1936 Presidential General Election Results," in *Atlas of U.S. Presidential Elections*.

39. For an account of Roosevelt's relationship with the Chicago party leadership, see Jones, Gene Delon, "The Origin of the Alliance Between the New Deal and the Chicago Machine," *Journal of the Illinois State Historical Society,* vol. 67, no. 3 (1974), 253–274.

40. The experience in Pittsburgh was unique—as the town went from being a Republican machine to a Democratic one. For a great account of this transformation, see Stave, Bruce M., *The New Deal and the Last Hurrah: Pittsburgh Machine Politics*. Pittsburgh, PA: University of Pittsburgh Press, 1970.

41. See Greenstein, Fred I., "The Changing Pattern of Urban Party Politics," *The Annals of the American Academy of Political and Social Science*, vol. 353 (*City Bosses and Political Machines*) (1964), 1–13; Havard, William C., "From Bossism to Cosmopolitanism: Changes in the Relationship of Urban Leadership to State Politics," *The Annals of the American Academy of Political and Social Science*, vol. 353 (*City Bosses and Political Machines*) (1964), 84–94.

42. See Conway, M. Margaret, and Frank B. Feigert, "Motivation, Incentive Systems, and the Political Party Organization," *The American Political Science Review,* vol. 62, no. 4 (1968), 1159–1173; Erie, 140–190; Sorauf, Frank J., "State Patron-

age in a Rural County," *The American Political Science Review*, vol. 50, no. 4 (1956), 1046–1056; Sorauf, Frank J., "The Silent Revolution in Patronage," *Public Administration Review*, vol. 20, no. 1 (1960), 28–34; Wilson, James Q., "The Economy of Patronage," *The Journal of Political Economy*, vol. 69, no. 4 (1961), 369–380; and Wilson, James Q., *The Amateur Democrat* (Chicago: University of Chicago Press, 1962).

43. The following account of the South and the Democratic party is based primarily on the classics of southern politics and economics: Cash, W. J., *The Mind of the South* (New York: Vintage, 1991); Key, V. O., *Southern Politics in State and Nation: A New Edition* (Knoxville: University of Tennessee Press, 2006); Kousser, J. Morgan, *The Shaping of Southern Politics: Suffrage Restriction and the Establishment of the One-Party South, 1880–1910* (New Haven, CT: Yale University Press, 1976); Tindall, George Brown, *The Emergence of the New South, 1913–1945* (Baton Rouge: Louisiana State University Press, 1992); Woodward, C. Vann, *The Strange Career of Jim Crow* (Oxford, England: Oxford University Press, 2001); and Wright, Gavin, *Old South, New South: Revolutions in the Southern Economy Since the Civil War* (Baton Rouge: Louisiana State University Press, 1986).

44. We shall discuss the relationship between African Americans and the Republican party in greater detail in Chapter 6.

45. See Burnham, 83.

46. Ibid., 163 and 173.

47. For an excellent review of the South's role in the New Deal, see Biles, Roger, *The South and the New Deal.* Lexington: University Press of Kentucky, 1994.

48. Myrdal, Gunnar, *An American Dilemma: The Negro Problem and Modern Democracy.* New York: Transaction Publishers, 1995, 260. See also Whatley, Warren C., "Labor for the Picking: The New Deal in the South," *Journal of Economic History,* vol. 48, no. 4 (1983), 905–929.

49. See Leuchtenburg, 138–139.

50. Alston, Lee J., and Joseph P. Ferrie, *Southern Paternalism and the American Welfare State.* New York: Cambridge University Press, 1999, 19.

51. Schlesinger, *The Politics of Upheaval,* 437–438.

52. See Wilentz, Sean, *Chants Democratic: New York City and the Rise of the American Working Class, 1788–1850.* Oxford, England: Oxford University Press, 1986.

53. See Landis, James M., and Marcus Manof, *Cases on Labor Law.* Chicago: Foundation Press, 1942, 30–34.

54. See Morris, Richard B., *Government and Labor in Early America.* New York: Columbia University Press, 1946, 522–523.

55. Dubofsky, Melvyn, and Foster Rhea Dulles, *Labor in America*, 6th ed. Wheeling, IL: Harlan Davidson, 1999, 125. For a discussion of the rise and fall of the Knights of Labor, see ibid., 116–137; and Raybeck, Joseph G., *A History of American Labor* (New York: The Free Press, 1966), 142–167.

56. See "*Loewe* v. *Lawlor,* 208 U.S. 274 (1908)," *FindLaw;* and Morris, 522–524.

57. See Raybeck, 272 and 295.

58. See Dubofsky and Dulles, 138–140; and Raybeck, 194–206.

59. Dubofsky and Dulles, 185. For a discussion of the AFL's political strategy in this period, see Greenstone, J. David, *Labor in American Politics.* Chicago: University of Chicago Press, 1977, 5–13.

60. See Dubofsky and Dulles, 211–214.

61. For the decline of labor following World War I, see Raybeck, 294–298.

62. For a discussion of 7(a), see Dubofsky and Dulles, 250–252; Milton, David, *The Politics of U.S. Labor from the Great Depression to the New Deal* (New York: Monthly Review Press, 1982), 29–31; and Ziegler, Robert H., and Gilbert J. Gall, *American Workers, American Unions*, 3rd ed. (Baltimore: Johns Hopkins University Press, 2002), 79–80.

63. Schlesinger, *The Coming of the New Deal,* 403. Wagner was "the driving force behind the New Deal's great achievements in social welfare reform" and in many respects remains the ideal type of the modern liberal. That quotation is taken from Biles, Roger, "Robert F. Wagner, Franklin D. Roosevelt, and Social Welfare Legislation in the New Deal," *Presidential Studies Quarterly*, vol. 28, no. 1 (*Wheeling and Dealing in the White House*) (1998), 140.

64. See Ziegler and Gall, 76–77.

65. See Greenstone, 47–49.

66. Milton, 69–73.

67. See Dubofsky and Dulles, 272–288.

68. Ibid., 288–293; Rosenbloom, Joshua L., "Work Stoppages and Workers Involved, by Major Issue: 1881–1981," in *Historical Statistics of the United States,* 2–357; and Wilson, Graham K., *Unions in American National Politics* (New York: St. Martin's Press, 1979), 288–293.

69. See Flynt, J. Wayne, "The New Deal and Southern Labor," in *The New Deal and the South,* ed. James C. Cobb and Michael V. Namorato (Jackson: University of Mississippi Press, 1984), 97–117; and Halpern, Rick, "Organized Labor, Black Workers, and the Twentieth Century South: The Emerging Revision," *Social History*, vol. 19, no. 3 (1994), 359–383.

70. See Dubofsky and Dulles, 325; and Rosenbloom, Joshua L., "Union Membership, by Affiliation: 1897–1955," in *Historical Statistics of the United States*, 2–341.

71. See "1936 Presidential General Election," in *Atlas of U.S. Presidential Elections.*

72. Raybeck, 357.

73. See Greenstone, 34 and 50–52. Labor gave $770,000 in the 1936 election, almost all of which went to fund the Democratic side. What's more, 61 percent came from the UMW, with major contributions from the Amalgamated Clothing Workers of America and the International Ladies' Garment Workers' Union. See Overacker, Louis, "Labor's Political Contributions," *Political Science Quarterly,* vol. 54, no. 1 (1939), 56–68.

74. See Fones-Wolf, Elizabeth, "Industrial Unionism and Labor Movement Culture in Depression-Era Philadelphia," *The Pennsylvania Magazine of History and Biography,* vol. 109, no. 1 (1985), 3–26.

75. See "1936 Presidential General Election," in *Atlas of U.S. Presidential Elections.*

76. See Ziegler and Gall, 144–147.

77. Lewis, John L., "What Labor Is Thinking," *The Public Opinion Quarterly,* vol. 1, no. 4 (1937), 27.

78. Quoted in Milton, 134.

79. See Dubofsky and Dulles, 301–305.

80. See Dark, Taylor E., *The Unions and the Democrats: An Enduring Alliance*. Ithaca, NY: Cornell University Press, 2001.

81. See Burnham, 177.
82. Biles, *The South and the New Deal,* 101. For more on the FLSA, see Leuchtenburg, 261–263.
83. See Smith, 390–392.
84. Ibid., 408–435.
85. See Poole.

CHAPTER 4: He Just Dropped into the Slot

1. Burnham, Walter Dean, with Thomas Ferguson and Louis Ferleger, *Voting in American Elections: The Shaping of the American Political Universe Since 1788.* Bethesda, MD: Academica Press, 2010, 178–179.
2. See McCullough, David, *Truman.* New York: Simon & Schuster, 1992, 193–252.
3. Truman was featured on the cover of *Time* in March 1943. The magazine celebrated the Truman Committee in this way:

   They had served as watchdog, spotlight, conscience and spark plug to the economic war-behind-the-lines. They had prodded Commerce Secretary Jesse Jones into building synthetic-rubber plants, bludgeoned the president into killing off doddering old SPAB and setting up WPB. They had called the turn on raw-materials shortages, had laid down the facts of the rubber famine four months before the famed Baruch report. One single investigation, of graft and waste in Army camp building, had saved the U.S. $250,000,000 (according to the Army's own Lieut. General Brehon B. Somervell). Their total savings ran into billions, partly because of what their agents had ferreted out in the sprawling war program, partly because their hooting curiosity was a great deterrent to waste.

   See "Billion-Dollar Watchdog," *Time,* March 8, 1943.
4. Ferrell, Robert H., *Choosing Truman: The Democratic Convention of 1944.* Columbia: University of Missouri Press, 1994, 1–3.
5. Ibid., 14–18.
6. Ibid., 12–14. See also Poole, Keith, "Roll Call Data," *VoteView.* University of Georgia, 2011. http://voteview.com. Accessed September 21, 2011.
7. See McCullough, 322–323.
8. Ibid., 375. According to Arthur Krock of the *New York Times,* Sidney Hillman of the CIO had the final say on the choice of Truman. "Clear everything with Sidney," FDR was reported to have said. See Krock, Arthur, "In the Nation: The Inflammatory Use of a National Chairman," *New York Times,* July 25, 1944.
9. McCullough tells the story of FDR on the phone with DNC chairman Robert Hannegan. Truman was in the room with Hannegan, and Roosevelt spoke so loudly that Truman could hear FDR say, "Bob, have you got that fellow lined up yet?" "No. He is the contrariest goddamn mule from Missouri I ever dealt with," Hannegan replied. FDR exclaimed, "Well, you tell the Senator that if he wants to break up the Democratic party in the middle of the war, that's his responsibility!" Then Roosevelt hung up, and that was that. McCullough, 314.
10. "American Presidents: Greatest and Worst," Siena Research Institute, July 1, 2010. http://siena.edu. Accessed September 21, 2011.
11. See Ambrose, Stephen E., *Eisenhower, Volume Two: The President* (New York: Simon & Schuster, 1984), 13; and Donovan, Robert J., *Tumultuous Years: The*

Presidency of Harry S. Truman, 1949–1953 (Columbia: University of Missouri Press, 1982), 393.

12. See Savage, Sean J., *Truman and the Democratic Party.* Lexington: University Press of Kentucky, 1997, 94.

13. As economist Neil Chamberlain argued, "Union leaders no longer regard themselves as a force merely reacting to managerial decisions in certain areas of business operation, but as a force which itself can influence the whole range of industrial activity." Quoted in Lichtenstein, Nelson, "Labor in the Truman Era: Origins of the 'Private Welfare State,'" in *The Truman Presidency*, ed. Michael James Lacey. New York: Cambridge University Press, 1989, 132.

14. Ibid., 138–139.

15. See Donaldson, Gary A., *Truman Defeats Dewey.* Lexington: University Press of Kentucky, 1999, 12.

16. McCullough, 602. Truman was referring to A. F. Whitney of the Brotherhood of Railroad Trainmen and Alvanley Johnston of the Brotherhood of Locomotive Engineers. The original draft of the address was much more intemperate. It closed, "Let's give the country back to the people. Let's put transportation and production back to work, hang a few traitors, and make our country safe for democracy." Quoted in Patterson, James T., *Grand Expectations: The United States, 1945–1974.* Oxford, England: Oxford University Press, 1997, 48.

17. See Truman, Harry, "Truman Speaks on the Railroad Strike," in *History Matters.* George Mason University, March 31, 2006. http://historymatters.gmu.edu. Accessed September 22, 2011. The House passed Truman's proposal, but Robert Taft blocked it in the Senate, arguing that it went "farther toward Hitlerism, Stalinism, totalitarianism than I have ever seen." Quoted in Lee, R. Alton, *Truman and Taft-Hartley: A Question of Mandate.* Lexington: University of Kentucky Press, 1966, 38.

18. See Donaldson, 74; and Donovan, Robert J., *Conflict and Crisis: The Presidency of Harry S. Truman, 1945–1948* (Columbia: University of Missouri Press, 1977), 209.

19. See Lee, 37–44.

20. Donovan, *Conflict and Crisis*, 125.

21. "Presidential Job Approval, F. Roosevelt (1941)–Obama," in *American Presidency Project*, ed. John T. Woolley and Gerhard Peters. University of California at Santa Barbara, 2011. http://presidency.ucsb.edu. Accessed September 21, 2011.

22. "The G.O.P. Trend," *Life*, November 4, 1946.

23. See Martis, Kenneth C., *The Historical Atlas of Political Parties in the United States Congress, 1789–1989.* New York: Macmillan Publishing Co., 1989, 198–201. The GOP victory in 1946 was impressive considering that the party already controlled the typical swing congressional districts in midwestern states like Ohio, Indiana, and Illinois. In 1946, the gains came largely in urban areas—the Republicans picked up seats in Los Angeles, St. Louis, Milwaukee, Detroit, and New York City, and, amazingly, they swept the field in the Philadelphia districts as anti-Communist Catholic voters backed the GOP for the first time in more than a decade.

24. See Donaldson, 17; and Martis, 201.

25. See Woods, Randall Bennett, *Fulbright: A Biography*. New York: Cambridge University Press, 2007, 125.

26. As *Time* put it after the election in 1946:

Harry Truman, his party rejected, would have trouble functioning effectively as President. Many of the Executive functions, for all practical purposes, must be taken over by Arthur Vandenberg and Robert Taft in the Senate; Joe Martin in the nation's most representative body, the House. There was little that Harry Truman could or probably would do to prevent this assumption of power. He could lay about him with his veto, and the Republican majority alone would not be strong enough to override him. But Mr. Truman said he would not follow such tactics. If the Republicans would work with him he would work with them. The major conflicts might well come within the Republican Party. In any case, the Republican legislators, led by Martin, Vandenberg and Taft, will have the task of guiding the nation for the next two years, at least.

"The Congress: Mr. Speaker," *Time,* November 18, 1946.

27. For more on the "Missouri Gang," see Donovan, *Conflict and Crisis,* 15–25. Wallace (in)famously said: "I am neither anti-British nor pro-British—neither anti-Russian nor pro-Russian. And just two days ago, when President Truman read these words, he said that they represented the policy of his administration." See Wallace, Henry A., "The Way to Peace," *The New Deal Network*. Franklin and Eleanor Roosevelt Institute. http://newdeal.feri.org. Accessed September 22, 2011.

28. See Hamby, Alonzo L., *Beyond the New Deal: Harry S. Truman and American Liberalism* (New York: Columbia University Press, 1973), 224–229; and Karabell, Zachary, *The Last Campaign: How Harry Truman Won the 1948 Election* (New York: Vintage, 2000), 152–153.

29. See Savage, 95–96.

30. See Clifford, Clark, *Counsel to the President: A Memoir*. New York: Random House, 1991, 189–194. Clifford was careful to give it to Truman without mentioning its author, as Rowe was working at the time for Tommy "the Cork" Cocoran, whom Truman disliked immensely.

31. See Ross, Irwin, *The Loneliest Campaign: The Truman Victory of 1948*. New York: New American Library, 1968, 26–27.

32. Rowe, James H., "The Politics of 1948," in *Oral History Interviews*. The Harry S. Truman Library and Museum. http://www.trumanlibrary.org. Accessed September 22, 2011.

33. See Burnham, 10.

34. See Lee, 49–105.

35. Truman, Harry, "Veto of the Taft-Hartley Labor Bill, June 20, 1947," in *The American Presidency Project*.

36. The override in the House was 331 to 83, with only 71 Democrats (including John F. Kennedy) supporting Truman. See Donovan, *Conflict and Crisis*, 302.

37. See "Historical Census Browser," University of Virginia Library. http://mapserver.lib.virginia.edu. Accessed September 21, 2011.

38. See Smith, Richard Norton, *Thomas Dewey and His Times*. New York: Simon & Schuster, 1982, 443–448.

39. See Donaldson, 98–99. The Republican platform in 1944 declared: "We unre-

servedly condemn the injection into American life of appeals to racial or religious prejudice. We pledge an immediate Congressional inquiry to ascertain the extent to which mistreatment, segregation and discrimination against Negroes who are in our armed forces are impairing morale and efficiency, and the adoption of corrective legislation. We pledge the establishment by Federal legislation of a permanent Fair Employment Practices Commission." In contrast, the 1944 Democratic platform included this ambiguous plank: "We believe that racial and religious minorities have the right to live, develop and vote equally with all citizens and share the rights that are guaranteed by our Constitution. Congress should exert its full constitutional powers to protect those rights." See "Republican Party Platform of 1944" and "Democratic Party Platform of 1944," in *The American Presidency Project.*

40. See Donaldson, 9–10.
41. Truman, Harry, "Executive Order 9808—Establishing the President's Committee on Civil Rights, December 5, 1946," in *The American Presidency Project.*
42. See Gardner, Michael R., *Harry Truman and Civil Rights: Moral Courage and Political Risks.* Carbondale: Southern Illinois University Press, 2002, 43–64.
43. Ibid., 71–86.
44. See Donovan, *Conflict and Crisis*, 406.
45. See Burnham, 94–97.
46. See Donaldson, 158–163.
47. See Humphrey, Hubert, "1948 Democratic National Convention Address, Delivered 14 July 1948, Philadelphia, PA," in *American Rhetoric,* ed. Michael E. Eldenmuller. University of Texas at Tyler, 2011. http://americanrhetoric.com. Accessed September 22, 2011.
48. See *Congressional Quarterly's Guide to U.S. Elections*, 4th ed., vol. 1. Washington, DC: Congressional Quarterly Press, 2001, 616. In his diary, Truman wrote the following about the affair: "Platform fight in dead earnest. Crackpot (Andrew J.) Biemiller from Wisconsin offers a minority report on civil rights. Moody from Texas offers states rights amendment. . . . The Convention votes down States Rights and votes for the crackpot amendment to the Civil Rights Plank." Truman, Harry, *Off the Record: The Private Papers of Harry S. Truman*, ed. Robert H. Ferrell. New York: Harper & Row, 1980, 143.
49. Truman, Harry, "Address in Philadelphia upon Accepting the Nomination of the Democratic National Convention, July 15, 1948," in *The American Presidency Project.*
50. See Goldzwig, Steven R., *Truman's Whistle-stop Campaign* (College Station: Texas A&M Press, 2008); and Truman, Harry, *Miracle of '48: Harry Truman's Major Campaign Speeches & Selected Whistle-stops*, ed. Steve Neal (Carbondale: Southern Illinois University Press, 2003).
51. See "1948 Presidential General Election Results," in *Atlas of U.S. Presidential Elections,* David Leip. http://uselectionatlas.org. Accessed September 21, 2011.
52. Truman, Harry, "Annual Message to the Congress on the State of the Union, January 5, 1949," in *The American Presidency Project.*
53. See Burnham, 98.
54. See Hamby, 312–315.
55. See ibid., 444–445 ; and Donovan, 120–122.

56. See Donovan, 123–127.

57. See Hamby, 303–310.

58. See Donovan, 126.

59. See Savage, 28–30.

60. See Donovan, 127.

61. "Presidential Job Approval, F. Roosevelt (1941–Obama," in *The American Presidency Project.*

CHAPTER 5: Let Us Continue

1. See *Congressional Quarterly's Guide to U.S. Elections*, 4th ed., vol. 1. Washington, DC: Congressional Quarterly Press, 2001, 515–516.

2. See Broadwater, Jeff, *Adlai Stevenson and American Politics*. New York: Twayne Publishers, 1994, 90–91.

3. See *Congressional Quarterly's Guide to U.S. Elections*, 516–517.

4. See "1952 Presidential General Election Results," in *Atlas of U.S. Presidential Elections*, David Leip. http://uselectionatlas.org. Accessed September 21, 2011. For a detailed analysis of the 1952 election, see Janowitz, Morris, and Dwaine Marvick, *Competitive Pressure and Democratic Consent*. Chicago: Quadrangle Books, 1964.

5. See "Data Center," *American National Election Studies*. Stanford University and the University of Michigan, 2011. http://electionstudies.org. Accessed September 22, 2011.

6. See Burnham, Walter Dean, with Thomas Ferguson and Louis Ferleger, *Voting in American Elections: The Shaping of the American Political Universe Since 1788*. Bethesda, MD: Academica Press, 2010, 182–184.

7. The basic premise of Eisenhower's middle-way approach was that the federal government had to provide some basic social welfare functions but not become so onerous that it would encumber individual effort. Ike also did not like the Democratic propensity to play favorites with key pressure groups. See Wright, Steven T., *Eisenhower Republicanism*. DeKalb: Northern Illinois University Press, 2006.

8. See "1960 Presidential General Election Results," in *Atlas of U.S. Presidential Elections*.

9. His only real success to date had been to finish in second place in the 1956 Democratic veepstakes, losing to Kefauver for the "privilege" of being Stevenson's running mate in his disastrous campaign. JFK's brother Robert Kennedy followed Stevenson's organization around in 1956 to learn the mechanics of political campaigning, but he was so disgusted by the ineptitude that he ended up voting for Eisenhower. See Thomas, Evan, *Robert Kennedy: His Life*. New York: Touchstone, 2000, 72–74.

10. See Dallek, Robert, *An Unfinished Life: John F. Kennedy, 1917–1963*. Boston: Little, Brown and Co., 2003, 134–228.

11. Some contemporaries doubted the legitimacy of the surgery, which pulled Kennedy out of a difficult political problem, seeing as how McCarthy was quite popular with JFK's Catholic constituency back in Massachusetts. See Parmet, Herbert S., *Jack: The Struggles of John F. Kennedy*. New York: The Dial Press, 1980, 307–311.

12. Dallek, 232.

13. See "Life Goes Courting with a U.S. Senator," *Life*, July 20, 1963.

14. See Rorabaugh, W. J., *The Real Making of the President: Kennedy, Nixon, and the 1960 Election*. Lawrence: University Press of Kansas, 2009, 49.

15. West Virginia would be the critical contest for JFK, as it was a traditionally Democratic state with only a small proportion of Catholic voters. See Fleming, Dan B., Jr., *Kennedy vs. Humphrey, West Virginia, 1960: The Pivotal Battle for the Democratic Presidential Nomination*. Jefferson, NC: McFarland & Co., 1992.

16. Johnson himself had tossed in for the presidential nod, planning to build a coalition of southern and western delegates, but he had waited too long, and as he learned when he started making calls on western party leaders, the Kennedys already had the jump on him. In the early balloting in Los Angeles, LBJ finished in second place, with half as many delegates as Kennedy. See *National Party Conventions, 1831–2004*. Washington, DC: Congressional Quarterly Press, 2005, 123–124 and 228.

17. Donaldson, Gary, *The First Modern Campaign: Kennedy, Nixon, and the Election of 1960* (Lanham, MD: Rowman & Littlefield, 2007), 71–82; Pietrusza, David, *1960—LBJ vs. JFK vs. Nixon: The Epic Campaign That Forged Three Presidencies* (New York: Union Square Press, 2008), 194–206; and White, Theodore H., *The Making of the President 1960* (New York: Harper Perennial, 2009), 150–179.

18. See "Gallup Presidential Trial-Heat Trends, 1936–2004," Gallup. September 24, 2008. http://gallup.com. Accessed September 22, 2011.

19. The debate itself is especially boring, lacking any sharp policy differences between the two candidates. See "Presidential Debate in Chicago, September 26, 1960," in *The American Presidency Project,* ed. John T. Woolley and Gerhard Peters. University of California at Santa Barbara, 2011. http://presidency.ucsb.edu. Accessed September 21, 2011.

20. See "1960 Presidential General Election," in *Atlas of U.S. Presidential Elections*. Law professor Gordon Tullock has argued that Nixon *did* win the popular vote, when one corrects the common errors in counting the votes in Alabama and Mississippi. See Tullock, Gordon, "Nixon, Like Gore, Also Won Popular Vote, but Lost Election," *PS: Political Science and Politics,* vol. 37, no. 1 (2004), 1–2.

21. See "Data Center," Stanford and University of Michigan.

22. See *The Gallup Poll: Public Opinion, 1935–1997*. Gallup, 2000. CD-ROM.

23. Again, the southern Democrats' raw numerical power was enhanced by their adept manipulation of the committee system, especially the House Rules Committee. This critical legislative junction point had an 8–6 Democratic majority in the Eighty-seventh Congress, which gave the two southern Democrats, including committee chair Judge Howard Smith, nearly total control. See Dallek, 329; and Giglio, James N., *The Presidency of John F. Kennedy* (Lawrence: University Press of Kansas, 1991), 101.

24. See Kennedy, John F., "Address to the Economic Club of New York. Delivered December 14, 1962," in *American Rhetoric*, ed. Michael E. Eldenmuller. University of Texas at Tyler, 2011. http://americanrhetoric.com. Accessed September 22, 2011.

25. See Bernstein, Irving, *Promises Kept: John F. Kennedy's New Frontier*. New York: Oxford University Press, 1991, 246–258.

26. See Giglio, 101–102.

27. Ibid., 107–117.

28. See Bernstein, 192–218.

29. See "Data Center," Stanford and University of Michigan.

30. See Dallek, 184.

31. See Giglio, 45.

32. See *The Gallup Poll: Public Opinion, 1935–1997.*

33. See Schlesinger, Arthur M., *A Thousand Days: John F. Kennedy in the White House.* New York: Mariner Books, 2002, 379–405 and 794–819.

34. Kennedy, John F., "Inaugural Address, January 20, 1961," in *The American Presidency Project.*

35. For instance, on its April 26, 1963, cover, *Life* ran a picture of a young Jackie Kennedy with the line "Her secret is out—and here's a story of the First Lady as a child herself. . . . Charming Album of Jackie Growing Up." Inside, readers were treated to an eight-page spread of photographs from Jackie's childhood. See "Hers Was a Gentle World," *Life,* April 26, 1963.

36. See "Presidential Job Approval, F. Roosevelt (1941)–Obama," in *The American Presidency Project.*

37. See Burnham, 185.

38. See "Real Gross Domestic Product, Chained Dollars, 1929–2011." Bureau of Economic Analysis, 2011. http://bea.gov. Accessed September 21, 2011.

39. Kennedy was worried that his support of civil rights legislation would weaken him in Texas and Florida. In the Lone Star State, the party was divided along ideological lines, with Governor John Connally on the right and Senator Ralph Yarborough on the left. Kennedy was in Texas in late November to mend these fences and promote party unity. See Cox, Patrick L., *Ralph W. Yarborough: The People's Senator.* Austin: University of Texas Press, 2009, 188–193.

40. See Dallek, Robert, *Flawed Giant: Lyndon Johnson and His Times, 1961–1973.* New York: Oxford University Press, 1998, 69–70.

41. See Johnson, Lyndon, "Address Before a Joint Session of Congress, November 27, 1963," in *The American Presidency Project.*

42. Goodwin, Doris Kearns, *Lyndon Johnson and the American Dream.* New York: Harper & Row, 1976, 178.

43. Dallek, *Flawed Giant,* 71–72.

44. See Bernstein, Irving, *Guns or Butter? The Presidency of Lyndon Johnson.* New York: Oxford University Press, 1996, 36–42.

45. Lyndon Johnson was substantially less liberal on civil rights than the Senate as a whole during his term. However, he was much more liberal than the likes of John Sparkman of Alabama and James Eastland and John Stennis of Mississippi. See Poole, Keith, "Roll Call Data," *VoteView.* University of Georgia, 2011. http://voteview.com. Accessed September 21, 2011.

46. See Dallek, *Flawed Giant,* 114.

47. The original House bill passed 290–131, with the only significant opposition coming from southern Democrats and the handful of southern Republicans. See Poole.

48. As it turned out, the South would not fall entirely into line. Texas Democrat Ralph Yarborough, one of the most liberal members of the chamber, supported the cloture motion. See ibid.

49. See Bernstein, *Guns or Butter?* 71.

50. Dirksen gave a memorable speech in which he famously said:

    It is said that on the night he died, Victor Hugo wrote in his diary, substantially this sentiment: "Stronger than all the armies is an idea whose time has come." The time has come for equality of opportunity in sharing in government, in education, and in employment. It will not be stayed or denied. It is here.

    Dirksen, Everett, "The Time Has Come," in *Landmark Speeches of the American Conservative Movement,* ed. Peter Scweizer and Wynton C. Hall. College Station: Texas A&M University Press, 2007, 23.

51. See Bernstein, *Guns or Butter?, 75–77.*

52. See Galbraith, John Kenneth, *The Affluent Society* (New York: Mariner Books, 1998); and Harrington, Michael, *The Other America: Poverty in the United States* (New York: Scribner, 1997).

53. Johnson would introduce this concept during a speech at the University of Michigan in May 1964:

    Your imagination, your initiative, and your indignation will determine whether we build a society where progress is the servant of our needs, or a society where old values and new visions are buried under unbridled growth. For in your time we have the opportunity to move not only toward the rich society and the powerful society, but upward to the Great Society.

    See Johnson, Lyndon, "Remarks at the University of Michigan (May 22, 1964)," in *American President: A Reference Resource.* Miller Center of the University of Virginia, 2011. http://millercenter.org. Accessed September 22, 2011.

54. The roll call vote in the Senate serves as a good reminder of how the ideological cleavages of the 1960s cut across party lines. Northern Democrats broke uniformly in favor of the bill in the Senate, but southern Democrats opposed it slightly. Meanwhile, almost all of the Republican support for the bill came from the Northeast. See Poole.

55. See Johnson, Robert David, *All the Way with LBJ: The 1964 Presidential Election.* New York: Cambridge University Press, 2009, 1.

56. See Donaldson, Gary, *Liberalism's Last Hurrah: The Presidential Campaign of 1964* (Armonk, NY: M.E. Sharpe, 2003), 184–200; and White, Theodore H., *The Making of the President 1964: A Narrative History of American Politics in Action* (New York: Atheneum, 1965), 243–293. LBJ managed to defuse a controversy over the Mississippi delegation to the convention. The regular state party had sent an all-white delegation to Atlantic City, while the rival Mississippi Freedom Democratic Party (MFDP) sent an alternative group, many of whom were poor black sharecroppers. LBJ was terrified of a southern walkout that would dramatize the party's internal divisions, so he arranged a compromise in which two of the MFDP delegates would be seated as at-large delegates. See Dallek, *Flawed Giant,* 163–164.

57. See Johnson, *All the Way with LBJ,* 199–247.

58. That phrase comes from Middendorf, William, II, *Glorious Disaster: Barry Goldwater's Presidential Campaign and the Origins of the Conservative Movement.* New York: Basic Books, 2006.

59. For more on the shift in the balance of power in the Republican party, see Brennan, Mary C., *Turning Right in the Sixties: The Conservative Capture of the GOP*

(Chapel Hill: University of North Carolina Press, 1995); and Rae, Nicol C., *The Decline and Fall of the Liberal Republicans, from 1952 to the Present* (New York: Oxford University Press, 1989).

60. Perlstein, Rick. *Before the Storm: Barry Goldwater and the Unmaking of the American Consensus.* New York: Hill and Wang, 2001, 273.

61. On the eve of the election, Goldwater gave a speech in Columbia, South Carolina, in which he denounced the Civil Rights Act. It was a peculiar crowd for a Republican candidate because, as the *New York Times* noted, "there were as many Confederate as United States flags" in the audience. The Goldwater speech was telecast in the "11 states of the old Confederacy plus Kentucky, West Virginia and Oklahoma." See "Carolina Crowds Hail Goldwater," *New York Times,* November 1, 1964. In the end, Goldwater's performance in the South was quite unlike any Republican haul before or since—he won the Deep South states, but performed terribly in rising Republican areas in the peripheral South. Much of the 1964 Goldwater vote had gone for Stevenson in 1952 and 1956, then for Kennedy in 1960; and it would finally go for Wallace in 1968.

62. Johnson, *All The Way with LBJ*, 203.

63. See "Peace Little Girl (Daisy) (Johnson, 1964)," *The Living Room Candidate.* Museum of the Moving Image, 2010. http://livingroomcandidate.org. Accessed September 22, 2011.

64. See "1964 Presidential General Election Results," in *Atlas of U.S. Presidential Elections.*

65. See "Data Center," Stanford and University of Michigan.

66. See Burnham, 185.

67. See Dallek, *Flawed Giant*, 192.

68. See "*Everson v. Board of Education of Ewing Township,* 330 U.S. 1 (1947)," *FindLaw.* Thomson Reuters, 2011. http://findlaw.com. Accessed September 22, 2011.

69. The opposition was the old remnants of the conservative coalition: southern Democrats aligned with Republicans from the Midwest and the Mountain West. In the Eighty-ninth Congress, this opposition was simply not sufficient to stop the liberal agenda. See Poole.

70. This substantially less controversial bill passed the Senate with just three senators—all southern Democrats—opposed. See ibid.

71. See Bernstein, *Guns or Butter,* 183–21; Bornet, Vaughn Davis, *The Presidency of Lyndon B. Johnson* (Lawrence: University Press of Kansas, 1983), 123–127; and Woods, Randall B., *LBJ: Architect of American Ambition* (Cambridge, MA: Harvard University Press, 2006), 565–568.

72. See Bernstein, *Guns or Butter?* 156–182; and Woods, *LBJ,* 569–573. Opposition came primarily from southern Democrats and Republicans from the Midwest and the Mountain West. See Poole.

73. See Burnham, 186.

74. Quoted in Dallek, *Flawed Giant*, 231.

75. Rowe, James H., "The Politics of 1948," in *Oral History Interviews.* The Harry S. Truman Library and Museum. http://www.trumanlibrary.org. Accessed September 22, 2011.

CHAPTER 6: They Can Count

1. Hamilton, Alexander, James Madison, and John Jay, *The Federalist*. Cambridge, MA: The Belknap Press of Harvard University Press, 2009, 514.
2. See "*U.S. v. Reese,* 92 U.S. 214 (1875)," *FindLaw*. Thomson Reuters, 2011. http://findlaw.com. Accessed 22 September 2011.
3. See "*Plessy v. Ferguson,* 163 U.S. 537 (1896)," *FindLaw*.
4. Rees, Matthew, *From the Deck to the Sea: Blacks and the Republican Party*. Wakefield, NH: Longwood Academic, 1991, 1.
5. DeSantis, Vincent, "The Republican Party and the Southern Negro, 1877–1897," *The Journal of Negro History*, vol. 45, no. 2 (1960), 73.
6. Ibid., 74–75; and Abbott, Richard H., *The Republican Party and the South, 1855–1877: The First Southern Strategy* (Chapel Hill: University of North Carolina Press), 233–244.
7. See DeSantis, Vincent, "Republican Efforts to 'Crack' the Democratic South," *The Review of Politics*, vol. 14, no. 2 (1952), 257.
8. See DeSantis, Vincent, "President Hayes's Southern Policy," *The Journal of Southern History*, vol. 21, no. 4 (1955), 476–480; and Tindall, George Brown, *The Disruption of the Solid South* (New York: W.W. Norton & Co., 1973), 11–12.
9. In particular, Arthur reached out to the "Readjuster" Movement in Virginia during the 1880s. See DeSantis, Vincent, "President Arthur and the Independent Movements in the South in 1882," *The Journal of Southern History*, vol. 19, no. 3 (1953), 346–363.
10. See DeSantis, Vincent, "Benjamin Harrison and the Republican Party in the South, 1889–1893," *Indiana Magazine of History*, vol. 51, no. 4 (1955), 287–288.
11. See Burnham, Walter Dean, with Thomas Ferguson and Louis Ferleger, *Voting in American Elections: The Shaping of the American Political Universe Since 1788*. Bethesda, MD: Academica Press, 2010, 159–174.
12. For the sad history of post-Harrison Republican uninterest in the condition of southern African Americans, see Bacote, Charence A., "Negro Officeholders in Georgia Under President McKinley," *The Journal of Negro History*, vol. 44, no. 3 (1959), 217–239; Blair, John L., "A Time for Parting: The Negro During the Coolidge Years," *Journal of American Studies*, vol. 3, no. 2 (1969), 177–199; Day, David S., "Herbert Hoover and Racial Politics: The DePriest Incident," *The Journal of Negro History*, vol. 65, no. 1 (1980), 6–17; DeSantis, "Republican Efforts to 'Crack' the Democratic South," 257–264; Scheiner, Seth M., "President Theodore Roosevelt and the Negro, 1901–1908," *The Journal of Negro History*, vol. 47, no. 3 (1962), 169–182; Sherman, Richard B., "The Harding Administration and the Negro: An Opportunity Lost," *The Journal of Negro History*, vol. 49, no. 3 (1964), 151–168; and Topping, Simon, *Lincoln's Lost Legacy: The Republican Party and the African American Vote, 1928–1952*. (Gainesville: University Press of Florida, 2008), 9–28.
13. Ferrie, Joseph P., "Interstate Migration—Native-Born Population, by Race and Residence Within or Outside the State of Birth: 1850–1990," in *Historical Statistics of the United States*, ed. Susan B. Carter, Scott Sigmund Gartner, Michael R. Haines, Alan L. Olmstead, Richard Sutch, and Gavin Wright. New York: Cambridge University Press, 2006, 1–497.

14. Dubin, Michael J., *United States Congressional Elections, 1788–1997: The Official Results of the Elections of the 1st through 105th Congresses.* Jefferson, NC: McFarland & Co., 1998, 471.

15. See Weiss, Nancy J., *Farewell to the Party of Lincoln: Black Politics in the Age of FDR.* Princeton, NJ: Princeton University Press, 1983, 30–31.

16. See Fishel, Leslie H., Jr., "The Negro in the New Deal Era," *The Wisconsin Magazine of History,* vol. 48, no. 2 (1964–65), 111–126.

17. See Blumenthal, Henry, "Woodrow Wilson and the Race Question," *The Journal of Negro History,* vol. 48, no. 1 (1963), 1–21; and Wolgemuth, Kathleen L., "Woodrow Wilson and Federal Segregation," *The Journal of Negro History,* vol. 44, no. 2 (1959), 158–173.

18. The GOP pledged: "that our American citizens of Negro descent shall be given a square deal in the economic and political life of this nation. Discrimination in the civil service, the army, navy, and all other branches of the Government must cease. To enjoy the full benefits of life, liberty and pursuit of happiness universal suffrage must be made effective for the Negro citizen." See "Republican Party Platform of 1948," in *The American Presidency Project,* ed. John T. Woolley and Gerhard Peters. University of California at Santa Barbara, 2011. http://presidency.ucsb.edu. Accessed September 21, 2011.

19. For a discussion of the political games played on civil rights by both parties during the 1948 campaign season, see Topping, 121–139.

20. During the Eisenhower administration, the Supreme Court finally declared the southern system of "separate but equal" schools unconstitutional, though it would be decades before desegregation was complete, in part because, as political scientist Gerald Rosenberg has cogently argued in *The Hollow Hope,* the court was in a uniquely poor position to lead on the issue of civil rights, lacking the enforcement powers of the executive branch or the powers of the purse that only Congress controls. According to Rosenberg, there is "little evidence that *Brown* helped produce positive change"; what's more, there is "some evidence that it hardened resistance to civil rights among both elites and the white public." Rosenberg, Gerald M., *The Hollow Hope: Can Courts Bring About Social Change?* 2nd ed. Chicago: University of Chicago Press, 2008, 155.

21. See Nichols, David A., *A Matter of Justice: Eisenhower and the Beginning of the Civil Rights Revolution.* New York: Simon & Schuster, 2007, 143–168.

22. See "Democratic Party Platform of 1960," in *The American Presidency Project.*

23. The first lasting civil rights advocacy group was the National Association for the Advancement of Colored People (NAACP), founded in 1909 out of the Niagara Movement. The NAACP was not a mass movement in the common sense of the phrase. Instead, its membership was never more than 2 percent of the black community, its locus was New York City, and its main goal was legal action to get the courts to undo the "separate but equal" doctrine of *Plessy.* See Morris, Aldon D., *The Origins of the Civil Rights Movement: Black Communities Organizing for Change.* New York: The Free Press, 1984.

24. See Graham, Hugh Davis, *The Civil Rights Era: Origins and Development of National Policy, 1960–1972.* New York: Oxford University Press, 1990, 10.

25. See Williams, Juan, *Eyes on the Prize: America's Civil Rights Years, 1954–1965.* New York: Penguin, 2002, 121–132. One of the conditions that helped make

this new movement so effective was the urbanization of the South. As we saw in Chapter 3, labor union activists in Dixie had a terrible time organizing rural farmworkers who were geographically dispersed and often difficult to reach. But by the mid-1950s, the migration of black farmers into the cities had been ongoing for more than a decade, and it was easier to organize mass protests in places like Atlanta, Baton Rogue, and Birmingham than in the Mississippi Delta. See Morris, 26.

26. Morris, 234–235; see also Schlesinger, Arthur M., *A Thousand Days: John F. Kennedy in the White House* (New York: Mariner Books, 2002), 286–316, for his discussion of the meetings between Robert Kennedy and civil rights leaders.

27. Even Kennedy's hagiographer Arthur Schlesinger was forced to admit that "some of his Southern judicial appointments in 1961 were unfortunate." Schlesinger, 321.

28. Hansen, Drew D., *The Dream: Martin Luther King, Jr., and the Speech That Inspired a Nation.* New York: Harper Perennial, 2005, 12.

29. See Graham, 74; and Williams, 163–195.

30. Kennedy, John F., "Address on Civil Rights (June 11, 1963)," in *American President: A Reference Resource.* Miller Center of the University of Virginia, 2011. http://millercenter.org. Accessed September 22, 2011.

31. See Dallek, Robert, *An Unfinished Life: John F. Kennedy, 1917–1963.* Boston: Little, Brown and Co., 2003, 642–644.

32. See "Historical Census Browser." University of Virginia Library. http://mapserver.lib.virginia.edu. Accessed September 21, 2011. See also "Presidential General Election Results Comparison—Dallas County," in *Atlas of U.S. Presidential Elections.*

33. Williams, 273.

34. Woods, Randall B., *LBJ: Architect of American Ambition.* Cambridge, MA: Harvard University Press, 2006, 480.

35. Quoting Abigail Thernstrom:

Why the figure of 50 percent? Because those who wrote the legislation knew the states they wanted to "cover" and, by a process of trial and error, determined the participation level that would single them out. Those central, temporary provisions of the 1965 act—suspension of the literacy test chief among them—applied to six southern states in their entirety, a seventh in substantial part, and only scattered counties elsewhere. And why not an outright ban on all literacy tests, without the intervening, indirect test for Fifteenth Amendment violations? Because it was assumed that such a ban would not survive a constitutional challenge.

Thernstrom, Abigail M., *Whose Votes Count? Affirmative Action and Minority Voting Rights.* Cambridge, MA: Harvard University Press, 1987, 17.

36. For a concise summary of the Voting Rights Act, see Bullock, Charles S., III, and Ronald Keith Gaddie, *The Triumph of Voting Rights in the South.* Norman: University of Oklahoma Press, 2009, 10–13.

37. Data for these conclusions come from the *Atlas of U.S. Presidential Elections;* "Election Statistics," Office of the Clerk of the U.S. House of Representatives (clerk.house.gov, accessed September 24, 2011); and "Historical Census Browser."

38. See "Data Center," *American National Election Studies.* Stanford University and the University of Michigan, 2011. http://electionstudies.org. Accessed September 22, 2011.

39. Rae, Nicol C., *Southern Democrats.* New York: Oxford University Press, 1994, 73.

40. Ibid., 80–81.

41. Ibid., 74.

42. See Poole, Keith T., "Polarized America," *VoteView*. University of Georgia, 2011. http://voteview.com. Accessed September 21, 2011.

43. See Rae, 74.

44. See Light, Steven Andrew, *"The Law Is Good": The Voting Rights Act, Redistricting, and Black Regime Politics*. Durham, NC: Carolina Academic Press, 2010, 68–69.

45. For an incisive critique of the *White-Zimmer* test, see Thernstrom, Abigail, *Voting Rights—And Wrongs: The Elusive Quest for Fair Elections*. Washington, DC: The AEI Press, 2009, 78–80.

46. *"Mobile* v. *Bolden,* 446 U.S. 55 (1980)." *FindLaw*.

47. See Thernstrom, *Whose Votes Count?*, 79–136; as well as King, Desmond S., and Rogers M. Smith., "Strange Bedfellows? Polarized Politics? The Quest for Racial Equity in Contemporary America," *Political Research Quarterly*, vol. 61, no. 4 (December 2008), 694–698.

48. See Lloyd, Mark Kevin, *The Battle for Virginia's 5th District: How the Ancestral Spirit of Patrick Henry Inspired Me to Join the Tea Party*. New York: Broadside e-Books, April 19, 2011. http://amazon.com. Accessed September 26, 2011.

49. See "New York Exit Poll. President, 2008," CNN. http://cnn.com. Accessed September 26, 2011.

50. See Barone, Michael, with Richard E. Cohen and Grant Ujifusa, *The Almanac of American Politics, 2010*. Washington, DC: National Journal, 2009, 58–60.

51. See *"Baker* v. *Carr,* 369 U.S. 186 (1962)," *FindLaw*.

52. *"Thornburg* v. *Gingles,* 478 U.S. 30 (1986)," *FindLaw*.

53. See Barone, Michael, and Grant Ujifusa, *The Alamanac of American Politics, 1994* (Washington, DC: National Journal, 1993), 10–24; Bullock, Charles S., III, *Redistricting: The Most Political Activity in America* (Lanham, MD: Rowman & Littlefield, 2010), 70–79.

54. Those who think majority-minority representation has harmed African American representation in Congress include: Cameron, Charles, David Epstein, and Sharyn O'Halloran, "Do Majority-Minority Districts Maximize Substantive Black Representation in Congress?" *The American Political Science Review,* vol. 90, no. 4 (1996), 794–812; Epstein, David, Michael C. Herron, Sharyn O'Halloran, and David Part, "Estimating the Effect of Redistricting on Minority Substantive Representation," *The Journal of Law, Economics, and Organization,* vol. 23, no. 2 (2007), 499–518; Epstein, David, and Sharyn O'Halloran, "Measuring the Electoral and Policy Impact of Majority-Minority Districts," *American Journal of Political Science,* vol. 43, no. 2 (1999), 367–395; Overby, Marvin, and Kenneth M. Cosgrove, "Unintended Consequences? Racial Redistricting and the Representation of Minority Interests," *The Journal of Politics,* vol. 58, no. 2 (1996), 540–550; Lublin, David, *The Paradox of Representation: Racial Gerrymandering and Minority Interests in Congress* (Princeton, NJ: Princeton University Press, 1997), 98–119; Lublin, David, and D. Stephen Voss, "The Missing Middle: Why Median-Voter Theory Can't Save Democrats from Singing the Boll-Weevil Blues," *The Journal of Politics,* vol. 65, no. 1 (2003), 227–237; and Lublin, David, and D. Stephen Voss, "Racial Redistricting and Realignment in Southern State

Legislatures," *American Journal of Political Science,* vol. 44, no. 4 (2000), 792–810. Some argue that the effects have been overstated: see Petrocik, John R., and Scott W. Desposato, "The Partisan Consequences of Majority-Minority Districting in the South, 1992 and 1994," *The Journal of Politics,* vol. 60, no. 3 (1998), 613–633; Shotts, Kenneth W., "Does Racial Redistricting Cause Conservative Policy Outcomes? Policy Preferences of Southern Representatives in the 1980s and 1990s," *The Journal of Politics,* vol. 65, no. 1 (2003), 216–226; Shotts, Kenneth W., "The Effect of Majority-Minority Mandates on Partisan Gerrymandering," *American Journal of Political Science,* vol. 45, no. 1 (2001), 120–135; and Shotts, Kenneth W., "Gerrymandering, Legislative Composition, and National Policy Outcomes," *American Journal of Political Science,* vol. 46, no. 2 (2002), 398–414.

55. The liberalism of the Congressional Black Caucus can be appreciated by looking at the ideological scores developed by political scientists Keith Poole and Howard Rosenthal. They track legislator ideology through a complicated system that produces a simple result: +1.0 is basically a perfect conservative, -1.0 is a perfect liberal, 0 is a moderate. From 1970 to 1990, the Congressional Black Caucus scored on average -0.60. In comparison, northern white Democrats scored -0.34, southern white Democrats scored -0.13, and Republicans scored +0.28. See Poole, Keith T., and Howard Rosenthal, *Ideology and Congress.* Piscataway, NJ: Transaction Publishers, 2007.

56. For more on the Congressional Black Caucus, see Canon, David T., *Race, Redistricting, and Representation: The Unintended Consequences of Black Majority Districts* (Chicago: University of Chicago Press, 1999), 143–201; Canon, David T., "Redistricting and the Congressional Black Caucus," *American Politics Research,* vol. 23, no. 2 (1995), 159–189; Gile, Roxanne L., and Charles E. Jones, "Congressional Racial Solidarity: Exploring Congressional Black Caucus Voting Cohesion, 1971–1990," *Journal of Black Studies,* vol. 25, no. 5 (1995), 622–641; Jones, Charles E., "United We Stand, Divided We Fall: An Analysis of the Congressional Black Caucus' Voting Behavior, 1974–1980," *Phylon,* vol. 48, no. 1 (1987), 26–37; and Pinney, Neil, and George Serra, "The Congressional Black Caucus and Vote Cohesion: Placing the Caucus Within House Voting Patterns," *Political Research Quarterly,* vol. 52, no. 3 (1999), 583–608.

57. The research of political scientist Richard Fenno also suggests that black legislators are aware of a larger set of black interests to which they are responsible. See Fenno, Richard F., *Going Home: Black Representatives and Their Constituents.* Chicago: University of Chicago Press, 2003.

58. Yet on other issues, there are few differences between the races. Black and white voters support increased spending on science and technology in about equal proportions (35 percent to 34 percent); ditto increased defense spending (25 percent to 33 percent). They are also about equal on increased environmental regulations (46 percent to 43 percent) and on their demand for greater emphasis on traditional values (80 percent to 84 percent). Blacks and whites are also generally in agreement on abortion (49 percent of black voters think it should be illegal or strictly prohibited, compared with 44 percent of whites), though black voters are less supportive of gay adoption than whites (29 percent to 47 percent). See "Data Center," Stanford and University of Michigan.

CHAPTER 7: There's No Party That Can Match Us

1. See "Real Gross Domestic Product, Chained Dollars, 1929–2011." Bureau of Economic Analysis, 2011. http://bea.gov. Accessed September 21, 2011.

2. See "Establishment Survey Data." FRED Economic Data, Federal Reserve Bank of St. Louis. http://research.st.louisfed.org. Accessed September 22, 2011.

3. See U.S. Bureau of the Census, *Historical Statistics of the United States: Colonial Times to 1970, Part 1*. Washington, DC: U.S. Government Printing Office, 1975, 178.

4. See "Union Members—2010." Bureau of Labor Statistics, January 21, 2011. http://bls.gov. Accessed September 22, 2011.

5. See Greenstone, J. David, *Labor in American Politics*. Chicago: University of Chicago Press, 1977, 25.

6. It is worth pointing out that a relatively small number of unions were and are politically active. Many have no role in the subsequent discussion, and most local unions still to this day follow the voluntaristic approach—preferring negotiations with local employers over activity in state and federal governments. Ibid., 5.

7. See "Labor: Partisan League," *Time*, August 24, 1936.

8. See Robinson, Archie, *George Meany and His Times*. New York: Simon & Schuster, 1981, 40.

9. In fact, many leaders of these groups, like "Big" Bill Hutcheson of the UBC, were actually Republican. Hutcheson supported every Republican nominee from Coolidge to Eisenhower. See "Milestones," *Time*, November 2, 1953.

10. See Buffa, Dudley W., *Union Power and American Democracy: The UAW and the Democratic Party, 1935–72* (Ann Arbor: University of Michigan Press, 1984), 4–9; and Dubofsky, Melvyn, and Foster Rhea Dulles, *Labor in America: A History*, 6th ed. (Wheeling, IL: Harlan Davidson, 1999).

11. For a good, if not entirely persuasive, argument on how the New Deal was actually quintessentially American, see Hartz, Louis, *The Liberal Tradition in America*. San Diego: Harcourt Brace Jovanovich, 1991, 250–283.

12. See Filippelli, Ronald L., *Labor in the USA: A History*. New York: Alfred A. Knopf, 1984, 205.

13. See Raybeck, Joseph G., *A History of American Labor*. New York: The Free Press, 1966, 400.

14. Robinson, 154.

15. Rosenbloom, Joshua L., "Union Membership, by Affiliation: 1897–1955," in *Historical Statistics of the United States*, ed. Susan B. Carter, Scott Sigmund Gartner, Michael R. Haines, Alan L. Olmstead, Richard Sutch, and Gavin Wright. New York: Cambridge University Press, 2006, 2–341.

16. See Robinson, 163.

17. See Rosenbloom.

18. See Dubofsky and Dulles, 349; and Galenson, Walter, *The American Labor Movement, 1955–1995* (Westport, CT: Greenwood Press, 1996), ix.

19. Eisenhower, Dwight, "Annual Message to Congress on the State of the Union, February 2, 1953," in *American Presidency Project*, ed. John T. Woolley and Gerhard Peters, University of California at Santa Barbara, 2011. http://www.presidency.ucsb.edu. Accessed September 21, 2011.

20. See Draper, Alan, *A Rope of Sand: The AFL-CIO Committee on Political Education, 1955–1967.* New York: Praeger, 1989, 30–31.

21. See Dubofsky and Dulles, 353.

22. See Troy, Leo, *The New Unionism in the New Society: Public Sector Unions in the Redistributive State.* Fairfax, VA: George Mason University Press, 1994, 100–130.

23. No other political activity of the leadership so inflamed the party base. In 1962, COPE director James McDevitt went so far as to offer a bald-faced lie to local members regarding COPE's work on behalf of civil rights. That year, the Oil, Chemical and Atomic Workers local of Memphis, Tennessee, asked the AFL-CIO to confirm or deny reports that COPE was planning to conduct a registration drive in coordination with Dr. Martin Luther King Jr. Despite the fact that COPE was doing exactly that, McDevitt responded: "I emphatically deny that we will give any part of our registration to these minority groups or any other minority group. I assure you that we are not associated with these groups." See Draper, 106–110.

24. See Dark, Taylor E., *The Unions and the Democrats: An Enduring Alliance.* Ithaca, NY: Cornell University Press, 1999, 1–49.

25. See Draper, 106; and Wilson, Graham K., *Unions in American National Politics* (New York: St. Martin's Press, 1979), 18.

26. Wilson, 21.

27. See Dark, 51; and Schiavone, Michael, *Unions in Crisis? The Future of Organized Labor in America* (Westport, CT: Praeger, 2008), 16–21.

28. See Rosenbloom, Joshua L., "Union Membership, by Affiliation: 1955–1983," in *Historical Statistics of the United States,* 2–342. Some old-line unions saw modest increases in their numbers; for instance, the construction industry saw the addition of about 600,000 unionized workers. However, those gains must be viewed in the context of the rapidly expanding American workforce, which grew by nearly 33 percent during this period, meaning that even unions with growing membership often saw their relative presence in the workforce decline.

29. See Dubofsky and Dulles, 367.

30. See Poole, Keith, "Roll Call Data," *VoteView.* University of Georgia, 2011. http://voteview.com. Accessed September 21, 2011.

31. Ibid., 362.

32. See Bernstein, Irving, *Guns or Butter? The Presidency of Lyndon Johnson* (New York: Oxford University Press, 1996), 309; and Buffa, Dudley W., *Union Power and American Democracy: The UAW and the Democratic Party, 1972–1983* (Ann Arbor: University of Michigan Press, 1984), 63–67.

33. See Bernstein, 310.

34. Ibid., 312

35. Ibid., 205–217.

36. See Kearney, Richard C., with David G. Carnevale, *Labor Relations in the Public Sector,* 3rd ed. New York: Marcel Dekker, 2001, 15–17.

37. Freeman, Richard B., "Unionism Comes to the Public Sector," *Journal of Economic Literature,* vol. 24 (1986), 44.

38. See U.S. Bureau of the Census, 137.

39. See Slater, Joseph E., *Public Workers: Government Employee Unions, the Law and the State, 1900–1962.* Ithaca, NY: Cornell University Press, 2004, 158–192.

40. See Kearney, 63.

41. Kennedy, John, "Executive Order 10988, January 17, 1962," in *The American Presidency Project.*

42. See Bernstein, 205–217.

43. Rosenbloom, "Union Membership, by Affiliation: 1955–1983." See also Lieberman, Myron, *Teacher Unions: How the NEA and the AFT Sabotage Reform and Hold Students, Parents, Teachers and Taxpayers Hostage to Bureaucracy.* New York: The Free Press, 1997, 29–40.

44. See Murphy, Marjorie, *Blackboard Unions: The AFT and the NEA, 1900–1980.* Ithaca, NY: Cornell University Press, 1990, 209–231.

45. See U.S. Bureau of the Census, 178.

46. See Troy, 133–140.

47. See Greenhouse, Steven, "Most U.S. Union Members Are Working for the Government, New Data Shows," *New York Times,* January 22, 2010.

48. Dubofsky and Dulles, 373.

49. See Galenson, 21.

50. See Battista, Andrew, "Political Divisions in Organized Labor, 1968–1988," *Polity,* vol. 24, no. 2 (1991), 173–197; and Dark, 70–73.

51. Battista., 180.

52. To appreciate the lasting effects of Taft-Hartley, consider that in the states of the old Confederacy, which all have right-to-work laws on the books, the average proportion of union members in the workforce is just 5 percent. In contrast, the Great Lake states have an average unionization density of 16 percent. See "Union Members by State, 2010." AFL-CIO, 2011. http://afl-cio.org. Accessed September 22, 2011.

CHAPTER 8: The Share-Out Runs Its Course

1. See, for instance, Wilentz, Sean, *The Age of Reagan: A History, 1974–2008.* New York: Harper, 2008.

2. The change in the southern electorate is extraordinary. In Mississippi, for instance, about 400,000 people voted in the 1964 presidential election. Four years later, after the enactment of the Voting Rights Act, that number had jumped to more than 650,000, with many counties in the Mississippi Delta doubling the size of their electorates. See "Presidential General Election Results Comparison—Mississippi," in *Atlas of U.S. Presidential Elections,* David Leip. http://uselectionatlas.org. Accessed September 21, 2011.

3. See Dallek, Robert, *Flawed Giant: Lyndon Johnson and His Times, 1961–1973.* New York: Oxford University Press, 1998, 371.

4. According to the American National Election Studies (ANES), more than 50 percent of Americans indicated that foreign affairs were their primary concern that year. This was the fourth straight election cycle in which the ANES found that foreign concerns had been dominant, but all through the 1970s the economy would top the list of voter concerns. See "Data Center," *American National Election Studies.* Stanford University and the University of Michigan, 2011. http://electionstudies.org. Accessed September 22, 2011.

5. See Herring, George C., *America's Longest War: The United States and Vietnam,*

4th ed. Boston: McGraw Hill, 2002, 69. In fact, even before the fall of Dien Bien Phu and the end of French colonial domination, the United States was shouldering as much as 40 percent of the cost of fighting off the Communists. Herring, 24–45.

6. See "The Tonkin Gulf Resolution," International Relations Department, Mount Holyoke College. http://www.mtholyoke.edu. Accessed September 22, 2011.

7. Johnson, Lyndon Baines, "Report on the Gulf of Tonkin Incident (August 4, 1964)," *American President: A Reference Resource*. Miller Center of the University of Virginia, 2011. http://millercenter.org. Accessed September 22, 2011.

8. See Herring, 182.

9. *Time* offered a typical example of how and why the phrase "credibility gap" became a commonplace term. In its May 5, 1967, edition, regarding a bombing raid on a North Vietnamese MiG air base, *Time* reported:

   Barely three days before the bases were bombed, Illinois' Republican Senator Charles H. Percy was assured by both the State and Defense Departments that they would not be touched. Moreover, Defense Secretary Robert S. McNamara had said only a few weeks earlier that "under present circumstances—and this belief can change as time goes by—we think the loss in U.S. lives will be less if we pursue our present target policy than they would, were we to attack those airfields."

   See "The War: Cards on the Table," *Time*, May 5, 1967.

10. See *The Gallup Poll: Public Opinion, 1935–1997*. Gallup, 2000. CD-ROM.

11. See Herring, 232.

12. Significant in the shift in public opinion was the reaction to Tet of the news media, which previously had been supportive of the Johnson administration's efforts. On the *CBS Evening News* on February 27, Walter Cronkite told millions of home viewers:

   It seems now more certain than ever that the bloody experience of Vietnam is to end in a stalemate. This summer's almost certain standoff will either end in real give-and-take negotiations, or terrible escalation. And for every means we have to escalate, the enemy can match us, and that applies to invasion of the North, the use of nuclear weapons, or the mere commitment of 100 or 200 or 300 thousand American troops to the battle. . . . To say that we are mired in stalemate seems the only realistic, yet unsatisfactory, conclusion.

   Walter Cronkite, "We Are Mired in Stalemate . . ." in *Reporting Vietnam: Part One, American Journalism,* compiled by Milton J. Bates, Lawrence Lichty, Paul Miles, Ronald H. Spector, and Marilyn Young. New York: Library of America, 1998, 581–582.

13. See Gould, Lewis L., *1968: The Election That Changed America,* 2nd ed. Chicago: Ivan R. Dee, 2010, 17.

14. See *Congressional Quarterly's Guide to U.S. Elections,* vol. 1, 4th ed. Washington, DC: Congressional Quarterly Press, 2001, 351.

15. Thomas, Evan, *Robert Kennedy: His Life*. New York: Touchstone, 2000, 360.

16. See Johnson, Lyndon Baines, "Remarks on Decision Not to Seek Re-Election (March 31, 1968)," in *American President: A Reference Resource*.

17. See "Estimated Crime in United States—Total." Uniform Crime Reporting Statistics, Department of Justice, September 22, 2011. http://www.ucrdatatool.gov. Accessed September 22, 2011.

18. "John Lindsay's Ten Plagues," *Time*, November 1, 1968.

19. For details on the riots through 1968, see National Advisory Commission on Civil Disorders, *Report of the National Advisory Commission on Civil Disorders*. Washington, DC: U.S. Government Printing Office, 1968, 19–87.

20. Ibid., 1–2.

21. See *The Gallup Poll: Public Opinion, 1935–1997*.

22. See Patterson, James T., *Grand Expectations: The United States, 1945–1974*. New York: Oxford University Press, 1996, 685–686.

23. See "*Green v. County School Board*, 391 U.S. 430 (1968)," *FindLaw*. Thomson Reuters, 2011. http://findlaw.com. Accessed September 22, 2011.

24. See Milstein, Mike M., and Dean E. Hoch, "A Landmark in School Racial Integration: Berkeley, California," *The Phi Delta Kappan*, vol. 50, no. 9 (1969), 524–599.

25. See "Public Schools: Boston's Busing Battle," *Time*, September 24, 1965; and Useem, Bert, "Models of the Boston Anti-Busing Movement: Polity/Mobilization and Relative Deprivation," *The Sociological Quarterly*, vol. 22, no. 2 (1981), 263–274.

26. According to historian Randall Woods, the Daley machine in Chicago got a special carve-out: LBJ intervened when HEW planned to withhold $30 million from the schools. See Woods, Randall B., *LBJ: Architect of American Ambition*. Cambridge, MA: Harvard University Press, 2006, 696–697.

27. See Rodgers, Harrell R., Jr., and Charles S. Bullock III, "School Desegregation: A Policy Analysis," *Journal of Black Studies*, vol. 2, no. 4 (1972), 418–419.

28. See "Data Center," Stanford and University of Michigan.

29. See Dallek, 381.

30. See "California: Proposition 14," *Time*, September 25, 1964.

31. See Cannato, Vincent, *The Ungovernable City: John Lindsay's New York and the Crisis of Liberalism*. New York: Basic Books, 2001, 504–515.

32. See Woods, 840.

33. Humphrey took 1759¼ delegates to 601 for McCarthy, 146½ for McGovern, and 67½ for the Reverend Channing Smith of the District of Columbia. Thanks to his tight connection to the Johnson administration, Humphrey nearly swept the delegates of the old Confederacy; this is ironic because it was his speech at the 1948 convention that helped sway the delegates to adopt a liberal civil rights plank that, in turn, induced the southern delegates to walk out. See *National Party Conventions, 1831–2004*. Washington, DC: Congressional Quarterly Press, 2005, 231.

34. Most, but not all. The National Election Study found that the third of the electorate most comfortable calling themselves liberal gave Humphrey 70 percent of their vote, while Nixon would take 25 percent. In 1964, LBJ had scored 90 percent of this vote to Goldwater's 9 percent. Still, the liberals would come back in force four years later, giving South Dakota senator George McGovern 90 percent of their vote in 1972. See "Data Center," Stanford and University of Michigan.

35. Humphrey promised a halt to the bombing if North Vietnam would offer "direct or indirect" evidence "by deed or by word" that it was interested in serious peace talks. He called this an "acceptable risk for peace." The *New York Times* reported, "Mr. Humphrey's advisers hope that his statement will be interpreted by the peace faction in the Democratic party as a break with the Johnson admin-

istration. They hope that it might prompt Senator Eugene J. McCarthy of Minnesota to endorse the Vice President in the next few weeks." McCarthy finally did so, albeit tepidly, in late October. Apple, R. W., "Humphrey Vows Halt in Bombing If Hanoi Reacts," *New York Times,* October 1, 1968.

36. Wallace, George C., "The 1963 Inaugural Address of Governor George C. Wallace, January 14, 1963, Montgomery, Alabama," Alabama Department of Archives and History, April 12, 2002. http://archives.state.al.us. Accessed September 26, 2011.

37. Welsh, Matthew E., "Civil Rights and the Primary Election of 1964 in Indiana: The Wallace Challenge," *Indiana Magazine of History*, vol. 75, no. 1 (1979), 25.

38. In Wisconsin, Governor John Reynolds, LBJ's stand-in, predicted right before the campaign that Wallace would receive about 100,000 votes. The Alabama governor ended up pulling more than 250,000, thanks in no small part, according to the *New York Times,* to "defecting Democrats from Milwaukee's large Polish population . . . [that] fears that Negroes will move into their neighborhoods." See "Heavy Vote Today Seen in Wisconsin," *New York Times,* April 6, 1968.

39. Outside the states of the old Confederacy, Thurmond won just 0.03 percent of the popular vote. See Burnham, Walter Dean, with Thomas Ferguson and Louis Ferleger, *Voting in American Elections: The Shaping of the American Political Universe Since 1788.* Bethesda, MD: Academica Press, 2010, 98.

40. See Kovenock, David M., James W. Prothro, and Associates, *Explaining the Vote: Presidential Choices in the Nation and the States, 1968,* vol. 2. Chapel Hill, NC: Institute for Research in Social Sciences, 1973, 98–99 and 222–223. Wallace's high point in the Gallup Poll had him clocking in at more than 20 percent of the vote in late September. See "Gallup Presidential Trial-Heat Trends, 1936–2004," Gallup, September 24, 2008. http://gallup.com. Accessed September 22, 2011. By this point, labor had grown highly concerned with Wallace's appeals to AFL-CIO members. As one UAW official reported, "The men in the plants want to zap the Negroes by voting for Wallace" (Gould, 125). The AFL-CIO was also worried about the anemic campaign organization of Humphrey-Muskie and the DNC, which had atrophied during the LBJ years and seemed unable to mount the kind of advertising blitz to counter the Wallace and Nixon onslaughts. Accordingly, organized labor (once again) mounted a significant effort to bring its voters home to the Democratic party, specifically targeting Wallace by highlighting his anti-union record as governor of Alabama as well as the state's relative lack of strong social welfare regulations. Gould, 135.

41. "Busing/Law and Order (Wallace, 1968)," *The Living Room Candidate.* Museum of the Moving Image, 2010. http://livingroomcandidate.org. Accessed September 22, 2011.

42. See Lesher, Stephen, *George Wallace: American Populist.* Cambridge, MA: Perseus Publishing, 1994, 427.

43. See, for instance, Rohler, Lloyd, *George Wallace: Conservative Populist.* Westport, CT: Praeger, 2004, 151–163.

44. "American Independent Party Platform of 1968," in *American Presidency Project,* ed. John T. Woolley and Gerhard Peters. University of California at Santa Barbara, 2011. http://www.presidency.ucsb.edu. Accessed September 21, 2011.

45. White, Theodore, *The Making of the President 1968.* New York: Atheneum, 1969, 68.

46. These numbers are calculated by running the figures of Kovenock and Prothro, 98–99 and 222–223, through the Westegg Inflation Calculator. See http://www .westegg.com.

47. See "2008 Exit Polls." CNN Politics, November 5, 2008. http://cnn.com. Accessed September 22, 2011.

48. Blumenthal, Sidney, *The Strange Death of Republican America: Chronicles of a Collapsing Party.* New York: Union Square Press, 2008, 8.

49. There is an extensive literature that advocates this position, with varying degrees of sophistication. See, for instance, Benen, Steve, "Barbour Explains the South with Baseless, Revisionist History," *Washington Monthly,* September 2, 2010. http://washingtonmonthly.com. Accessed September 22, 2011. It also has been the dominant scholarly view for some time. See Aistrup, Joseph A., *The Southern Strategy Revisited: Republican Advancement in the South* (Lexington: University of Kentucky Press, 1996); Black, Earl, and Merle Black, *The Rise of Southern Republicans* (Cambridge, MA: Harvard University Press, 2002); Carmines, Edward G., and James A. Stimson, *Issue Evolution: Race and the Transformation of American Politics* (Princeton, NJ: Princeton University Press, 1989); Carmines, Edward G., and James A. Stimson, "Issue Evolution, Population Replacement, and Normal Partisan Change," *The American Political Science Review,* vol. 75, no. 1 (1981), 107–118; Carter, Dan T., *From George Wallace to Newt Gingrich: Race in the Conservative Counterrevolution, 1963–1964* (Baton Rouge: Louisiana State University Press, 1996); and Carter, Dan T., *The Politics of Rage: George Wallace, the Origins of the New Conservatism, and the Transformation of American Politics* (New York: Simon & Schuster, 1994). These works promote the idea that the GOP's growing appeal in the South has been largely racial, depending upon either overt appeals (à la Goldwater in 1964) or coded appeals, which include in this analysis Reagan's referencing "states' rights" in Philadelphia, Mississippi, or George H. W. Bush airing the "Willie Horton" ad in the latter stages of the 1988 campaign.

Our analysis here will favor more recent literature that either questions the salience of purely racial issues or emphasizes the importance of class-based issues in the development of southern Republicanism. See Abramowitz, Alan I., "Issue Evolution Reconsidered: Racial Attitudes and Partisanship in the U.S. Electorate," *American Journal of Political Science,* vol. 38, no. 1 (1994), 1–24; Lassiter, Matthew D., *The Silent Majority: Suburban Politics in the Sunbelt South* (Princeton, NJ: Princeton University, 2006); Lublin, David, *The Republican South: Democratization and Partisan Change* (Princeton, NJ: Princeton University Press, 2004); Voss, Stephen, "Beyond Racial Threat: Failure of an Old Hypothesis in the South," *The Journal of Politics,* vol. 58, no. 4 (1996), 1156–1170; Shafer, Byron E., and Richard Johnston, *The End of Southern Exceptionalism: Class, Race, and Partisan Change in the Postwar South* (Cambridge, MA: Harvard University Press, 2006); and Shafer, Byron E., and Richard Johnston. "The Transformation of Southern Politics Revisited: The House of Representatives as a Window," *British Journal of Political Science,* vol. 31, no. 4 (October 2001), 601–625.

The principal reason for the focus on this latter literature is that GOP strength appeared first and most lastingly in the suburban areas of the peripheral South, which historically were less tied to the old Jim Crow system and thus were not really part of the clientelistic relationship the region had with the Democratic party. These areas become partial to the Republican party as early as 1952, and they remain to this day the core areas of GOP strength. Goldwater actually lost these areas with his overt racial appeals in 1964, doing worse than Eisenhower throughout the South and being crushed in the North. So it is not realistic to expect national Republican candidates—who, it must be recalled, still had most of their coalition situated in the North—to make racial appeals.

Much of the confusion with this issue ultimately traces back to the fact that the meaning of "racial conservatism" changed abruptly during the 1960s. Previously, it meant opposition to antidiscrimination laws, antilynching laws, laws to abolish Jim Crow instruments like the poll tax, etc. After these civil rights are secured, the racial divide begins to resemble a class divide—in particular, the extent to which middle-income whites would be responsible for the social welfare of lower-income blacks. Thus, the racial divides in the North and South became increasingly indistinguishable; the racial tensions in metro Detroit are also present in metro Atlanta—issues of school busing, open housing, affirmative action, etc. The older literature does a poor job of dealing with this shift in the meaning of "racial conservatism," and often one will find the term used to describe opposition to affirmative action *as well as* opposition to antilynching laws, without appropriate qualifiers.

50. Olmstead, Alan L., and Paul W. Rohde, "Farm Population, by Region and State: 1890–1969," in *Historical Statistics of the United States,* ed. Susan B. Carter, Scott Sigmund Gartner, Michael R. Haines, Alan L. Olmstead, Richard Sutch, and Gavin Wright. New York: Cambridge University Press, 2006, 4–44–45.

51. Ferrie, Joseph P, "Net Intercensal Migration, by Race and State: 1940–1990," in *Historical Statistics of the United States,* 1–505–506.

52. Ibid.

53. See Grady, Henry, "Henry Grady to the Bay State Club of Boston, 1889," *History Matters.* George Washington University. http://historymatters.gmu.edu. Accessed September 26, 2011.

54. See Sale, Kirkpatrick, *Power Shift: The Rise of the Southern Rim and Its Challenge to the Eastern Establishment.* New York: Random House, 1976, 17–88.

55. See Black, Earl, and Merle Black, *Politics and Society in the South.* Cambridge, MA: Harvard University Press, 1987, 33–34. LBJ, in particular, was a master of this, particularly when as vice president he chaired the National Aeronautics and Space Council, an excellent opportunity to funnel pork barrel projects to his native Texas. See Dallek, *Flawed Giant,* 22.

56. Black and Black, *Politics and Society in the South,* 53. These authors quantify the rise of the new southern middle class by coding census data on employment, and conclude, "Southerners with professional, technical, managerial, administrative, sales, and clerical positions constitute the new middle class." Black and Black, 52.

57. Ibid., 59.

58. See "Census of Population and Housing," United States Census Bureau, 2011. http://census.gov. Accessed September 22, 2011.

59. For more on the rise of the conservative wing of the Republican party, see Brennan, Mary C., *Turning Right in the Sixties: The Conservative Capture of the GOP* (Chapel Hill: University of North Carolina Press, 1995); McGirr, Lisa, *Subur-*

ban Warriors: The Origins of the New American Right (Princeton, NJ: Princeton University Press, 2002); Rae, Nicol C., *The Decline and Fall of the Liberal Republicans, from 1952 to the Present* (New York: Oxford University Press, 1989); Reinhard, David W., *The Republican Right Since 1945* (Louisville: The University of Kentucky Press, 1983). The best barometer for the change in the GOP was Nixon, who was always careful to find the center of gravity in the party. In 1960 Nixon won the nomination but was concerned that liberal Republican Nelson Rockefeller, governor of New York, would not offer his full support in November. So Nixon hammered out with the New York governor the so-called Treaty of Fifth Avenue, in which the two agreed on a fairly liberal reform program. See "Republicans: The Bold Stroke," *Time,* August 1, 1960. Eight years later, in pursuit of the nomination, Nixon was worried about the rising conservatism of the Sunbelt in the South and West, so this time he traveled to Atlanta to come to terms with Republican senators John Tower of Texas and Strom Thurmond of South Carolina, who had switched to the Republican party in 1964. The fact that Nixon traveled to Atlanta, not New York City, to make a deal with Thurmond and Tower, not Rockefeller, is a sign of just how the balance in the party power structure had tipped south and west. See White, 137–138.

60. See "1952 Presidential General Election Results," in *Atlas of U.S. Presidential Elections;* and Burnham, 99.

61. See Burnham, 194.

62. See Shafer and Johnston, *The End of Southern Exceptionalism*, 22–50.

63. See Poole, Keith, "Roll Call Data," *VoteView.* University of Georgia, 2011. http://voteview.com. Accessed September 21, 2011. Theodore White records the nature of the "deal" between Nixon and the southern Republicans and dispels the notion that the Republican nominee brokered a "Faustian bargain" with Dixie:

Mr. Nixon agreed that the Supreme Court phrase "all deliberate speed" needed re-interpretation; he agreed also that a factor in his thinking about new Supreme Court Justices was that liberal-interpretationists had tipped the balance too far against the strict-construction interpreters of the Constitution; and he averred, also, that the compulsory bussing of school students from one district to another for the purpose of racial balance was wrong. On schools, however, he insisted that no Federal funds would be given to a school district which practiced clear segregation; but, on the other hand, he agreed that no Federal funds should be withheld from school districts as a penalty for tardiness in response to a bureaucratic decision in Washington which ordained the precise proportions of white or black children by a Federal directive that could not be questioned in the provinces. . . .

The southerners, in general, wanted to be "in" on decisions, not to be treated like pariahs on the national scene as Negroes had previously been treated. On this, too, Nixon gave reassurance. No particular veto[es] on Vice-President or Cabinet were requested, although Mr. Nixon assured them they would be in on consultations. To their desire that he campaign heavily throughout the South, Nixon could not give entire assurance—Deep South states like Mississippi and Alabama he felt were lost, but he *would* stump the Border South. The Southerners wanted some clearance on Federal patronage; they agreed that a new administration ought, indeed, to include large personalities from the South; and some would have to be

Democrats, since the Democrats are still the Establishment in the South. But the Southerners wanted no appointments that would nip the growth of the Southern Republican Party; they did not insist on veto, only on consultation.

    White, 137–138.

64. See Lassiter, 2.

65. In fact, countywide data suggest that LBJ's frontlash strategy was successful in the rising suburbs of the major southern cities. Johnson carried Greater Charlotte, Dallas, Houston, Miami, and Tampa, all of which Eisenhower had won in 1952 and 1956. See "1952 Presidential General Election Results" and "1964 Presidential General Election Results," in *United States Election Atlas*.

66. The GOP convention in 1968 is a telling example of the Republican strategy moving forward. It avoided any mention of the Civil Rights or Voting Rights acts, and demanded tough anti-crime measures and solutions to the urban poverty that emphasized individual initiative and local control. See "Republican Party Platform of 1968," in *The American Presidency Project*. In his convention address, Richard Nixon said:

> [L]et us build bridges, my friends, build bridges to human dignity across that gulf that separates black America from white America. Black Americans, no more than white Americans, they do not want more government programs which perpetuate dependency. They don't want to be a colony in a nation. They want the pride, and the self-respect, and the dignity that can only come if they have an equal chance to own their own homes, to own their own businesses, to be managers and executives as well as workers, to have a piece of the action in the exciting ventures of private enterprise. I pledge to you tonight that we shall have new programs which will provide that equal chance.

    Nixon, Richard, "Address Accepting the Presidential Nomination at the Republican National Convention in Miami Beach, August 8, 1968," in *The American Presidency Project*.

67. Bush won 56 percent of white Catholics, 53 percent of those without a college degree, and 58 percent of southerners. See "2004 Exit Polls—President, United States," MSNBC. http://msnbc.com. Accessed September 26, 2011.

CHAPTER 9: Too Much Hair and Not Enough Cigars

1. See Hartz, Louis, *The Liberal Tradition in America*. San Diego: Harcourt Brace Jovanovich, 1991, 57–58.

2. See Dahl, Robert A., *Who Governs? Democracy and Power in an American City*. New Haven, CT: Yale University Press, 1961, 85.

3. Polsby, Nelson, *Community Power and Political Theory*. New Haven, CT: Yale University Press, 1970, 118.

4. See Crotty, William J., and John S. Jackson III, *Presidential Primaries and Nominations*. Washington, DC: Congressional Quarterly Press, 1985, 16. Of these primaries, a good portion of them were "delegate primaries," in which voters did not select a candidate but rather a delegate for the party convention—a confusing process that enabled the regulars to retain control over the process. In fact, by 1968 just 23 percent of all delegates were chosen through the kind of candidate-centered primaries that we take for granted today. See Shafer, Byron E., *Bifur-*

cated Politics: Evolution and Reform in the National Party Convention. Cambridge, MA: Harvard University Press, 1988, 86.

5. Wilson, James Q., *The Amateur Democrat.* Chicago: University of Chicago Press, 1962, 33.

6. Shafer, Byron E., *Quiet Revolution: The Struggle for the Democratic Party and the Shaping of Post Reform Politics.* New York: Russell Sage Foundation, 1983, 538.

7. See White, Theodore, *The Making of the President 1972.* New York: Atheneum, 1973, 38.

8. See Rising, George, *Clean for Gene: Eugene McCarthy's 1968 Presidential Campaign.* Westport, CT: Praeger, 1997.

9. Friedan, Betty, *The Feminine Mystique.* New York: W.W. Norton, 2001, 463–464.

10. See Sale, Kirkpatrick, *The Green Revolution: The American Environmental Movement, 1962–1992.* New York: Hill and Wang, 1993, 3–46.

11. See Unger, Irwin, *The Movement: A History of the American New Left, 1959–1972* (New York: Dodd, Mead and Co., 1974), 9; and Diggins, John P., *The American Left in the Twentieth Century* (New York: W.W. Norton, 1992), 150.

12. See Bachrach, Peter, and Morton S. Baratz, "Decisions and Nondecisions: An Analytical Framework," *The American Political Science Review,* vol. 57, no. 3 (1963), 632–642; and Bachrach, Peter, and Morton S. Baratz, "Two Faces of Power," *The American Political Science Review,* vol. 56, no. 4 (1962), 947–952.

13. See Harrington, Michael, *The Other America: Poverty in the United States* (New York: Scribner, 1997); and Mills, C. Wright, *The Power Elite* (Oxford, England: Oxford University Press, 2000).

14. See Gaventa, John, *Power and Powerlessness: Quiescence & Rebellion in an Appalachian Valley* (Urbana: University of Illinois Press, 1982); and Lukes, Steven, *Power: A Radical View* (New York: Palgrave Macmillan, 2004).

15. See Unger, 23.

16. Ibid., 93–101.

17. See Piven, Frances Fox, and Richard A. Cloward, "The Weight of the Poor: A Strategy to End Poverty," *The Nation,* May 2, 1966.

18. For a time, NWRO was successful, but eventually states and localities responded by eliminating special subsidies. See Piven, Frances Fox, and Richard A. Cloward, *Poor People's Movements: Why They Succeed, How They Fail.* New York: Vintage, 1977, 264–362.

19. See Moynihan, Daniel Patrick, *Maximum Feasible Misunderstanding: Community Action and the War on Poverty.* New York: The Free Press, 1969, 114.

20. Ibid., 133.

21. See Braun, Mark Edward, *Social Change and the Empowerment of the Poor: Poverty Representation in Milwaukee's Community Action Programs, 1964–1972.* Lanham, MA: Lexington Books, 2001, 110–139.

22. Alinsky, Saul, *Rules for Radicals: A Practical Primer for Realistic Radicals.* New York: Vintage, 1989, 4.

23. See Moynihan, 144–145.

24. Gillette, Michael L., *Launching the War on Poverty: An Oral History.* New York: Simon & Schuster, 2010, 348–349.

25. As William Styron put it in a blistering critique of the Windy City boss in the *New York Review of Books:*

No one should ever have been surprised that [Daley] set loose his battalions against the kids; it was the triumphant end-product of his style, and what else might one expect from this squalid person whose spirit suffused the great city as oppressively as that of some Central American field marshal?

Styron, William, "In the Jungle," *New York Review of Books,* September 26, 1968.

26. See Crotty, William J., *Decision for the Democrats: Reforming the Party Structure* (Baltimore: Johns Hopkins University Press, 1978), 14–19; and Polsby, Nelson, *Consequences of Party Reform* (Oxford, England: Oxford University Press, 1983), 22–27.

27. Crotty, 5–6. As Byron Shafer puts it:

The 1968 convention was determinedly regular in its political orientation; indeed, it was the last such convention in our era. Yet its dominant participants, regular-party delegates and leaders of the Humphrey campaign as well, while they could surely have defeated the Rues minority report as they had defeated all other minority reports at the convention, did not mobilize against it. And they did not do so because they wanted to provide a sop to the losing side, in the hope that it might be brought around for the general election; because they felt that the reform realm was comparatively inconsequential, especially if they continued to control the party after the convention; and because they viewed this sort of compensation as an appropriate part of ongoing politics.

Shafer, *Quiet Revolution,* 528.

28. See White, 40–41.

29. See *National Party Conventions, 1831–2004.* Washington, DC: Congressional Quarterly Press, 2005, 231.

30. Ceaser, James W., *Presidential Selection: Theory and Development.* Princeton, NJ: Princeton University Press, 1979, 263.

31. See Polsby, *Consequences of Party Reform,* 34–51.

32. See Ceaser, 291; and Crotty, 257.

33. See Polsby, *Consequences of Party Reform,* 59–62.

34. See Shafer, *Quiet Revolution,* 100–105.

35. William Crotty offers an interesting take on the considerations of the AFL-CIO:

Organized labor feared that reform was simply a device through which a new, and more liberal, faction would assume control of the party and its nominating procedures, threatening labor's power and even expelling it from its position of dominant influence within party ranks. This position came far closer to labor's principal concern and accounts for its prolonged and bitter opposition: the AFL-CIO fought the reforms at every stage; it chose never to accommodate itself to the guidelines once they were adopted; it refused to accept or support the nominees of the Democratic convention (the fact that one of them was McGovern, the early reform leader and a politician personally disliked by Meany, did not help matters), who [were] chosen through the new procedures, thus giving latent support to Nixon, labor's arch rival for decades; and it led an assault on the new delegate selection regulations once the 1972 election year ended.

Crotty, 110.

Also of importance to organized labor in 1972 was the fact that McGovern, who had promised them he would vote with them to repeal the right-to-work provisions of Taft-Hartley, actually voted with Senate Republicans to sustain the filibuster discussed in the previous chapter. See White, 223–224.

36. See Crotty, 255–256; and Shafer, *Bifurcated Politics,* 255–256.

37. For a good description of the post-1970 reforms, which saw the creation of the "superdelegates," i.e., the return of ex officio status to party members in government, see Crotty, William, *Party Reform* (New York: Longman, 1983), 40–43; and Davis, James W., *U.S. Presidential Primaries and the Caucus-Convention System: A Sourcebook* (Westport, CT: Greenwood Press, 1997), 25–27. More generally, Marty Cohen and his colleagues offer an apt description of the new party:

The individuals who . . . now control nominations include "politicians"—governors, big-city mayors, members of party committees, and legislators—but not only politicians. In opening the process to rank-and-file voters, the reforms opened it to many other players as well. These include organized interests—unions, religious organizations, civil rights groups, and business. Also included are people whose technical skills are necessary to win mass elections, such as organizers, fund-raisers, pollsters, and media specialists. Finally, and perhaps as important as anyone else, [there] are citizen activists who join the political fray as weekend warriors.

Cohen, Marty, David Karol, Hans Noel, and John Zaller, *The Party Decides: Presidential Nominations Before and After Reform*. Chicago: University of Chicago Press, 2008, 4.

38. White, 101.

39. "Gonzo" journalist Hunter S. Thompson, with his usual flair, described the absurd scene from the floor as the convention wasted hours over pointless vice-presidential nominations: "All over the floor I saw people caving in to the lure of booze, and in the crowded aisle between the California and Wisconsin delegations a smiling freak with a bottle of liquid THC was giving free hits to anybody who still had the strength to stick their tongue out." Thompson, Hunter S., *Fear and Loathing: On the Campaign Trail '72*. New York: Warner Books, 1973, 319.

40. Crotty, *Decision for the Democrats*, 148.

41. See Remini, Robert V., *The House: The History of the House of Representatives*. New York: HarperCollins, 2006, 376–377.

42. Ibid., 423–443.

43. See Cooper, Joseph, and David W. Brady, "Institutional Context and Leadership Style: The House from Cannon to Rayburn," *The American Political Science Review,* vol. 75, no. 2 (1981), 419.

44. See Rohde, David W., *Parties and Leaders in the Postreform House*. Chicago: University of Chicago Press, 1991, 17–28.

45. Ibid., 15.

46. See Rozell, Mark J., Clyde Wilcox, and David Madland, *Interest Groups in American Campaigns: The New Face of Electioneering* (Washington, DC: Congressional Quarterly Press, 2006), 73–74; and Wright, John R., *Interest Groups and Congress: Lobbying, Contributions, and Influence* (New York: Longman, 2003), 118–121.

47. See Hall, Richard L., and Frank W. Wayman, "Buying Time: Moneyed Interests and the Mobilization of Bias in Congressional Committees," *The American Political Science Review,* vol. 84, no. 3 (1990), 797–820.

48. See Berry, Jeffrey M., *The New Liberalism: The Rising Power of Citizen Groups*. Washington, DC: The Brookings Institution Press, 1999, 45.

49. See Wright, 8.

50. These groups have also had a similar influence on the mainstream media, which regularly turns to New Left advocacy groups for seemingly nonpartisan information on public policy problems. See Berry, 118–152.

51. Ibid., 55.

CHAPTER 10: Hard Choices and Scarce Resources

1. Lowi, Theodore J., *The End of Liberalism: Ideology, Policy, and the Crisis of Public Authority*. New York: W.W. Norton & Co., 1969, 71 and 72.

2. See Mason, Robert, *Richard Nixon and the Quest for a New Majority* (Chapel Hill: University of North Carolina Press, 2004), 28–57; and Small, Melvin, *The Presidency of Richard Nixon* (Lawrence: University Press of Kansas, 2004), 164–190.

3. See Burnham, Walter Dean, with Thomas Ferguson and Louis Ferleger, *Voting in American Elections: The Shaping of the American Political Universe Since 1788*. Bethesda, MD: Academica Press, 2010, 187–188.

4. See Greene, John Robert, *The Presidency of Gerald R. Ford*. Lawrence: University Press of Kansas, 1995, 77.

5. Jordan, Hamilton, "Hamilton Jordan Original Strategy Memo for Jimmy Carter's Run for President, November 4, 1972," C-SPAN. http://c-span.org. Accessed September 22, 2011.

6. Schram, Martin, *Running for President 1976: The Carter Campaign*. New York: Stein and Day, 1977, 10.

7. As Stephen Skowronek put it: "Carter's drive for the White House revolutionized the political art of self-presentation and set the mold for the plebiscitary politics of our day. His was an 'autobiographical' campaign which blurred received images of the Democratic party to project a national political identity that was wholly idiosyncratic." Skowronek, Stephen, *The Politics Presidents Make: Leadership from John Adams to Bill Clinton*. Cambridge, MA: The Belknap Press of Harvard University Press, 1997, 374.

8. "New Day A'Coming in the South," *Time,* May 31, 1971.

9. See Murphy, Reg, and Hal Gulliver, *The Southern Strategy*. New York: Charles Scribner's Sons, 1971, 177–179.

10. See Bourne, Peter G., *Jimmy Carter: A Comprehensive Biography from Plains to Postpresidency*. New York: Scribner, 1997, 192–193.

11. Ibid., 196.

12. See Kaufman, Burton I., and Scott Kaufman, *The Presidency of James Earl Carter*. Lawrence: University Press of Kansas, 2006, 10–15.

13. See Jones, Charles O., *The Trusteeship Presidency: Jimmy Carter and the United States Congress*. Baton Rouge: Louisiana State University Press, 1988, 14.

14. See Witcover, Jules, *Marathon: The Pursuit of the Presidency, 1972–1976*. New York: Signet, 1977, 164.

15. As Hamilton Jordan commented: "I felt like there was going to be an overreaction to the new rules of the Democratic Party, that people were going to pick and choose, to shape strategies that presumed a brokered convention. We shaped a

strategy that presumed there was *not* going to be a brokered convention." Ibid., 209.

16. See Aldrich, John H., *Before the Convention: Strategies and Choices in Presidential Nomination Campaigns.* Chicago: University of Chicago Press, 1980, 104–105.

17. See Alexander, Herbert E., *Financing the 1976 Election* (Washington, DC: Congressional Quarterly Press, 1979), 160; Levantrosser, William F., "Financing Presidential Campaigns: The Impact of Reform Campaign Finance Laws on the Democratic Presidential Nomination of 1976," *Presidential Studies Quarterly,* vol. 11, no. 2 (1981), 285; and Schram, 7.

18. Bartels, Larry M., *Presidential Primaries and the Dynamics of Public Choice.* Princeton, NJ: Princeton University Press, 1988, 183.

19. See Schram, 123.

20. See *Congressional Quarterly's Guide to U.S. Elections,* 4th ed., vol. 1. Washington, DC: Congressional Quarterly Press, 2001, 364.

21. See Bartels, 202. Carter's momentum produced not only extra votes, but extra dollars. It wasn't until after his early victories that his fund-raising finally picked up. See Alexander, 231.

22. Alexander, 237–238.

23. Brill, Steven, "Jimmy Carter's Pathetic Lies: The Heroic Image Is Made of Brass." *Harper's,* March 1976. Also, liberal strategist Bob Shrum quit the campaign just days after joining because of Carter's caginess, and his resignation memo, leaked to the press, read in part:

> You say you wish to keep your options open. Within reason that is understandable. But an election is the only option the people have. After carefully reflecting on what I have seen and heard here, I do not know what you would do as President. I share the perception that simple measures will not answer our problems; but it seems to me that your issue strategy is not a response to that complexity, but an attempt to conceal your true positions. I am not sure what you truly believe in other than yourself.

> Schram, 136.

> See also Lydon, Christopher, "A Carter Writer Quits in Protest," *New York Times,* May 3, 1976.

24. See Kaufman and Kaufman, 122.

25. See Alexander, 122; and Shafer, Byron E., *Bifurcated Politics: Evolution and Reform in the National Party Convention* (Cambridge, MA: Harvard University Press, 1988), 119–120.

26. See Alexander, 365.

27. See "Gallup Presidential Trial-Heat Trends, 1936–2004," Gallup, September 24, 2008. http://gallup.com. Accessed September 22, 2011.

28. See Burnham, 97–105.

29. Charles O. Jones describes the trusteeship president thus: "[A] president who views his background and electoral record as incongruent with those of legislators . . . [and] who will be less tolerant of the electoral connection and of inconsistencies in representational roles. He sees his job as representing all the people, and as a 'counterforce to special interests.' " Jones, 4. See also Hargrove, Erwin, *Jimmy Carter as President: Leadership and the Politics of the Public Good.* Baton Rouge: Louisiana State University Press, 1988, 34.

30. See "Real Gross Domestic Product, Chained Dollars, 1929–2011," Bureau of Economic Analysis, 2011. http://bea.gov. Accessed September 21, 2011.

31. Biven, Carl W., *Jimmy Carter's Economy: Politics in an Age of Limits*. Chapel Hill: University of North Carolina Press, 2002, xi.

32. See "Business Sector: Output per Person, 1947–2011," FRED Economic Data, Federal Reserve Bank of St. Louis, September 1, 2011 (http://research.st.louisfed .org, accessed September 22, 2011); and "Disposable Personal Income: Per Capita, Chained (2005) Dollars, 1959–2011," FRED Economic Data, Federal Reserve Bank of St. Louis, September 1, 2011 (http://research.st.louisfed.org, accessed September 22, 2011).

33. "Consumer Price Index for All Urban Consumers: All Items, 1947–2011," FRED Economic Data. Accessed September 22, 2011.

34. See Jones, 124; and Hargrove, 11.

35. Carter, Jimmy, "Remarks of President Jimmy Carter," John F. Kennedy Presidential Library and Museum. http://jfklibrary.org. Accessed September 22, 2011. As Carter's adviser Stu Eizenstat put it: "Far from being a traitor to his party, as some on the left insinuated, he realized that only by changing the party could he save it. The tragedy is that he did not have the chance to finish the job." Eizenstat, Stuart E., "President Carter, the Democratic Party, and the Making of Domestic Policy," in *The Presidency and Domestic Policies of Jimmy Carter,* ed. Herbert D. Rosenbaum and Alexej Ugrinsky. Westport, CT: Greenwood Press, 1994, 3.

36. See "(Seas) Unemployment Rate," Bureau of Labor Statistics, January 21, 2011 (http://bls.gov, accessed September 22, 2011); and "Real Gross Domestic Product, Chained Dollars, 1929–2011."

37. See Biven, 70.

38. Kaufman and Kaufman, 33–34. See also Dark, Taylor, "Organized Labor and the Carter Administration: The Origins of Conflict," in Rosenbaum and Ugrinsky, *The Presidency and Domestic Policies of Jimmy Carter,* 765; and Hargrove, 89–91. In a sign of Carter's uneasiness about inflation, the president actually withdrew the proposal for a $50 tax rebate after he had submitted the bill to the Congress. This was also an example of Carter's poor management of Congress. The rebate was an unpopular proposal, and Democratic leaders had pushed for it as a sign of party unity, yet Carter withdrew it abruptly without consultation. See Jones, 134.

39. See "History of Federal Minimum Wage Rates Under the Fair Labor Standards Act," United States Department of Labor. http://www.dol.gov. Accessed September 22, 2011.

40. See Biven, 211–217; and Haas, Garland A., *Jimmy Carter and the Politics of Frustration* (Jefferson, NC: McFarland & Co., 1992), 73.

41. See Dubofsky, Melvyn, "Jimmy Carter and the Politics of Productivity," in *The Carter Presidency: Policy Choices in the New Deal Era*, ed. Gary M. Fink and Hugh Davis Graham. Lawrence: University Press of Kansas, 1998, 101.

42. See Lynn, Laurence E., Jr., and David deF. Whitman, *The President as Policymaker: Jimmy Carter and Welfare Reform*. Philadelphia: Temple University Press, 1981, 40.

43. Ibid., 229.

44. See Patterson, James T., "Jimmy Carter and Welfare Reform," in Fink and Graham, *The Carter Presidency*, 120.

45. See Lynn and Whitman, 231–235.

46. Ibid., 239.

47. See Dubofsky, 795.

48. See Haas, 120–124.

49. Two items on the labor agenda during the Carter tenure were a "common-site" picketing bill that would have allowed workers to strike an entire site even if their dispute was with only one contractor of many and a reform of the National Labor Relations Act to enable unions to form more quickly. Carter backed both bills, yet both of them failed to secure passage, as the anti-labor coalition in Congress was still strong, despite the large Democratic majorities. Many in labor blamed Carter for not lobbying hard enough for the passage of these bills, but the fact is that labor was simply not the force it had been as recently as a decade before. See Dark, 766–767; and Dubofsky, 106.

50. For more on Carter's battle over the Department of Education, see Dark, 768; Hargrove, 60–62; Jones, 184–185; and Shafer, 119–120.

51. See Flint, Andrew R., and Joy Porter, "Jimmy Carter: The Re-Emergence of Faith-Based Politics and the Abortion Rights Issue," *Presidential Studies Quarterly*, vol. 35, no. 1 (2005), 28–51; and Hartmann, Susan M., "Feminism, Public Policy, and the Carter Administration," in Fink and Graham, *The Carter Presidency*, 224–243.

52. See Haas, 92.

53. See Kaufman and Kaufman, 92–94.

54. See Jones, 180.

55. See Dark, 762; Kaufman and Kaufman, 121; and Schulman, Bruce J., "Slouching Toward the Supply Side: Jimmy Carter and the New American Political Economy," in Fink and Graham, *The Carter Presidency*, 58.

56. See Ranney, Austin, "The Carter Administration," in *The American Elections of 1980*, ed. Austin Ranney. Washington, DC: American Enterprise Institute for Public Policy Research, 1981, 28.

57. "Nation: Jimmy's Party in Memphis," *Time*, December 18, 1978.

58. Kennedy, Edward M., "Remarks of Senator Edward M. Kennedy, Workshop on Health Care, Democratic National Committee Midterm Convention, Memphis, Tennessee, December 9, 1978," Edward M. Kennedy Institute, 2009. http://ted kennedy.org. Accessed September 22, 2011.

59. See Biven, 190–191; Dubofsky, 110; and Kaufman and Kaufman, 138.

60. As Meany said, "We are ready to have our wages controlled by an act of Congress. But we want dividends controlled. We want the middle man controlled. We want insurance rates controlled. We want interest rates controlled. We went everything that goes into the cost controlled." Fink, Gary M., "Fragile Alliance: Jimmy Carter and the American Labor Movement," in Rosenbaum and Ugrinsky, *The Presidency and Domestic Policies of Jimmy Carter*, 797.

61. See Biven, 194; Dark, 772; and Schulman, 60.

62. Haas, 95. For more on the FY 1980 budget, see Kaplowitz, Craig Allan, "Struggles of the First 'New Democrat': Jimmy Carter, Youth Employment Policy, and the Great Society Legacy," *Presidential Studies Quarterly*, vol. 28, no. 1 (1998), 187–206.

63. See Kaufman and Kaufman, 169.

64. See Haas, 97. For more on the FY 1981 budget battle, see "Jimmy Carter vs. Inflation," *Time,* March 24, 1980.

65. See Busch, Andrew E., *Reagan's Victory: The Presidential Election of 1980 and the Rise of the Right.* Lawrence: University Press of Kansas, 2005, 37.

66. See Germond, Jack W., and Jules Witcover, *Blue Smoke and Mirrors: How Reagan Won and Why Carter Lost the Election of 1980.* New York: Viking, 1981, 55.

67. Busch, 38–39.

68. See Abramson, Paul R., John H. Aldrich, and David W. Rohde, *Change and Continuity in the 1980 Elections.* Washington, DC: Congressional Quarterly Press, 1982, 20.

69. See "Presidential Job Approval, F. Roosevelt (1941)–Obama," in *American Presidency Project,* ed. John T. Woolley and Gerhard Peters. University of California at Santa Barbara, 2011. http://www.presidency.ucsb.edu. Accessed September 21, 2011.

70. See "The Kennedy Challenge," *Time,* November 4, 1979.

71. See Polsby, Nelson, *Consequences of Party Reform.* Oxford, England: Oxford University Press, 1983, 51–52.

72. See Stanley, Timothy, *Kennedy vs. Carter: The 1980 Battle for the Democratic Party's Soul.* Lawrence: University Press of Kansas, 2010, 141.

73. See Alexander, Herbert E., *Financing the 1980 Election.* Lexington, MA: Lexington Books, 1983, 383–384.

74. See Dark, 773.

75. See Germond and Witcover, 48–78.

76. *Congressional Quarterly's Guide to U.S. Elections,* 630.

77. Kennedy, Edward M., "1980 Democratic National Convention." The Edward M. Kennedy Institute.

78. Eizenstat, 14–15.

79. "Democratic Party Platform of 1980," in *American Presidency Project.*

80. See "Gallup Presidential Trial-Heat Trends, 1936–2004."

81. See Abramson et al., 98–99.

82. See Fallows, James, "The Passionless Presidency," *The Atlantic Monthly*, May 1979.

CHAPTER 11: A Temporary Triangle

1. See Woodward, Bob, *The Agenda: Inside the Clinton White House.* New York: Simon & Schuster, 1994, 40–41.

2. See Alexander, Herbert E., and Brian A. Haggerty, *Financing the 1984 Election* (Washington, DC: Lexington Books, 1987), 93; "PAC Contributions to House Campaign by Type of Campaign, Through December 31 of the Election Year," Federal Election Commission (http://fec.gov, accessed September 24, 2011); and "PAC Contributions to Federal Candidates: 1992, 1994, and 1996 Election Cycles," Federal Election Commission (accessed September 24, 2011).

3. See Eismeier, Theodore J., and Philip H. Pollock III, "Money in the 1994 Elections and Beyond," in *Midterm: The Elections of 1994 in Context*, ed. Philip A. Klinker. Boulder, CO: Westview Press, 1996, 91.

4. See Alexander and Haggerty, 181–203. The AFL-CIO spent about $3.1 million

on Mondale's behalf during the pre-nomination period, while the NEA dispatched workers to mobilize the organization's members.

5. Ibid., 219; and Abramson, Paul R., John H Aldrich, and David W Rohde, *Change and Continuity in the 1984 Elections,* revised ed. (Washington, DC: Congressional Quarterly Press, 1987), 32. A notable twist during this cycle was the candidacy of civil rights advocate Jesse Jackson, who managed to carry 77 percent of the black vote.

6. See Mondale, Walter F., "Address Accepting the Presidential Nomination at the Democratic National Convention in San Francisco, July 19, 1984," in *American Presidency Project,* ed. John T. Woolley and Gerhard Peters, University of California at Santa Barbara, 2011 (http://www.presidency.ucsb.edu, accessed September 21, 2011); and Plotkin, Henry A., "Issues in the Campaign," in *The Election of 1984: Reports and Interpretations*, ed. Gerald M. Pomper (Chatham, NJ: Chatham House Publishers, 1985), 44.

7. See Abramson et al., 136–137. The Reagan victory in 1984 underscores a persistent trend that has been in place for thirty years: even though labor union money flows almost entirely to the Democratic party, Republicans do fairly well with rank-and-file members. Union workers had begun drifting away from the Democratic party in 1968, but what was notable about 1984 was Reagan's strong haul among union workers, despite the all-out effort that labor leaders put in for Mondale, a longtime friend of the AFL-CIO.

8. See Baer, Kenneth S., *Reinventing Democrats: The Politics of Liberalism from Reagan to Clinton* (Lawrence: University Press of Kansas, 2000), 130–134; and Goldman, Peter, Thomas M. DeFrank, Mark Miller, Andrew Murr, and Tom Matthews, with Patrick Rogers and Melanie Cooper, *Quest for the Presidency, 1992* (College Station: Texas A&M University Press, 1994), 25.

9. See Baer, 59–68; and "The New Orleans Declaration, March 1, 1990," The Democratic Leadership Council (http://www.dlc.org, accessed September 24, 2011).

10. See Ceaser, James, and Andrew Busch, *Upside Down and Inside Out: The 1992 Elections and American Politics* (Lanham, MD: Rowman and Littlefield, 1993), 55; and Plotkin, 46. Jackson had hoped to form a "Rainbow Coalition" of many groups, not just African Americans, who had all felt put upon by the economic system in the country.

11. For more on the 1988 Democratic primary vote, see Abramson, Paul R., John H. Aldrich, and David W Rohde, *Change and Continuity in the 1988 Elections.* Washington, DC: Congressional Quarterly Press, 1990, 34.

12. Ibid.,44.

13. See Abramson, Paul R., John H Aldrich, and David W Rohde, *Change and Continuity in the 1992 Elections,* revised ed. (Washington, DC: Congressional Quarterly Press, 1995), 16; Goldman et al., 48–49; and Ceaser and Busch, 56–57.

14. See Baer, 164; and Abramson et al., *Change and Continuity in the 1992 Elections*, 32.

15. Berman, William C., *From the Center to the Edge: The Politics and Policies of the Clinton Presidency.* Lanham, MD: Rowman and Littlefield, 2001, 10.

16. See Ceaser and Busch, 71–72.

17. Clinton, William J., "Address Accepting the Presidential Nomination at the Democratic National Convention in New York," in *The American Presidency Project.*

18. Pitney, John J., Jr., "Clinton and the Republican Party," in *The Postmodern Presidency: Bill Clinton's Legacy in U.S. Politics*, ed. Steven E. Schier. Pittsburgh, PA: University of Pittsburgh Press, 2000, 168.

19. See Wilson, Graham K. "The Clinton Administration and Interest Groups," in *The Clinton Presidency: First Appraisals*, ed. Colin Campbell and Bert A. Rockman. Chatham, NJ: Chatham House Publishers, 1996, 218.

20. For more on Clinton's battle with organized labor in Arkansas, see Berman, 7.

21. See Abramson et al., *Change and Continuity in the 1992 Elections*, 132–135.

22. See Drew, Elizabeth, *On the Edge: The Clinton Presidency*. New York: Touchstone Books, 1994, 47.

23. See Cohen, Richard E., *Changing Course in Washington: Clinton and the New Congress* (New York: Macmillan College Publishing, 1994), 68–69; Harris, John F., *The Survivor: Bill Clinton in the White House* (New York: Random House, 2005), 16; and Jones, Charles O., *Clinton and Congress, 1993–1996: Risk, Restoration, and Reelection* (Norman: University of Oklahoma Press, 1999), 74–75.

24. See Drew, 41; and Jones, 76.

25. See Drew, 198. These and other early actions, combined with continuing ethical questions, contributed to a swift decline in Clinton's job approval rating, which had sunk below 40 percent in the Gallup Poll by early summer. Yet in the long run, Clinton's early symbolic and substantive gestures created goodwill with African Americans, environmentalists, and feminists—all of whom would stand by Clinton during the impeachment process. See Hine, Darlene Clark, "African Americans and the Clinton Presidency: Reckoning with Race, 1992–2000," in *The Clinton Riddle: Perspectives on the Forty-second President*, ed. Todd G. Shields, Jeannie M. Whayne, and Donald R. Kelly (Fayetteville: The University of Arkansas Press, 2004), 82–85; Jones, Charles O., "Campaigning to Govern: The Clinton Style," in Campbell and Rockman, *The Clinton Presidency: First Appraisals*, 24; Kraft, Michael E., *Environmental Policy and Politics,* 3rd ed. (New York: Pearson, 2004), 114; Stetson, Dorothy McBride, "The Women's Movement Agenda and the Record of the Clinton Administration," in Shields et al., *The Clinton Riddle: Perspectives on the Forty-Second President*, 140–141; and Wickham, DeWayne, *Bill Clinton and Black America* (New York: Ballantine, 2002).

26. See Brady, David W., and Craig Volden, *Revolving Gridlock* (Boulder, CO: Westview Press, 1998), 117; and Drew, 116.

27. See Cohen, 130.

28. See Woodward, 83.

29. See Tatalovich, Raymond, and John Fredreis, "Clinton, Class, and Economic Policy," in Schier, *The Postmodern Presidency,* 48–49. At one point during the fractious debate over the deficit, Clinton noted sarcastically, "I hope you're all aware we're all Eisenhower Republicans. . . . We stand for lower deficits and free trade and the bond market. Isn't that great?" Quoted in Woodward, 165.

30. See Jones, "Campaigning to Govern," 29.

31. See Cohen, 80, 136–138, and 197; Drew, 73–74 and 166; Sinclair, Barbara, *Unorthodox Lawmaking: New Legislative Processes in the United States Congress,* 2nd ed. (Washington, DC: Congressional Quarterly Press, 2000), 165–176; and Woodward, 88–89.

32. See Gimpel, James G., *Legislating the Revolution: The Contract with America in the First 100 Days*. Boston: Allyn and Bacon, 1996, 58.

33. Ibid., 56.

34. In a politically shrewd move, the CBC produced an alternative bill called the Racial Justice Act, which attracted wide support among House liberals. The CBC alternative had no chance in the Senate, but it served as excellent leverage for the CBC to ensure that Clinton and the congressional leadership kept most of the social spending intact. See Windlesham, Lord David James George Hennessy, *Politics, Punishment, and Populism*. Oxford, England: Oxford University Press, 1998, 30–40 and 89–90.

35. Ibid., 104.

36. See *The Gallup Poll: Public Opinion, 1935–1997*. Gallup, 2000. CD-ROM.

37. See Brady and Volden, 112.

38. See Drew, 297; Engel, Steven T., and David J. Jackson, "Wielding the Stick Instead of the Carrot: Labor PAC Punishment of Pro-NAFTA Democrats," *Political Research Quarterly*, vol. 51, no. 3 (September 1998), 822; and Grayson, George W., *The North American Free Trade Agreement* (New York: Foreign Policy Association, 1993), 50–55. Interestingly, organized labor once supported free trade—when its position in the global economy was much stronger. But with the movement having fallen on hard times, the AFL-CIO embraced protectionism. See Wilson, 224.

39. See Jacobson, Gary C., "The 1994 House Elections in Perspective," in *Midterm: The Elections of 1994 in Context*, ed. Philip A. Klinker. Boulder, CO: Westview Press, 1996, 1–20. Also, for more on the AFL-CIO's financial punishment of pro-NAFTA Democrats, see Kahane, Leo H., "Congressional Voting Patterns on NAFTA: An Empirical Analysis," *American Journal of Economics and Sociology*, vol. 55, no. 4 (1996), 406.

40. The fact that Clinton chose health care reform before welfare reform was a signal to New Democrats that his heart was not really with them. See Baer, 214. Clinton did not even propose a welfare reform bill until June 1994—far too late in the session to do anything about it. See Quirk, Paul J., and Joseph Hinchliffe, "Domestic Policy: The Trials of a Centrist Democrat," in Campbell and Rockman, *The Clinton Presidency: First Appraisals*, 281.

41. The secrecy of the task force made for an easy Republican talking point, and even Ralph Nader's Public Citizen group complained that it was a "political mistake." See Rovner, Julie, "Congress and Health Care Reform, 1993–1994," in *Intensive Care: How Congress Shapes Health Policy*, ed. Thomas Mann and Norman J. Ornstein. Washington, DC: American Enterprise Institute, 1995, 186.

42. The government would form a series of regional health "alliances" that would pool risk—all companies with fewer than five thousand employees would be required to join these alliances, with smaller companies receiving subsidies. There would be no more denial of insurance based on preexisting conditions, and companies would have to charge premiums based on "community rating." To control costs, the government would impose caps on Medicare and Medicaid spending, and a government board would set insurance premium targets. See Berman, 27; Drew, 304; Laham, Nicholas, *A Lost Cause: Bill Clinton's Campaign for National Health Insurance* (Westport, CT: Praeger, 1996), 30–32; and Rovner, 189.

43. See Laham, 2.

44. See Berman, 28; Johnson, Haynes, and David S. Broder, *The System: The Ameri-*

can Way of Politics at the Breaking Points (Boston: Little, Brown, and Co., 1996), 198; Rovner, 181–197; and Sinclair, Barbara, "Trying to Govern Positively in a Negative Era: Clinton and the 103rd Congress," in Campbell and Rockman, *The Clinton Presidency: First Appraisals*, 114–115.

45. See Rovner, 200.

46. These dollars went to well-placed members of key committees, Democratic and Republican alike; Senate Democrats Bill Bradley, Tom Daschle, Chris Dodd, Tom Harkin, Barbara Mikulski, John D. Rockefeller, and Paul Simon all received at least $100,000 from health care PACs in the 1992 cycle. Plus, the anti-reform interests had well-connected, highly experienced lobbyists working for them—like Bill Gradison, formerly of the House Ways and Means Committee, who labored on behalf of the HIAA. See Laham, 47–55.

47. See Clymer, Adam, Robert Pear, and Robin Toner, "The Health Care Debate: What Went Wrong?" *New York Times,* August 29, 1994; and Wilson, 227–228.

48. See Jacobson.

49. See Klinker, Philip A., "Court and Country in American Politics: The Democratic Party and the 1994 Election," in Klinker, *Midterm: The Elections of 1994 in Context*, 72.

50. Morris, Dick, *Behind the Oval Office: Getting Reelected Against All Odds*. Los Angeles: Renaissance Books, 1999, 80–81.

51. See Fenno, Richard F., Jr., *Learning to Govern: An Institution View of the 104th Congress*. Washington, DC: Brookings Institution Press, 1997, 38.

52. See Morris, 160.

53. Harris, 185.

54. See Berkowitz, Edward D., *America's Welfare State: From Roosevelt to Reagan* (Baltimore: The Johns Hopkins Press, 1991), 92–93; and Office of the Assistant Secretary for Planning and Evaluation, "Aid to Families with Dependent Children: The Baseline, 1998," Department of Health and Human Services, June 1998 (http//:aspe.hhs.gov, accessed September 23, 2011). By 1962, some 3.5 million people were on AFDC; by 1972 the number had nearly tripled, to 10.5 million. Presidents Nixon, Carter, and Reagan had all tried to reform the program, with little or no success. Worse, welfare had taken on a racial dimension—by the 1980s some 40 percent of all AFDC recipients were African American, and increasingly there was evidence that some—though certainly not all or even most—welfare recipients had come to depend on it as a permanent source of support.

55. See Haskins, Ron, *Work over Welfare: The Inside Story of the 1996 Welfare Reform Law*. Washington, DC: The Brookings Institute, 2006, 266–267.

56. The Republicans proposed to replace AFDC with the Temporary Assistance for Needy Families (TANF) program, which would limit participation to five years. What's more, they would give the funds to the states in the form of block grants, allowing the states to design their own programs, so long as they stayed within federally mandated boundaries, which were much less stringent than the liberals would have liked. See Harris, 238; Haskins, 364–370; and Gimpel, 82.

57. Noted African American history professor Robin D. G. Kelley, for instance, argued that "perhaps the most draconian measure of the late twentieth century is the welfare reform bill, signed not by a Republican president but by a self-proclaimed liberal Democrat: Bill Clinton." Kelley, Robin D. G., *Yo' Mama's*

Disfunktional! Fighting the Culture Wars in Urban America. Boston: Beacon Press, 1998, 82.

58. See Berman, William C., *America's Right Turn: From Nixon to Clinton*, 2nd ed. (Baltimore: The Johns Hopkins University Press, 2001), 179–182; Ceaser, James W., and Andrew E. Busch, *Losing to Win: The 1996 Elections and American Politics* (Lanham, MD: Rowman & Littlefield, 1997), 41; Clinton, William J., "Address on Affirmative Action (July 19, 1995)," in *American President: A Reference Resource,* Miller Center of the University of Virginia, 2011 (http://miller center.org, accessed September 22, 2011); and Stetson, Dorothy McBride, "The Women's Movement Agenda and the Record of the Clinton Administration," in Shields et al., *The Clinton Riddle: Perspectives on the Forty-Second President*, 143.

59. The closest any prominent Democrat came to challenging Clinton was former Pennsylvania governor Robert Casey, who was a prominent opponent of abortion. Casey set up an "exploratory committee" to begin raising funds, but ultimately he declined to challenge Clinton. See Ceaser and Busch, *Losing to Win*, 49.

60. See Abramson, Paul R., John H. Aldrich, and David W. Rohde, *Change and Continuity in the 1996 Elections*, revised ed. (Washington, DC: Congressional Quarterly Press, 1999), 25; Berman, *America's Right Turn,* 185; Corrado, Anthony, "Financing the 1996 Elections," in *The Election of 1996: Reports and Interpretations*, ed. Gerald M. Pomper (Chatham, NJ: Chatham House Publishers, 1997), 142; and Dwyre, Diana, "Interest Groups and Issue Advocacy in 1996," in *Financing the 1996 Election,* ed. John C. Green (Armonk, NY: M.E. Sharpe, 1999), 200.

61. Berman, *America's Right Turn,* 184–185; Berman, *From the Center to the Edge*, 52–53; Ceaser and Busch, *Losing to Win,* 15; and Rae, Nicol C., "Clinton and the Democrats: The President as Party Leader," in Schier, *The Postmodern Presidency*, 194.

62. Gillon, Steven M., *The Pact: Bill Clinton, Newt Gingrich, and the Rivalry That Defined a Generation*. Oxford, England: Oxford University Press, 2008, 137.

63. "Democratic Party of 1996," in *The American Presidency Project*.

64. See Rae, 195.

65. The role of organized labor in the 1996 congressional election deserves special attention. The congressional Republicans basically froze the AFL-CIO out of the policy-making role and initiated investigations into the activities of organized labor. This freezing of congressional relations helped prompt a major change in the leadership of the AFL-CIO. John Sweeney, of the Service Employees International Union, defeated Tom Donohue, the protégé of Lane Kirkland, for the presidency of the organization, and he initiated an aggressive new political campaign called Labor '96. The organization redesigned its PAC allocations to channel more funds to challengers, redoubled its efforts to educate and mobilize its grassroots workers, and even bankrolled a $35 million ad campaign against congressional Republicans. See Biersack, Robert, and Melanie Haskell, "Sitting on the Umpire: Political Parties, the Federal Election Campaign Act, and the 1996 Campaigns," in Green, *Financing the 1996 Election*, 174; Cantor, David, "The Sierra Club Political Committee," in *After the Revolution: PACs, Lobbies, and the Republican Congress,* ed. Robert Biersack, Paul S. Herrnson, and Clyde Wilcox (Needham Heights, MA: Allyn and Bacon, 1999), 102–117; Corrado, 162; Dwyre, 203; Gerber, Robin, "Building to Win, Building to Last: AFL-CIO COPE Takes On the Republican

Congress," in Biersack et al., *After the Revolution,* 77–89; Herrnson, Paul S., "Financing the 1996 Congressional Elections," in Green, *Financing the 1996 Election,* 107; Mundo, Philip A., "League of Conservation Voters," in Biersack et al., *After the Revolution,* 130; Thomas, Sue, "NARAL PAC: Battling for Women's Reproductive Rights," in Biersack et al., *After the Revolution,* 140–141.

66. Clinton essentially won the core New Deal coalition—African Americans, liberals, and working-class Catholics—while pulling in a very impressive share of the vote from the middle class, which had historically backed Republicans. He did particularly well with middle-class women. See Abramson et al., *Change and Continuity in the 1996 Elections,* 93.

67. Clinton, William J., "Inaugural Address, January 20, 1997," in *The American Presidency Project.*

68. See Gillon, 195–200. The 1997 budget deal was a triumph of Clinton's "Third Way" politics, or as Joseph Stiglitz, the chair of Clinton's Council of Economic Advisers, put it, a position "somewhere between the New Deal and Reaganomics":

    On the one hand, we must acknowledge that the world has changed. The kind of strong government intervention associated with the New Deal is clearly inappropriate now. On the other hand, Reaganomics led to its own problems—such as deregulation. To a large extent, the banking crisis of 1989 was related to regulatory lapse. Maybe more important, the implicit assumptions of trickledown economics and social Darwinism clearly have problems for the long run strength of the country. Arriving at an economic philosophy that lies between these two represents an achievement in the sense that it lays a new course, a direction for our time.

    Stiglitz, Joseph, "Defending the Clinton Administration: Interview with Joseph Stiglitz," *Challenger,* May–June 1997, 22–23.

69. See Gillon, 213.

70. Ibid., 236–237.

71. See Mayer, William G., "The Presidential Nominations," in *The Election of 2000,* ed. Gerald M. Pomper. New York: Seven Bridges Press, 2001, 16.

72. See Abramson, Paul A., John H. Aldrich, and David W. Rohde, *Change and Continuity in the 2000 and 2002 Elections.* Washington, DC: Congressional Quarterly Press, 2003, 14–15.

73. See Berman, *From the Center to the Edge,* 105.

74. See Ceaser, James W., and Andrew E. Busch, *The Perfect Tie: The True Story of the 2000 Presidential Election.* Lanham, MD: Rowman & Littlefield, 2001, 72–73.

75. Ibid., 85–86.

76. Ibid., 103; and Hershey, Marjorie Randon, "The Campaign and the Media," in Pomper, *The Election of 2000,* 63.

77. See Martin, Justin, *Nader: Crusader, Spoiler, Icon.* New York: Basic Books, 2002, 40–189.

78. In response, Nader turned away from Washington politics and aligned with the American Trial Lawyers Association—another important star in the Democratic constellation—to stop tort reform proposals in the states. Ibid., 201–223.

79. Nader had developed a rather dim view of Gore by the end of the 1990s, writing:

    Gore may be called a Pavlovian politician. By displaying obeisance to corporate power, he and Clinton have been rewarded. They win special-interest-money-saturated elections and avoid having the varieties of corporate powers arrayed against them as would occur if they were progressive political figures having what professor James MacGregor Burns called "transforming leadership" qualities.

Nader, Ralph, *In Pursuit of Justice: Collected Writings, 2000–2003.* New York: Seven Stories Press, 2004, 494–495.

80. See Martin, 240–271.
81. Gore, Albert, Jr., "Address Accepting the Presidential Nomination at the Democratic National Convention in Los Angeles, August 17, 2000," in *The American Presidency Project.*
82. See Martin, 263; and Nader, Ralph, *Crashing the Party: How to Tell the Truth and Still Run for President* (New York: St. Martin's Press, 2002), 240–271.
83. See Corrado, Anthony, "Financing the 2000 Elections," in Pomper, *The Election of 2000,* 109; and Herrnson, Paul S., "The Congressional Elections," in Pomper, *The Election of 2000,* 169.
84. Nader does particularly well among younger voters, the professional and semi-professional classes, the wealthy, and union members. See Abramson, *Change and Continuity in the 2000 and 2002 Elections,* 98–100.

CHAPTER 12: You're on the Menu

1. See Remnick, David, *The Bridge: The Life and Rise of Barack Obama.* New York: Vintage, 2011, 290–293.
2. Ibid., 261 and 370; and Kurtz, Stanley, *Radical-in-Chief: Barack Obama and the Untold Story of American Socialism* (New York: Threshold Editions 2010), 194.
3. See Hodge, Roger D., *The Mendacity of Hope: Barack Obama and the Betrayal of American Liberalism,* New York: HarperCollins, 2010, 23.
4. See Ceaser, James W., Andrew E. Busch, and John J. Pitney Jr., *Epic Journey: The 2008 Elections and American Politics.* Lanham, MD: Rowman & Littlefield, 2009, 19.
5. See Corrado, Anthony, "Financing the 2008 Presidential General Election," in *Financing the 2008 Election,* ed. David B. Magleby and Anthony Corrado (Washington, DC: Brookings Institution Press, 2011), 134–136; Currinder, Mariam, "Campaign Finance: Fundraising and Spending in the 2008 Elections," in *The Elections of 2008,* ed. Michael Nelson (Washington, DC: Congressional Quarterly Press, 2010), 163–186; and Green, John C., and Diana Kingsbury, "Financing the 2008 Presidential Nomination Campaigns," in Magleby and Corrado, *Financing the 2008 Election,* 98–99.
6. See Ceaser et al., 22.
7. See Abramson, Paul R., John H. Aldrich, and David W. Rohde, *Change and Continuity in the 2008 Elections* (Washington, DC: Congressional Quarterly Press, 2010), 20–32; and Cost, Jay, "How Obama Won the Nomination," *Policy Review,* August–September 2008, 59–73. Importantly, Speaker of the House Nancy Pelosi—the country's top-ranking Democrat—subtly signaled her support for Obama in the spring by urging the superdelegates to support the candidate who won the most pledged delegates, i.e., Obama. See Connor, Patrick, "Pelosi: Su-

perdelegates Should Reflect Voters' Will," *Politico,* March 16, 2008. http://www.politico.com. Accessed September 24, 2011.

8. See Gasparino, Charles, *Bought and Paid For: The Unholy Alliance Between Barack Obama and Wall Street.* New York: Sentinel, 2010, ix–xi.

9. See Cigler, Allan, "Interest Groups and the Financing of the 2008 Elections," in Magleby and Corrado, *Financing the 2008 Election,* 261–275.

10. The only notable exception to the seniority rule occurred when Henry Waxman of Hollywood successfully pushed out John Dingell of Dearborn as chairman of the House Energy and Commerce Committee. Pelosi and Obama backed the coup, believing that Waxman would be a more forceful advocate for their planned environmental regulations. See Broder, John M., "In Obama's Team, 2 Camps on Climate." *New York Times,* January 3, 2009.

11. As Matt Bai of the *New York Times* reported about the stimulus:
    Obama's policy advisers . . . decided to offer only the vaguest outlines of their plan, laying out broad categories on spreadsheets rather than in binder-length written proposals. They were surprised when aides to David Obey, the House Appropriations Committee chairman, soon complained that the Obama plan was, in fact, too vague. The suspicion in the House, perhaps not entirely unfounded, was that Obama wasn't really being sensitive to Congressional prerogative when he punted on the details; instead, he was trying to dump the whole spending bill—and the potentially onerous responsibility for throwing around billions in taxpayer money—on lawmakers, so he wouldn't have to own it.
    Bai, Matt, "Taking the Hill," *New York Times Magazine,* June 7, 2009.

12. See Newton-Small, Jay, "Obama's Stimulus: Jump-Starting His Long-Term Agenda," *Time,* January 8, 2009. See also "Breakdown of Funding," Recovery Accountability and Transparency Board (http://recovery.gov, accessed September 22, 2011); Weisman, Jonathan, and Greg Hitt, "Stimulus Plan Would Expand Tax Credit for Poor—President-elect Seeks Input from Republicans as He Begins Effort to Win Lawmakers' Backing for Possible $775 Billion Package," *Wall Street Journal,* January 6, 2009.

13. See Miller, Peyton R., "In the Tank for Big Labor," *The Weekly Standard,* July 19, 2010; Recovery Accountability and Transparency Board; and Weisman, Jonathan, Greg Hitt, and Naftali Bendavid, "House Passes Stimulus Package—$819 Billion Jolt to Economy Aims to Reshape Education, Health Care; Deficit to Soar," *Wall Street Journal,* January 29, 2009.

14. See Kaus, Mickey, "Hello? GOP? Your Favorite Wedge Issue Is Coming Back," *Slate,* February 7, 2009 (http://slate.com, accessed September 24, 2011); The Editors, "Ending Welfare Reform As We Knew It," *National Review,* February 12, 2009 (http://nationalreview.com, accessed September 24, 2011); and Weisman et al.

15. See Alter, Jonathan, *The Promise: President Obama, Year One* (New York: Simon & Schuster, 2010), 129; Mullins, Brody, and Elizabeth Williamson, "The Stimulus Plan: From Yachts to Textiles, Perks for Special Interests," *Wall Street Journal,* January 29, 2009; Sinclair, Barbara, "Congressional Leadership in Obama's First Two Years," in *Obama in Office,* ed. James A. Thurber (Boulder, CO: Paradigm Publishers, 2011), 94; "A 40-Year Wish List," *Wall Street Journal,* January 28, 2009.

16. Elmendorf, Douglas W., "Letter to the Honorable Nancy Pelosi," Congressional Budget Office, February 13, 2009. http://cbo.gov. Accessed September 24, 2011.

17. See Taylor, John B., "An Empirical Analysis of the Revival of Fiscal Activism in the 2000s," Stanford University (http://stanford.edu, accessed September 24, 2011); and Wilson, Daniel J., "Fiscal Spending Jobs Multipliers: Evidence from the 2009 American Recovery and Reinvestment Act," Federal Reserve Bank of San Francisco, May 2011 (http://frbsf.org, accessed September 24, 2011).

18. See "Failed Stimulus," *Investor's Business Daily,* August 16, 2011 (http://investors. com, accessed September 24, 2011); Glantz, Aaron, "Number of Green Jobs Fails to Live Up to Promises," *New York Times,* August 18, 2011; Mead, Walter Russell, "Feeding the Masses on Unicorn Ribs," *The American Interest,* August 20, 2011 (http://blogs.the-american-interest.com, accessed September 24, 2011).

19. Krueger, Alan B., and Bruce D. Meyer, "Labor Supply Effects on Social Insurance," *Handbook of Public Economics,* vol. 4., ed. A. J. Auerbach and M. Feldstein. Amsterdam: North Holland, 2002, 2328.

20. Meltzer, Allan H., "Why Obamanomics Has Failed," *Wall Street Journal,* June 20, 2010; and Taylor.

21. Feyrer, James, and Bruce Sacerdote, "Did the Stimulus Stimulate? Real Time Estimates of the Effects of the American Recovery and Reinvestment Act." National Bureau of Economic Research, February 2011. http://nber.org. Accessed September 24, 2011.

22. See "Union Members—2010," Bureau of Labor Statistics, January 21, 2011. http://bls.gov. Accessed September 22, 2011.

23. See Davis, Susan, "SEIU's Stern Tops White House Visitor List," *Wall Street Journal,* October 30, 2009.

24. See Dennis, Brady, and Peter Wallsten, "Obama Joins Wisconsin's Budget Battle, Opposing Republican Anti-Union Bill," *Washington Post,* February 18, 2011.

25. See Greenhouse, Steven, "Democrats Drop Key Part of Bill to Assist Unions," *New York Times,* July 17, 2009. It's a testament to the dire straits of unionism today that organized labor would even back a provision like "card check" in the first place. One of the most important reforms of the National Labor Relations Act was the secret ballot provision, which allowed workers to vote to form a union without fear of reprisal from their employers. So desperate are the unions for new members that they were willing to do away with this once sacred provision.

26. See Meckler, Laura, "Obama to Reverse Bush Labor Policies," *Wall Street Journal,* January 30, 2009.

27. See Stout, David, "Obama Moves to Reverse Bush's Labor Policies," *New York Times,* January 31, 2009.

28. See McArdle, Megan, "More Love for Big Labor," *The Atlantic,* February 7, 2009. http://theatlantic.com. Accessed September 24, 2011.

29. See Morley, Jefferson, "Labor Wins 'Prevailing Wages' in Stimulus," *Washington Independent,* March 31, 2009. http://washingtonindependent.com. Accessed September 24, 2011.

30. See Bevan, Tom, "The Newest Labor War: Union, Feds Attack Boeing," *RealClearPolitics,* April 22, 2011. http://realclearpolitics.com. Accessed September 24, 2011.

31. See "Our View: Boeing vs. Union Threatens Dreamliner Investment," *USA Today,* June 23, 2011. Even some liberals were upset by the move. See, for instance, Nocera, Joe, "How Democrats Hurt Jobs," *New York Times,* August 22, 2011.

32. See Alter, 177.

33. See Rattner, Steve, *Overhaul: An Insider's Account of the Obama Administration's Emergency Rescue of the Auto Industry.* Boston: Houghton Mifflin, 2010, 149.

34. See Kouwe, Zachery, "The Lenders Obama Decided to Blame," *New York Times,* April 30, 2009.

35. Quoted in Clarke, Connor, "What Obama Said About Chrysler," *The Atlantic,* April 30, 2009. http://theatlantic.com. Accessed September 24, 2011.

36. See Freddoso, David, *Gangster Government: Barack Obama and the New Washington Thugocracy.* Washington, DC: Regnery, 2011, 31.

37. See Gasparino, 50–61.

38. Heilemann, John, "Obama Is from Mars, Wall Street Is from Venus," *New York,* May 22, 2010.

39. See Barr, Colin, "Geithner Unveils New Bank Rescue Plan," CNN, February 2, 2009 (http://cnn.com, accessed September 24, 2011); and Carney, Timothy P., *Obamanomics: How Barack Obama Is Bankrupting You and Enriching His Wall Street Friends, Corporate Lobbyists, and Union Bosses* (Washington, DC: Regnery, 2009), 160.

40. Gasparino, 210.

41. See Carney, 110.

42. See "The Economic Efforts of Legislation to Reduce Greenhouse-Gas Emissions," Congressional Budget Office, September 2009. http://cbo.gov. Accessed September 24, 2011.

43. Ibid.; and Eilperin, Juliet, "Cap-and-Trade Would Slow Economy, CBO Chief Says," *Washington Post,* October 15, 2009.

44. Reportedly, this was a big reason why Larry Summers was so hesitant about pursuing cap and trade. See Broder.

45. See "New York Exit Poll. President, 2008," CNN. http://cnn.com. Accessed September 26, 2011.

46. See Obama, Barack, "Address Before a Joint Session of the Congress, February 24, 2009," in *American Presidency Project,* ed. John T. Woolley and Gerhard Peters. University of California at Santa Barbara, 2011. http://www.presidency.ucsb.edu. Accessed September 21, 2011.

47. Carney, Timothy P., "Tick, Tick, Tick: The Cost of Obamacare Is a Time Bomb," *Washington Examiner,* January 16, 2011. http://washingtonexaminer.com. Accessed September 24, 2011.

48. See Connolly, Ceci, "How We Got Here," in *Landmark: The Inside Story of America's New Health-Care Law and What It Means for All of Us* (New York: Public Affairs, 2010), 11–64; Eggen, Dan, and Ceci Connolly, "In Health Plan, Industry Sees Good Business; Lure of New Customers Creates Unexpected Support for Obama," *Washington Post,* March 5, 2009; and Jacobs, Lawrence R., and Theda Skocpol, *Health Care Reform and American Politics: What Everyone Needs to Know* (Oxford, England: Oxford University Press, 2011), 69.

49. See Newton-Small, Jay, "Obama Moves Health Care to the Front Burner," *Time,* February 26, 2009.

50. See Eggen, Dan, "Industry Cash Flowed to Drafters of Reform; Key Senator Baucus Is a Leading Recipient," *Washington Post,* July 21, 2009; Eggen, Dan, "Health Sector Has Donated Millions to Lawmakers," *Washington Post,* March 8, 2009; and Hernandez, Raymond, "As Special Interests Aid Dodd, He Distances Himself from Them," *New York Times,* July 28, 2009.

51. See Eggen, Dan, and Kimberly Kindy, "Familiar Players in Health Bill Lobbying; Firms Are Enlisting Ex-Lawmakers, Aides," *Washington Post,* July 6, 2009; and Rucker, Philip, and Anne E. Kornblut, "Oval Office Visit Hints at Daschle's Role; President Consulting Man He Once Wanted as Czar on the Issue," *Washington Post,* August 22, 2009.

52. See Greenhouse, Steven, "New Yorker Leads Labor Charge for Health Reform," *New York Times,* August 27, 2009; and Rutenberg, Jim, "Liberal Groups Flexing Muscle in Lobby Wars," *New York Times,* March 1, 2009.

53. See Connolly, "How We Got Here," 16–17; Connolly, Ceci, "In Pitch to AMA, Obama Paints Mixed Picture," *Washington Post,* June 16, 2009; Connolly, Ceci, "Wal-Mart Endorses Employer Mandate," *Washington Post,* July 1, 2009; Jacobs and Skocpol, 69; and Meckler, Laura, "What Docs, Insurers, Pharma and Businesses Agree On," *Wall Street Journal*, March 27, 2009 (http://blogs.wsj.com, accessed September 24, 2011).

54. See Connolly, Ceci, "Health-Care Dialogue Alarms Obama's Allies," *Washington Post,* April 21, 2009; Connolly, Ceci, "Key Feature of Obama Health Plan May Be Out; Administration Hints That Public Option Isn't Only Way to Go," *Washington Post,* August 17, 2009; and Pear, Robert, "Doctors' Group Opposes Public Health Insurance Plan," *New York Times,* June 11, 2009.

55. See Alter, 253; Jacobs and Skocpol, 71; Kirkpatrick, David D., "Drug Industry to Run Ads Favoring White House Plan," *New York Times,* August 9, 2009; and Pear, Robert, and Jackie Calmes, "Senate Panel Rejects Bid to Add Drug Discount," *New York Times,* September 25, 2009.

56. See Connolly, "In Pitch to AMA, Obama Paints Mixed Picture"; Connolly, "How We Got Here," 21; Jacobs, Lawrence R., "The Privileges of Access: Interest Groups and the White House," in *The Obama Presidency: Appraisals and Prospects,* ed. Bert A. Rockman, Andrew Rudalevige, and Colun Campbell (Washington, DC: Congressional Quarterly Press, 2011), 162–163; and Jacobs and Skocpol, 70–74.

57. Quoted in Jacobs and Skocpol, 72. See also Connolly, Ceci, "Health Industry Concerned About Reform Measures; Leaders Warn That Democrats' Bills Would Leave Too Many Uncovered," *Washington Post,* October 9, 2009; and Jacobs, 163.

58. See MacGillis, Alec, "Health Overhaul Puts Obama in Union Bind," *Washington Post,* January 12, 2010; Meyerson, Harold, "For Unions, a Messy Bargain," *Washington Post,* December 23, 2009; Montgomery, Lori, and Michael D. Shear, "Obama, Labor Reach Deal on Health Care; Union Members Would Get Reprieve from Tax on High-Cost Insurance," *Washington Post,* January 15, 2010; and Pear, Robert, "Rangel Bars Any Taxes on Workers' Health Care," *New York Times,* May 7, 2009.

59. See Allen, Jared, Jeffrey Young, and Molly K. Hooper, "Pro-Choice Caucus Livid at Talk of Deal with Stupak on Abortion," *The Hill,* March 19, 2010. http://thehill.com. Accessed September 24, 2011.

60. Singhai, Shubham, Jerise Stueland, and Drew Ungerman, "How U.S. Health Care Reform Will Affect Employee Benefits," *McKinsey Quarterly* (http://www .mckinseyquarterly.com, accessed September 24, 2011); Turner, Grace-Marie, James C. Capretta, Thomas P. Miller, and Robert E. Moffit, *Why Obamacare Is Wrong for America* (New York: Broadside Books, 2011), 5; and Holtz-Eakin, Douglas, and Cameron Smith, "Labor Markets and Health Care Reform: New Results," American Action Forum, May 2010 (http://americanactionforum.org, accessed September 24, 2011).

61. See Elmendorf, Douglas W., "An Analysis of Health Insurance Premiums Under the Patient Protection and Affordable Care Act," Congressional Budget Office, November 30, 2009. http://cbo.gov. Accessed September 24, 2011.

62. See Foster, Richard S., "The Estimated Effect of the Affordable Care Act on Medicare and Medicaid Outlays and Total National Health Care Expenditures," Testimony Before the House Committee on the Budget, January 26, 2011 (http:// budget.house.gov, accessed September 24, 2011); and Shatto, John D., and M. Kent Clemmons, "Projected Medicare Expenditures Under an Illustrative Scenario with Alternative Payment Updates to Medicare Providers," Centers for Medicare and Medicaid Services, August 5, 2010 (http://www.cms.gov, accessed September 24, 2011). A similar problem with cost control is that the tax on high-end insurance plans, while delayed until 2019, is not indexed to the historical inflation we've seen in insurance cost. Thus, in 2019 only "high-end" insurance policies will be taxed, but ten years later the tax will hit much more modest policies. Again, it's unrealistic to expect Congress to allow this to happen. Just as it regularly "patches" the Alternative Minimum Tax, which has a similar indexing problem, it will surely patch the Cadillac tax, driving the total costs of PPACA even higher. See Turner et al., 155.

63. See Cost, Jay, "If Our Food Stamp Recovery Persists, Obama Will Lose Big," *The Weekly Standard,* May 6, 2011. http://weeklystandard.com. Accessed September 24, 2011.

64. Morris, Roy, Jr., *Fraud of the Century: Rutherford B. Hayes, Samuel Tilden, and the Stolen Election of 1876.* New York: Simon & Schuster, 2004, 35.

65. Connolly, "How We Got Here," 17.

Conclusion

1. Fowler, Mayhill, "Obama: No Surprise That Hard-Pressed Pennsylvanians Turn Bitter," *Huffington Post*, April 11, 2008. http://huffingtonpost.com. Accessed September 26, 2011.

Index

ABOUT THE AUTHOR

JAY COST writes the twice-weekly "Morning Jay" column for the *Weekly Standard* and was previously a writer for *RealClearPolitics* and a popular political blogger. Cost received a BA in government from the University of Virginia and an MA in political science from the University of Chicago. He lives in Pennsylvania.